1991

Mainstreaming Exceptional Students

A Guide for Classroom Teachers

THIRD EDITION

JANE B. SCHULZ
Western Carolina University

C. DALE CARPENTER
Western Carolina University

ANN P. TURNBULL
The University of Kansas

ALLYN AND BACON
Boston London Toronto Sydney Tokyo Singapore

Series Editorial Assistant: Carol Craig
Production Administrator: Annette Joseph
Production Coordinator: Holly Crawford
Editorial-Production Services: Grace Sheldrick, Wordsworth Associates
Cover Administrator: Linda K. Dickinson
Cover Designer: Susan Slovinsky
Manufacturing Buyer: Megan Cochran

Copyright ©1991 by Allyn and Bacon
A division of Simon & Schuster, Inc.
160 Gould Street / Needham Heights, MA 02194-2310

Previous editions, by Jane B. Schulz and Ann P. Turnbull, were published under the title *Mainstreaming Handicapped Students: A Guide for Classroom Teachers,* ©1984, 1979 by Allyn and Bacon, Inc.

Library of Congress Cataloging-in-Publication Data

Schulz, Jane B., date
    Mainstreaming exceptional students : a guide for classroom
teachers / Jane B. Schulz, C. Dale Carpenter, Ann P. Turnbull. —
3rd ed.
      p. cm.
    Rev. ed. of: Mainstreaming handicapped students. c1984.
    Includes bibliographical references and index.
    ISBN 0-205-12377-5
    1. Handicapped children—Education—United States.
2. Mainstreaming in education—United States. I. Carpenter, C.
Dale. II. Turnbull, Ann P., date. III. Schulz, Jane B., date
Mainstreaming handicapped students. IV. Title.
LC4031.S38 1991
371.9′046—dc20   90-36692
                                            CIP

Printed in the United States of America

10 9 8 7 6 5 4 3 2 1   95 94 93 92 91 90

Illustrations by Mary de Wit

Figure 9.3: Collage by David Gates; photo by Richard Cloontz.

Photo Credits: Photos on pages 55, 341 © Media Vision; photo on page 409 by Anthony Taro. All other photos by Jos de Wit.

Contents

iii

Preface

THE FIRST EDITION of this book, *Mainstreaming Handicapped Students* (1979), was one of the first books to address the concerns and needs of classroom teachers as students with handicaps were being integrated into their programs. The orientation of the first edition was toward curriculum needs and teaching strategies. This is still the intent of the book and the base from which the authors operate.

The second edition was a major revision, reflecting needs expressed by teachers for a stronger orientation toward teachers in secondary settings and toward increased practical suggestions. The addition of numerous photographs and artwork enhanced that edition.

This third edition, *Mainstreaming Exceptional Students*, encompasses additional changes. After teaching courses in mainstreaming for an extended period of time, we have learned more about what students need and what people teaching such courses are requesting. Accordingly, this edition reflects two major changes. We have found that teachers and prospective teachers want more information about exceptionalities. First, while still keeping the curriculum emphasis, we have expanded the chapters on definitions, characteristics, and educational implications of exceptionalities for teachers who work with mainstreamed students. We do not want this book to be an introduction to special education, but we do want to give prospective teachers more information that we hope will increase their observational skills, their abilities to make appropriate referrals, and their abilities to integrate exceptional students into regular classes.

The second change is the addition of the area of gifted and talented to the range of exceptionalities. The first and second editions, in accordance with Public Law 94–142, were based on the needs of students with handicaps. However, students who are gifted and talented are also exceptional and are also integrated into regular classrooms. Many states now provide for their needs and require Individualized Education Programs for them. Chapter 5 is devoted to a discussion of their unique requirements. Each subject-area chapter also now incorporates discussions of their educational needs and of strategies to meet those needs. This major addition resulted in changing the book's title to *Mainstreaming Exceptional Students*.

Mainstreaming Exceptional Students, Third Edition, is organized into two parts. Part One, "Exceptional Students," develops the legal and educational rationale for mainstreaming and includes five chapters describing students who have orthopedic and health impairments, students who have sensory impairments and communication disorders, students who have learning and behavior disorders, and students with exceptional gifts and talents.

Part Two, "Educational Strategies," is devoted to helping teachers work with exceptional students. A discussion of the Individualized Education Program is followed by general strategies for adapting instruction within the classroom. Specific curriculum areas follow, with descriptions of problems that may be encountered and helpful suggestions for dealing with them.

We have seen many outstanding teachers who work well with students who are exceptional. We believe that good teachers will continue to be good teachers in mainstreaming situations and that they will meet the challenge of ensuring that *all* students have the best educational opportunities available.

We acknowledge and appreciate the work of our reviewers, Richard Dickson, Rhode Island College, Dianne Hoffbauer, Mankato State University, and Eleanor Wright, University of North Carolina at Wilmington. We are also grateful to Raymond G. Short, Senior Series Editor at Allyn and Bacon, and to Grace Sheldrick, Managing Editor, Wordsworth Associates, for their encouragement and valuable suggestions. Mary de Wit has again provided illustrations that represent our concepts so well and that demonstrate her understanding of our efforts. We also acknowledge the many experiences and ideas that teachers and university students have shared with us. We appreciate our families and their patience with us and are aware of the contributions they have made to our lives and to this book.

We also acknowledge each other and feel that each of us has made unique contributions to *Mainstreaming Exceptional Students*. We respect our different areas of expertise and remain, through it all, good friends.

—PART ONE—
Exceptional Students

—1—

Introduction

Diversity characterizes regular classrooms—students are different. They possess unique characteristics along the dimensions of achievement levels, language acquisition, social interaction, physical size, motor development, general health, vision, hearing acuity, and other personal attributes. The students in each classroom have a distinctive mixture of abilities/disabilities, strengths/weaknesses, likes/dislikes, and successes/failures.

Individual differences among children and youth in regular classrooms fall along a continuum. The differences among the great majority are not extreme and can be accommodated within the usual routine of the regular class program. Other students deviate significantly from the expected norm at a given grade level along varying dimensions. This deviation may single them out as being gifted or handicapped in learning capability, communication, motor development, sensations, and/or emotional adjustment. These deviations are what constitute exceptionality.

Regardless of the definition of the difference, the majority of students with unusual gifts and those with handicaps spend most of their school day in regular classrooms. The integration of exceptional students (mainstreaming) into regular classrooms has evolved through years of social pressure and legal action. In spite of controversy over mainstreaming practices, present and future trends support the concept. Wang and Baker (1986) indicate calls for action in two areas affecting regular and special education. The first call is to bring students now enrolled in segregated special education programs back into the mainstream; the second action calls for not moving exceptional students out of regular classes. Both actions involve providing special education and related services in regular classes to the maximum extent possible and appropriate. These calls for action reflect a major trend away from questioning the advisability of mainstreaming and toward efforts to provide more effective special education services within the regular classroom.

This focus, referred to as the Regular Education Initiative, is an effort to review and improve instruction for mildly handicapped students in the regular classroom. As stated by the former assistant secretary of the Office of Special Education and Rehabilitative Services:

> The heart of this commitment is the search for ways to serve as many of these children as possible in the regular classroom by encouraging special education and other special programs to form a partnership with regular education. The objective of the partnership for special education and the other special programs is to use their knowledge and expertise to support regular education in educating children with learning problems. (Will, 1986, p. 20)

Successful integration of exceptional students requires that people change. It requires the acquisition of knowledge about exceptional students, the use of effective teaching strategies, and the necessity for collaboration among educators, other professionals, parents, and communities.

It also requires an understanding of the background, nature, and rationale for mainstreaming.

RATIONALE FOR MAINSTREAMING

In exploring the rationale for mainstreaming exceptional students, it is necessary to define the terms *exceptional* and *mainstreaming*.

Exceptional Students

Exceptionality is a condition of difference (Lynch & Lewis, 1988). Exceptional students include those who are handicapped by disabilities and those who are distinguished by special gifts and talents. Because both groups of students spend a majority of their school day in the regular classroom, their needs fall within the mainstreaming concept. However, federal and state support for the two groups has differed widely. Public Law 94–142, discussed in the following section, is an act for the education of all handicapped children, but it does not include students who are gifted and/or talented. Therefore, support for programs for gifted and talented students comes mainly from state funds. In states in which *gifted* is included with *handicapped* in the definition of *exceptional children*, the support appears to be greater (Gallagher, 1985).

Because of the difference in legal provisions and requirements, the backgrounds of the process of mainstreaming students with handicaps and mainstreaming students with exceptional gifts are discussed separately.

Education of Handicapped Students

Under the provisions of PL 94–142, handicapped students are defined as

> those children evaluated as being mentally retarded, hard of hearing, deaf, speech impaired, visually handicapped, seriously emotionally disturbed, orthopedically impaired, other health impaired, deaf-blind, multi-handicapped, or as having specific learning disabilities, who because of those impairments need special education and related services. (*Federal Register*, 1977, pp. 42478–42479)

Approximately 11 percent of the nation's public school population receive special education services designed for handicapped students. This group of students is extremely diverse; almost 70 percent are classified as learning disabled or speech impaired; the remainder fall into the range of classifications listed above (Singer, Butler, Palfrey, & Walker, 1986). Reynolds and Birch (1977) describe the history of the education of handicapped students that has preceded their placement in regular classes as characterized by "progressive inclusion." This concept is illustrated by the rough historical breakdown in Table 1.1. A clear trend from more to less restrictive settings is evidenced by Table 1.1. There were some very specific reasons for questioning the value of special class placement for the majority of handicapped students during the seventies. These reasons are outlined briefly.

Efficacy of Special Classes

During the late 1960s and early 1970s, research studies were conducted to assess the academic progress and social adjustment of handicapped stu-

TABLE 1.1   Approximate History of Progressive Inclusion of Handicapped Students in Regular Classes

General Time Frame	Predominant Education Service
1. Ancient times	No education. Handicapped indivuduals were generally neglected and abused.
2. 1850–1900	Development of residential schools for the purpose of providing education and training.
3. 1900–1950	Special schools and special classes became more prevalent; residential schools continued to grow and expand.
4. 1950–1970	Special classes became the preferred type of educational service for students with mental retardation, emotional disturbance, and learning disabilities. Residential institutions and special schools flourished for blind, deaf, and physically handicapped students.
5. 1970–1977	Movement toward placement in regular classes of handicapped students who were able to be socially and instructionally integrated (mainstreaming). Development of special classes in public schools for some moderately and severely handicapped students formerly placed in residential institutions and special schools.
6. 1977–present	Major national effort directed to implementing federal and state legislation in providing a free appropriate public education to handicapped students in the least restrictive environment (including mainstreaming a substantial number of handicapped students in regular class settings).

dents placed in special classes as contrasted to handicapped students who remained in regular classes. Most of the efficacy studies were conducted on mentally retarded students rather than on a broad sampling of children with various types of handicaps. Regarding academic progress, it was found that the achievement of retarded students in special classes was very similar to that of retarded students in regular classes (Bradfield, Brown, Kaplan, Rickert, & Stannard, 1973; Budoff & Gottlieb, 1976). Some studies, however, did indicate slightly higher gains in reading for students attending the regular class program (Carroll, 1967). Research on social adjustment resulted in mixed findings (Budoff & Gottlieb, 1976; Goodman, Gottlieb, & Harrison, 1972; Iano, Ayers, Heller, McGettigan, & Walker, 1974). The trends apparent in the research findings have shown that retarded students generally have low social status whether they are placed in special or regular classes (Corman & Gottlieb, 1979).

Thus, the efficacy studies were interpreted as failing to document specific beneficial outcomes for retarded students in special class placements. During the mid-1970s, these studies added momentum to the parental and court actions (discussed subsequently) that placed pressure on the public school systems to curtail the separation of handicapped and nonhandicapped students.

It is paradoxical that after the establishment of legal requirements pertaining to mainstreaming, the efficacy studies have been severely criticized in a number of reviews because of the methodological problems (Corman & Gottlieb, 1979; Jones, Gottlieb, Guskin, & Yoshida, 1978; MacMillan, Jones, & Aloia, 1974; Meyers, MacMillan, & Yoshida, 1980). The efficacy studies, however, were interpreted in the 1970s as providing empirical justification for mainstreaming.

Minority Imbalance

One of the first major criticisms of special classes regarding minority imbalance was made by Dunn (1968), who pointed out that 60 to 80 percent of the students in special classes are from "low status background," including Mexican American, Puerto Rican American, black, and poverty-level homes. Such imbalance has largely been attributed to the use of standardized intelligence tests, which has resulted in a disproportionately large number of students from minority backgrounds being labeled as intellectually subnormal and a strikingly small number of these students being considered gifted (Mercer, 1973). Because most intelligence tests generally reflect the culture and language patterns of middle-class Anglo-Americans and are mostly standardized on this population, persons from other socioeconomic groups or backgrounds are automatically put at a disadvantage for performing successfully on these tests.

On a frequently used IQ test, one of the general information questions is: "What does the stomach do?" When the psychologist asked this question to Walter, his response was "it growls." Walter was from a low socioeconomic background. He routinely did not have food at home for breakfast and often his only meal was his free lunch at school. Based on Walter's life experience, his response was accurate; although the item was scored as "failed."

Racial desegregation contributed to focusing attention on special classes predominantly composed of students from minority backgrounds. In carrying out the decision of the Supreme Court in *Brown* v. *Board of Education* (1954), the Office of Civil Rights in the federal government has required some school systems to eliminate special classes that were interpreted to be vehicles for de facto segregation.

Parental and Judicial Action

On the basis of a combination of the foregoing reasons questioning the value and effects of special class placements, many parents of handicapped students began to seek help through the judicial system for what they considered to be educational inequities. They were joined by groups of parents whose handicapped children had been completely denied any type of appropriate free public education. These parents had essentially been told that the schools offered no programs for their children. The National Association for Retarded Citizens, a parent organization, initiated strong advocacy efforts based on the philosophical premise of equal educational opportunities for handicapped students. The first legal suits against schools for failing to provide appropriate educational programs for handicapped students were brought by parent organizations and were based on this philosophy.

The precedent for many of the court cases involving educational discrimination of handicapped students was the landmark case of *Brown* v. *Board of Education* (1954). It was argued that special education was a separate and unequal system of education. The court cases resulted in rulings that all handicapped children have a right to an education (*Mills* v. *D.C. Board of Education*, 1972; *Pennsylvania Association for Retarded Children* v. *Commonwealth of Pennsylvania*, 1971, 1972), that students may not be inappropriately evaluated with tests reflecting cultural bias and subsequently placed in special classes based on the results (*Hobson* v. *Hansen*, 1967; *Diana* v. *State Board of Education*, 1970, 1973), and that tracking is discriminatory (*Hobson* v. *Hansen*, 1967).

The judicial decisions in these special education cases provided a strong impetus to mainstreaming. The decision of *Pennsylvania Association for Retarded Children* v. *Commonwealth of Pennsylvania* (1971, 1972), the first right-to-education case, provides an example of this impetus.

It is the Commonwealth's obligation to place each mentally retarded child in a free, public program of education and training appropriate to the child's capacity, within the context of the general educational policy that, among the alternative programs of education and training required by statute to be available, placement in a regular public school class is preferable to placement in a special public school class and placement in a special public school class is preferable to placement in any other type of program of education and training. (334 F. Supp. 1257, 1260, E.D. Pa. 1971).

Court cases involving the right to education were brought in almost every state with very similar results. The social context of the 1970s in which these court cases were embedded is important to consider in understanding the widespread judicial preference for mainstreaming. The push to establish rights for handicapped persons was highly consistent with public sensitivity to establish rights for other groups, such as racial minorities and women who had previously been the targets of discrimination. Thus, it can be concluded that the *primary* judicial rationale for mainstreaming was based on sociopolitical factors rather than on scientific-pedagogical ones (Miller & Switzky, 1979; Turnbull, 1982).

The judicial decisions resulted in every state's (except New Mexico) adopting legislation regarding the education of handicapped students. (Readers are encouraged to get a copy of their state legislation on the education of handicapped students from their State Department of Public Instruction, the attorney general's office, or the legislative library.) A further result of parental and judicial action was the passage of federal legislation in November 1975, referred to as Public Law 94–142, the Education for All Handicapped Children Act. This legislation sets forth regulations and requires actions by teachers and school systems. These actions can be interpreted as legislative remedies to some of the past failures of schools in providing appropriate education to handicapped students. PL 94–142 has a striking correspondence to the legislation of most states regarding the education of handicapped students in terms of legal and educational principles. A summary of the major principles and requirements follows (*Federal Register*, 1977).

LEGISLATIVE PRINCIPLES AND REQUIREMENTS

The provision of a *free appropriate public education* is the central consideration of PL 94–142. Six major principles of PL 94–142 define the parameters of what is meant by this key phrase—free appropriate public education. These six principles include zero reject, nondiscriminatory evaluation, individualized education, least restrictive environment, due process, and parental participation. These principles are discussed individually, along with an overview of specific requirements associated with each one.

Zero Reject

The principle of zero reject requires public school systems to serve *all* handicapped students, regardless of the type of handicap they have or the level of its severity. In terms of age, handicapped students between the ages of 3 and 21 must be provided with a free appropriate public education. The only exception to this requirement is for the age ranges of 3 to 5 and 18 to 21; states that do not provide educational services to nonhandicapped students in these age ranges are exempt from being required to provide such services to handicapped students.

The zero reject principle prevents both total and functional exclusion of handicapped students. Total exclusion refers to cases in which handicapped students were denied the opportunity of attending school at all in the past. Functional exclusion occurs when handicapped students are allowed to attend school but are provided with inappropriate programs that are not responsive to their special needs. In order to prevent the occurrence of functional exclusion (and thus to insure that handicapped students receive an appropriate education), PL 94–142 requires that special education and related services be provided to them. Special education is defined as

> specially designed instruction, at no cost to the parent, to meet the unique needs of a handicapped child, including classroom instruction, instruction in physical education, home instruction, and instruction in hospitals and institutions. (*Federal Register,* 1977, p. 42480)

In addition to special education, public school systems are required to provide handicapped students with all related services that they need to enable them to benefit from special education. Related services are defined as

> transportation and such developmental, corrective and other supportive services as are required to assist a handicapped child to benefit from special education, and includes speech pathology and audiology, psychological services, physical and occupational therapy, recreation, early identification and assessment of disabilities in children, counseling services, and medical service for diagnostic or evaluation purposes. The term also includes school health services, social work services in schools, and parent counseling and training. (*Federal Register,* 1977, p. 42473)

The legal definitions of these services are included in Table 1.2.

It is important for classroom teachers to know that handicapped students in their classes are entitled to special education and related services designed to meet their individual needs. Entitling handicapped students to such services implies that classroom teachers are assured of

TABLE 1.2   Related Services in Special Education: Legal Definitions

Audiology	(a) Identification of children with hearing loss;
	(b) Determination of the range, nature, degree of hearing loss, including referral for medical or other professional attention for the habilitation of hearing;
	(c) Provision of habilitative activities, such as language habilitation, auditory training, speech reading (lip reading), hearing evaluation, and speech conservation;
	(d) Creation and administration of programs for prevention of hearing loss;
	(e) Counseling and guidance of pupils, parents, and teachers regarding hearing loss; and
	(f) Determination of the child's need for group and individual amplification, selecting and fitting an appropriate aid, and evaluating the effectiveness of amplification.
Counseling Services	Services provided by qualified social workers, psychologists, guidance counselors, or other qualified personnel.
Early Identification	Implementation of a formal plan for identifying a disability as early as possible in a child's life.
Medical Services	Services provided by a licensed physician to determine a child's medically related handicapping condition which results in the child's need for special education and related services.
Occupational Therapy	(a) Improving, developing, or restoring functions impaired or lost through illness, injury, or deprivation;
	(b) Improving ability to perform tasks for independent functioning when functions are impaired or lost; and
	(c) Preventing, through early intervention, initial or further impairment of loss of function.
Parent Counseling and Training	Assisting parents in understanding the special needs of their child and providing parents with information about child development.
Physical Therapy	Services provided by a qualified physical therapist.

(continued)

TABLE 1.2   (continued)

Psychological Services	(a) Administering psychological and educational tests, and other assessment procedures;
	(b) Interpreting assessment results;
	(c) Obtaining, integrating, and interpreting information about child behavior and conditions related to learning;
	(d) Consulting with other staff members in planning school programs to meet the special needs of children as indicated by psychological tests, interviews, and behavioral evaluations; and
	(e) Planning and managing a program of psychological services, including psychological counseling for children and parents.
Recreation	(a) Assessment of leisure function;
	(b) Therapeutic recreation services;
	(c) Recreation programs in schools and community agencies; and
	(d) Leisure education.
School Health Services	Services provided by a qualified school nurse or other qualified person.
Social Work Services	(a) Preparing a social or developmental history on a handicapped child;
	(b) Group and individual counseling with the child and family;
	(c) Working with those problems in a child's living situation (home, school and community) that affect the child's adjustment in school; and
	(d) Mobilizing school and community resources to enable the child to receive maximum benefit from his or her educational program.
Speech Pathology	(a) Identification of children with speech or language disorders;
	(b) Diagnosis and appraisal of specific speech or language disorders;
	(c) Referral for medical or other professional attention necessary for the habilitation of speech or language disorders;
	(d) Provisions of speech and language services for the habilitation or prevention of communicative disorders; and

	(e) Counseling and guidance of parents, children, and teachers regarding speech and language disorders.
Transportation	(a) Travel to and from school and between schools;
	(b) Travel in and around school buildings; and
	(c) Specialized equipment (such as special or adapted buses, lifts, and ramps), if required to provide special transporation for a handicapped child.

Source: Federal Register. August 23, 1977, pp. 42479–42480.

receiving assistance from special education teachers and related services providers (e.g., speech therapist, school counselor) in designing and delivering an appropriate educational program to handicapped students.

Another assurance to teachers to help provide appropriate educational programs to handicapped students is the availability of inservice training. PL 94–142 requires the state education agency to develop and implement *innovative* inservice training programs to insure that teachers are qualified to carry out their responsibilities. Furthermore, incentives for teachers (e.g., release time, payment for participation, options for academic credit, salary step credit, and certification renewal) must be incorporated into the inservice programs according to the legislative requirements.

Nondiscriminatory Evaluation

Federal and state legislative guidelines specify the manner in which evaluations are administered to handicapped students. The following legal definition of evaluation is important to consider. It includes

> procedures used . . . to determine whether a child is handicapped and the nature and extent of the special education and related services that the child needs. The term means procedures used selectively with an individual child and does not include basic tests administered to or procedures used with all children in a school, grade, or class. (*Federal Register*, 1977, p. 42494)

Evaluation is thus used to classify students as handicapped and to plan appropriate educational programs for them.

The timeline for evaluations is an important consideration. An evaluation must be conducted before placing or denying placement of a handicapped student in a special education program or transferring or denying transfer to a student in a special education class to a regular class setting. After students have been initially evaluated and classified as handicapped, they must be reevaluated every 3 years or more frequently if requests are made by the students' teachers or parents.

Most of the requirements pertaining to the principle of nondiscriminatory evaluation are aimed at assuring fairness in testing procedures, particularly in consideration of racial and cultural factors. Four examples of evaluation requirements include:

1. testing specific areas of educational need rather than focusing only on general intelligence;
2. making the decision for educational placement on the basis of giving a minimum of two tests or types of tests;
3. considering information concerning physical development, sociocultural background, and adaptive behavior in conjunction with test scores; and
4. setting up a *team* of persons in the school who possess knowledge about the student being evaluated and the placement alternatives.

In most school systems, responsibility for developing procedures that adhere to these legislative requirements regarding evaluation is assigned to one of the central administrators in charge of special education, special services, school psychology, or another related area. Classroom teachers are encouraged to ask for a copy of the system's written policies on evaluation, if this information is not routinely provided. One right of classroom teachers in this area is to have their questions concerning the handicapped students for whom they are responsible considered by the evaluation committee and answered to their satisfaction. Teachers responsible for instructing handicapped students are entitled to complete information on the curriculum implications of these evaluation results, appropriate resource materials, and behavior management programs. Strategies for teachers to use in working with the multidisciplinary evaluation committee are included in chapter 6.

Individualized Education

To assure that educational programs are appropriate to the individual needs of handicapped students, PL 94–142 and state legislation require the development of individualized education programs, or IEPs. The IEP requirements can be subdivided into two parts: the IEP document and the IEP meeting.

The components of the IEP document are specified by law (*Federal Register*, 1977):

1. a documentation of the student's current level of educational performance,

2. annual goals or the attainments expected by the end of the school year,
3. short-term objectives, stated in instructional terms, which are the intermediate steps leading to the mastery of annual goals,
4. documentation of the particular special education and related services that will be provided to the student,
5. an indication of the extent of time a student will participate in the regular education program,
6. projected dates for initiating services and the anticipated duration of services, and
7. appropriate objectives criteria, evaluation procedures, and schedules for determining mastery of short-term objectives, at least on an annual basis.

An IEP document must be developed for each handicapped student receiving special education. All curriculum areas that must be specially designed to meet the particular needs of the handicapped student should be included on the IEP. In regard to timelines, IEPs must be in effect for each handicapped student receiving special education at the beginning of the school year. "Be in effect" is typically interpreted to mean that the IEP is less than 1 calendar year old.

The second aspect of IEP regulations is the meeting held for the purpose of developing the IEP document. The following individuals are required participants at the IEP meeting (*Federal Register,* 1977):

1. a representative of the school system, other than the student's teacher, who has qualifications to provide or supervise special education,
2. the student's teacher,
3. one or both of the student's parents,
4. the student, when appropriate,
5. other individuals at the request of the parents or school representatives, and
6. for handicapped students evaluated for the first time, either a member of the evaluation team or another individual (representative of the school system, the student's teacher) who is knowledgeable about the evaluation procedures used with the student and the results of the evaluation.

Parent participation in decision making is an extremely important aspect of the IEP meeting; thus, the legislation requires that parents be notified of the purpose, time, and location of and other participants in the meeting. Meetings may be held without parent participation only when school personnel have documentation of their unsuccessful attempts to encourage parents to attend.

Because the IEP document and meeting are so central to the development of an appropriate education for handicapped students, chapter 6 outlines the requirements in more detail and suggests strategies to implement them.

Least Restrictive Environment

The law requires that state and local education agencies set up policies to insure that handicapped students are educated to the maximum extent appropriate in programs with nonhandicapped students and that they be placed in special classes or special schools only when the handicap is so severe that education cannot be satisfactorily accomplished in the regular education program with the use of supplementary aids and services. It is important to recognize that restrictiveness is a relative issue based on the special needs of each student. For some moderately and severely handicapped students, the regular classroom is a highly restrictive environment. Thus, the most normal environment is not always the least restrictive. Two factors must be considered in determining the least restrictive environment for a handicapped student. The first factor involves identifying the range of placements (e.g., regular class, resource room, special class) in which the student's instructional and social needs could be appropriately met. The second factor is the identification of the particular placement from the range of placements identified that provides the handicapped student with the greatest opportunity to interact meaningfully and successfully with persons who are nonhandicapped (Turnbull, 1982).

School systems are required to include a range of educational alternatives, including instruction in regular classes, resource rooms, special classes, special schools, hospitals and homes, and institutions. In regard to implementing the least restrictive requirement, schools should review the placement of handicapped students at least annually. The placement decision should be based on student IEPs. Unless the IEPs require some other arrangement, handicapped students should be educated in the same school they would attend if they were not handicapped. Further, handicapped students should be integrated into nonacademic and extracurricular activities with nonhandicapped students to the maximum extent appropriate.

Due Process

The principle of due process entitles both parents and professionals to *fair* procedures in the identification, evaluation, and placement of handicapped students. The specific due process requirements comprise a system of checks and balances regarding decisions made by parents and professionals concerning the education of handicapped students.

Prior written notice must be provided to parents of handicapped students whenever a change is proposed or refused regarding the identification, evaluation, or placement of handicapped students. Additionally, prior parental consent is necessary when a student is *initially* evaluated for special education placement with psychological or educational tests that are over and above those routinely given to nonhandicapped students.

A due process hearing may be initiated by parents or school personnel when conflicting points of view exist on the identification, evaluation, or placement of a handicapped student. Examples of such conflicts are whether the student is, indeed, handicapped or whether the student should be placed in a regular or special class. When conflicts cannot be resolved in the IEP meeting and all other attempts to reach a satisfactory resolution are unsuccessful, the school system is responsible for appointing an impartial hearing officer and conducting a due process hearing. At the hearing, both parties have the right to be represented by counsel or by persons having expertise in the area of handicapping conditions and to present evidence and cross-examine witnesses. They are entitled to a written record after the hearing. Either the parents or the school system may appeal the hearing decision from the local school system to the state education agency, and beyond to the appropriate state or federal court. While the proceedings of the hearing are pending, the handicapped student should remain in the current educational placement.

Only a relatively small number of cases involving handicapped students actually progress to the stage of a due process hearing. Thus, the vast majority of teachers will never be involved in such a hearing. It is important, however, for teachers who are involved in due process hearings to be prepared for this role. More detailed information on the hearing and the teacher's role in it can be found in Turnbull and Strickland (1981).

Parental Participation

The final legislative principle is parental participation. Although the five preceding principles are all directly or indirectly linked with parental participation, this principle is considered separately because some parental rights cannot be classified in the other five categories. These rights include the involvement of parents in the development of educational policy and parental access to records.

Parents of handicapped students have the opportunity to participate in the development of educational policy by attending required public hearings on the state's special education plan and serving on local and state advisory panels. Thus, parents can influence program priorities, budgets, and other organizational factors.

Access to educational records is an extremely important parental right. Parents have the right to review *all* educational records maintained on their handicapped child. (The only exceptions to this right are under state law requirements pertaining to situations involving guardianship, separation, and divorce.) Parents may also request that the contents of their child's records be explained and justified, and they may request that the contents be changed if they believe recorded information is inaccurate or represents an invasion of privacy. Furthermore, no personally identifiable information on a handicapped student may be released to anyone who is not involved with developing or implementing the student's educational program without obtaining the written consent of parents. Thus, parents have the right to control the flow of information on their handicapped child to persons who are not directly involved in the education of their child. Parental decisions, however, can be questioned by school personnel through the proceedings of a due process hearing.

In addition to the principles presented in the foregoing sections, provisions have been made to accommodate changes in the direction and purposes of special education.

PL 94–142 periodically undergoes reauthorization and amendment to respond to changing needs and circumstances. Congress allocates funds to each state on a yearly basis, enabling the states to provide financial support for programs for handicapped students in each school district.

Education of Preschool Handicapped Children

The Education of the Handicapped Act Amendments of 1986 constitutes a major change in the education of children who are handicapped. This act, Public Law 99–457, amends PL 94–142 to provide special education services to handicapped infants and toddlers (children from birth through age 2) who have developmental delays or physical or mental impairments that put them at risk for developmental delay. The law states that Congress has found "an urgent and substantial need" to

1. enhance the development of handicapped infants and toddlers and to minimize their potential for developmental delay.
2. reduce the educational costs to our society, including our Nation's schools, by minimizing the need for special education and related services after handicapped infants and toddlers reach school age.
3. minimize the likelihood of institutionalization of handicapped individuals and maximize their potential for independent living in society, and
4. enhance the capacity of families to meet the special needs of their infants and toddlers with handicaps. (PL 99–457, sec. 1471)

An emphasis on early identification was incorporated in PL 94–142, mandating that communities identify all children with handicaps as early as possible. The passage of PL 99–457 underscores the initiative for early identification and early intervention.

Rather than mandating special services for preschool children, PL 99–457 encourages each state to "develop and implement a statewide, comprehensive, coordinated, multidisciplinary, interagency program of early intervention services for handicapped infants and toddlers and their families" (Heward & Orlansky, 1988, p. 51). Teachers who are interested in working with this population will need to investigate the procedures adopted by the state in which they work. This area presents a new and exciting challenge, with the possibility of helping many children overcome their problems prior to school entrance.

In summary, federal and state legislative requirements have far-reaching implications for all teachers. Knowledge of these requirements can help teachers provide appropriate educational programs and insure their own professional behavior in teaching handicapped students. For more detailed information on legislative requirements and their educational implementation, refer to Turnbull (1986), Turnbull, Strickland, and Brantley (1982), and Weintraub (1986).

Education of Gifted Students

Gifted students, discussed in chapter 5, are not included under the provisions of PL 94–142 (unless they are also handicapped), and they remain without meaningful assistance from federal sources. In 1980, for example, the amount spent by the federal government on programs for gifted students was less than 1 percent of the total spent on handicapped students (Kirk & Gallagher, 1983).

In 1977, representatives of the Council for Exceptional Children (CEC) called on Congress to realize that the education of gifted and talented children should become a federal priority (Zettel & Ballard, 1978). CEC had also adopted a policy statement declaring that

> special educators should vigorously support programs for the gifted as consistent with their concept of the need for special assistance for all exceptional children. (Zettel & Ballard, 1978, p. 262)

A 1972 federal study referred to as the Marland Report revealed that approximately 2 million children had been identified as gifted and that the needs of only a few of them were being met. For the first time, the federal government officially recognized gifted and talented children and established the Office of Gifted and Talented (Silverman, 1988). The national study set goals for the education of gifted students but made no efforts toward implementation.

The official federal policy toward gifted and talented students recommends, but does not mandate, special educational services. The primary responsibility for developing and implementing these special services lies with local and state educational agencies; the national role remains one of technical assistance (Ysseldyke & Algozzine, 1984).

At the present time, 30 states categorize gifted children as exceptional either in statute or in the state department of education regulations to support the provision of programs (Wolf & Stephens, 1982). Thirty-nine states have developed guidelines for the identification of students for gifted programs, and 14 states currently require special certification for teachers of students who are gifted (Parker, 1989). Many state programs have the same provisions for referral, evaluation, and IEP development as those provided under PL 94–142 for students who are handicapped.

The lack of federally mandated provisions for the education of gifted children may be due in part to misconceptions about the children and their parents (Callahan & Kauffman, 1982). Many people believe that gifted children can be adequately educated without benefit of special programs or parent involvement. Some people assume that the parents of these students are also gifted and thus can provide appropriate resources for them. This may be true in some cases, but it cannot be assumed to be the rule.

The special needs of gifted children should be recognized and granted the same urgency as the needs of handicapped children. The same right should be accorded to parents of gifted children as to parents of handicapped children: the right to share in the decisions made concerning the education of their children. Parent and professional groups are advocating for this right; perhaps they will soon be recognized on a national level (Schulz, 1987).

MAINSTREAMING

Mainstreaming is the term used to describe the least restrictive environment clause of PL 94–142. This act does not use the term *mainstreaming*, but it does call for the integration of disabled and nondisabled students to the maximum extent appropriate. In practice, mainstreaming means different things in different educational settings and districts and can take many forms.

From studies of schools ranging from preschools to high schools, from rural to suburban to urban, and in wealthy districts as well as poor ones, Biklen (1985) describes four different models of mainstreaming. The first model is referred to as teacher deals. In this model, one teacher approaches another and suggests that a particular student is ready for placement in a regular class. If the regular class teacher agrees, mainstreaming takes place. The teacher who integrates a student may receive no support from the school system or the administration.

The second type of mainstreaming is characterized by the special education classroom in a regular school. Because there is no programmatic or social integration in this model, it may be referred to as island in the mainstream.

In a third model, many states have established intermediate school districts to serve multischool districts. Individual districts share in these services, which include special education, vocational education programs, computer services, and diagnostic services. Although there are some advantages in this system, it precludes mainstreaming and serves to isolate and segregate special populations.

In the model called unconditional mainstreaming, teachers and staff speak about integration and learning as correlated goals. Mainstreaming is a part of the setting, just as physical education, recess, grouping of children by their ages, and the determination of hours in a school day are parts of the setting. What makes this approach possible is

> not only the prior planning but also the presence of a problem solving attitude. People share an unconditional commitment to try and make it work, to discover the practical strategies to make it successful. (Biklen, 1985, p. 61)

The philosophy of this book is based on unconditional mainstreaming. We define mainstreaming as the social and instructional integration of exceptional students in a regular education class for at least a portion of the school day. For an exceptional student to be mainstreamed, this definition requires that two criteria be met: (1) physical inclusion in a regular class (for an unspecified portion of the day), and (2) functional inclusion as evidenced by social and instructional integration with students who are not identified as exceptional.

In 1976 the Council for Exceptional Children announced its official definition of mainstreaming and the philosophy underlying it. The major tenets of the CEC position are that

- Exceptional children have a wide variety of special educational needs, varying greatly in intensity and duration.
- There is a recognized continuum of educational settings that may, at any given time, be appropriate for a particular child's needs.
- Each exceptional child should be educated in the least restrictive environment in which his or her needs can be satisfactorily met.
- Exceptional children should be educated with nonexceptional children.

- Special classes, separate schooling, or other removal of an exceptional child from education with nonexceptional children should occur only when the intensity of the child's special needs is such that they cannot be satisfied in an environment including nonexceptional children even when supplementary aids and services are provided. (Cartwright, Cartwright, & Ward, 1989, p. 11)

Although most exceptional students receive their education in regular classes, mainstreaming does not mean that all special education settings will be eliminated. Rather, it means that new and different alternatives for exceptional students will be created. The following settings are used in many school systems:

1. regular class with no supplementary services
2. regular class with direct or indirect services
3. resource room
4. self-contained special class
5. special school
6. hospital–home instruction
7. residential school

These alternatives are illustrated in Figure 1.1 and described in the following sections.

1. *Regular class with no supplementary services.* For some handicapped students, the regular class, with no modifications, is an appropriate learning environment. The nature and degree of the student's handicap and the coping skills demonstrated by the student are factors determining the appropriateness of such a placement.

Educating gifted and talented students in regular classroom settings is a controversial topic. Some educators firmly believe that this placement is inappropriate (Parke, 1989). However, most gifted students are in regular classrooms at least part of their school day, and many are there for the majority of the day.

2. *Regular class with direct or indirect services.* Supplementary services can be added to the regular classroom to enable handicapped and gifted students to be instructionally and socially integrated. Among the alternatives are consulting teachers, methods and materials specialists, and itinerant teachers. Supplementary services within the regular classroom can be categorized as direct or indirect. Direct services are those provided to the student; indirect services may be delivered as help for teachers in developing techniques and obtaining materials.

3. *Resource room.* The resource room is designed to provide more support, more specialized services, and individual or small-group instruction to students whose total needs are not being met in the regular classroom. Handicapped students receive instruction from a special educator

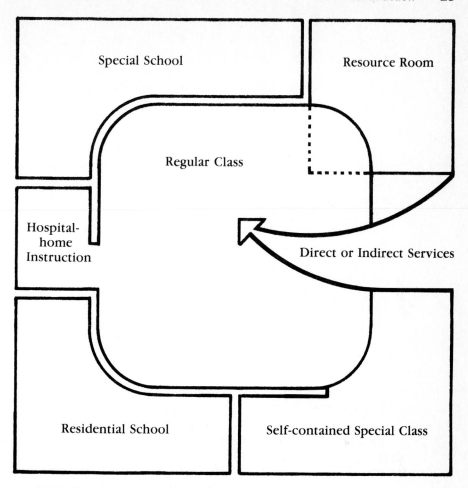

FIGURE 1.1 Placement Alternatives

and are usually grouped together for remediation in a particular subject area. Close communication between the special teacher and the classroom teacher is essential to insure that students are not penalized by missing class instruction or pleasurable activities such as physical education, art, or music.

In this model, gifted students are taken out of the regular classroom for a specified amount of time (often 1 class period or an hour a day) on a regular basis. The resource room is used most often at the upper elementary grade levels, because the structure of the secondary school by content subjects makes the resource-room concept difficult to apply (Gallagher, 1985).

4. *Self-contained special class.* Many handicapped students have been moved from self-contained special classes back to the regular classroom;

however, there are other students for whom the self-contained special class is still an appropriate setting. Students who are severely handicapped or who have unusual curriculum needs may be served better in a special classroom.

Another use for the self-contained special class is on a transitional basis. Some students who have behavior problems may be so distracting and distractible that they cannot be served in a regular classroom or resource room. After a period of intense training in a structured setting, it may be possible for them to return to regular classrooms on a part- or full-time basis. Blind students may need a specialized setting to acquire mobility and other skills before progressing into the mainstream of regular classes, and students who are deaf may need concentrated training in the acquisition of communication skills.

When this model is used for gifted students, the special-class teacher is responsible for the primary instruction of the gifted students in the major subject areas. Differentiated experiences for these students might include independent projects, accelerated subjects, and small-group enrichment activities, all of which aim at developing creative and other high-level thinking skills (Davis & Rimm, 1989).

5. *Special school.* In the continuum of services, there may still be a need for special schools. Facilities may be available at special schools that offer greater opportunities for some students. A school for children who are severely mentally retarded may offer vocational, physical education, or home living programs appropriate to their needs. The trend, however, is toward providing these services in schools attended by nonhandicapped students.

Special schools for the gifted are typically a big-city alternative. An entire elementary or secondary school may be designated for gifted students. The curriculum includes both traditional academic content plus special training in whatever academic, artistic, scientific, or personal development areas the school chooses to emphasize (Davis & Rimm, 1989).

6. *Hospital-home instruction.* Some handicapped students are absent from school for extended periods because of health impairments or medical interventions. In these instances (discussed in chapter 2), a teacher hired by the school system provides special education to the student in the hospital or home setting. This instruction is coordinated with the teacher who usually provides instruction to the student in the school setting.

7. *Residential school.* The residential school represents the most restrictive environment in the continuum of services for students who are handicapped. Even though there has been a concerted national effort toward deinstitutionalization, some children and adults still need residential services. Such services may include medical care as well as comprehensive educational and vocational programming; some may be part of a hospital setting. Two factors usually lead to the choice of a residential placement. The handicapped person may have severe or multiple hand-

icaps or there may not be a suitable living situation available with the individual's family.

Evidence from empirical studies of the past decade supports the effectiveness of mainstreaming in improving the performance of handicapped students and in attitudes toward them (Wang & Baker, 1986). Such evidence calls for increased efforts to unify regular and special education. Wang, Reynolds, and Walberg (1986) state the present situation and issue a challenge:

> The aspiration expressed in PL 94–142 has been the provision of appropriate education for all children and youth—even those most difficult to teach—within the regular schools of the community. Remarkable progress is evidenced in the facts that very nearly all school-age children and youth are in school and that the majority are in regular schools most of the time. Current practices, however, still leave a good deal of separateness, disjointedness, and inefficiency. What we must do is restructure school programs to more completely integrate students with special learning needs into regular school programs, using all forms of knowledge on how best to proceed with instruction. (p. 31)

The former assistant secretary for Special Education and Rehabilitative Services, the U.S. Department of Education, has spoken of the need to remove the barriers that exclude students with special needs from full integration into the life of the school and the larger society (Will, 1986). Such a task calls for the establishment of new partnerships in education—partnerships between states and the federal government, between states and local districts, between regular and special educators, and between educators and parents. It calls for communication and sharing of responsibility.

SHARED RESPONSIBILITY

The implementation of mainstreaming requires a team approach. In many school systems, classroom teachers have been expected to possess all the skills and have the time to accomplish the successful mainstreaming of students representing the full range of exceptionality—in most cases an impossible expectation. A sound approach to mainstreaming requires shared responsibility on the part of all educators in the school.

Classroom Teachers

Classroom teachers are undoubtedly expected to assume major responsibility in the mainstreaming process. As they teach handicapped students for a portion of the school day or in some cases for the entire day, they coordinate the students' instructional and social integration, which is the essence of mainstreaming. It is very important for these teachers to know where help is available. The following sections briefly outline responsibilities that might generally be shared with other team members. These suggestions are offered as a general guide and must be adapted to the particular staffing pattern of each school.

Special Educators

Resource Teachers

Many handicapped students in regular classes receive individual or small-group instruction from a special education resource teacher. Handicapped students may leave the regular class to receive instruction in the resource room for a specified period of time each day or each week, or the resource teacher may come into the regular class and instruct handicapped students in the everyday setting. To insure maximum educational progress, resource and regular teachers need to coordinate their programs carefully and maintain close communication about student performance. Classroom teachers can expect resource teachers to give them suggestions or instructional techniques and curriculum adaptations that are appropriate for students when they are in the regular class.

Itinerant Teachers

Itinerant teachers usually function like resource teachers. They are considered itinerant because they travel from one school to another to work with individual students. This model is usually followed in sparsely populated areas or in schools that have too few handicapped students to justify a full-time resource teacher. Also, many therapists (e.g., speech, occupational, and physical) are employed on an itinerant basis.

Self-Contained Class Teachers

Special class teachers are responsible for working with handicapped students in the self-contained class setting and also for integrating these students into school activities and curriculum blocks as appropriate. Although self-contained class teachers usually do not have the consultative duties of the resource or itinerant teacher, they do share instructional suggestions and materials readily with classroom teachers in many situations.

Special Education Consultants

Larger school systems often employ a special education consultant whose job might be to provide inservice training to classroom teachers and to offer backup support to classroom and resource teachers. Consultants usually have advanced training and are knowledgeable about a variety of instructional strategies. Systems that do not directly employ a consultant are likely to have consultative services available from the Division of Exceptional Children in the State Department of Public Instruction (agency titles vary from state to state) or from a regional educational service agency.

Director of Special Education

School systems usually have either a part-time or full-time director or coordinator of special education. This person is responsible for knowing the legal requirements and for administering, and often supervising, special education services. Classroom teachers who have specific questions about obtaining needed services, resources, or evaluations of handicapped students should consider working through their principal to contact the director of special education.

Principals

Principals have been identified as one of the keys to mainstreaming success (Payne & Murray, 1974). They might be called on to arrange inservice training, consider hiring additional personnel, instigate a volunteer program to help with individualization, locate appropriate instructional resources, and/or work toward the reduction of the student-teacher ratio. Teachers should share their concerns about mainstreaming constructively with principals so that principals can respond most effectively to teachers' needs.

Counselors

Counselors have various roles to play in the implementation of mainstreaming. They often serve as chairpersons of evaluation teams and IEP committees. They might help teachers with problems of social adjustment or coordinate activities associated with parent involvement. Specific responsibilities vary from school to school, but the important thing for teachers to remember is that counselors share in the responsibility for mainstreaming.

School Psychologists

Many schools employ part-time or full-time psychologists. Frequently psychologists, like itinerant teachers, are responsible for serving more than one school. Psychologists typically assume major responsibility in evaluation and placement decisions, in addition to participating in the development of the IEP. Other mainstreaming involvement could be working with teachers on behavior management programs and on ways to individualize instruction effectively.

Librarians

Librarians can be of great assistance in curriculum adaptation, particularly in helping to identify textbooks and a large variety of supplementary materials appropriate to student achievement levels and interests. Many handicapped students who read significantly below grade level need books of a high interest/low vocabulary nature. Librarians are qualified to identify such materials and to make them available to students and teachers.

Therapists

Mainstreaming requires the expertise of many specialists, such as those in speech, physical development, occupational development, dramatics, art, and music. Many schools do not employ therapists in these areas on a full-time basis; however, they may contract for services with mental health clinics, hospitals, special schools, colleges and universities, and state department consultants. When it is documented in IEP conferences that the needs of handicapped students require the expertise of therapists, such help must be made available by the school system. Therapy sessions should be coordinated with the students' academic schedules. Therapists can also train teachers in special techniques that teachers can provide routinely in the regular class.

Paraprofessionals

Paraprofessionals or teacher aides can contribute significantly to the quality and quantity of individualized instruction. Even if their help is available for only a portion of the school day or week, every bit of extra-hands time can be helpful. When working with a handicapped student, paraprofessionals should be thoroughly aware of the IEP and the other educational placements in which the student is included (resource program). Suggestions for preparing paraprofessionals to work with handicapped students are provided by Boomer (1980) and Kahan (1981).

Students

Students, both handicapped and nonhandicapped, play a significant role in successful mainstreaming. Handicapped students should be involved in the development of their IEPs when appropriate, considering their age and maturity. They should be encouraged to share their perspectives on their social acceptance in the regular class. Problems can often be pinpointed and eliminated in early stages if students bring them to the attention of teachers before they reach a crisis point. Handicapped students often know how to adapt the curriculum or school environment to their needs most effectively. For example, sometimes teachers waste time by trying to second-guess the needs of a blind student. Asking the student directly about when help is needed and when it is not can assist teachers in getting on with the task of appropriate instruction. Mainstreaming should be viewed not as an arrangement to be imposed on handicapped students, but rather as a process involving reciprocal information sharing and responsibility.

Parents

Parents can be invaluable partners to teachers in mainstreaming programs. First, they have a significant responsibility as members of the team developing the IEP. As they participate in specifying priority instructional goals, they help shape the curriculum through which their children will progress. Educational decision making and accountability, therefore, become shared responsibilities with parents. Other participatory involvement of parents might include serving as classroom volunteers in their child's class or in another class in the school; sharing information on helpful hints regarding possible classroom/environmental adaptations or motivational suggestions; making instructional materials to be used at school; reviewing and reinforcing classroom concepts after school; and helping to foster their child's social adjustment.

Community Volunteers

Volunteers from the community have made beneficial contributions to mainstreaming in some school systems by serving, like parents, as classroom volunteers. They might work individually or in small groups with handicapped students needing extra help or might be involved in projects or assignments with other class members in order to free teachers to spend more time with students having special problems. Some communities have organized volunteer programs for the purpose of making instructional materials needed by handicapped students or raising money to purchase equipment, such as auditory trainers for hearing-impaired students, wheelchairs, large-print typewriters, or braille readers. Civic groups and service clubs in many communities have a particular interest in the needs of handicapped persons. One of the best examples of this interest on a

national basis is the Lions Club, an organization that has made a tremendous contribution to services for blind persons. Other interested target groups could include college students and retired people. For readers interested in guidelines for recruiting and training volunteers to work with handicapped students, information is provided by Adams and Taylor (1980), Buffer (1980), and Cuninggim (1980).

Professional and Consumer Organizations

Educators involved in mainstreaming should call on the resources of professional and consumer organizations. These organizations are many in number, and most have information dissemination as one of their major goals. The names and addresses of some of these organizations are included in Appendix B. Readers with particular interest in a certain type of exceptionality or a focused area of mainstreaming are encouraged to write the organizations with corresponding target groups and concerns. A wealth of information is available from these sources. Additionally, many of these organizations have local and state chapters that can provide on-site contributions to the implementation of mainstreaming, such as providing consultants to conduct inservice training, offering specific instructional suggestions for particular handicapped students, or sharing information on appropriate instructional materials.

Team Approach

Mainstreaming requires shared responsibility involving many team members working cooperatively with classroom teachers to provide quality educational programs to handicapped and gifted students. Mainstreaming does not mean that classroom teachers must assume all the responsibility; rather, special educators, principals, counselors, school psychologists, librarians, therapists, paraprofessionals, students, parents, community volunteers, and professional/consumer organizations all have responsibilities and opportunities in planning and implementing mainstreaming for exceptional students. Emphasis is directed to the need to coordinate all involvement carefully in order to maximize the ultimate benefit to students. Coordination, communication, and cooperation are keys to shared responsibility and successful programming.

Organization for Categories of Exceptionality

Knowledge about the characteristics of their students who are handicapped or gifted also empowers teachers to be successful in mainstreaming situations. It is important to provide all school personnel with basic information about the categories of exceptionalities they are likely to encounter in the school.

Even though it is not expected that teachers become experts in areas of exceptionality, it is important for them to recognize indications of exceptionality, to be able to make appropriate referrals, and to understand and respond to characteristics of the exceptional students they teach. Chapters 2, 3, 4, and 5 present definitions, characteristics, and educational implications of the various exceptionalities. The categories include students with orthopedic and health impairments, students with sensory impairments and communication disorders, students with learning and behavior disorders, and students with exceptional gifts and talents.

REFERENCES

Adams, P. K., & Taylor, M. K. (1980). Volunteer help in the classroom. *Education Unlimited, 2,* (1), 26–27.

Biklen, D. P. (1985). Mainstreaming: From compliance to quality. *Journal of Learning Disabilities, 18,* (1), 58–61.

Boomer, L. W. (1980). Special education paraprofessionals: A guide for teachers. *Teaching Exceptional Children, 12,* (4), 146–149.

Bradfield, H. R., Brown, J., Kaplan, P., Rickert, E., & Stannard, R. (1973). The special child in the regular classroom. *Exceptional Children, 39,* 384–390.

Brown v. Board of Education, 347 U.S. 483 (1954).

Budoff, M., & Gottlieb, J. (1976). Special class students mainstreamed: A study of an aptitude (learning potential) × treatment interaction. *American Journal of Mental Deficiency, 81,* (1), 1–11.

Buffer, L. C. (1980). Recruit retired adults as volunteers in special education. *Teaching Exceptional Children, 12,* (3), 113–115.

Callahan, C. M., & Kauffman, J. M. (1982). Involving gifted children's parents: Federal law is silent, but its assumptions apply. *Exceptional Education Quarterly, 3,* (2), 50–55.

Carroll, A. (1967). The effects of segregated and partially integrated school programs on self concept and academic achievement of educable mental retardates. *Exceptional Children, 34,* (2), 93–99.

Cartwright, G. P., Cartwright, C. A., & Ward, M. E. (1989). *Educating special learners* (3rd ed.). Belmont, CA: Wadsworth.

Corman, L., & Gottlieb, J. (1979). Mainstreaming mentally retarded children: A review of research. In N. R. Ellis (Ed.), *International review of research in mental retardation* (Vol. 9) (pp. 251–275). New York: Academic.

Cuninggim, W. (1980). Citizen volunteers: A growing resource for teachers and students. *Teaching Exceptional Children, 12,* (3), 108–112.

Davis, G. A., & Rimm, S. B. (1989). *Education of the gifted and talented* (2nd ed.). Englewood Cliffs, NJ: Prentice-Hall.

Diana v. State Board of Education, No. C–70–37 RFP (N.D. Cal., Jan. 7, 1970, and June 18, 1973).

Dunn, L. M. (1968). Special education for the mildly retarded: Is much of it justifiable? *Exceptional Children, 35,* (1), 5–22.

Federal Register (1977). Washington, DC: U.S. Government Printing Office.

Gallagher, J. J. (1985). *Teaching the gifted child* (3rd ed.). Boston: Allyn and Bacon.

Goodman, H., Gottlieb, J., & Harrison, R. H. (1972). Social acceptance of EMRs integrated into a non-graded elementary school. *American Journal of Mental Deficiency, 76,* (4), 412–417.

Heward, W. L., & Orlansky, M. D. (1988). *Exceptional children* (3rd ed.). Columbus, OH: Merrill.

Hobson v. Hansen, 269 F. Supp. 401 (1967), *affd sub nom.* Smuck v. Hobson, 408 F. 2d 175 (D. C. Cir. 1969).

Iano, R. P., Ayers, D., Heller, H. B., McGettigan, J. F., & Walker, V. S. (1974). Sociometric status of retarded children in an integrative program. *Exceptional Children, 40,* (4), 267–271.

Jones, R. L., Gottlieb, J., Guskin, S., & Yoshida, R. K. (1978). Evaluating mainstreaming programs: Models, caveats, considerations and guidelines. *Exceptional Children, 44,* (8), 588–601.

Kahan, E. H. (1981). Aides in special education—a boon for students and teachers. *Teaching Exceptional Children, 14,* (3), 101–105.

Kirk, S. A., & Gallagher, J. J. (1983). *Educating exceptional children* (4th ed.). Boston: Houghton Mifflin.

Lynch, E. W., & Lewis, R. B. (1988). *Exceptional children and adults.* Glenview, IL: Scott, Foresman.

MacMillan, D. L., Jones, R. L., & Aloia, G. F. (1974). The mentally retarded label:

A theoretical analysis and review of research. *American Journal of Mental Deficiency, 79*, (3), 241–261.

Mercer, J. R. (1973). *Labeling the mentally retarded: Clinical and social system perspectives on mental retardation.* Berkeley: University of California Press.

Meyers, C. E., MacMillan, D. L., & Yoshida, R. K. (1980). Regular class education of EMR students, from efficacy to mainstreaming: A review of issues and research. In J. Gottlieb (Ed.), *Educating mentally retarded persons in the main-stream* (pp. 176–206). Baltimore: University Park Press.

Miller, T. L., & Switzky, H. N. (1979). P.L. 94-142 and the least restrictive alternative: An interim progress report for educators. *Journal of Education, 161*, (3), 60–80.

Mills v. D.C. Board of Education, 348 F. Supp. 866 (D.D.C. 1972).

Parke, B. N. (1989). *Gifted students in regular classrooms.* Boston: Allyn and Bacon.

Parker, J. P. (1989). *Instructional strategies for teaching the gifted.* Boston: Allyn and Bacon.

Payne, R., & Murray, C. (1974). Principals' attitudes toward integration of the handicapped. *Exceptional Children, 41*, (2), 132–135.

Pennsylvania Association for Retarded Children v. Commonwealth of Pennsylvania, 334 F. Supp. 1257 (E.D.Pa. 1971) and 343 F. Supp. 279 (E.D. Pa. 1972).

Reynolds, M. C. & Birch, J. (1977). *Mainstreaming in all America's schools.* Reston, VA: Council for Exceptional Children.

Reynolds, M. C., Wang, M. C., & Walberg, H. J. (1987). The necessary restructuring of special and regular education. *Exceptional Children 53*, (5), 391–398.

Schulz, J. B. (1987). *Parents and professionals in special education.* Boston: Allyn and Bacon.

Silverman, L. K. (1988). Gifted and talented. In E. L. Meyen & T. M. Skrtic (Eds.), *Exceptional children and youth* (3rd ed.) (pp. 264–291). Denver: Love.

Singer, J. D., Butler, J. A., Palfrey, J. S., & Walker, D. K. (1986). Characteristics of special education placements: Findings from probability samples in five metropolitan school districts. *The Journal of Special Education, 20*, (3), 319–337.

Turnbull, A. P. (1982). Preschool mainstreaming: A policy and implementation analysis. *Educational Evaluation and Policy Analysis, 4*, (3), 281–291.

Turnbull, A. P., & Strickland, B. (1981). Parents and the educational system. In J. L. Paul (Ed.), *Understanding and working with parents of children with special needs* (pp. 231–263). New York: Holt, Rinehart and Winston.

Turnbull, A. P., Strickland, D. B., & Brantley, J. (1982). *Developing and implementing individualized education programs.* Columbus, OH: Merrill.

Turnbull, H. R. (1986). *Free appropriate public education: The law and children with disabilities.* Denver: Love.

Wang, M. C., & Baker, E. T. (1986). Mainstreaming programs: Design features and effects. *The Journal of Special Education, 19*, (4), 503–520.

Wang, M. C., Reynolds, M. C., & Walberg, H. J. (1986). Rethinking special education. *Educational Leadership, 44*, (1), 26–31.

Weintraub, F. J. (1986). *Goals for the future of special education.* Reston, VA: Council for Exceptional Children.

Will, M. (1986). *Educating students with learning problems—a shared responsibility: A report to the Secretary.* Washington, DC: U.S. Dept. of Education, Office of Special Education and Rehabilitative Services.

Wolf, J. S., & Stephens, I. M. (1982). *Effective skills in parent/teacher conferencing: The parents' perspective.* Columbus: Ohio State University, National Center for Educational Materials and Media for the Handicapped.

Ysseldyke, J. E., & Algozzine, B. (1984). *Introduction to special education.* Boston: Houghton Mifflin.

Zettel, J. J., & Ballard, J. (1978). A need for increased federal effort for the gifted and talented. *Exceptional Children, 44* (4), 261–267.

—2—

Students with Orthopedic and Health Impairments

Case Study: Orthopedic Impairment

I was about five minutes into my lecture the second day of school when out of the corner of my eye, I sensed a movement at the door. I turned and was greeted by the arrival of Eric—wheelchair, backpack, support staff member and all. His name had not appeared on my class roll, and the staff member introduced us. She encouraged me to treat him as any other student but also offered her assistance if I felt he was in a situation where he needed additional time to complete an assignment or test. I had no trouble being genuine in welcoming Eric to my classroom; however, I did wish I had known earlier. The immediate problem, which could have been anticipated and solved, was where to place him. Eric needed a table which would enable him to sit comfortably in his wheelchair and do written work. But it was also important to me that this table be placed so that he would not feel any sense of isolation from the other students. I had a suitable table in the room, but at that moment it was piled high with over 100 textbooks. I had no choice but to put him at the back of the room. I relate this to emphasize the importance of communication with the classroom teacher before the student arrives in class.

I remember well the day I gave out the textbooks. I asked the students to come get the books, being sure to record their names in them. As I called out for Eric, I wrote his name in the book myself and then looked up. He still sat at the back of the room. Numerous ideas rushed into my mind at the speed of thought. "Treat him like any other student. Why is he just sitting there? Should I get someone to take his book to him?" The next second I heard myself saying, "Eric, come get your book." He did so willingly, and in my mind in that instant I made the commitment that insofar as possible, I would treat Eric as a student first, as orthopedically handicapped second.

Eric's writing is slow, labored, and large. He needs more space as well as more time to write. I have realized that I will have to adjust some assignments and tests to accommodate this. For example, while others are rewriting a paragraph for logical order, Eric just numbers the sentences in order. When I gave a standardized diagnostic test which required a machine-scored answer sheet, Eric went to the library where the support staff member marked the answers for him. However, the reading of the test was his responsibility, and he worked in the same time frame as the others since recording the answers was no longer a problem.

At the end of this year I hope Eric will feel he has learned much in the area of communication skills, but I hope even more that he will feel he has had a teacher who led her class in responding to him as a person, capable in his own way. I already sense we are kindred spirits in humor. About a week after he first rolled in, he was preparing to leave at the end of class. I had been working with an overhead projector that day, and the hot August weather necessitated the placement of a fan near my desk also. All of this equipment was blocking his exit. He politely asked if I would move the projector. I put my hands on my hips and with pretended exasperation replied, "Gee, you're a lot of trouble!" He never missed a beat. He smiled and with eyes twinkling replied, "No, I'm just wide!"

Hey, I like this kid!

Dee Grantham
Smoky Mountain High School

A number of years ago, one of the authors visited a class designated for physically handicapped children. Included in the class was a young woman with cerebral palsy who was noncommunicative and extremely physically limited; a 12-year-old boy who was deaf and very bright; a teenage girl who had epilepsy; and a young boy who was thought to be autistic. These students had nothing in common except their label. They were functioning on widely different educational levels and presented an overwhelming challenge to their teacher.

Today, students with physical or health impairments are successfully integrated into an increasing number of regular classrooms. In some cases, their intellectual ability and learning potential are limited; in other cases, their educational level is equal to or above that of their peers.

Freiberg (1988) points out that even though students with physical or health impairments are being included in regular classrooms in increasing numbers, school physicians and school nurses are less frequently available to students and to faculty as resource personnel. Therefore, teachers and other school personnel are required to provide more special services to physically and health impaired students than they have in the past.

The guidelines of PL 94–142 divide children with physical impairments into two groups: students with orthopedic impairments and those with health impairments. Orthopedic impairments refer to disorders of the skeleton, joints, and muscles; health impairments are conditions affecting strength, vitality, and alertness.

ORTHOPEDIC IMPAIRMENTS

An orthopedic impairment is defined as a condition that

> adversely affects a child's educational performance. The term includes impairments caused by a congenital anomaly (e.g., clubfoot, absence of some member, etc.), impairments caused by disease (e.g., poliomyelitis, bone tuberculosis, etc.), and impairments from other causes (e.g., cerebral palsy, amputations, and fractures or burns which cause contractures). (*Federal Register*, 1977, p. 42478)

It is obvious from this definition that orthopedic handicaps can be congenital (present from birth) or acquired during childhood or adult years, sometimes resulting from accidents. Like all other handicapping conditions, orthopedic handicaps vary greatly depending on the age of onset, the level of severity, the extent of involvement, and the treatment provided by special therapists, the family, and teachers. Sometimes students with such handicaps also have secondary problems in the areas of speech, vision, or mental retardation. In other cases, students may have the singular disadvantage of an orthopedic handicap, such as dwarfism, but have gifted intelligence and accelerated academic achievement.

It is also important to realize that orthopedic impairments may be educationally and socially debilitating to one student but not to another. Different persons have differing coping abilities in minimizing handicaps. Consider the student who has paralyzed legs and has satisfactory or above-average academic achievement; who adapts such games as basketball, tennis, and softball to be played from the wheelchair; and who participates in peer and family activities. Another student with an identical physical impairment may be academically deficient, physically inactive, and socially excluded. The difference lies in personality traits unique to each individual, plus the support the student has received from parents, teachers, other helping professionals, and peers.

Although it is not the purpose of this chapter to focus on the medical bases of physical disabilities, it is important to understand the characteristics and implications of a variety of orthopedic and neurological impairments. The following impairments are most commonly encountered in school settings.

Cerebral Palsy

Cerebral palsy is one of the physical impairments found most frequently in school-age children. By definition, cerebral palsy is a nonprogressive disorder of movement or posture that begins in childhood and is caused by a malfunctioning of, or damage to, the brain (Bleck, 1982a).

Henderson and Bryan (1984) report that 700,000 persons in the United States have cerebral palsy. The damage to the brain, resulting in motor impairment, may occur before birth, at or near the time of birth, or soon after birth. The causes of cerebral palsy are not clearly understood, but factors most likely to be associated with it are mental retardation of the mother, premature birth, low birth weight, and a delay of 5 minutes or more after birth before the baby's first cry (Heward & Orlansky, 1988).

Cerebral palsy is classified into several types according to patterns of motor dysfunction. The most common types expressed in children are spasticity, athetosis, and ataxia. About 90 percent of the conditions are spastic and athetoid. Muscles are tense and frequently contracted in spastics, resulting in difficulty controlling body movements. Athetoid cerebral palsy is characterized by involuntary and uncontrollable movements, and ataxia is a condition of imbalance and a distorted sense of direction (Henderson & Bryan, 1984). Individuals may have mixed types of cerebral palsy, and different portions of the body may be affected, as described in the following section on the locus of involvement.

Cerebral palsy occurs in a wide variety of degrees and may be accompanied by other disorders. Common problems that may be present include mental retardation, visual defects, and communication disorders. The majority of persons who have cerebral palsy have normal or above normal intelligence; their motor involvement may be slight or severe. It is important for teachers and other school personnel to look at the individual and to ask the following questions before planning for instruction:

- What is the expected intelligence range?
- What kind of speech communication should be expected?
- How does the condition affect hearing?
- How does the condition affect vision?
- Where is the site of the condition, or how does the condition manifest itself?
- What is the prognosis, while the student is in an educational setting?
- What kind of mobility will the child have?
- What general classroom considerations should be anticipated? (McCoy & Prehm, 1987, p. 63)

It is helpful if the classroom teacher can observe the student who has cerebral palsy and talk with parents and other people who have worked with the student. Frequently, the student may have adapted to his or her surroundings and will be able to let the teacher know in what areas help is needed.

Students who have cerebral palsy, as well as students described in the following sections, may require various types of orthotic and prosthetic appliances (usually called braces or artificial limbs) to minimize the effects of their disabilities. When a teacher first encounters an orthopedic appliance, the plethora of straps, joints, fasteners, and other hardware may be intimidating (Frederick & Fletcher, 1985). In order to monitor the fit and effect of the orthotic or prosthetic appliance, the teacher will need information about its function and maintenance. Parents, physicians, and physical therapists can provide the necessary information. Teachers who become informed about the devices help increase the student's adjustment to the appliance and help provide a more positive, successful learning environment.

Muscular Dystrophy

Muscular dystrophy is a "progressive, diffuse weakness of all muscle groups, which is characterized by a degeneration of muscle cells and their replacement by fat and fibrous tissue" (Bleck, 1982b, p. 385). The most common form of muscular dystrophy is the Duchenne, or childhood form. This disability mainly affects boys and can be traced to a recessive gene carried by the mother and transmitted to sons.

Because muscular dystrophy is progressive, it may not be diagnosed until the child is at least 3 years old. Children who have not been diagnosed before they enter school may have slow motor development, awkward and clumsy movement, and difficulty in learning. Students who have this disability will become more and more disabled and may be unable to walk by 10 to 12 years of age (Seibel, 1989). The disease is fatal, and children who have it rarely live beyond later teen years.

Teachers should be aware of the fatigue associated with muscular dystrophy and should plan for periods of rest. A more sensitive situation arises in dealing with a student who is terminally ill. One teacher expressed the dilemma this way: "I don't know whether to expect him to do the same work or not. On one hand, I know he will never live to pursue his education; on the other hand, I want him to learn while he is here."

Teachers and fellow students may need counseling to help them deal with the knowledge that a classmate will not live long. If death should occur, many questions need to be answered and complicated issues faced.

Spina Bifida

Spina bifida is a congenital defect in the development of the spinal cord in which part of the spinal cord and the nerves that normally control muscles and feeling in the lower part of the body fail to develop normally (Heward

& Orlansky, 1988). If the lining of the spinal cord bulges through an opening in the infant's back at birth, the condition is called *meningocele.* If the spinal lining, spinal cord, and nerve roots all protrude, the condition is called *myelomeningocele,* which is a more serious condition (Pieper, 1983).

Spina bifida may be accompanied by hydrocephalus, which means that cerebrospinal fluid has accumulated in tissues surrounding the brain. This fluid may be diverted away from the brain and into the bloodstream by inserting a shunt. The shunt must be monitored and cleared or replaced if it malfunctions.

Children with spina bifida usually have some degree of paralysis of the lower limbs and lack full control of their bladder and bowel functions. Most children with spina bifida learn to use a catheter to collect their urine so they can empty their bladders at convenient times.

Limb Deficiency

Missing limbs or amputations affect a number of students. Absence of a limb may be congenital or may have occurred after birth. Usually, early intervention by rehabilitation personnel is critical, with the location and severity of limb deficiency determining the extent and potential of the rehabilitation process (Sirvis, 1988a).

Frequently students with missing limbs are fitted with artificial limbs (prostheses). Such devices are important to physical and psychological adjustment of the individuals, enabling them to function in a normal environment and to appear physically intact. Some people, however, prefer to use the remaining portion of a limb. For example, a young woman who played the guitar was missing a hand and used the remaining rounded wrist effectively in playing musical instruments.

Juvenile Rheumatoid Arthritis

Although it is not considered as debilitating as conditions discussed above, arthritis is a major disability. *Juvenile rheumatoid arthritis* is a term used to refer to a group of diseases characterized by chronic arthritis of unknown cause (Miller, 1982). Arthritis is an inflammation of the joints of the body and may occur in infants as young as 6 weeks of age. The symptoms of arthritis that apply to an adult do not always apply to children. Childhood arthritis is complicated because the patient may be too young to describe the symptoms fully and accurately (Hollister, 1985).

The most important difference between rheumatoid arthritis in adults and in children is that 60 to 70 percent of children will be free of active disease after a period of 10 years. The length of time that a child will remain affected is unpredictable and can vary from months to years. With good care, less than 20 percent of children should be left with real functional limitations (Miller, 1982).

The student who has rheumatoid arthritis may experience a great deal of pain and may be irritable and distressed during the school day. Lack of sleep because of pain may contribute to poor achievement and inattentiveness. Because people with rheumatoid arthritis may have morning stiffness, students who have this disability are frequently unable to move their joints for several hours. This stiffness also occurs with prolonged sitting or remaining in one particular position. Teachers can help this condition by planning for and permitting frequent movement from one seat or activity to another. It is also important to allow adequate transition time for students whose movement may be slow or painful.

Juvenile rheumatoid arthritis is usually treated with aspirin and physical therapy.

Educational Implications

From the brief descriptions above, it is obvious that a disability may be mild or severe, temporary, permanent, or terminal. Regardless of the origin or description of the handicap, there are implications for the classroom teacher. The primary educational implications center around mobility and adaptive equipment.

Mobility

Mobility basically refers to a person's capacity to move about, stand, or to use the hands in manipulating environmental objects. Students with limited mobility may need to develop compensatory ways of moving around the classroom, entering and leaving the school building, going to the school cafeteria, participating in playground activities, or learning to write. In educational implications, mobility must be considered in light of three factors: the locus of involvement, the nature of the handicap, and the rate and stability of motion.

The locus of involvement can occur in various parts of the body and in various combinations of body parts. The following terms are used to describe the involvement:

monoplegia: paralysis of one limb
paraplegia: paralysis of both lower extremities
hemiplegia: paralysis of both extremities on the same side
quadriplegia: paralysis of all four extremities
diplegia: paralysis of all four extremities; greater involvement in the
lower limbs.

The educational implications and the resulting adaptations planned by the physical therapist, occupational therapist, and teacher depend on the student's particular locus of involvement.

Disadvantages of mobility differ, depending on the nature of a student's handicap. One way to view the nature of these disadvantages is from the perspectives of paralysis, problems with coordination, and loss of limbs. Paralysis results in the limitation of moving parts of the body, ranging from mild limitations to total incapacity. Students whose legs are paralyzed gain mobility through the use of a wheelchair, braces, and crutches. The elimination of architectural barriers in schools is necessary for these students to gain access to educational services and opportunities. Minimizing the disadvantages of these students means creating accessibility through ramps, aisles, and doorways; adjusting desks to the comfort of the students; and accommodating toilet facilities and water fountains. Plans for fire drills and other emergency procedures sometimes have to be adapted according to the particular needs of orthopedically handicapped students and the physical plant of the school.

Students with handicaps related to coordination may have too much movement as opposed to the limited movement resulting from paralysis. Coordination problems might also be characterized by tenseness, jerkiness, or difficulty in directing one's movements in desired patterns. Helping these students to position themselves while sitting, standing, or moving about can contribute significantly to their adaptability to coordination handicaps. Correct positioning is an individual matter based on the particular needs of each orthopedically handicapped student. Teachers should discuss positioning with the student's parents, physical therapist, or occupational therapist for specific classroom guidelines. Academically, impairment in coordination of the arms and hands is usually reflected in a student's writing.

Mobility rate is an important factor in classroom success. Some students with no major, overt orthopedic impairment may generally have slow mobility. These students are usually chosen last on the playing field because they can never make it to first base before the ball gets there; or they rarely have time to complete classwork or tests because of the slow pace at which they write. These students are at a definite disadvantage in attaining school success. The characteristics of mobility problems previously discussed also may result in lowered rates of motion.

Curriculum accommodations can be fairly simple. If a student requires significantly more time to complete a written assignment, the teacher might reduce the length of the assignment so it is not physically overwhelming. All classroom tasks can be reduced in length if necessary. This practice often allows the student with low mobility rate to complete tasks and to achieve success.

As to the stability of motion, some students with orthopedic handicaps become tired more quickly than do other students. Teachers should be alert to this factor and minimize it by making provisions for such students to rest at necessary intervals throughout the school day. Some teachers have successfully used a cot or lounge chair in the corner of the classroom for this purpose.

Adaptive Equipment

Orthopedically handicapped students (e.g., those with cerebral palsy, rheumatoid arthritis, muscular dystrophy, or spina bifida) vary greatly in the ability to handle their bodies. Being able to move prevents discomfort, presents people with a variety of visual stimuli, and facilitates awareness and attentiveness. Therefore, teachers working with orthopedically handicapped students should be knowledgeable about basic physical management strategies (Parette & Hourcade, 1986).

Students with paralysis use a variety of adaptive equipment to enhance their mobility. Types of equipment include wheelchairs, braces, and crutches. Teachers who have had no previous contact with orthopedically handicapped students need to learn about the use and maintenance of these devices. The best procedure for teachers is to gather this information from discussions with the student, parents, physical therapist, and occupational therapist. Teachers of young children, who will likely need to assume more responsibility for helping the student maneuver a wheelchair (and for helping peers develop this skill), should ask for demonstrations of how to lock the braces, fold the chair when it is not being used, open it again, remove the arms, and assist the student in moving from the wheelchair to a regular chair. Examples of other areas of information related to moving around the school grounds include getting up and down curbs and boarding elevators.

Teachers should not hesitate to ask any questions that will help them feel more confident and competent in helping a student with mobility impairments. Further, teachers may be surprised at how much of this information they already possess. Manipulating wheelchairs around the environment is very similar to manipulating baby strollers (Pieper, 1983), an experience many adults have had.

Teachers and parents are concerned about the psychological aspects of orthopedic and health impairments as well as the physical aspects. It is commonly acknowledged that students who are orthopedically impaired frequently have low self-esteem related to being disabled among able-bodied peers (Walker & Jacobs, 1984). In the elementary school years, children strive to conform to behavior set by their small circles of friends; during adolescence, they are also conscious of the larger community and its expectations for their behavior and appearance.

Young children are usually more open and accepting of differences than are older students. The following example illustrates the uninhibited attitude found in young children:

> *Jason, who has cerebral palsy, was entering kindergarten. His parents and teachers were concerned about the other children's reactions to his crutches, but decided to wait and see what would happen. He came into the classroom, sat on the floor and put his crutches aside. One little girl asked, "What are those things?" "They're crutches, dummy." "Could I use them?" "I don't know; it's kinda hard, but I'll show you." (Schulz, 1983, p. 127)*

Adolescence is a particularly trying time for students who are increasingly sensitive to peers' reactions to their differences. The teacher's attitude toward the disabled student and efforts to create an open and accepting environment are primary factors in the total integration of the student with an orthopedic impairment. Suggestions for facilitating social integration are made in chapter 13.

HEALTH IMPAIRMENTS

Conditions affecting a student's health may be permanent, temporary, or intermittent. Most of the health impairments discussed in this section are chronic—they are present over long periods of time and tend not to get better or to disappear (Heward & Orlansky, 1988). This category of handicaps is defined by PL 94–142 as

> having an autistic condition which is manifested by severe communication and other developmental and educational problems or having limited strength, vitality or alertness, due to chronic or acute health problems such as a heart condition, tuberculosis, rheumatic fever, nephritis, asthma, sickle cell anemia, hemophilia, epilepsy, lead poisoning, leukemia, or diabetes, which adversely affects a child's educational performance. (*Federal Register*, 1981, pp. 3865–3866)

Students with a variety of health problems are enrolled in public schools. Some of the problems, such as asthma, may not require special education services. Whether or not the students are identified within the regulations of PL 94–142, teachers need to be aware of and concerned about their health problems and the effect of these problems on school performance and psychological well-being. Among the health impairments encountered in the school population are seizure disorders (epilepsy), cystic fibrosis, sickle cell anemia, juvenile diabetes mellitus, and asthma. There also are a number of diseases (e.g. cancer and hemophilia) that could occur; the following brief descriptions provide an introduction.

Seizure Disorders (Epilepsy)

Seizures are disturbances of movement, sensation, behavior, and/or consciousness caused by abnormal electrical activity in the brain. Seizures can occur in people when they have high fevers or drink excessive amounts of alcohol or experience a blow to the head. When seizures occur chronically and repeatedly, the condition is called *epilepsy* (Heward & Orlansky, 1988).

When nerve cells in the brain are charged with excessive electricity, the brain may temporarily lose control of such functions as attention, sensation, perception, and muscle control. This phenomenon is referred to as a *seizure*. The two most common types of seizures teachers might encounter in the classroom are petit mal and grand mal seizures.

When petit mal seizures occur, a student is likely to appear to be daydreaming. The student might stare straight ahead, blink his or her eyes, drop books or pencils, or nod for a few seconds. The student does not comprehend classroom information for the brief period of the petit mal seizure. First, the teacher must realize that the student is not just failing to pay attention. A teacher who suspects the possibility of seizures should discuss this concern with the school nurse and the student's family. The teacher's second responsibility is to make sure the student has an opportunity to get the information missed in class. Both the teacher and the student's classmates can help fill the gaps in classroom activities and instruction caused by the occurrence of the seizure.

A grand mal seizure is a more severe manifestation. It is usually preceded by an aura, a strange sensation that can alert the person that a seizure is about to occur. The student probably will first stiffen the muscles of the body and then proceed into a stage of jerking movements. During this period, he or she will lose consciousness, perhaps emit sounds and/or saliva, and possibly lose bladder and bowel control, which can result in extreme embarrassment to the student. The actual seizure lasts from 5 to 10 minutes and is followed by the need for rest or sleep. Teachers can help manage seizures that occur at school by following these guidelines:

1. Collect information and plan your classroom response so that you can remain calm when the seizure occurs. Talk with the student, parents, and doctor to make sure your questions about the student's particular seizure pattern are answered. Write to the Epilepsy Foundation of America (see Appendix B for the address) to obtain pamphlets and visual material for classroom teachers and students and information on school management of seizures.
2. Try to help the student respond to the aura or warning signal by getting to an open space away from desks and tables. The student should lie on the floor and be free to move around. The teacher should not attempt to restrict movement or place anything in the student's mouth other than possibly a soft handkerchief between

the teeth. It is important for the teacher to remember that the seizure is painless to the student.

3. After the seizure occurs, the student may need to sleep (but not necessarily need to be sent home). The teacher should always report the seizure to the student's parents and the school nurse.

Most seizures are controlled very effectively by medication and rarely occur in classrooms. Unfortunately, students with histories of seizures are often stigmatized. Teachers have a major responsibility to help classmates understand the nature of seizures as well as the strengths and talents of students who have seizures.

Cystic Fibrosis

It is estimated that 1 in every 500 children is born with cystic fibrosis and approximately 1 in every 25 Caucasians carries the gene for this disorder (Harvey, 1982b). Characterized by chronic pulmonary (lung) involvement and pancreatic deficiency, its major effects include a dry cough, bronchial obstruction by abnormal secretions, and susceptibility to acute infections. Although people with cystic fibrosis have a poor prognosis, recent medical advances have increased their potential life span into adulthood. Treatment includes antibiotics, modified diet, and respiratory exercises (Sirvis, 1988a). A regular educational program is appropriate, but exercise may need to be limited.

Sickle Cell Anemia

A hereditary blood disease, sickle cell anemia predominantly affects black persons. About 10 percent of blacks in the United States are carriers of the disease. Characteristics of sickle cell anemia are anemia (insufficiency of red blood cells); swelling of the hands, feet, and joints; bouts of severe pain in the abdomen, legs, or arms; impairment of liver function; loss of appetite; painful, slow-healing sores; and general weakness. Various types of episodes may occur in children with sickle cell anemia. These episodes, or crises, may require hospitalization and result in prolonged absences from school (Seibel, 1989).

Juvenile Diabetes Mellitus

Another disorder influenced by heredity is juvenile diabetes mellitus, in which sugar cannot be used normally by the body due to a failure of the pancreas to produce insulin. Abnormal amounts of sugar in the blood and in the urine cause continuous thirst, passing of large amounts of urine, and loss of weight and strength (Henderson & Bryan, 1984).

Although the discovery that a child has diabetes mellitus may come as a shock to both child and parents, a thorough understanding of the nature of the disease and its treatment can allow the student to lead a normal life. The person who has diabetes mellitus learns to inject insulin, to recognize insulin reactions, and to pay close attention to diet and exercise. Christiansen and Hintz (1982) contend that patients with juvenile diabetes mellitus can be made into "miniphysicians" equipped to provide their own care. In this way, students can achieve the freedom from diabetes required for living a normal and useful life.

The major concern for classroom teachers is to watch out for signs of insulin reactions. The symptoms and treatment should be made clear to all school personnel when a student who has juvenile diabetes mellitus is enrolled.

Asthma

Asthma is a condition frequently encountered in the classroom. Described as a labored, wheezing breathing caused by interference with the normal flow of air into and out of the lungs, it is one of the most common chronic diseases of childhood (Harvey, 1982a).

The severity, frequency, and onset of asthma attacks vary with individuals. Treatment consists of medication, keeping asthmatics away from allergens that may trigger an attack, and monitoring the individual's exercise. With effective treatment, the majority of children obtain complete relief from the symptoms of asthma or a significant lessening in the severity of attacks.

Classroom adaptations may need to be made in such areas as the choice of a pet, choices of foods to be served at a class party, and the availability of medicine to control attacks. In most cases, the student who has asthma will be able to engage fully in the regular class program and activities.

Other Considerations

The conditions described, as well as other impairments, can vary in age of onset, severity, and prognosis. Some conditions (e.g., asthma) can result in students' going through periods of heightened or decreased symptoms and problems. Other conditions (e.g., tuberculosis) can be cured through proper treatment, and others (e.g., epilepsy) can be effectively controlled through medication. Autism is an example of a health impairment that must be managed largely through behavioral, as contrasted to medical, intervention.

Services once thought to be outside the responsibility of the public schools are now legally mandated: administering medications, providing physical and occupational therapy, transporting children to school buildings, and revising classroom protocols and curricula to suit an individual child's physical capacity (Walker & Jacobs, 1984). These responsibilities require that school personnel be aware of the medical implications as well as of the educational implications when students with health impairments are mainstreamed.

Medical Implications

Inclusion of children with severe and mild health problems necessitates a close collaboration between education and medical professionals. Although some students with identified disabilities require little more than the routine medical care received by nondisabled peers, others may require frequent, intensive, and recurrent medical service. As a general standard, the American Academy of Pediatrics now recommends that all children identified as disabled have their care coordinated by a pediatrician (Butler, Singer, Palfrey, & Walker, 1987). Although school personnel may debate the appropriate role for physicians in educational decisions about chronically ill children, their role as primary referral agents is clear (Walker & Jacobs, 1984).

Children who have complex medical conditions are entitled to related services, including any medical or nursing interventions that may be performed by a school nurse or other trained personnel. There is, however, a wide variation within school districts and between states in the manner in which such services are delivered. A 1985 national survey of directors of the 50 state departments of education and public health asked if guidelines governing the practice of selected nursing procedures in schools existed at the state level. The procedures included were catheterization, seizure management, medication administration, respiratory care, tube feeding, positioning, colostomy/ileostomy care, and "other" (including allergy shots). Results indicated that 13 states had no written guidelines, 13 states had guidelines only for medication administration, and 6 states had guidelines for the selected nursing procedures (Wood, Walker, & Gardner, 1986). Other states had guidelines at the local level or were developing guidelines.

Some health impairments have social as well as medical implications. For example, much public attention has focused on the increasing number of sexually transmitted diseases. These diseases include gonorrhea, syphilis, herpes, and acquired immune deficiency syndrome (AIDS). AIDS in particular has raised serious issues for school authorities. A number of authors and agencies have developed guidelines to insure that the provisions of PL 94–142, as well as confidentiality guaranteed by the Buckley Amendment, are afforded to all children (Seibel, 1989).

Another consideration is the incidence of health problems among all children with handicaps. A survey of five large urban school systems revealed that 47.8 percent of special education students were reported to have at least one health problem, and 17.8 percent were reported to have more than one. The most prevalent were vision problems, hearing problems, and asthma or other breathing disorders (Palfrey, Singer, Walker, & Butler, 1986). The findings of this study suggested that the objectives of PL 94–142 have not been totally fulfilled in the provision of comprehensive health services for all school children with disabilities.

Although equal education for all children is mandated, serious questions remain about implementation of these laws with regard to medically involved children. Teachers who have students with health impairments in their classes need to learn about the procedures used in their own school district and to maintain close contact with the parents and physician of the particular student.

For some students, there will be little change in classroom organization and management. For others, modifications will be necessary to insure an appropriate education. It is important to identify the implications of the health impairment for classroom programming and to develop guidelines on how specific problems should be handled.

Educational Implications

Although degree of impairment, prognosis for improvement, and type of problem dictate individual needs, there are some general implications for teachers who have students with health impairments in their classes. Factors to be considered include educational placement, scholastic achievement, absenteeism, scheduling, medication, and attitudes.

Educational Placement
Students who have special health care needs must have their immediate medical needs accommodated before their educational needs can be addressed (Sirvis, 1988b). When their medical condition is stable, they should participate in the educational programs that best meet their needs. In some cases, this means providing instruction in specialized medical settings, in home-based situations, or in special class placement. In most cases, students can be placed in regular classroom settings. Table 2.1 indicates classroom placements usually needed by children with various chronic conditions.

Scholastic Achievement
As a group, children with health impairments are expected to be of normal intelligence. However, there is evidence of significant differences in

TABLE 2.1 Classroom Placements Needed by Children with Various Chronic Conditions during Their School Careers

Chronic Condition	Regular Only	Special Only	Both Regular and Special	Homebound/ Hospital
Asthma	XX			X
Diabetes	XX			X
Cystic fibrosis	XX			X
Hemophilia	XX			X
Leukemia	XX			X
Sickle cell anemia	X			X
Congenital heart disease	XX			X
Kidney problems	X			X
Cleft palate	XX	X	X	
Muscular dystrophy		X	XX	X
Spina bifida		X	XX	X

XX–Most frequent placement

X–Possible placement during school career, depending on course of illness or condition

Source: "Chronically Ill Children In school by D. K. Walker and F. H. Jacobs, 1984, *Peabody Journal of Education, 61* p. 49. Copyright 1984 by *Peabody Journal of Education.* Reprinted by permission.

achievement between chronically ill and healthy groups of children with normal intelligence (Walker & Jacobs, 1984). Factors contributing to lack of achievement are frequent or prolonged school absence, limited alertness or stamina, psychosocial maladjustment, and the disorienting effects of medication.

Absenteeism

Chronically ill students are more likely to experience academic difficulties resulting from interrupted school attendance than are children with other disabilities. Conditions associated with excessive absence are asthma, hemophilia, cystic fibrosis, nephrosis, leukemia, and sickle cell anemia (Walker & Jacobs, 1984). Difficulties with school work arise from prolonged absences and from frequent but brief absences. Both are disruptive to learning content material and to sustaining peer relationships.

In most states, students absent from school for more than 2 weeks receive homebound or hospital instruction. During this time, the classroom teacher can maintain contact with the homebound teacher to insure as much carry-over from the classroom as possible. When the student returns to school, it is helpful if the teacher or a peer can spend extra time with the student who has been absent in an effort to minimize the time lost. Making up missed work can add stress to an already difficult situation.

Scheduling

Classroom schedules should be adjusted for students with limited vitality to create maximum on-task learning time (Sirvis, 1988b). As much as possible, interruptions for medical intervention should be nondisruptive to classroom activities. It may be necessary to provide a rest period for students who have limited vitality or for those who are experiencing temporary fatigue, such as following a seizure. Such considerations should be discussed with the student, the student's parents, the physician, and administrative school personnel. These considerations should also be made clear to other students, who may interpret the teacher's flexibility as preferential treatment.

Medication

Many students with health impairments are required to take daily medication. Frequently, schedules can be arranged so that medication is administered only at home; however, in some cases teachers and students will need to assume the responsibility for administering medication at school. In these instances, school nurses or teachers should obtain written instructions from parents or the student's physician about the schedule and written consent from parents for the medication to be administered at school. A safe and convenient place must be found at school to store the medication, and it should be carefully labeled. Many schools have the policy that only the school nurse can dispense medication. Teachers are therefore advised to check their local policies. Regardless of the role of the person who dispenses the medication, accurate records of dosage and time of administration should be kept.

When a student is started on medication for a health problem, teachers may be asked to keep anecdotal records of the observed behavior of the student. For example, drugs used for several types of medical problems cause hyperactivity as an undesirable side effect. For example, children who are taking a theophylline preparation may be restless and unable to concentrate for their usual length of time, and they may disturb classmates with their overactivity (Lindsey, Leibold, Ladd, & Ownby, 1988).

Some side effects may lead the teacher to believe that the student is ill; others can cause vomiting or loss of appetite; others can cause lethargy and fatigue and interfere with learning. Obviously, such effects have an impact on the teacher, on the student, and on the student's self-image.

The teacher and parents need to maintain frequent communication on how the medication seems to be working and on any unanticipated side effects. Sometimes it is necessary to change the dosage of a drug; such a change may be based on the teacher's observations.

Attitudes

Although students who are health impaired do not have the visible disabilities that orthopedically handicapped students have, the effects can be just as great. The attitude of the student who is health impaired may reflect embarrassment, insecurity, and rejection. The attitude of the student's peers may be equally negative as the result of revulsion to the effects of chemotherapy, the manifestations of epilepsy, or the fear of contagion.

Obviously, the attitude of the teacher sets the tone of acceptance or rejection for the student and for the entire class. The student's achievement may suffer because of the teacher's overindulgence or low scholastic expectations; the student may be socially ostracized because of the teacher's overprotectiveness. Information and open communication provide an atmosphere in which teachers can support students who are health impaired, help them acquire normalization, and work toward peer acceptance and understanding.

REFERENCES

Bleck, E. E. (1982a). Cerebral palsy. In E. E. Bleck & D. A. Nagel (Eds.), *Physically handicapped children: A medical atlas for teachers* (2nd ed.) (pp. 59–132). New York: Grune & Stratton.

Bleck, E. E. (1982b). Muscular dystrophy—Duchenne type. In E. E. Bleck & D. A. Nagel (Eds.), *Physically handicapped children: A medical atlas for teachers* (2nd ed.) (pp. 385–394). New York: Grune & Stratton.

Butler, J. A., Singer, J. D., Palfrey, J. S., & Walker, D. K. (1987). Health insurance coverage and physician use among children with disabilities: Findings from probability samples in five metropolitan areas. *Pediatrics, 79,* (1), 89–98.

Christiansen, R. O., & Hintz, R. L. (1982). Juvenile diabetes mellitus. In E. E. Bleck & D. A. Nagel (Eds.), *Physically handicapped children: A medical atlas for teachers* (2nd ed.) (pp. 269–277). New York: Grune & Stratton.

Federal Register. (1981). Washington, DC: U.S. Government Printing Office.

Federal Register. (1977). Washington, DC: U.S. Government Printing Office.

Fredrick, J., & Fletcher, D. (1985). Facilitating children's adjustment to orthotic and prosthetic appliances. *Teaching Exceptional Children, 17,* (3), 228–230.

Freiberg, K. L. (1988). *Educating exceptional children* (4th ed.). Guilford, CT: Dushkin Publishing Group.

Harvey, B. (1982a). Asthma. In E. E. Bleck & D. A. Nagel (Eds.), *Physically handicapped children: A medical atlas for teachers* (2nd ed.) (pp. 31–42). New York: Grune & Stratton.

Harvey, B. (1982b). Cystic fibrosis. In E. E. Bleck & D. A. Nagel (Eds.), *Physically handicapped children: A medical atlas for teachers* (2nd ed.) (pp. 255–263). New York: Grune & Stratton.

Henderson, G., & Bryan, W. V. (1984). *Psychosocial aspects of disability.* Springfield, IL: Charles C Thomas.

Heward, W. L., & Orlansky, M. D. (1988). *Exceptional children* (3rd ed.). Columbus, OH: Merrill.

Hollister, J. R. (1985). When arthritis strikes, children are no exception. *USA Today, 113,* (May), 79–81.

Lindsey, C. N., Leibold, S. R., Ladd, F. T., & Ownby, R. (1988). Children on medication: A guide for teachers. In K. L. Freiberg (Ed.), *Educating exceptional children* (4th ed.) (pp. 226–228). Guilford, CT: Dushkin Publishing Group.

McCoy, K. M., & Prehm, H. J. (1987). *Teaching mainstreamed students.* Denver: Love.

Miller, J. J. (1982). Juvenile rheumatoid arthritis. In E. E. Bleck & D. A. Nagel (Eds.), *Physically handicapped children: A medical atlas for teachers* (2nd ed.) (pp. 423–430). New York: Grune & Stratton.

Palfrey, J. S., Singer, J. D., Walker, D. K., & Butler, J. A. (1986). Health and special education: A study of new developments for handicapped children in five metropolitan communities. *Public Health Reports, 101,* (4), 379–388.

Parette, H. P., & Hourcade, J. J. (1986). Management strategies for orthopedically handicapped students. *Teaching Exceptional Children 18,* (4), 283–286.

Pieper, E. (1983). *The teacher and the child with spina bifida* (2nd ed.). Rockville, MD: Spina Bifida Association of America.

Schulz, J. B. (1983). Social integration of handicapped children. In S. Heekin & P. Mengel (Eds.), *New friends.* Chapel Hill, NC: Chapel Hill Training–Outreach Project.

Seibel, P. (1989). Physical handicaps and health problems. In G. P. Cartwright, C. A. Cartwright, & M. E. Ward (Eds.), *Educating special learners* (3rd ed.) (pp. 180–216). Belmont, CA: Wadsworth.

Sirvis, B. (1988a). Physical disabilities. In E. L. Meyen & T. M. Skrtic (Eds.), *Exceptional children and youth* (3rd ed.) (pp. 387–411). Denver: Love.

Sirvis, B. (1988b). Special health care needs. *Teaching Exceptional Children, 20,* (4), 40–44.

Walker, D. K., & Jacobs, F. H. (1984). Chronically ill children in school. *Peabody Journal of Education, 61,* (2), 28–74.

Wood, S. P., Walker, D. K., & Gardner, J. (1986). School health practices for children with complex medical needs. *Journal of School Health, 56,* (6), 215–217.

—3—

Students with Sensory Impairments and Communication Disorders

Case Study: Visual Impairment

When I learned that I would have a blind student in my home room and social studies class, my first thought was "What can I do for him?" I had misgivings about things I would say, such as "Look at the board," or "We're going to see a film." After talking with a friend, I decided that the first day I would tell David that I would treat him just like the other students. This worked out well; his attitude made it easy for me and we both relaxed.

David wants to learn more than any kid in my class. He wants to learn because he's behind. He will have to work hard just to finish high school.

Before David came into the class and the home room, I talked with the other students. At first he was a curiosity to them but soon it was evident that the others liked him and wanted to help in any way they could. David talks about his handicap and thus there is no pressure on the other kids; they don't view him as very different.

Actually, David has been an asset to the class. I put him at a table of boys who like him; they are conscious that they must verbalize so David can take part in whatever is going on. As they read or look for answers for questions, they talk about it for David's benefit and they all profit. He has helped the whole class verbalize their feelings and their findings.

I have had to take a good look at my instructional techniques and I am not altogether happy with what I am doing. For one thing, I like showing "war movies"; the kids like them and are motivated by them. But I feel David is cheated when we have movies and that this emphasizes his disability.

Sometimes I feel that I neglect David, and that I need to let him know I'm there. The lack of eye contact makes me feel he may think I have forgotten him.

I have not been easy on David; I feel it would be demeaning to expect less of him than I do of the other students. I have given him tests equal to the ones the rest of the class took. We started with verbal tests, then I asked him to type the answers. He didn't like this, but I required him to do it. I don't feel I've measured his understanding of concepts, such as on the subject of communism.

Next year I will be better prepared for David. The best thing David and I have going is that we like each other. He's helped me more than I've helped him.

Mr. Dewey Rayburn
Fairview Elementary School

Sensory impairments (vision and hearing disorders) and communication disorders can have serious impacts on the learning process. Most information acquired in the environment, and certainly in the schools, is processed through the visual and auditory systems. The abilities to label, attach meaning, and describe impressions of such information are possible through communication.

Difficulties in these three areas range from mild to severe, with individual adaptations varying widely. In terms of numbers, students who have vision and hearing impairments are relatively rare, whereas students with communication disorders comprise one of the largest categories of exceptionality.

VISUAL IMPAIRMENTS

We live in a visually oriented society. Our vision constantly informs us of the beauties (and imperfections) in our environment and of the appearances of people. Much of our information comes from printed material in books, newspapers, magazines, and pamphlets. Add to this array the numerous technological devices designed for visual use, including computers, television, films, and calculators. In educational settings we use all of these materials and equipment, plus the chalkboard, charts, overhead projectors, and workbooks. It is no wonder that the prospect of mainstreaming a student who has a visual impairment can be daunting for both the teacher and the student.

Visual impairments occur in about 20 percent of the general population. However, a large majority of the problems are corrected with prescriptive lenses. Educationally significant, noncorrectable vision impairments are found in only about 1 student in 1,000. Fewer than 1 percent of the students receiving special education and related services in the United States are visually handicapped (Reynolds & Birch, 1988).

Definitions

A functional definition of the term *visual handicaps* is included in PL 94–142:

> Visually handicapped means a visual impairment which, even with correction, adversely affects a child's educational performance. The term includes both partially seeing and blind children. (*Federal Register,* 1977, p. 42479)

For education purposes, there is a vast difference between students who are blind and those who are partially sighted. In addition, a number of students have visual defects.

Blindness

The medical-legal definition of blindness, adopted by the American Medical Association, states that

> a person shall be considered blind whose central visual acuity does not exceed 20/200 in the better eye with correcting lenses or whose visual acuity, if better than 20/200, has a limit in the central field of vision to such a degree that its widest diameter subtrends an angle of no greater than 20 degrees. (Hardman, Drew, & Egan, 1987, p. 291)

In this definition, the term *visual acuity* refers to the distance from which an individual can see and identify symbols. The referrant 20/20 means the distance at which a person with normal vision can identify symbols on a wall chart—20 feet. Thus, the term *20/200 vision* refers to the distance of 20 feet at which a blind person must stand in order to read the symbol a normal person can read at 200 feet. The term *field of vision* refers to the area an individual can see when looking straight ahead. Field of vision is described in terms of the angle from the center to the periphery or edge of that area. A normal person has peripheral vision to the extent of approximately 180 degrees, whereas a person with a 20-degree arc would have tunnel vision or could see only what is directly in front (Aserling & Browning, 1987).

Because students with severe visual problems traditionally have received their education in residential schools, many public-school teachers have had limited contact with them. These teachers are often understandably uncomfortable about situations for which they have little information. It is difficult for sighted people to imagine how blind people are able to get around and participate in their environment.

As with other handicapping conditions, the capabilities of blind persons are frequently underestimated. Many blind people make their way around busy city streets, engage in advanced academic study, make significant contributions in their career, participate in sports of all kinds, and have a meaningful and enjoyable family life.

In the majority of cases, severe visual problems are identified early in the first years of life. The age of onset is critical to the impact of the loss of vision. Concept development is extremely difficult for children who have never seen, whereas children who became blind after birth have concepts of color, shape, and area that facilitate their adjustment after blindness occurs.

Partial Sight

Partially sighted students are unable to perform tasks ordinarily requiring detailed vision without using special aids, such as magnifiers, special lighting, or large type. These students usually have limited distance vision but frequently can see objects and materials held a few inches from their eyes (Ward & McCormick, 1981).

Visual Defects

Visual defects affect visual acuity. The most common disorders are astigmatism, which causes a generalized blurring of the vision and is often the result of irregular corneal curvature; myopia, or nearsightedness, in which sight is clear in proximity but blurred at far distances; and hyperopia, or farsightedness, in which sight is clear at a distance but blurred in proximity. Referred to as *refractive* errors, these defects can usually be corrected by corrective lenses, which can help the eyes to focus and reduce eye strain but may fail to provide normal vision. When corrected by lenses, these errors do not constitute handicaps.

Characteristics

Because of the wide range of severity and adaptability in visually impaired students, it is difficult to generalize about their characteristics. However, some common characteristics occur in physical symptoms, cognitive functioning, and orientation and mobility.

Physical Symptoms

Physical signs of visual problems may be observed in students already identified as visually impaired and also may help the teacher identify students whose vision problems have not been identified. Teachers may observe a student rubbing the eyes excessively, shutting or covering one eye and tilting or thrusting the head forward, having difficulty in reading or in other work requiring close use of the eyes, blinking more than usual, squinting eyelids together and frowning, and/or having difficulty seeing objects at a distance.

The physical appearance of the student may also indicate problems. The eyes may be crossed; they may be red-rimmed, encrusted, or swollen; they may be inflamed or watery; and sties may occur frequently. The student may complain of itching, burning, or scratchy eyes; of not seeing well; of experiencing dizziness, headaches, or nausea following close eye work; or of blurred or double vision.

Teachers should refer students who demonstrate any of these characteristics. If the school does not provide adequate visual screening, county health departments are usually willing to come to the school or to see students in their clinics.

Cognitive Functioning

Visually handicapped students have been found, in general, to be within the normal range of intelligence (Bateman, 1963; Scholl & Schnur, 1976).

Their school achievement, however, tends to fall behind that of their normal-sighted classmates (Bateman, 1963; Hayes, 1941; Lowenfeld, Abel, & Hatlen, 1969). Underachievement could be attributable to a number of reasons, including slower concept development associated with impaired vision, slower reading rates, and inappropriate instructional procedures.

Concept development refers to the process of attaching meaning to ideas and clustering the ideas into units of information to form a conceptual framework. A concept can be thought of as the hook on which students can attach ideas when the ideas are first perceived. This type of concept formation adds clarity, meaning, and organization to the thousands of inputs students receive each day. Vision contributes significantly to the quality of concept development; it is considered to be the unifier of experience. When a student's vision is impaired to the extent that visual sensory input is impossible, teachers must capitalize on the student's use of other sensory channels, such as listening, feeling, tasting, and smelling. It is also important for students who are visually impaired to use the remaining usable vision. In many cases, the more the vision is used, the more efficient it becomes.

Visually impaired students may also have learning problems not associated with vision. The same kinds of characteristics observed in sighted students with learning disabilities, mental retardation, and emotional problems (see chapter 4) may be observed in visually impaired students. Harley, Truan, and Sanford (1987) indicate the following five characteristics of visually impaired students with learning problems:

1. Academic achievement is below expected performance.
2. High distractibility interferes with learning.
3. Avoidance behaviors may develop.
4. Learning differences may be circumvented.
5. Learning in some academic areas may occur quickly. (p. 119)

Specific problem areas for these students include memory, perception, organization, concrete thinking, perseveration and fixation, generalization, and language.

Orientation and Mobility
The terms *orientation* and *mobility* are often confused when related to blind and partially sighted people. Orientation is the awareness of one's position in space as related to other objects and people in the environment. Mobility refers to one's movement within the environment in going from one place to another (Suterko, 1973).

Students with severe visual impairment may have started mobility training before entering school. Many students will have an orientation and mobility instructor who works with them, their families, and their teachers in helping prepare them to get around the classroom and school independently.

Students who are blind and have attended public schools report on the horror of walking down the steps when a mass of students is thundering past them. Teachers should encourage sighted classmates to take precautions against possible collisions or should schedule the blind student's transition time between classes a few minutes earlier or later than that of other students.

Educational Implications

A school district with 20,000 pupils might expect about 20 to have moderate to severe visual impairments that will require special educational programs and services. Because of the heterogeneity of this population, it might not be possible to group these 20 students for educational purposes. The following reasons would make such grouping difficult:

- They might represent the entire age span from birth through high school.
- They are very likely to have other impairments that may be more educationally handicapping than their visual impairments.
- They have a broad range of visual abilities.
- They have a broad range of intellectual abilities.
- They have educational needs that might require different service delivery systems.
- They may come from families with a wide variety of socio-economic and cultural characteristics.
- They may have a minimal support system provided by their families.
- They may reside in geographical locations that preclude having a full continuum of services available to them. (Scholl & Schnur, 1976, p. 33)

To insure that their various needs are met, visually impaired students require individual assessment and instruction.

Assessment

Because routine vision screening programs may not be adequate for complete diagnosis of visual impairment, parents and teachers must be aware of the signs of possible eye trouble as discussed in the previous section. Following visual assessment, a determination must be made as to whether the impairment is educationally handicapping. Other areas of functioning also need to be assessed in order to determine placement and develop the IEP. Areas to be assessed should include:

Current Eye Medical Information

Academic Skills—Learning Style

Compensatory Skills

Academic compensatory skills: those special skills a visually handicapped student needs to cope with the school academic curriculum such as braille, use of math aids, tactile devices, sensing devices, light probes, etc.

Personal compensatory skills: those areas of skills a visually handicapped person needs to cope with the environment in general such as personal grooming, independence of travel, recreation tools, environmental awareness, normalcy information, etc.

Functioning Level

Communication Skills

Orientation and Mobility Skills

Social Adjustment Skills

Sensory Skills (including functional vision from the perspective of an educator)

Visual Efficiency

Physical Education and Leisure Activities

Career, vocational or pre-vocational skills

Language of the Home. (Spungin, 1981, p. 4)

Teachers of students who are visually handicapped should participate in planning the assessment so the comprehensive evaluation of the student's abilities can lead to an appropriate IEP. Observation, interviews, and curriculum-based assessment may add to the formal assessment (Scholl & Schnur, 1976).

Instruction

Adaptations in general classroom procedures are necessary for students with visual impairment. Some helpful considerations, depending on the individual student, include seating close to the teacher and chalkboard; avoiding glare by having the student work facing away from a window; keeping doors either opened or closed (ajar doors can be a potential safety hazard in mobility); providing adequate space for the storage of special equipment (e.g., braille books and typewriters) and adequate desk space for using it; providing a verbal explanation of board work, filmstrips, or other visual presentations; and alternating periods requiring the use of residual vision with other educational experiences to reduce fatigue and strain. More specific suggestions deal with the use of braille, special equipment, and advanced technology.

BRAILLE Because reading requires visual reaction to graphic symbols, the student who is visually impaired is at a great disadvantage. Provisions must be made for an adequate alternative method for the input of information or for an adequate method to develop the student's ability to see.

In the case of the student who is blind, a complicated skill must be acquired—learning to read by touch. Braille, a system of six embossed dots arranged in two vertical rows of three, is used for this purpose (see Figure 3.1). These dots can be covered simultaneously by the pad of the finger tip. Grade-one braille is written with full spelling; grade-two braille makes use of contractions and short forms.

Classroom teachers may think that the responsibility of teaching students to read braille is overwhelming. Even though braille is difficult to learn by touch, using it visually is quite simple. Sighted students are

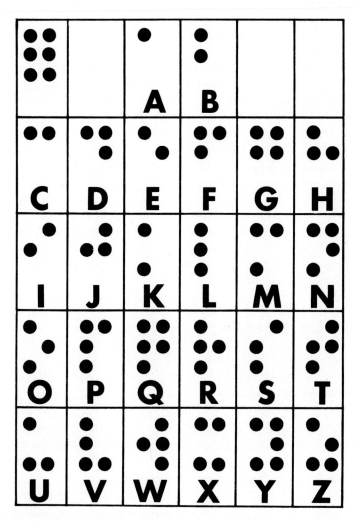

FIGURE 3.1   Braille Alphabet

curious about it and often view it as a code to be broken (see chapter 7). Teachers and students can decode braille by referring to the chart.

A majority of students who are partially sighted, including those identified as legally blind, read print rather than braille materials. Many students who are partially sighted can read regular-size print, particularly at the first- and second-grade levels, where the print is rather large. With appropriate teaching approaches, these students can use many of the same materials as their peers and reach comparable levels.

The quality of print is an important determinant of legibility. Teachers should do everything possible to insure that print materials are clear, attractive, and meaningful. Reading materials that display the greatest contrast between the print and the paper are the easiest to see. Black print on white paper with fairly large letters and good spacing is best; purple ink used in commercial duplicating is often difficult to see. Teachers should make duplicated copies on white paper and give the darkest, clearest copies to the visually impaired students. Readability can be improved by using black masters and primary type with good spacing. Elite or fancy type, handwriting, crowded letters, colored paper, and blurred or faint copies all add to difficulties for visually impaired students.

SPECIAL EQUIPMENT   A substantial amount of adapted instructional equipment has been developed for students who are partially sighted and blind. Two tactual aids for students who are blind are the braillewriter and the slate and stylus. The braillewriter is a six-key machine that is manually operated to type braille. The slate and stylus can be used to take notes in class. The slate is a metal frame with small openings. Braille dots can be embossed through these openings with the use of a pointed stylus. Aids for students who are partially sighted include glasses with special prescriptions and magnifiers either held in the hand or attached to the glasses.

Catalogs of materials and adaptive equipment are available free of charge from the Commission for the Blind in each state. Materials are also distributed free of charge from regional and subregional libraries of the Library of Congress, Division for the Blind and Physically Handicapped (see Appendix B for the address of the Library of Congress). Teachers are urged to write the Library of Congress to obtain reference brochures on these available materials.

ADVANCED TECHNOLOGY   A variety of new materials has been provided for persons with visual impairments through advanced technology. The following materials are examples.

1. The *laser cane* is an electronic improvement on the traditional long cane. The long cane is limited by its length to the distance which can be scanned. In contrast, the laser cane sends out three beams

ahead of the traveler, assisting the individual in perceiving objects straight ahead, at head height, and downward.

2. The *Sonicguide* is used with a long cane. It sends out ultrasonic impulses from a transmitter mounted in an eyeglass frame and supplies the wearer with information about the direction, distance, and surface characteristics of an object.

3. The *Mowat Sensor* is a hand-held device which sends out a narrow beam of ultrasound. If the beam is reflected back, the device gently vibrates, helping the user perceive openings such as doorways.

4. The *Kurzweil Reading Machine* converts print directly to synthetic speech. When an open book is placed over a glass surface, a high-resolution camera scans the lines of print. The image from the camera is processed by a computer, which identifies words and activates a speech synthesizer. Most large library systems or university libraries have these reading machines available.

5. The *Optical to Tactile Converter* (Opticon) translates an image from a small camera into a vibrating image of the same shape that can be felt with the index finger. As the reader moves the camera along a line of print, words are read through feeling the letters. (Bauer & Shea, 1989, p. 239)

Talking computers and terminals are meeting the demands of students who are blind and visually impaired in many communities, and they look to being more available in the future. By using talking terminals, typewriters, calculators, microprocessors, and other talking products, students who are blind and visually impaired have the same access to information as do nonhandicapped students and have many more opportunities available to them in education and careers. Williams (1984) underscores the importance of technological equipment:

> Students, particularly disabled ones, have to learn to view technology as their equalizer or compensator. They have to embrace it and master it. Having done so, they are the equal of nondisabled people. (p. 28)

In the past, it has been difficult for students with visual impairment who use braille as their primary reading medium to gain access to microcomputers. One way now available for such students is through electronic braille devices. These microprocessor-based devices use magnetic audio cassette tapes or disks to store and retrieve information written in braille. The user can send information to the computer using the six keys ordinarily used in braille-writing devices. The user views information sent from the computer via a renewable braille display of 20 or more characters in a line of movable pins representing braille dots (Ruconich, 1984). These devices enable the user to send as well as receive information through a single instrument.

Resources

In most states there are agencies for persons who are blind or visually impaired. These groups offer services including counseling, allocations for equipment and eye care, direction and funding for programs offering appropriate services for students who are visually impaired, and early intervention programs for children from birth to age 3. These programs are designed to maximize a child's development in areas that might be delayed because of the visual impairment (Silberman, Trief, & Morse, 1988).

Not many teachers have had experience teaching students who are visually impaired. An experienced special education teacher expressed her initial reaction to having a student with this problem:

> *Although I have taught special education for many years, last year was the first time I have ever had a blind student. My first reaction was panic: Would I have to learn braille? How could I teach him math? To my surprise, I found that there were many resources available to me and to Josh. I found that there was a teacher of braille from Social Services; that the State Division for the Blind would send tapes, talking books, and the necessary equipment; and I even had an offer one day from a retired teacher who was willing to braille any textbook material I needed. Josh taught me how to use an abacus effectively, and together we worked out his mobility problems. I learned to think through problems with him. This was good for both of us. (Schulz, 1989, p. 253)*

Collaborative consultation between a resource teacher of students with visual handicaps and a classroom teacher can insure that the students are provided with the support needed in a mainstream program (Erin, 1988). Because visual impairment is a low incidence condition, many school systems may not have an expert on staff. In such cases, an itinerant teacher may cover several counties or school systems, providing guidance to the special educator and to the classroom teacher.

Case Study: Hearing Impairment

My experiences in mainstreaming hearing-impaired children had a terrible beginning and a very happy ending. It all started last year when Dave, a severely hearing-impaired student, was placed in my class. Prior to the first day of school with Dave, I had received no training in teaching children with hearing handicaps.

When Dave started in the third-grade class, I thought I could adapt my program to meet his needs. Although I was promised consultation and help from a special education teacher, I received none. Dave's language and reading skills were very low and his handwriting was all done in tall manuscript letters. I shudder now to think of all the mistakes I made with him. For example, we always give standardized achievement tests to students in the third grade. Not knowing any better, I gave him a group test on the third-grade level. Dave scored very low, and I recommended him for possible placement in a special class for mentally retarded children. His mother got very upset and contacted the state department of education. Someone from the hearing-impaired program in the state department called and fussed at me for using a test that required third-grade reading and language skills with Dave. I could then understand that the test was inappropriate for him and that his hearing handicap had penalized his performance. I did not mean to treat him unfairly, but I simply did not know what was best for him. I developed a very negative attitude about teaching Dave.

Just when I was relieved that the school year was over and I had made it through the year, the principal asked me to move up to the fourth grade and teach the same class the following year. This meant another year of having Dave in class. The only hope I had was that a new special education teacher had been hired to work with me and with other classroom teachers. I was very skeptical, but I agreed to give it a try. Ms. Goulding, the new teacher, held a short workshop before school started and gave me lots of suggestions on good instructional tips to use with Dave. I don't want to sound like I am overstating it, but she was truly like a ray of sunshine. All of a sudden I knew help was close by and that she had much to offer. She started working with Dave every day in reading and math. He seemed to do well in programmed series like the Sullivan. Instead of always taking Dave out of the room, she frequently came into my class and worked with him there. She then could remind me of important considerations, like facing the children when I talk, avoiding standing in front of the window, and writing assignments on the board. Even though she had told me these things before, sometimes I would forget and not even realize it. Another thing that I really appreciate is that she always gives me suggestions in such a nice way. There's nothing threatening or negative about them.

I am responsible for the social studies and science portion of Dave's program. I use the overhead projector frequently to introduce vocabulary, and I always try to put new words into context for him. He enjoys captioned films and supplementary library books. Dave always wears an auditory trainer at school. I wear the microphone so that my voice is amplified for him and background noises are screened out. At first he tended to wear his coat over the trainer to hide it, but now it is a normal thing in our classroom. I have never heard any teasing by the other students. One thing that has helped tremendously is that hearing-impaired children have been attending our school for the last 10 years. It is nothing new for the other children.

As I look back on this year, I realize that I have made great strides

as a teacher. I can honestly say that the key has been Ms. Goulding.
The great thing about it is that the techniques I have learned for Dave
have benefited all the students. I am excited over what has happened
this year. It seems that all of us have made gains in different ways.

Ms. Sandra Fracker
Cary Elementary School

HEARING IMPAIRMENTS

The development of young children is influenced by many factors, including innate capacity, motivation, maturation, and parental input and response. In a healthy environment, the child develops needs, skills, and
abilities commensurate with family and societal expectations. When the
child's hearing is absent or defective, however, development follows a
different course (Boothroyd, 1982). Developmental patterns emerge at
different rates, and parents, teachers, and the child are frequently confused by the lack of conformity. Appropriate detection and intervention
are essential to a successful school experience and adult life for the person
who is hearing impaired.

Definitions

The generic germ *hearing impairment* includes all disorders of hearing,
regardless of their nature, cause, or severity. The two major subgroups of
hearing impairment are hearing loss and auditory processing disorder. A
hearing loss is an impairment of sound detection; an auditory processing
disorder is an impairment of sound interpretation. Other terms frequently
used are *hard of hearing* and *deaf*, defined by PL 94–142 as follows:

> "Hard of hearing" is a hearing impairment, whether permanent or fluctuat-
> ing, which adversely affects a child's educational performance but which is
> not included under the definition of "deaf" in this section.
> "Deaf" means a hearing impairment which is so severe that the child is
> impaired in processing linguistic information through hearing, with or with-
> out amplification, which adversely effects educational performance. (*Federal
> Register*, 1977, p. 42478).

Like visual impairment, hearing impairment is a low incidence handicapping condition. Only 1 child in 1,000 is deaf, and only 3 to 4 children in
1,000 are severely hard of hearing (Kirk & Gallagher, 1989).

Characteristics

Characteristics of students who have hearing impairments are related to three factors: the nature of the impairment, the degree of hearing impairment, and the age at which it occurred.

Nature of Hearing Impairment

The nature of the hearing impairment refers to a person's hearing pattern as it relates to frequency and intensity. Frequency can be thought of as pitch (high versus low sounds); intensity refers to loudness. Frequency must be considered in terms of the pitch range needed for communication purposes in order to understand the nature of the hearing loss. Some students may be able to hear the majority of sounds, missing those at one or the other extreme of pitch. Students with the greatest educational handicap are unable to hear the pitch range of normal conversation. Referring to intensity, students vary in their ability to hear different levels of amplification. Some students, unable to hear faint or even conversational intensity, can hear when these sounds are amplified by the use of a hearing aid.

The nature of a hearing impairment is influenced by the type of hearing loss and by the part of the ear that is affected. A conductive hearing loss, which occurs in the middle ear, reduces the intensity of sound reaching the inner ear, where hearing occurs. This is the most common type of hearing loss in school-age children and frequently is transient. It can be caused by otitis media (middle-ear infection), by a blockage in the middle ear or by other conditions. Conductive hearing losses can be effectively reduced through prompt medical care and by amplification of sound when the severity of the condition warrants.

Although conduction hearing losses may not be permanent, they can interfere with learning. Students who appear not to pay attention or who are not picking up on class activities and information may have a temporary conductive loss and can miss important sequences in instruction.

A sensorineural hearing loss results from damage to the cochlea or auditory nerve and is usually greater than conductive loss. A sensorineural loss can be caused by a virus (such as rubella, meningitis, mumps, measles, chicken pox, or flu), by RH incompatibility, ototoxic medications (such as kanamycin, neomycin, gentamycin, streptomycin, or vancomycin), or by hereditary factors. The aging process and exposure to loud noises can also contribute to sensorineural losses. As a rule, sensorineural hearing losses are not medically or surgically treatable and require rehabilitative efforts. However, medical technology has advanced to such a degree that plastic cochleas can now be implanted, and other conditions previously thought incurable may be able to be treated in the future.

Central auditory disorders, which may result from damage to the central nervous system, result in problems with auditory comprehension and discrimination. Students who have central auditory disorders exhibit problems in correctly perceiving spoken language and other meaningful sounds in their environments, even though they have auditory systems that operate normally in response to basic measures of auditory functions (Willeford & Burleigh, 1985). Students who exhibit such problems may be identified as learning disabled (see chapter 4).

Degree of Hearing Impairment

Students who are hard of hearing can be described as having mild, moderate, or moderately severe hearing losses. At the mild level, they may have difficulty hearing distant sounds and may need preferential seating and speech therapy. Students who have moderate losses may understand conversational speech but may miss class discussions. They may require hearing aids and speech therapy. With a moderately severe loss, students may require hearing aids, auditory training, and intensive speech and language training.

Students who are deaf are described as either severely or profoundly deaf. A person who is severely deaf can only hear loud sounds close up and will probably need intensive special education, hearing aids, and speech and language training. A person who is profoundly deaf may be aware of loud sound and vibrations but relies on vision rather than hearing for instruction (Kirk & Gallagher, 1989).

Age of Onset

The age at which the hearing loss occurs is a critical factor, particularly because hearing influences the acquisition of language. A hearing impairment creates more significant educational handicaps when it is congenital (present from birth) or when it occurs in the first or second year of development. Early onset is more significant because language has not yet been learned; therefore, the child has no frame of reference for understanding language. When the impairment occurs later, after the age of 10, for example, the child's vocabulary and syntax of language and reading achievement are developed to the point at which continued, steady growth can be anticipated.

Secondary Impairments

Although the number of students with severe hearing impairments is small, the consequences are great. Boothroyd (1982) describes nine secondary impairments that can occur:

1. *A perceptual problem.* The children cannot identify objects and events by the sounds they make.

2. *A speech problem.* The children do not learn the connection between the movements of their speech mechanisms and the resulting sounds. Consequently, they do not acquire control of speech.
3. *A communication problem.* The children do not learn their native language. They cannot, therefore, express thoughts to other people except by gesture or other concrete acts; they cannot understand what people say to them; and they cannot participate in conversational exchange.
4. *A cognitive problem.* Children with language have access to their world through the minds of other people, through abstract ideas, and through information about distant times and distant places. Children without language must learn about their world only from the concrete—the "here and now."
5. *A social problem.* Hearing-impaired children have difficulty developing appropriate behaviors towards other people. As toddlers they do not hear the tone of voice that indicates emotional state or signals the fact that they are about to transgress parental limits. At a later age they cannot have social rules explained to them. Even more importantly, they use manipulative and ritualistic behaviors as substitutes for language in their attempts to influence others.
6. *An emotional problem.* Unable to satisfy their evolving needs with spoken language; unable to make sense of the seemingly precipitous and capricious reactions of parents and peers; constantly feeling acted upon rather than acting upon others; hearing-impaired children become confused and angry and develop poor self-images.
7. *An educational problem.* Children without language gain minimal benefit from educational experiences.
8. *An intellectual problem.* Although it will be possible by suitable testing to demonstrate normal nonverbal intelligence, our subjects will be deficient in general knowledge and language competence—both of which are included in a broad definition of intelligence.
9. *A vocational problem.* Lacking in verbal skills, general knowledge, academic training, and social skills, hearing-impaired children will reach adulthood with severely limited possibilities for gainful employment.[1]

Although the characteristics cited above appear to be all negative, parent training, early intervention, and appropriate educational programs have prevented the development of many secondary problems and have served the needs of the hearing-impaired child.

Sometimes hearing-impaired students are not identified before entering school. Some hearing problems follow immediately after diseases or

1. From *Hearing Impairments in Young Children* (pp. 4–5) by A. Boothroyd, 1982. Englewood Cliffs, NJ: Prentice Hall. Copyright 1982 by A. Boothroyd. Reprinted by permission.

accidents. Upper respiratory diseases, chronic middle-ear infections, or infected tonsils and adenoids can create temporary or sometimes permanent hearing loss. The teacher should carefully observe any behaviors indicative of hearing problems. Some behaviors include turning one side of the head toward the speaker or touching the ears when trying to listen; delayed language development; standing very close to whoever is talking; frequently asking for comments or instructions to be repeated; lack of attention; inappropriate responses to questions, signaling a lack of understanding; and complaints of earaches, runny discharges from ears, sore throat, and constant colds. The teacher who observes these symptoms should contact the student's parents and the school nurse. Initial screening of problems might indicate the need for medical, audiological, and educational evaluations.

Although the numbers of students who are hearing impaired are small, the educational adaptations required for them are great.

Educational Implications

Surveys indicate that classroom teachers have limited knowledge about hearing disorders (Martin, Bernstein, Daly, & Cody, 1988), that few teachers have had exposure to people wearing hearing aids (Lass, Tecca, & Woodford, 1987), and that teachers initially express anxiety about working with a student who is hearing impaired in a regular school setting (Chorost, 1988). Teachers thus should be aware of the kinds of adaptations required to accommodate students who are hearing impaired. The difficulties these students encounter most frequently occur in communication, academic achievement, and social integration.

Communication
Hearing impairment is primarily a communication problem (Champie, 1986). The degree and kind of hearing impairment greatly affect the ability to communicate. For people who have a considerable hearing loss, there are several approaches to communication. The basic approaches are oral, manual, and total communication.

The oral method of communication requires the student with a hearing impairment to use a combination of residual hearing, a hearing aid, and speech reading (the ability to understand another person by watching the lips and face) in order to comprehend. For self-expression, the student using the oral approach verbalizes. Oral communication enables the hearing-impaired person to communicate with hearing people who do not use manual systems. Teaching speech to children who are deaf or hard of hearing is very difficult, and many of them never acquire understandable speech.

The manual method of communication includes finger spelling and sign language. Finger spelling has a movement for each letter; words are spelled using particular movements for different letters. This method is slow and requires the ability to spell. However, it can be used by following a chart and is frequently a good way for hearing-impaired children to begin to communicate with their peers. The manual alphabet appears in Figure 3.2.

American Sign Language (ASL) is the most popular of several sign language systems. ASL is a gestural language with units composed of

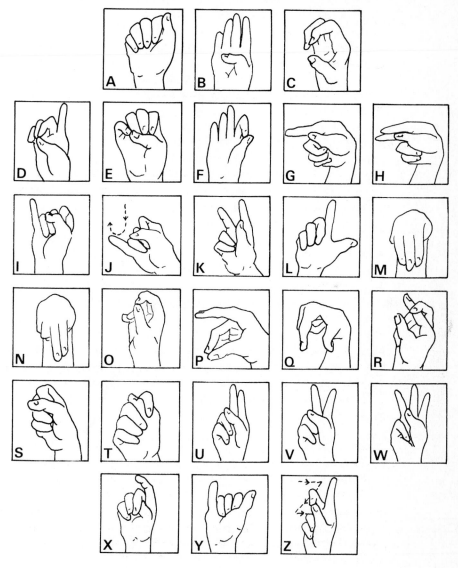

FIGURE 3.2 Manual Alphabet

specific movements and shapes of the hands and arms, eyes, face, head, and body posture (Baker & Padden, 1978). It has its own grammar and syntax. Many educators feel that ASL inhibits the acquisition of English; others believe it should be the native language of deaf children (Kirk & Gallagher, 1989).

Total communication includes the simultaneous presentation of signs (including finger spelling when necessary) and speech (through residual audition and speech reading). The theory is that learning both oral and manual codes is mutually reinforcing. Research does not support this philosophy, but it does indicate that no one method or collection of methods can meet the individual needs of all children (Ling, 1984).

The form of communication a student uses has important implications for the classroom. Although there is some debate about the most advantageous approach, may specialists seem to follow the pattern of intensively stimulating oral communication with hearing-impaired students during preschool and early elementary years (Nix, 1976). If the child has not developed adequate language by the age of 9 or 10, consideration is then given to teaching the two forms of manual communication. The oral approach to language facilitates mainstreaming in that the student with a hearing handicap can understand and be understood by classroom peers. When signing is necessary, however, hearing students often enjoy the intrigue of learning to sign as a way of communicating with their friends. In some mainstream situations, teachers also have learned signs for basic classroom terminology. In other cases, an interpreter accompanies the student to class.

Different children communicate in different ways. Some children who are hearing impaired have experienced frustration and failure because of their school's rigid adherence to an all oral program. Others have not been given an adequate opportunity to develop their auditory and oral skills because they were placed in educational programs that did not provide good oral instruction (Heward & Orlansky, 1988). Regardless of the means of communication used, surveys published by Gallaudet College (for the deaf) show that the linguistic and academic performance of students who are hearing impaired tends to be appallingly low (Ling, 1984).

Academic Achievement

Many academic skills draw on a student's general awareness of language. Individuals who are hearing impaired are at risk for reading and writing difficulties because the hearing loss affects their ability to construct accurate representations of sound-letter correspondences (Wray, Hazlett, & Flexer, 1988). Because of their conceptual limitations, they may have problems interpreting the language of others and expressing themselves in oral and written modes (Degler & Risko, 1979).

One strategy for teaching writing skills to students who are hearing impaired began with maximal auditory input through the use of hearing aids and frequency modulation (FM) auditory training units. Students were encouraged to listen before looking. The writing program consisted of four stages: (1) prewriting, (2) drafting, (3) revising and editing, and (4) final drafting. This program led to improvement of the students' academic status (Wray, Hazlett, & Flexer, 1988).

One investigation of the mathematics achievement of hearing-impaired adolescents reached three conclusions:

> First, because of the differential selection process for mainstreaming, student background factors are a primary determinant of achievement. Second, mainstreaming with an interpreter has no specific effect on achievement for hearing impaired students. Third, the quality of instruction a hearing impaired child receives is the prime determinant of achievement. (Kluwin & Moores, 1989, p. 334)

Social Integration

Hearing-impaired students have the same social needs as other students. They need interaction with peers in academic and extracurricular activities. They need to share sports, games, drama, clubs, and competitions; they need to stand in the halls between classes to discuss a test or to gossip and also to have the usual experiences in dating and in selecting a friend from a large group (Champie, 1986).

Several studies indicate that students who are hearing impaired initiate more interactions during free activities than during structured language periods and that hearing students interact with a significantly greater number of peers than do the hearing-impaired students (Antia, 1985). Teachers need to plan for the social integration of their students who are hearing impaired and encourage them to initiate contacts with their hearing peers. Suggestions for social integration appear in chapter 13.

Special Equipment in the Classroom

Students who are hearing impaired frequently wear hearing aids. Therefore, teachers must have a basic understanding of how hearing aids work and of basic maintenance operations. The hearing aid itself is composed of three parts: a receiver for picking up the sound, an amplifier for making it louder, and a speaker for transmitting the sound to the hearing-impaired person. The aid runs on batteries. Any specific questions about its operation or maintenance, and all major repairs, should be directed to the hearing aid dealer who sold it. General guidelines important for the classroom are discussed in this section (Birch, 1975).

Hearing aids cannot be assumed to enable the user to achieve normal hearing. Aids do make sounds louder, including background noises. Preferential seating should be assigned to students wearing aids to accommodate their need to hear classroom discussions and instructions; this will also prevent sounds from being drowned out by loud background noises. Sometimes it is difficult to know the best seating location. Perhaps the special education teacher in the school could offer some suggestions. A good strategy is to start with the best guess and place students in a particular seating arrangement. Seek feedback from them as to their ability to hear, and also observe their behavior to see if they seem to be straining or missing important information. Make modifications in the seating pattern until the optimal location is identified.

If a hearing aid has been prescribed for a student, it should be worn at all times unless otherwise directed by the student's audiologist. When a student repeatedly tries to remove an aid at school, it may indicate that the aid is not doing the proper job reproducing sounds. The teacher can listen to the aid to get an idea of possible disturbances. Aids should be checked intermittently.

Students who wear a hearing aid should learn early to care for it. When they first detect a change in functioning, they should report it to their parents and teacher. Teachers should keep extra batteries and cords at school. As students advance in elementary years, they usually are able to change batteries or insert cords themselves. Teachers should be knowledgeable in these procedures and carry them out for young children. Audiologists and hearing aid dealers are usually the best people to give teachers and parents detailed information on this type of maintenance.

In addition to hearing aids, some schools purchase auditory training units, which generally have stronger amplification and a wider frequency range than do hearing aids. The student wears the trainer, which has the same three parts as the hearing aid—receiver, amplifier, and speaker. Additionally, the teacher wears a portable microphone that transmits the voice directly to the student wearing the auditory trainer. The FM auditory trainer creates a listening situation that is comparable to the teacher's being only 6 inches from the student's ear at all times. The use of this device promotes both speech intelligibility and audibility. A distinct advantage of trainers is that they can be adjusted to close off all sound except the teacher's voice. With background distractions cut down, the student is able to focus completely on what the teacher is saying. In addition to the use of the auditory trainer, teachers can use facilitating strategies such as repeating and rephrasing information and saying the cue word "listen" before presenting instruction (Ireland, Wray, & Flexer, 1988). Typically, trainers are used for speech and language development. Hearing aid dealers can give teachers more specific information on the use of auditory trainers.

Adaptations in Classroom Procedures
In considering necessary adaptations in classroom procedures, the teacher must realize that the needs of students who are hearing impaired vary according to the details of their particular handicap. Here are some general

suggestions for classroom adaptations that might be considered and modified for a particular student in a regular classroom.

If the student needs specialized services to keep up with achievement in the classroom or to develop communication skills, help should be obtained from the resource teacher, audiologist, or speech therapist. The student may receive individual tutoring outside the classroom, or the resource teacher and/or speech therapist might work with the student within the regular class. Total coordination of the program will be a key to success.

The teacher (classroom, resource, or both) may have to introduce the vocabulary of lessons to hearing-impaired students ahead of time, or seek the help of the student's parents in this preliminary preparation for the lesson. This language orientation can facilitate speech reading and understanding. Another helpful hint is to write key words and phrases on the chalkboard as an outline for the student during a class discussion.

The teacher should try to remain stationary when talking and not stand near a window that creates a glare for the student. Light on the teacher's face is most helpful to students with hearing impairments. Of course, it is important to face students when talking. Using an overhead projector rather than the chalkboard can increase the amount of time a teacher faces a class.

Fancy hairstyles, mustaches, beards, and excessive jewelry worn by teachers often create distractions and interfere with the hearing-impaired student's ability to read lips. Other facial obstructions to avoid include pencils, books, cigarettes, pipes, and coffee cups.

Teachers should not exaggerate lip movements, speech rate, or voice volume. Complete sentences should be used so that individual words can be interpreted in the context of their meaning.

Visual aids are extremely helpful. Consider using captioned films, pictures, and the chalkboard.

Students who work very hard to hear in the classroom often tire more quickly than do other students. Academic subjects should be interwoven with physical activity and short intervals of free time to minimize fatigue and frustration.

A hearing-impaired student in the class can benefit significantly from having a hearing buddy make an outline or carbon copy of notes, repeat directions, clarify concepts, or point out the correct page in a book. Hurwitz (1979), a deaf adult, described the notetaking assistance he received during his college years:

> The registrar could not find an academically strong student to work with me, so we settled for a weak-C student who happened to be enrolled in all of my classes. He agreed to help me, since he needed the money which was financed by the Office of Vocational Rehabilitation. At first, he would use

carbon copy papers, and I would sit next to him to read his notes. It did not work out well because I was bored. The teacher's lecture was often not relevant to the textbooks I had before me on my desk. My notetaker would take the kind of notes he felt would be useful for me and himself. So we agreed to eliminate the carbon papers and I would copy his notes in the class as he took them. I would try to analyze the notes with my textbooks. Whenever I needed to ask a question, I would write it down on scratch paper and give it to my notetaker to ask the teacher for me. It worked out well. At the end of the academic year my notetaker became an honor student! I did well myself, too. The support services program worked out well not only for myself but also for my notetaker. It enabled him to take better notes for himself too. (p. 51)

Buddies can be rotated on a weekly or biweekly basis. The teacher has to instruct classroom peers carefully on how much help is needed or when help is not needed. Striking the proper balance is an important educational decision.

Sometimes students who are hearing impaired make unintentional noises, interrupt conversations, and speak too loudly or not loudly enough without being aware of it. They need guidance in appropriate verbal interactions. Overlooking or excusing these types of behaviors with students who are perfectly capable of appropriate communications skills denies them an opportunity to learn otherwise.

Case Study: Communication Disorders

Jane is the brightest student in my third-grade class. In every subject area, her achievement is outstanding to the point that every assignment is practically perfect. In contrast to all these strengths, she has a significant stuttering problem. At the beginning of school, it was immediately apparent. I was concerned because I have never before encountered this type of handicap. I was relieved when Jane's mother asked to meet with me during the second week of school. She openly discussed Jane's problem, which helped me understand it. It seems that Jane started talking very early and was using complete sentences long before her second birthday. Around the age of three she started stuttering and went through periods of mild to more obvious disfluencies. She has been receiving therapy since she was five. Since I was unsure how to handle the stuttering in the classroom, she suggested that I listen carefully to Jane, let her finish what she is trying to say, and try to be relaxed about it. I really appreciate being able to talk about this directly with Jane's mother.

As the school year has progressed, the stuttering has become worse. I have noticed that it seems to be very bad during spontaneous conversation in the classroom and during oral reading. Sometimes she jerks her neck and twists her mouth as she is struggling to say something. She seems to stutter less in free-play situations on the playground and with her peers. Lately her stuttering has been so severe that I have difficulty understanding her. I realize that I am having a problem handling the stuttering, because I feel uncomfortable when I see her struggling so much. Sometimes I almost want to skip over her in the reading group. I realize that this is a problem I must deal with.

The other children in the class are very sensitive. They have great respect for Jane's intelligence and would never tease or mock her. She is popular with her peers and very friendly. It concerns me that she rarely discusses her feelings. She's very closed about her personal reactions. Sometimes she looks sad and alone, but during these times she never will open up with me. She seems to be very conscious of the stuttering, yet she never mentions it. Her therapist has suggested that I not call attention to her problem, but I would like to talk with her about it. I operate better when I can be open with the students. I want to talk with him again about the possibility of talking openly with Jane. Since her speech therapist is handling her program, it is important to coordinate things with him. At the same time, it is important for him to be aware of techniques and approaches that fit comfortably into my teaching style.

I will have to admit that I am concerned about Jane. Stuttering is a difficult handicap. I just hope that her problem can be decreased.

Ms. Linda Tully
Ephesus Road School

COMMUNICATION DISORDERS

Communication disorders include problems in speech and/or language. The term *language* is much broader than the term *speech*. Language encompasses the numerous ways we receive messages as well as the ways we express ourselves. For example, there is considerable interest in body language, and the previous section in this chapter discusses the concept of sign language. This section focuses on oral communication, which involves speech and language.

Speech includes various processes related to producing sounds, combining sounds into words, and further combining words into phrases and sentences. Language is the total system of symbols used in both the expression and comprehension of ideas. Speech and language processes involve receiving, associating, comprehending, analyzing, synthesizing, and evaluating concepts, and then transferring these concepts into the production of speech that other people can comprehend. Because this process can be very difficult for some children to master, deviations from oral communication commonly occur with students in regular classes. Sometimes it is difficult to determine when a difference in speech patterns falls outside the range of normality and is considered to be a handicap.

Definitions

Speech impairment is defined by PL 94–142 as

> a communication disorder, such as stuttering, impaired articulation, a language impairment, or a voice impairment, which adversely affects a child's education performance. (*Federal Register*, 1977, pp. 42478–42479)

A classic criterion generally accepted for speech handicaps was specified by Van Riper (1972): "Speech is defective when it deviates so far from the speech of other people that it calls attention to itself, interferes with communication, or causes the possessor to be maladjusted" (p. 29).

Language disorders occur when there is a serious disruption of the language process. Language problems may arise in the form of language delays or language disorders. Language delay refers to interruption of the normal rate of language development; language disorder occurs when the language acquisition is not systematic or sequential (Hardman, Drew, & Egan, 1987).

Speech and language impairments are related to other disabilities. Mentally handicapped students frequently have delayed language development. Conditions related to orthopedic handicaps, such as paralysis, can seriously impede the production of speech. Because children who are hearing impaired are at a distinct disadvantage in developing oral communication, these special concerns have been discussed previously. The significant contribution of language impairment to learning disabilities is presented in chapter 4. Almost across the board, speech and language factors are major considerations in every handicapping condition. For this reason, it is difficult to estimate the number of students who have speech and language impairments. Approximately 5 percent of the total population, including about 10 percent of the children in elementary school, have communication disorders of various types and severity (Owens, 1988). This represents the largest group of exceptional students served in the public schools. To avoid confusion in terminology and characteristics, speech impairments and language disorders are discussed separately.

Speech Impairments

Characteristics
Speech impairments or disorders can be classified as either organic or functional. Organic disorders have a physiological base and therefore constitute a medical problem. Examples of physical factors that frequently result in communication disorders include cleft palate, paralysis of the speech muscles, absence of teeth, enlarged adenoids, and neurological impairments (Heward & Orlansky, 1988).

Most speech disorders are classified as functional, meaning that they have no known physiological cause. Regardless of the cause, speech disorders are manifested as disorders in articulation, voice, or fluency.

ARTICULATION   Articulation problems generally refer to consistent mispronunciation of syllables or of entire words. These mispronunciations occur very commonly among children in the primary grades and frequently disappear as students mature. Other articulation disorders can create significant communication problems. Articulation problems can be categorized as substitutions, distortions, and omissions.

Examples of substitutions are *wove* for *love*, *tite* for *kite*, *yeth* for *yes*.

Some students consistently substitute at various word positions (initial, medial, and final).

Distortions of sounds can be considered one kind of substitution; however, their distinctiveness comes from being unidentifiable as any other consonant or vowel. Omissions occur when sounds are dropped from words, such as when *h* is dropped from *house.* When this problem is severe, language is extremely difficult to understand.

VOICE DISORDERS   Voice disorders refer to abnormal pitch, loudness, or quality of the voice. Voice disorders are more prevalent in adults than in children and are not usually considered to be serious problems. However, if a student's voice differs in quality, pitch, or loudness to a great extent, other people may feel uncomfortable and the student may be embarrassed. Speech pathologists may be able to suggest exercises to change the voice quality.

FLUENCY DISORDERS   Normal speech makes use of rhythm and timing, with words and sentences flowing easily. Fluency disorders interrupt the natural flow of speech with inappropriate pauses, hesitations, or repetitions. The most familiar fluency disorder is stuttering. Stuttering is manifested in disruptions in the normal flow of speech. These disruptions may be prolongations or repetitions of sounds and words. Stuttering can vary widely as to circumstances, particular sounds or words, and location of syllables in words or of words in sentences and also as to the speaker's fatigue and emotional comfort.

Educational Implications

ARTICULATION   Articulation disorders are the speech impairment most prevalent among school-age children. Phillips (1975) estimates that approximately 90 percent of all speech problems are articulation problems. The majority of articulation problems are functional and can be considered related to faulty learning. Two significant factors are (1) poor speech models and (2) lack of stimulation and motivation (Phillips, 1975).

In classroom situations, articulation errors can interfere with the student's performance in the following ways: expressive language can be difficult to understand, phonics training affecting spelling and reading skills can be held back, and the student's social interactions can be influenced. The teacher needs to be alert to these possibilities and to work cooperatively with the student and the school's speech pathologist to eliminate these problems as much as possible.

STUTTERING   Although a significant amount of research has been conducted on stuttering, resulting in numerous theories of causation, experts debate and disagree over its definitive causes (Brutten & Shoemaker, 1967; Van Riper, 1972). Some people believe it is learned, others that it represents a developmental lag, and still others that it is emotionally and environmentally based. These debates are likely to continue; however, the important consideration for teachers is learning to minimize the educational implications of stuttering in the classroom.

Teachers should remember that normal disfluencies occur in everyone's speech at various times. Also, prolongations and repetitions normally are more frequent in the speech of young children, generally up to the age of 8. Therefore, caution should be taken in interpreting normal disfluencies as actual stuttering.

Four general suggestions for the teacher include:

1. Avoid calling attention to the stuttering. Let students finish what they are trying to say and maintain good listening habits, such as eye contact and positive facial expressions.
2. Make a special note of the classroom circumstances (discussions, oral presentation, free play) and the times of day when the stuttering seems to be the most severe. On the basis of each student's particular pattern, minimize the difficult situations and maximize the situations characterized by more fluency as much as possible.
3. Talk with the student and parents and cooperatively discuss ways of helping other students in the class react positively to stuttering episodes. Chapter 13 contains many suggestions for conducting such discussions. Classroom peers may resort to teasing and mimicking if they do not know ways to react positively.
4. Reduce anxiety over speaking situations as much as possible. If students who stutter are particularly fearful of being called on to answer a question orally in class, the teacher can tell them that they will not be called on unless they volunteer. Often, this strategy can prevent students with stuttering problems from being overly concerned about every discussion period.

In addition to the educational implications of speech impairments, the psychological and social implications are equally important. The following account of a boy who had a fluency disorder offers insight into the trauma of speech impairment:

He could kick the ball higher and farther than most other children; he could run very fast; and he could climb the ropes almost without using his feet. Music was fun too because the boy liked to sing. But the boy often stuttered and he knew it. Even when he knew the answer to a question, he would not talk because he was sure the children would laugh when he tried to speak. One time, even the teacher laughed. When the boy tried to take his turn reading out loud, he simply could not say the words. He knew the words, but the sounds just would not come out. Sometimes, trying so hard, the boy sounded like a little grizzly bear. When the teacher said, "You do know how to read, don't you?" or "You do have a name, don't you?" the children laughed. . . . It hurt to be teased so much. . . . He always got good grades— usually 90 or 95 in all of the subjects, but a 65 in oral reading. That hurt too. (Shapiro, 1988, p. 4)

Teachers play a key role in the acceptance of students who have speech impairments. As emphasized in chapter 13, students frequently use the teacher as a model for acceptance of and assistance to students who have a handicap.

Language Disorders

Characteristics
Some children have real difficulty acquiring and using the language code of their particular language culture. The majority of language disorders in children occur in the preschool years (Boone, 1987). Language disorders are basically determined by comparing the child's language function with that of normal children the same age.

NORMAL LANGUAGE DEVELOPMENT   Frank and Rieber (1981) suggest three minimal requirements for a child to progress from stage to stage in acquiring language:

1. *Biological requirements:* Adequate brain growth and maturation in the first 2 years.
2. *Linguistic requirements:* Exposure to appropriate quantity and quality of language within the critical language-learning period.
3. *Psychological requirements:* A relationship with a nurturing person with adequate initial closeness, normal progress through separation-individuation and absence of other severe psychopathology in mother or child at early developmental periods. (pp. 181–182)

Understanding the pattern of normal language development is essential for diagnosis and treatment of language disorders. Language has been determined to develop through sequential predictable stages; although there is a wide age range of development, it is the same for all children except those who are severely disabled. The following are six principles of language development:

1. Between the ages of 1–4, the child acquires some 1,500 words and can understand 6,000.
2. By age 6, the child has acquired the basic forms used in adult language.

3. Language development seems to be governed by both heredity and the environment.
4. Because learning language involves cognition and interaction, children with mental retardation may need stimulation and remediation. A hearing loss would likewise disturb normal language acquisition.
5. By 2 years of age, children should be beginning to speak in two-word utterances.
6. A five-year-old may be just able to produce the "j" and "n" sound; the "th" sound is not acquired until 6 years, the "s" and "z" from 5 or 6 to 8, and the "zh" at 6–8 years. Thus it is normal for young children to have difficulties with these and other sounds which may not be acquired until 6–7 years, including the "r," "l," "ch," and "sh." (Aserling & Browning, 1987, p. 125).

DELAYED LANGUAGE   Some students are significantly behind chronological age expectations in production of language and/or comprehension of ideas. Sometimes the cause can be pinpointed as mental retardation, hearing loss, severe emotional problems, or environmental or bilingual considerations. In other cases, students can have language delays and it is impossible to identify the origin of the problem. Regardless of the particular cause, handicaps of this nature can put students at a distinct disadvantage in achieving classroom success. These handicaps are characterized by an insufficient vocabulary, difficulty expressing or comprehending complex sentence structures, problems with sequencing ideas or organizing information, or difficulty with inferring the meaning of words or sentences. Speech and language are developmental processes, and some children and youths proceed through the levels of higher-order functioning at slower rates than others.

Educational Implications

Children with delayed language could have delays in reading, writing, and spelling because these subjects depend on understanding the language process; difficulty in understanding classroom discussions or mastering concepts in content subjects such as science and social studies; and difficulty in following directions. Helping students overcome language delays and avoid these educational handicaps is the responsibility of teachers and speech pathologists.

Remediation of language deficits is one of the most challenging problems faced by teachers and speech pathologists. Recent research favors a naturalistic approach, in which language and communication skills are taught in the child's natural environment (e.g., home or school). An example of a naturalistic approach is suggested by Warren and Kaiser (1986), who describe a technique called incidental teaching. This technique refers to the interactions between an adult and a child that arise naturally in an unstructured situation. Incidental teaching as a language intervention involves arranging the environment to increase the likelihood that the child will initiate a conversation with the adult, selecting language targets suitable for the child's skill level and interest, responding to the child's initiations with requests for language resembling the target, and reinforcing the child's communicative attempts.

Young children learn language while pursuing their own social and intellectual goals; demands for language required by tests or practice drills are foreign to their perspective (Johnston & Heller, 1987). The importance of a rich, language-stimulating environment cannot be overemphasized.

The speech pathologist and the classroom teacher need to work together closely when planning for children who are language delayed or language impaired. Teachers provide the models for communication on a daily basis, whereas the speech pathologist will see the child only on a scheduled basis.

The teacher should provide a classroom environment that will encourage communication and not exclude children who have communication disorders; help identify children who have speech, language, or hearing problems; and send children to therapy at the time scheduled (Neidecker, 1987). In no area is teacher involvement more important than in language development—it is a part of every curriculum area and every social interaction.

REFERENCES

Antia, S. (1985). Social integration of hearing impaired children. *Volta Review, 87,* (6), 279–287.

Aserling, L., & Browning, E. R. (1987). *Minds into the mainstream.* Dubuque, IO: Kendall/Hunt.

Baker, C., & Padden, C. (1978). *American sign language.* Silver Spring, MD: T. J. Publishers.

Bateman, B. (1963). Reading and psycholinguistic processes of partially seeing children. *CEC Research Monograph,* Series A, No. 5. Reston, VA: Council for Exceptional Children.

Bauer, A. M., & Shea, T. M. (1989). *Teaching exceptional students in your classroom.* Boston: Allyn and Bacon.

Birch, J. W. (1975). Hearing impaired children in the mainstream. Minneapolis: Leadership Training Institute/Special Education, University of Minnesota.

Boone, D. R. (1987). *Human communication and its disorders.* Englewood Cliffs, NJ: Prentice-Hall.

Boothroyd, A. (1982). *Hearing impairments in young children.* Englewood Cliffs, NJ: Prentice-Hall.

Brutten, G. J., & Shoemaker, D. J. (1967). *The modification of stuttering.* Englewood Cliffs, NJ: Prentice-Hall.

Champie, J. (1986). Least restrictive environments for the deaf. *The Education Digest, L11,* (3), 43–45.

Chorost, S. (1988). The hearing-impaired child in the mainstream: A survey of the attitudes of regular classroom teachers. *Volta Review, 90,* (1), 7–12.

Degler, L. S., & Risko, V. J. (1979). Teaching reading to mainstreamed sensory impaired children. *Reading Teacher, 32,* (8), 921–925.

Erin, J. N. (1988). The teacher-consultant: The teacher of visually handicapped students and collaborative consultation. *Education of the Visually Handicapped, 20,* (2), 57–63.

Federal Register. (1977). Washington, DC: U.S. Government Printing Office, pp. 42478–42479.

Frank, S. M., & Rieber, R. W. (1981). Language development and language disorders in children and adolescents. In R. W. Rieber (Ed.), *Communication disorders* (pp. 179–200). New York: Plenum.

Hardman, M. L., Drew, C. J., & Egan, M. W. (1987). *Human exceptionality* (2nd ed.). Boston: Allyn and Bacon.

Harley, R. K., Truan, M. B., & Sanford, L. D. (1987). *Communication skills for visually impaired learners.* Springfield, IL: Charles C Thomas.

Hayes, S. P. (1941). *Contributions to a psychology of blindness.* New York: American Foundation for the Blind.

Heward, W. L., & Orlansky, M. D. (1988). *Exceptional children* (3rd ed.). Columbus, OH: Merrill.

Hurwitz, T. A. (1979). Reflections of a mainstreamed deaf person. In M. E. Bishop (Ed.), *Mainstreaming: Practical ideas for educating hearing-impaired students* (pp. 48–53). Washington, DC: The Alexander Graham Bell Association for the Deaf.

Ireland, J. C., Wray, D., & Flexer, C. (1988). Hearing for success in the classroom. *Teaching Exceptional Children, 20,* (2), 15–17.

Johnston, J. R., & Heller, A. B. (1987). Effectiveness of a curriculum for preschool language intervention specialists. *ASHA, 29,* (7), 39–43.

Kirk, S. A., & Gallagher, J. J. (1989). *Educating exceptional children* (6th ed.). Boston: Houghton Mifflin.

Kluwin, T. N., & Moores, D. F. (1989). Mathematics achievement of hearing impaired adolescents in different placements. *Exceptional Children, 55,* (4), 327–335.

Lass, N. J., Tecca, J. E., & Woodford, C. M. (1987). Teachers' knowledge of, exposure to, and attitudes toward hearing aids and hearing aid wearers. *Language, Speech, and Hearing Services in Schools, 18,* (1), 86–96.

Ling, D. (1984). Early total communication intervention: An introduction. In D. Ling (Ed.), *Early intervention for hearing-impaired children: Total communication options* (pp. 1–14). San Diego: College Hill Press.

Lowenfeld, B., Abel, G., & Hatlen, P. *Blind children learn to read.* Springfield, IL: Charles C Thomas.

Martin, F. N., Bernstein, M. E., Daly, J. A., & Cody, J. P. (1988). Classroom teachers' knowledge of hearing disorders and attitudes about mainstreaming hard-of-hearing children. *Language, Speech, and Hearing Services in Schools, 19,* (1), 83–95.

Neidecker, E. A. (1987). *School programs in speech-language.* Englewood Cliffs, NJ: Prentice-Hall.

Nix, G. W. (1976). *Mainstream education for hearing impaired children and youth.* New York: Grune & Stratton.

Owens, R. E., Jr. (1988). *Language development* (2nd ed.). Columbus, OH: Merrill.

Phillips, P. P. (1975). *Speech and hearing problems in the classroom.* Lincoln, NE: Cliff Notes.

Reynolds, M. C., & Birch, J. W. (1988). *Adaptive mainstreaming* (3rd ed.). New York: Longman.

Ruconich, S. (1984). Evaluating microcomputer access technology for use by visually impaired students. *The Pointer, 28,* (2), 44–47.

Scholl, G., & Schnur, R. (1976). *Measures of psychological, vocational, and educational functioning in the blind and visually handicapped.* New York: American Foundation for the Blind.

Schulz, J. B. (1989). Teaching handicapped students in the regular classroom. In J. A. Banks & C. A. Banks (Eds.), *Multicultural education,* (pp. 251–268). Boston: Allyn and Bacon.

Shapiro, D. A. (1988). A way through the forest: One boy's story with a happy ending. *Letting Go Jr., 2,* (3), 4–7.

Silberman, R., Trief, E., & Morse, A. R. (1988). What if your child has a visual impairment? *Exceptional Parent, 18,* (3), 41–45.

Spungin, S. J. (1981). *Guidelines for public school programs serving visually handicapped children.* New York: American Foundation for the Blind.

Suterko, S. (1973). Life adjustment. In B. Lowenfeld (Ed.), *The visually handicapped child in school* (pp. 279–317). New York: John Day.

Van Riper, C. (1972). *Speech correction: Principles and methods* (5th ed.). Englewood Cliffs, NJ: Prentice-Hall.

Ward, M., & McCormick, S. (1981). Reading instruction for blind and low vision children in the regular classroom. *The Reading Teacher, 34,* (4), 434–444.

Warren, S. F., & Kaiser, A. P. (1986). Incidental language teaching: A critical review. *Journal of Speech and Hearing Disorders, 51,* (Nov.), 291–299.

Willeford, J. A., & Burleigh, J. M. (1985). *Handbook of central auditory processing disorders in children.* New York: Grune & Stratton.

Williams, J. M. (1984). Technology and the handicapped. *American Education 20,* (5), 27–30.

Wray, D., Hazlett, J., & Flexer, C. (1988). Strategies for teaching writing skills to hearing-impaired students. *Language, Speech, and Hearing Services in Schools, 19,* (2), 182–189.

4

Students with Learning and Behavior Disorders

The three most prevalent categories of handicap in schools are learning disabilities, mental retardation, and behavioral disorders. Together, they account for 4.35 percent of the population age 3 to 21 and approximately 68 percent of the handicapped population age 3 to 21 being served (U.S. Department of Education, 1988), (see Table 4.1). Students with learning disabilities, mental retardation, or behavioral disorders can have mild to severe handicapping conditions. Those students in mainstream classrooms usually have mild to moderate handicaps.

Each section in this chapter describes the specific characteristics and educational implications for each category. However, some learning and behavioral features are common to the mildly handicapped learners described in this chapter. According to Schloss and Sedlak (1986):

- Handicapped learners do not acquire information at a rate commensurate with their nonhandicapped peers.
- Handicapped learners do not acquire the same amount of information over an extended period of instruction as nonhandicapped students.
- Handicapped students will forget acquired information sooner than their nonhandicapped peers. This is particularly true if the information is not used fairly often.
- Handicapped individuals are less likely to acquire information that is incidental to the central learning task.
- Information gained under one set of instructional conditions is less likely to transfer or generalize to different conditions. (pp. 35–36)

LEARNING DISABILITIES

Case Study: Learning Disabilities

Having Tom in my eighth-grade language arts class means that there is never a dull moment. At the beginning of the year, his capabilities and performance were not easy to figure out. With some students, all the pieces of information fall into place immediately. Tom puzzled me. I knew he had high ability, yet he demonstrated real problems in getting his work done. After observing his behavior closely and talking with the resource teacher in the school, I now seem to have a handle on some of his learning strengths and weaknesses.

In the language arts areas, Tom is able to read just slightly below grade level. Although he does not have the reading proficiency of most of his classmates, he is able to read his textbooks, rarely needing help

TABLE 4.1 Students Served under Chapter 1 of ECIA (SOP)[a] and EHA-B[b] by Handicapping Condition, 1986–87

Handicapping Condition	EHA-B		ECIA (SOP)		Total	
	Number	Percent[c]	Number	Percent[c]	Number	Percent[c]
Learning disabled	1,900,739	45.6	25,358	9.9	1,926,097	43.6
Speech or language impaired	1,114,410	26.7	26,012	10.2	1,140,422	25.8
Mentally retarded	577,749	13.9	86,675	34.0	664,424	15.0
Emotionally disturbed	341,294	8.2	43,386	17.0	384,680	8.7
Multihandicapped	75,730	1.8	23,686	9.3	99,416	2.2
Hard of hearing and deaf	45,060	1.1	21,701	8.5	66,761	1.5
Orthopedically impaired	46,692	1.1	11,636	4.6	58,328	1.3
Other health impaired	44,966	1.1	7,692	3.0	52,658	1.2
Visually handicapped	19,201	.46	7,848	3.1	27,049	.61
Deaf-blind	851	.02	915	.36	1,766	.04
All conditions	4,166,692	100	254,909	100	4,421,601	100

[a]Education Consolidation and Improvement Act—State Operated Programs
[b]Education of the Handicapped Act—Part B
[c]Percents are within column.
Source: *Tenth Annual Report to Congress on the Implementations of the Education of the Handicapped Act*, 1988. Washington, DC: U.S. Department of Education, p. 9. Child count information is for the school year 1986–87.

with a word. In written assignments, his handwriting can be neat; however, he usually approaches a written task in a harum-scarum fashion, writing quickly to get through as soon as possible. More often than not, his papers are messy and difficult to read. When he gets down to work, he is able to make a passing grade on his spelling test. That is the heart of the problem—"when he gets down to work."

It is basically organization that poses extreme difficulty for Tom. He seems almost constantly distracted, having a difficult time sitting down and getting settled. On some days I think he spends more time wandering around the classroom than sitting in his seat. When he goes to sharpen his pencil, he will look out the window and become captivated watching a bird, or he will pass the magazine rack and flip through several magazines before returning to his seat. He's fidgety, constantly turning in his seat and moving around. As to his work, he often does not complete it. Since it takes him longer because of his attention span, he sometimes will hand in work several days late. With that much delay and his general difficulty with organization, it is not unusual for him to lose assignments that he has started but not completed. I have to watch Tom about taking shortcuts with his work. If he has ten questions to answer, he sometimes will answer the first, a couple in the middle, and the last, and state that he has finished the assignment. Sometimes I purposefully shorten his assignments so that the length is adjusted to his learning pattern. In this way, he can achieve success and demonstrate a mastery of the content without being penalized for his distractibility. Another approach which seems to help him is for me to write instructions for the class period on the board and sometimes even an outline of class discussions. Since Tom does not always generate his own structure, he seems to benefit from as much as I can impose. I have been pleased with the encouragement and direction he gets from the other students in the class. They tell him things like, "Turn around and do your work," or "Come on, Tom, I don't have time to talk to you."

Tom has his good and bad days, just like all of us. He's got the ability, and it's a continual challenge for me to capitalize on his strengths.

Ms. Elaine Allison
Culbreth Junior High School

Definitions

One of the newest and most controversial exceptionalities is termed *learning disabilities*. The definition of learning disabilities is constantly being debated, and no real consensus exists. There is even significant debate about whether such a category exists or ought to exist. Like most exceptionalities, the term is rather heterogeneous; it is an umbrella for a variety of problems that do not seem to fit easily into other available categories.

Many classroom teachers have worked with students who have significant gaps between their educational achievement and their intellectual potential. These students may experience severe academic difficulty in one or two, but not all, subject areas. They may have difficulty attending to their assigned task, sitting still for seemingly brief intervals, decoding or comprehending in reading, using expressive and receptive language, writing legibly, solving math problems, or generally following instruction. They can be characterized by a large combination of these factors or by only one or two. Frequently, students who fit this description are described as underachievers, poorly motivated students, and reluctant learners. An adult with some of these educational disadvantages recalled her school career as a period of being labeled "everything from lazy to crazy" when, in fact, she was part of the student population appropriately referred to as learning disabled.

PL 94–142 defines a specific learning disability as

> a disorder in one or more basic psychological processes involved in understanding or in using language, spoken, or written, which may manifest itself in an imperfect ability to listen, think, speak, read, write, spell, or to do mathematical calculation. The term includes such conditions as perceptual handicaps, brain injury, minimal brain dysfunction, dyslexia, and developmental aphasia. The term does not include children who have learning problems which are primarily the result of visual, hearing or motor handicaps, of mental retardation, of emotional disturbance, or of environmental, cultural, or economic disadvantage. (*Federal Register*, 1977, p. 42478)

To gain a clearer understanding of learning disabilities, a closer examination of four of the component parts of this definition is warranted (Myers & Hammill, 1976).

1. "a disorder in one or more of the basic psychological processes involved in understanding or in using language, spoken or written." (*Federal Register*, 1977, p. 42478)

Because the term *psychological processes* is not operationally defined, it is open to different interpretations. Perhaps the most frequent referents are learning modalities, such as visual, auditory, tactile, and motor, in addition to learning processes, such as memory, comprehension, and generalization. For these processes, the disorder may result from a developmental lag or from impaired functioning. A developmental lag occurs when the learning process becomes refined at a slower rate than that of other students. For example, some students may not have the necessary fine motor skills for successfully learning to write in manuscript in the first grade, but the refinement of these readiness skills may be present one to two years later. Impaired functioning of modalities or processes refers to a basic distortion in interpretation, organization, and/or expression. An example of impaired functioning in the area of language is a student who routinely is unable to find the words he or she wants to respond to an oral or written question. This word-finding difficulty represents impaired functioning of learning processes. It is often difficult for teachers to distinguish accurately between the disorders representing a developmental lag, in which remediation might reasonably be expected to occur in the future, and impaired functioning, in which the possibility exists that the student will always experience difficulty.

2. "[a disorder] which may manifest itself in an imperfect ability to listen, think, speak, read, write, spell, or to do mathematical calculation." (*Federal Register*, p. 42478)

These skills form the core of academic success, and in them the learning disability may be evidenced. The majority of questions from classroom teachers concern methods and materials for teaching these skills to students with learning disabilities. Chapters 6 through 11 respond directly to these concerns.

3. "The term [*learning disabilities*] includes such conditions as perceptual handicaps, brain injury, minimal brain dysfunction, dyslexia, and developmental aphasia." (*Federal Register*, p. 42478)

These terms do not have operational meanings, and even experts in the field of learning disabilities do not agree on their definitions. Teachers are wise to develop the habit of discussing characteristics of the student in educational terms, such as the specific strengths and weaknesses in subject areas. This information is educationally relevant to classroom teachers. Jargon and labels are superficial and often confuse rather than clarify the development of the student's instructional program.

4. "The term [*learning disabilities*] does not include children who have learning problems which are primarily the result of visual, hearing, or motor handicaps, of mental retardation, or of environmental, cultural, or economic disadvantage." (*Federal Register*, p. 42478)

Learning disabilities are often diagnosed through the process of elimination. When the student's primary handicap is not attributable to other conditions, yet a wide gap exists between achievement and potential, the student is often considered to have a learning disability. The key word in this portion of the definition is *primarily*. The student with learning disabilities may have secondary problems related to other handicapping conditions (emotional problems, sensory deficits) and may also have secondary educational concerns that fit the description of a learning disability. The difference between primary and secondary handicapping conditions is not always clearcut. Again, the important considerations for teachers are pinpointing the student's individual strengths and weaknesses and developing a systematic instructional program geared to the student's needs.

Another definition, later formulated by the National Joint Committee on Learning Disabilities (NJCLD) (1987), was represented by several organizations:

> "Learning disabilities" is a generic term that refers to a heterogeneous group of disorders manifested by significant difficulties in the acquisition and use of listening, speaking, reading, writing, reasoning, or mathematical abilities. These disorders are intrinsic to the individual and presumed to be due to central nervous system dysfunction. Even though a learning disability may occur concomitantly with other handicapping conditions (e.g., sensory impairment, mental retardation, social and emotional disturbance) or environmental influences (e.g., cultural differences or inappropriate instruction, psycholinguistic factors), it is not the direct result of those conditions or influences. (p. 107)

This definition differs significantly from the federal definition. It states that students with learning disabilities may have several different problems. This disorder is due to factors within the student, not to external factors. The problem is believed to be due to a biological or organic source, and learning disabilities can occur along with other handicaps.

Educational Characteristics

Often when the variety of characteristics associated with learning disabilities is listed, two major drawbacks are obvious. First, the list can be overwhelming. So many characteristics are associated with learning disabilities that it is common for such a list to contain more than 20 items. Second, many of the characteristics associated with learning disabilities are also associated with students who may not be experiencing significant educational problems. The learning-disabled student usually has more of them and to a greater degree than do more able students.

Educational characteristics of learning-disabled students should also be considered in a developmental context. Some characteristics are more often associated with younger children than are other characteristics. Other characteristics are most often seen in older pupils. This difference probably occurs because students usually face different kinds of tasks as they get older. The central nervous system, which many researchers in education believe to be the origin of learning disabilities, matures developmentally. For this reason, some characteristics and manifestations of learning disabilities may not surface until the student is in high school or beyond.

The categories of characteristics are disorders of attention, failure to develop and mobilize cognitive strategies for learning, poor motor abilities, perceptual and information processing problems, academic difficulties, and inappropriate social behavior. Each category has several specific characteristics (Lerner, 1989).

Disorders of Attention

Attention disorders include hyperactivity, distractibility, and poor attention spans or inability to focus. Hyperactivity refers to an excessive amount of activity compared to peers. First-grade children are generally very active in motor activity compared to ninth-grade children. A child is not said to be hyperactive unless the exhibited behavior is markedly different from peers and is unfocused and unproductive. Students who are distractible or who have poor attention spans are usually not able to block out extraneous sights and sounds. They do not remain focused as long as their peers do on tasks and in some ways are easily susceptible to environmental distractions.

The *Diagnostic and Statistical Manual of Mental Disorders* (third edition, revised) (American Psychiatric Association, 1987) has identified attention-deficit hyperactivity disorder (ADHD) and undifferentiated attention-deficit disorder as problems. Some of the criteria for ADHD are having difficulty remaining seated when required to do so, awaiting a turn in games or group situations, and sustaining attention in tasks or play activities. Many but not all students diagnosed as having attention-deficit disorder (ADD) are also identified as having learning disabilities or behavioral disorders. Some ADD students are likely to need special considerations but may not qualify for special education (Duane, 1988). Suggestions for helping learning-disabled students or students with behavioral disorders are also likely to help ADD students. In addition, mainstream teachers are advised to help parents seek appropriate diagnosis and assistance from psychiatrists or psychologists.

Cognitive Strategy Deficits

Many students do not have or know how to use strategies to acquire, organize, and/or express information. They do not know how to monitor their own comprehension, how to attack new words, or how to study for spelling tests. They do not know how to memorize or question or how to retrieve. They do not know strategies for spelling, writing, or speaking. Left on their own they are not likely to develop their own strategies, and often after they have learned how to do something, such as regrouping in subtraction, they will use the newly learned strategy even when it is not appropriate. This is the sort of student who after reading several pages without comprehending is not likely to realize it.

Poor Motor Abilities

Poor motor abilities are evident in some younger children and cause them problems. Children with poor motor abilities may have problems with large muscles that control limb movement used in running, jumping, skipping, and throwing and/or with small muscles used in writing, drawing, or grasping. Children with poor motor abilities are clumsy and awkward.

> *Robert, a fifth grader, labeled* learning disabled, *was blond and disheveled. He had problems in reading and handwriting. The most obvious thing was Robert's awkwardness—always stumbling over chairs, dropping things and losing his books. Robert's teachers kept a supply of sharpened pencils because Robert had never learned to use a pencil sharpener. He didn't seem to have the coordination to learn.*

Spatial problems such as confusing right and left are also characteristic of students with poor motor problems. This is sometimes exhibited in not keeping written work properly aligned and in executing out-of-proportion drawings.

Perceptual and Information-Processing Problems

Children with perceptual problems may have trouble discriminating sounds and associating sounds with their source. Children with auditory perceptual problems have trouble with sound-letter association and sound blending. Children with visual perceptual problems have similar difficulties with visual stimuli. Such students may not be able to interpret the environment by sight or to recognize visual objects and pictures rapidly. They may see letters in words as reversed or inverted.

Information-processing problems include memory problems (particularly remembering what has been seen or heard). Learning-disabled students with information-processing problems have trouble integrating information from auditory, visual, and tactile stimuli. They may have trouble with such tasks as copying from the board, following oral directions, or taking notes.

Academic Difficulties

Learning-disabled students have difficulties in one or more academic areas. The seven academic criteria areas necessary for identification include (1) listening comprehension, (2) oral expression, (3) written expression, (4) basic reading skill, (5) reading comprehension, (6) mathematics calculation, and (7) mathematics reasoning. A learning-disabled student may have a severe discrepancy between achievement and aptitude in one or more of these areas. Each curriculum chapter details common problems of handicapped pupils and provides suggestions to help them. Academic difficulties are the most common problem of learning-disabled students.

Inappropriate Social Behavior
Learning-disabled students frequently exhibit such social behavior problems as poor interpersonal relationships, short attention spans, poor self-concept, personality problems, withdrawal, and hyperactivity (Wallace & McLoughlin, 1988). Inappropriate social behaviors among learning-disabled students are well-documented (Bryan, Pearl, Donahue, Bryan, & Pflaum, 1983; Deshler & Schumaker, 1983; Pearl, Donahue, & Bryan, 1986). What is not known is whether social problems are the result of learning disabilities or are the outcome of academic frustration. It is likely that at least some social difficulties are due to the same central nervous system deficit that has hindered other kinds of learning for learning-disabled students. These students do not seem to be able to master some basic communication codes necessary for learning particular academic skills. For educational implications of inappropriate social behavior, see the section on behavioral disorders in this chapter and also see chapters 8 and 13.

Educational Implications

Because of their diverse problems, learning-disabled students present different challenges to mainstream teachers. As with their characteristics, the needs of students with learning disabilities are varied because of the variety of problems and the differences due to their ages and the focus of the curriculum. The two overwhelming needs of learning-disabled students are structure/organization and skill development.

Structure
Mainstream teachers can provide immense help to students by providing structure and organization. Students need detailed schedules and directions. Teachers should be careful to deliver directions in small amounts so as not to overload students. Expressing expectations in simple, concrete terms can be helpful. Telling Kara to open her health book to page 16 and waiting for her to do so before giving the next direction is better than two- or three-step directions given at once. Providing adequate time for the completion of assignments reduces the confusion that results from not being able to finish tasks and being required to organize time to complete them. Helping students copy homework assignments and organizing such materials as pencils and paper, jacket, and books can eliminate time wasted looking for misplaced belongings.

Teachers can help students by scheduling more difficult and intense activities along with less difficult and less taxing activities. Providing specific things to do rather than allowing many choices keeps students on task rather than trying to decide what the task requires and how to respond.

Students with attention disorders can often be assisted by diet or drug therapy to help reduce hyperactivity and excessive distractibility. If these interventions are successful, students can better interpret their environment and understand classroom structure.

Skill Development

Students with learning disabilities benefit from careful, systematic skill development. Ysseldyke and Algozzine (1984) identify two approaches to teaching students with skill deficits—precision teaching and direct instruction. Precision teaching involves planning, using, and analyzing the effects of instruction techniques or methods to improve a student's performance on specified academic skills. The two key components of precision teaching are pinpointing aims and evaluating the effects of interventions.

Direct instruction has seven components (Haring & Schiefelbusch, 1976) and is similar to precision teaching.

1. Assessment of learner characteristics establishes the student's present level of skills.
2. Instructional goals are established and broken down into short-term objectives.
3. Instruction is systematically applied along with motivational sequences and reinforcement.
4. Goal-directed materials that maximize time-on-task are used.
5. Instruction is clearly and completely described with discrete and replicable steps.
6. Direct instruction emphasizes the use of motivating consequences that are effective for the individual.
7. Student success is continually monitored to assess the rate of skill acquisition.

Learning Strategies

In addition to skill development in specific areas, learning-disabled students need to learn strategies that focus on how to learn. Researchers at the University of Kansas (Deshler, Alley, Warner, & Schumaker, 1981) have developed an instructional strategy based on the following eight acquisition and generalization steps:

1. Pretest the student's skill level.
2. Describe the strategy to be learned.
3. Model the strategy for the student.
4. Verbally rehearse the strategy steps.
5. Practice in controlled materials.

6. Practice in grade-appropriate materials.
7. Posttest.
8. Generalize to other materials and settings.

Using this instructional sequence, students have been taught to use strategies to acquire, organize, and express information. The approach often uses strategies that are easily remembered with a mnemonic aid, such as a word in which the letters cue the student to remember the steps of the strategy. For instance, a strategy to teach students how to paraphrase the main idea and details of a paragraph is *R–A–P*. *Read a paragraph*. *Ask* yourself what is the main idea and two details. *Put* the main idea and two details into your own words (Schumaker, Denton, & Deshler, 1984). In this way, students are taught to improve reading comprehension.

Compensatory Techniques
Many students with learning disabilities have trouble with perception and academic areas. Teachers can help students bypass weak areas when remediation of weak areas seems impossible or requires so much time that the opportunity to work in other content areas is lost. Examples of compensatory techniques occur when students who have difficulty reading and/or writing are allowed to take oral rather than written examinations or when a student who had difficulty taking notes is allowed to tape-record lectures (Ysseldyke & Algozzine, 1984). Other examples for content areas may help learning-disabled students and other low achievers.

1. Students who do not read well may benefit from picture and graphic (e.g., schematic diagrams) surveys. Newer textbooks, particularly in science, lend themselves well to gaining information from graphic aids because publishers are using them more often.
2. Students who do not write well can dictate written assignments to other students or record on tape. This option is becoming increasingly available for standardized tests, and the availability of cassette recorders in classrooms makes it feasible.
3. Cassette recordings of textbooks for students with learning disabilities who do not read may be available from Recordings for the Blind in addition to their availability for blind students. If such recordings are not available, teachers can record their own tapes for a particular student or train others to record them. Deshler and Graham (1980) provide suggestions; see chapter 8.
4. Students who cannot take notes may benefit from carbon copies of no-carbon-required paper copies from another student's notes. It is important to use these techniques only when necessary and not just as an easy solution. Otherwise, they may contribute to exacerbating the feelings of helplessness often present in handicapped

pupils and contribute to the student's passive approach to learning.

MENTAL RETARDATION

Case Study: Mental Retardation

Larry is in my sixth-grade class, and teaching him is not always easy. His cumulative records state that he has been classified as EMH, which stands for educable mentally handicapped. Do not misunderstand or underestimate him. Although he does have learning and behavior problems, Larry is capable of far more than most people realize. His life history is a story of moving from one place to another. He has been in four different schools in six years and has moved away from his parents to live with his aunt.

From the time Larry entered first grade, he has been behind academically. He must have lacked the readiness that the teacher expected from the first day he set foot in the school door. Because his learning rate is slower, he has increasingly fallen behind over the years. Now in the sixth grade, he reads on a fourth-grade level and is learning to multiply in math. He has real problems with spelling but has nice handwriting and excels in physical education. Sometimes I am unsure if I am doing the right thing with him, but I have had some success hitting on some strategies that seem to work. First, he works with the special education resource teacher for one hour per day in reading. With this kind of intensive help, he seems to be making progress. I plan special work for him to do in math, since his achievement is below all the other students'. Recently he has been working with Cuisenaire rods, which seem to help him understand abstract concepts. In social studies, we are studying Europe. I found a fourth-grade textbook on Europe that Larry uses in place of the regular sixth-grade text. He really likes having a book he can read. Filmstrips and visual aids are his favorites. He seems to learn more effectively when we use them.

The biggest concerns I have about Larry are his short attention span and low frustration level. On most days he will work for a short while and then just give up. I try to accommodate this by giving him short tasks that can be completed before he runs out of steam. After he works, he sometimes will play a game like Easy or Monopoly, or read library books about sports. I let him do this because I think he is learning from these games and books.

Larry loves to help out with classroom tasks like giving out books or setting the room up for a special activity. He would work all day long to help me. He loves to do things and move about.

There is no doubt that Larry does have some strengths. I think he benefits from being around his classmates. I know he is making some progress, but sometimes I wonder if he is working up to his potential.

Ms. Julia Tyson
Glenwood Elementary School

Children and young people who are mentally retarded represent one of the largest groups of exceptionality. They also constitute a group that has been served for the longest period of time in the public school setting. Most people have only a vague idea of the concept of mental retardation, but identification and placement of students with mental retardation are based on legal definitions.

Definition

Professionals working in the field of mental retardation have worked individually and in groups in an effort to define mental retardation. In 1983, the American Association on Mental Deficiency (changed in 1987 to the American Association on Mental Retardation) published its eighth manual on classification and terminology of mental retardation. The following definition was presented:

> Mental retardation refers to significantly subaverage general intellectual functioning resulting in or associated with concurrent impairments in adaptive behavior and manifested during the developmental period. (Grossman, 1983, p. 11)

This definition is the most frequently cited and has been designated as the legal definition of the term *mental retardation*. However, difficulties have become apparent in developing a common understanding of mental retardation. Further difficulties have arisen in explaining such terms as *significantly subaverage general intellectual functioning, adaptive behavior,* and *developmental period*. Although explaining these terms helps clarify the intent of the definition, the explanations still do not meet with universal approval.

In an effort to provide a more useful definition of mental retardation, Zigler, Balla, and Hodapp (1984) suggest that the fundamental property of mental retardation is a cognitive system in which many cognitive processes are less efficient than those found in the average person, and that the IQ (intelligence quotient) be the sole criterion for the classification of mental retardation. In a rebuttal of this concept, Barnett (1986) proposes an interactive view of mental retardation, in which it is defined and identified within the context of interactions between an individual's characteristics and the demands of the social environment. This view is consistent with the AAMD (American Association on Mental Deficiency) references to "subaverage general intellectual functioning" and "impairments in adaptive behavior."

The term *significantly subaverage general intellectual functioning* is generally interpreted as having an IQ of 70 or below on standardized measures of intelligence. Individual intelligence tests, such as the Wechsler Intelligence Scale for Children–Revised (WISC–R) or the Stanford-Binet, are used to determine the IQ. In the AAMD manual, clinicians are cautioned to exercise judgment in using the upper limit of 70 as a guideline, extending it to an IQ of 75 or more if there is adequate reason to do so (Grossman, 1983).

The concept of *adaptive behavior* refers to a person's ability to meet standards of personal independence and social responsibility appropriate to the individual's needs and the requirements of the particular culture in which that person lives. This aspect of behavior may be equated to the interactive view of mental retardation referred to above. The following examples of adaptive behavior areas occur

During infancy and early childhood in:
1. Sensory-motor skills development and
2. Communication skills (including speech and language) and
3. Self-help skills and
4. Socialization (development of ability to interact with others) and

During childhood and early adolescence in:
5. Application of basic academic skills in daily life activities and
6. Application of appropriate reasoning and judgment in mastery of the environment and
7. Social skills (participation in group activities and interpersonal relationships) and

During late adolescence and adult life in:
8. Vocational and social responsibilities and performances. (Grossman, 1973, pp. 11–12)

The final major term in the definition of mental retardation, *developmental period*, refers to the fact that the student's mental impairment must be evident by the chronological age of 18 years. The definition specifies that the deficits in intellectual functioning and adaptive behavior occur during the developmental period in order to help distinguish mental retardation from other disorders (Heward & Orlansky, 1988).

Even though there is a degree of consistency in defining mental retardation, a great variability of terminology is used in schools throughout the United States. In a review of states' adherence to specific definitions, eligibility criteria, and classification schemes, Utley, Lowitzer, and Baumeister (1987) found that 56 percent of the states used the AAMD term, *mental retardation,* while the remaining states referred to a variety of terms, including *mental disability, educationally or intellectually handicapped, learning impaired, developmentally disabled, significant limited intellectual handicapped,* and *individuals with exceptional needs* (p. 37).

Part of the problem in establishing consistent terminology is the negative connotation of the term *mental retardation.* In a recent policy statement, the American Association on Mental Retardation urged professionals to use the phrase "people who have mental retardation" rather than "mentally retarded persons" (*Information for Authors,* 1988). This approach designates mental retardation as a characteristic in itself rather than as a definition of the person.

Characteristics

In spite of the differences in terminology and definition of mental retardation, the two basic components remain (1) measured intelligence that is below normal and (2) social behavior that is inappropriate to the age and culture of the individual. Obviously, an important aspect of mental retardation is the degree to which individuals deviate from the normal in these two dimensions.

According to the AAMD definition (Grossman, 1983), mental retardation occurs in four levels of severity: mild, moderate, severe, and profound. Although IQ levels are used as descriptors, other factors are more relevant to understanding the educational needs of students who are mentally retarded. Developmental characteristics are also depicted in Table 4.2 to indicate the four degrees of retardation. Note that more than 80 percent of all persons with mental retardation appear in the mild category.

The majority of students with mental retardation who attend regular classes are classified as mildly retarded or educably mentally handicapped. Additionally, some students with moderate retardation have been successfully integrated into regular classes, but such placement has been more the exception than the rule for these students. As discussed in chapter 6, students whose achievement substantially deviates from that of non-handicapped students are usually educated in specialized programs, such as full-time special classes. The majority of students with moderate, severe, and profound mental retardation fall into this group.

In addition to the traditional classifications, some students may be designated as ineligible for special services but still experience a great deal of difficulty in school. Forness and Kavale (1984) describe a special education "no man's land" (p. 241), in which large numbers of children, with IQs in the 70 to 85 range, still need special assistance.

TABLE 4.2 Degrees of Mental Retardation

Degree	Developmental Characteristics		
	Preschool (0–5 years)	School Age (6–20 years)	Adult (21 and over)
Mild (educable)	May not be diagnosed	Learns basic academic and pre-vocational skills with special help	Lives and works in community; may not be identified as retarded
Moderate (trainable)	Likely to have clinical diagnosis (e.g., Down Syndrome) and fair motor and communication skills	Learns self-help and functional academic skills; independent in familiar surroundings	Performs semiskilled work with supervision; may achieve competitive employment
Severe	Slow motor development; some communication; may have physical handicaps	May care for personal needs; may learn to communicate	Can contribute to self-maintenance with supervision in work and living situations
Profound	Minimal responsiveness; often has multihandicaps	Slow motor development; learns basic self-care skills	May acquire some communication skills; cares for basic needs; may perform highly structured work activities

Educational Implications

The more severe the handicap, the earlier the child is likely to be identified as having mental retardation. Most educational programs for infants and preschool-age children are designed for the moderately to profoundly handicapped, those with multiple handicaps, or those who can be identified as being at high risk for having significant delays by the time they reach school age (Patton, Payne, & Beirne-Smith, 1986).

On the other hand, children who are eventually identified as having mild mental retardation may appear normal until they enter school. There are several reasons for this late recognition. First, the tasks required of preschool children are minimal; they usually depend on the family customs and structure for definition. In most cases, preschool children have limited responsibilities and thus are not viewed as inadequate in their roles. Second, there is a great variance in children of school age. Some children are quite mature at age 5 whereas others are not. When presented with a structured situation, as in a school, children of different levels of maturity respond in different ways. A less mature response may indicate a lower level of intellectual functioning in the school situation. Finally, children come from very different home environments. Children who receive a great amount of language stimulation, whose parents have read to them a great deal, and who have had rich experiences outside the home are much more prepared for school than are children whose environments have been less stimulating.

In addition to the home environmental factors, family expectations vary a great deal. In a family in which intellectual pursuits or education are not valued highly, a child who has not developed according to normal standards may not be perceived as being even mildly retarded. When children enter school their differences become apparent. Such differences are manifested in cognitive development, learning characteristics, and environmental factors.

Cognitive Development
The work of Jean Piaget provides a useful framework from which to investigate cognitive functioning in people who are mentally retarded (Dougherty & Moran, 1983). Piaget's comprehensive theory of cognitive development suggests that there are four major periods in the development of intelligence. An examination of these periods has major implications for understanding and planning for children who are mentally retarded.

The first period, sensorimotor intelligence, begins at birth and lasts for about 2 years. The period of preoperational thought (2 to 7 years) represents significant gains in children's intellectual functioning. The thought forms are internalized and representational. The period of concrete operations (7 to 11 years) enables children to deal much more effectively with the environment, because at this stage they possess well-organized cognitive systems. The period of formal operations (11 years and older) starts with the hypothetical or theoretical rather than with the real; an important feature is the use of reasoning to examine the possible logical relations among elements.

In examining the typical child of elementary school age, it would be expected that some younger elementary children would be completing the preoperational thought period and that most would be functioning in the concrete operations period. During this time, children usually form ordering structures, develop the concept of conservation, and begin to develop meaningful communication with other children (Drew, Logan, & Hardman, 1988).

Piagetian stages have been used extensively as a key to understanding the intellectual functioning of children who are mentally retarded. Children with mild retardation are slower in progressing from the preoperational stage into concrete operations. Even when the period of concrete operations is reached, only the lower stages may be attained during the elementary school years, with higher functioning in the period not attained until adolescence. Perhaps the most significant aspect of Piaget's orientation as it applies to children with retardation is that it forces professionals to shift from looking at what the children are *not* to looking at what they *are* (Robinson & Robinson, 1976). As stated by Dougherty and Moran (1983):

> The use of behavioral descriptions based on Piagetian stages with an appreciation of the appropriateness of these behaviors for the child's developmental age places the emphasis on differences rather than deficits and recognizes the individuality of each child. (p. 264)

Learning Characteristics

Learning characteristics are individual; they are dependent on a number of variables, such as severity of retardation, quality of instruction, and motivation of the student. Factors that may be considered include memory, skill generalization, learning of concrete concepts, and attention level.

Memory processes can be conceptualized in two ways: short-term memory and long-term memory stores. Human memory has been compared to a refrigerator, with the bins representing short-term memory and the freezer, long-term memory. In both cases, systematic storage facilitates easy retrieval (Polloway, Payne, Patton, & Payne, 1985). Research on the memory performance of mentally retarded children indicates that their short-term memory is deficient across all levels of retardation (Ellis, 1970). The research on long-term memory is less clear; Ellis (1963, 1970) contends that long-term memory is equal between retarded and nonretarded persons.

The focus of most recent research has related to rehearsal strategies, which bridge the gap between short-term memory and long-term memory and organize to facilitate later retrieval (Polloway et al., 1985).

Skill generalization refers to the ability to apply learned responses and experiences from previous problems to new problems with similar components (Drew, Logan, & Hardman, 1988). Many educators have assumed that once retarded individuals have acquired skills in the classroom, they would automatically be able to transfer those skills to other settings. Research has demonstrated that this assumption may not be true and that teachers may need to be more aware of strategies that will help the student transfer skills and training (Langone, 1986).

The following four suggestions are made for working with students who are deficient in the development of generalization skills:

1. Age seems to make a difference in the ability to transfer learning for both retarded and nonretarded individuals. Younger children transfer learning with greater ease than do older children.
2. Research also suggests that the retarded individual can transfer learning best when both the initial task and the transfer task are

very similar. Transfer is most effective if a considerable number of the operations involved in the first task can be performed as a unit in the transfer task.

3. Meaningfulness seems extremely important to the retarded person's ability to transfer, with a more meaningful task being easier to learn initially as well as to transfer to a second setting.

4. Retarded individuals seem to be able to transfer learning more effectively if instructions are more general rather than detailed and specific. This seems to be an opposite trend to that found with nonretarded children, who perform better if more detail is involved. (Drew, Logan, & Hardman, 1988, pp. 250–251)

Concrete learning is one characteristic that is nearly always attributed to persons with mental retardation. It is generally agreed that the more meaningful and concrete the material, the more apt the retarded student is to learn it. Thus, activities need to be planned in a realistic setting, with actual objects used as teaching materials.

Learning rate is another consideration in planning for students with mental retardation. Considering the characteristics of intellectual functioning associated with students who have mental retardation, it follows that their learning rate would be slower than that of their classmates.

BEHAVIORAL DISORDERS

Case Study: Behavioral Disorders

I teach a beginning course in Naval Science. In addition to the academic component, the class offers a number of extracurricular activities, including military drill, competitive drill, and rifle team. The purposes of the course are to develop informed, responsible citizens, and to provide a theoretical and practical experience in leadership.

Until this year, I had no experience or training in special education. This year Charles, a 17-year-old junior, enrolled in the Naval Science course. At the beginning of the year, Charles was a constant behavior problem in the classroom, speaking out at will, insulting other students, threatening other students, and refusing to cooperate. He seemed to want to solve every problem by "meeting you after school." I informed him of the rules of our program and advised him that it was my responsibility to recommend the disenrollment of any student who did not meet these standards. He surprisingly said he wanted very much to stay in the program. I told him that I would recommend him for disenrollment if he did not cease making threats to the other students. He agreed to try.

Charles told me he didn't care what other people thought of him, since most people didn't like him anyway. He told me he was like General Patton (he saw the movie). I agreed that Patton demonstrated one type of leadership—fear and force. I pointed out to him that leadership by personal example and persuasion was much more successful in the long run and certainly more satisfying to the person. I suggested to him that he try a new method, since he was already very good at the Patton way. If the new way didn't work, he could always revert to his old ways. I suggested that the first step to becoming a good leader was to be an accomplished follower.

The entire class was divided into four squads, with one person serving as squad leader for about two weeks. No one wanted to be in a squad with Charles. I was able to convince three other students to accept the challenge. After a short conference, Charles agreed to experiment with the new method of personal example and persuasion.

The first week went well with my keeping a close eye on Charles. The day before the first competition Charles turned in his class project. It was very well done, and he received many nice compliments. His squad won first place and he was very proud of himself. The students took turns being the squad leader. The first leader of Charles's squad—Earl—was an experienced drill team member and pushed the other students very hard for perfection. Charles did not take to these harsh measures and began to rebel. I reminded him of his goals and suggested that this student was somewhat like Patton. The next day Charles reported to class limping and informed me that he wanted to be excused from drill. Since his ankle was bandaged, I agreed.

After several weeks, it became Charles's turn to be leader of the squad. I held my breath. He began by explaining to his squad that he had done his best to help them and he now needed their help. He even advised them that, when he found he could not stand Earl, he faked an ankle injury so as not to hurt their chances. With the cooperation of the students, he did very well as their leader and I believe now has at least three people who are much friendlier to him. Charles agrees that the new methods did work but are a lot of trouble. He still thinks it might have been better to punch Earl. He said that with a smile.

Charles and I have developed a close friendship, and he frequently comes to me to discuss problems. He had by no means conquered all. He was disciplined last week for fighting in gym class.

An important part of this year is the beginning success of one student. Another important part has been the education of Charles's teacher. I have learned that success can be achieved—even with difficult students.

Mr. Mike Lavin
Shawnee Mission West High School

Definition

Many experts and other educators prefer the term *behavioral disorders* (BD) over the term *seriously emotionally disturbed,* which, according to Huntze (1985), is used as the official nomenclature of the U.S. Department of Education:

> It is the official position of the Council for Children with Behavior Disorders that the term behaviorally disordered is more descriptive and useful to educators in identifying and planning appropriate placements and services for students who are handicapped by their behavior than is the term seriously emotionally disturbed. (p. 167)

This position focuses on overt behavior problems rather than on the state of emotional disturbance, which may be difficult to distinguish.

This federal definition is important because it influences funding for these students. The federal definition of seriously emotionally disturbed is as follows:

> The term [*seriously emotionally disturbed*] means a condition exhibiting one or more of the following characteristics over a long period of time and to a marked degree, which adversely affects educational performance:
>
> **a.** An inability to learn which cannot be explained by intellectual, sensory, or other health factors;
> **b.** An inability to build or maintain satisfactory interpersonal relationships with peers and teachers;
> **c.** Inappropriate types of behavior or feelings under normal circumstances;
> **d.** A general pervasive mood of unhappiness or depression;
> **e.** A tendency to develop physical symptoms or fears associated with personal or school problems;
> **f.** The term includes children who are schizophrenic. The term does not include children who are socially maladjusted, unless it is determined that they are seriously emotionally disturbed. (*Federal Register,* 1977, p. 42478)

There are two important factors to consider in interpreting this definition. First, this is the only definition in PL 94–142 that uses the term *serious.*

Thus, the population of students who have mild to moderate emotional problems are excluded from this classification. Many of these students were served in special education programs before the implementation of PL 94–142 (Yard, 1977). Second, many school systems have previously used the classification of socially maladjusted to refer to students who exhibit disruptive or antisocial behavior. It has been reported that socially maladjusted students between the ages of 10 and 17 commit more than 50 percent of all serious crimes in this country (Raiser & Van Nagel, 1980). Unless socially maladjusted students are also seriously emotionally disturbed, they do not qualify for special education services under the federal requirements. Education professionals have suggested that the definition of seriously emotionally disturbed be carefully reviewed and amended to broaden its application to students with mild to moderate problems and also to those who have social maladjustments (Raiser & Van Nagel, 1980; Yard, 1977).

The important point here is that students with serious emotional problems will be formally classified as handicapped. Students having less serious emotional problems or social problems will not be formally identified as handicapped; however, they still will require some systematic intervention programs to help them achieve success in the regular classroom. Such interventions could involve curriculum modification, classroom management programs, or strategies aimed at helping the student improve personal relationships. Teachers should plan such interventions based on the individual needs of students rather than on formal labels and classifications.

Some behaviors indicative of serious emotional problems may be situational (e.g., related to a family crisis), and others may occur over a long period of time. Students considered emotionally handicapped by one teacher in a given classroom may not be so considered by another teacher in a different classroom. Students perform differently in various situations according to expectations, guidelines, responses, and personality traits of teachers. Tolerance is a reciprocal factor between student and teacher. Some teachers are more tolerant of particular student behavior and vice versa. An important educational principle is matching student and teacher characteristics/styles to the greatest degree possible in order to maximize the potential of a comfortable fit (Forness, 1981).

A definition by educators that may be easier to understand is provided by Gresham (1985):

> A behavior disorder is said to be present when a child or adolescent exhibits behavioral excesses and/or deficits that authoritative adults in the child's or adolescent's environment judge to be too high or too low. These behaviors are considered to be atypical because the frequency, intensity, and/or duration deviates from a relative social norm. The excesses and/or deficits which constitute a behavior disorder can be expressed through one or all behavioral

systems or repertoires (cognitive/verbal, overt/motoric, or physiological/emotional) and occur across settings, situations, and time. (p. 500)

Notice that according to these definitions, students whose handicap is labeled *behaviorally disordered* exhibit behaviors that are usually the same as those of other students. The significant points are that the behaviors are inappropriate for the situation and that the behavior's (1) occurrence is more or less frequent than normal, (2) intensity is usually more than normal, and (3) duration is longer than normal. The key is that the behavior or behaviors interfere with the student's learning or with the learning of other students to the extent that the student needs special education.

Surveys show that fewer students are identified as behaviorally disordered (BD) than the 2 percent estimated by the U.S. Department of Education (Morgan & Jensen, 1988). Reasons for underidentification are not clear but may be that

1. Few education professionals feel qualified to identify BD students because of their lack of training in the area.
2. The BD label is unpopular with parents and professionals because it is perceived to be more stigmatizing than other labels (e.g., learning disabled).
3. Identifying more BD students would require more special programs, which are expensive, unpopular with administrators, and difficult to staff.

Characteristics

Children with behavioral disorders are a diverse group; their characteristics differ and cluster in combinations unique for each individual. A group of children identified as behaviorally disordered students are just as much like nonhandicapped students as they are like each other. The characteristics of behavioral disorders commonly fall into the categories of conduct disorders, personality disorders, learning disorders, and childhood psychosis (Morgan & Jensen, 1988).

Conduct Disorders

These include overt and usually aggressive problem behaviors, such as hitting, stealing, disobeying, abusing property, and verbally threatening. Students with these behaviors usually display excesses of behavior. The behaviors are more frequent and intense than is normal. Hyperactivity frequently accompanies these behaviors. More boys than girls exhibit conduct disorders. These students disturb others and frequently disrupt the classroom program. Most teachers have no trouble identifying behaviors considered to be conduct disorders.

Personality Disorders

These include students who are socially withdrawn, socially isolated, unresponsive, immature, depressed, and feel inadequate. Withdrawn and isolated children may not have skills for interacting with others. They may even retreat into fantasy and may exhibit excessive self-stimulation, which prevents interactions with others. These self-stimulating behaviors are repetitive, stereotyped behaviors, such as masturbation, hair twirling, pencil tapping, drumming fingers, and rocking. Even though these may be normal behaviors, students with personality disorders display excessive amounts in inappropriate situations. These students are not accepted by peers and are not included in peer activities.

Children who are excessively immature and who have feelings of extreme inadequacy may exhibit crying; tantrums; extreme fear of persons, objects, or situations; school phobia; bed wetting; and helplessness; and they may choose not to talk in specific situations (Kauffman, 1985). These behaviors, which present severe and difficult problems for teachers, are sometimes attributed to cognitive deficits resulting in students' being referred to services for mentally retarded children.

Depression is usually included in the category of personality disorders. Children experiencing severe depression may be sad, appear apathetic, and project pessimism. They are likely to avoid tasks and have physical complaints. Other symptoms include eating and sleeping irregularities.

Learning Problems

The most common characteristic of students with behavioral disorders is low levels of academic achievement (Kauffman, 1985; Mastropieri, Jenkins, & Scruggs, 1985). According to Kauffman (1985), "Low achievement and behavior disorders go hand in hand. It is not clear, however, whether disordered behavior causes underachievement or vice versa" (p. 145). These pupils are likely to have poor academic survival skills, such as attending to tasks, following directions, working on or responding to an assignment, staying in seat, and following classroom rules. Students with mild to moderate behavior disorders are also reported to have slightly below average levels of intelligence as measured by IQ tests (Morgan & Jensen, 1988).

Childhood Psychosis

A very small number of students display symptoms of childhood schizophrenia and childhood autism. Symptomatic behaviors for schizophrenia are delusions, hallucinations, thought disorders, and altered mood states. Autistic symptoms are bizarre behavior, including no interaction or communication with other people and stereotypical behaviors, such as rocking, head banging, and foot tapping. Because these behaviors are extremely rare, teachers are not likely to encounter psychotic students who will need intensive special education.

Of the characteristics noted, mainstream teachers are most likely to have students with learning problems and conduct disorders. These are most noticeable in children with mild to moderate behavior problems. Teachers are also likely to have students with personality disorders and students who are withdrawn and isolated. However, they are less likely to identify or refer these students for special assistance unless some overt behavior presents itself. Nevertheless, the students need assistance if their own behavior impedes learning progress in themselves or other students.

Educational Implications

The major educational implications of behavioral disorders are related to the specific problems each student exhibits. It cannot be accurately stated, as it might be for students with some other exceptionalities (e.g., learning disabilities, gifted, hearing impaired) that some general implications are appropriate for many. Therefore, implications are considered for each class of characteristics.

Conduct Disorders

Usually, students with conduct disorders function better when teachers provide structure and clearly set limits to classroom behavior and assignments. Teachers are advised to have few but clear rules and to remind students of them. More important, students who display conduct disorders need to know explicitly the consequences of rule-breaking behavior. Consequences must be consistently applied; such students usually challenge rules to determine if they are applied fairly. Because of the propensity of all students to test rules, teachers who have a few definite rules usually experience more success than do teachers who have more rules.

> *Ms. Martin's school had just adopted a schoolwide plan based on Assertive Discipline (Canter & Canter, 1976). Teachers posted rules applicable to their class and listed the consequences for breaking rules according to the schoolwide plan. While most teachers listed four to six rules as advised, Ms. Martin listed 14. During the fourth week of the policy, Jerry broke one of the rules three times in the same class. Ms. Martin said after the third time, "Jerry, if you don't do that any more for the rest of the period, I'll forget about it." "How come you didn't do that for me?" yelled another student. "I just don't have time to keep Jerry in during 4th period. I have too much to do," Ms. Martin replied, obviously tired of enforcing her own rules.*

Students with conduct disorders often respond well to behavior management strategies based on operant conditioning principles, such as positive reinforcement and ignoring attention-seeking behaviors. These students also benefit from direct instruction in learning new behaviors that are appropriate and taught in a systematic way (North Carolina State Department of Public Instruction, 1987). Some students exhibit conduct disorders because they do not know how to behave appropriately. They need to be taught appropriate behaviors, and mainstream classes provide many students who are good role models for such instruction.

Personality Disorders

Personality disorders may be severe or relatively mild; teachers should seek assistance for more severe problems. More moderate problems can be successfully helped by attempts to build self-esteem and interpersonal skill development.

Although there is some disagreement among educators and psychologists about the rationale for building self-esteem and the focus of instruction for behaviorally disordered students, there is little disagreement among educators and psychologists that personality disorders often include low self-esteem in children. Teaching students so that they become more successful in academics and in interpersonal skills can usually build self-esteem. Trying to improve self-concept without academic instruction or assistance with social skills is usually short-sighted and futile because the student is likely to continue experiencing failure and rejection, the probable causes for low self-esteem (Polsgrove & Nelson, 1982). Hence, one suggestion is to improve academic skills to allow students to achieve success.

A second suggestion is to improve interpersonal skills or social skills. Several commercially available programs for social skill improvement are popular and successfully used. These programs are designed to teach such important socially valid skills as giving positive feedback, giving negative feedback, accepting negative feedback, resisting peer pressure, problem solving, negotiations, following instructions, and conversation (Hazel, Schumaker, Sherman, & Sheldon-Wildgen, 1981). The following six tips for teaching interpersonal skills have been provided.

1. Focus on small component skills rather than attempting to develop global characteristics.
2. Provide small-group instruction in which each participant receives a substantial amount of attention.
3. Structure high levels of social reinforcement to motivate skill development and usage.
4. Provide frequent opportunities for students to model skills demonstrated by others.
5. Encourage students to practice interpersonal skills in a range of situations.

6. Provide learners with frequent, clear, and consistent feedback on their performance. (Schloss & Sedlak, 1986, p. 391)

Learning Problems

Students who suffer from poor academic achievement due to learning problems frequently have little interest or motivation to succeed, and the most thorough and well-planned academic programs will not help them without their interest or motivation. Students need to see clearly the benefits of academic tasks by having teachers explain them in terms they can understand. They need to feel they have some reasonable expectation for success. Students with learning problems linked to inappropriate behaviors have usually experienced much frustration and failure and have, in many cases, lost interest and engaged in behaviors in which they try to avoid academic tasks. They have little motivation to succeed in academic tasks and considerable motivation to avoid them and to engage in behaviors that bring attention to them in other ways. Setting up activities that virtually guarantee success and that initially do not take long to accomplish will help enhance a feeling of accomplishment. Along with these short tasks, teachers who frequently praise and reward students for their efforts and help them to attribute success and the accompanying rewards to their skills and efforts are taking positive steps with their students. Charting progress with the students is likely to be rewarding, also.

To overcome low academic achievement, there is no substitute for systematic direct instruction in the areas of inadequate progress. The academic instruction should depend on some basic assumptions (Paine & Anderson-Inman, 1988):

1. Behaviorally disordered students want to succeed in school. This might not always be apparent, but it is relatively safe to conclude that they would rather succeed than fail.
2. Behaviorally disordered students can succeed in school if they are given sufficient structure. Structure includes everything from rules to reinforcers, from praise to points, from time management to teacher expectations. Given enough structure in the initial stages of intervention, students will succeed.
3. Teaching behaviorally disordered students academic skills is very similar to teaching other students academic skills. It requires a curriculum, a teaching method, and an evaluation system. These students learn much like other students. The teaching/learning process is essentially the same; it is only the intensity of the process that may vary.
4. To enable behaviorally disordered students to experience long-term success, the structure that is so important to their early success must eventually be faded. (pp. 197–198)

Direct instruction accepts these assumptions; it provides the sort of structure handicapped students need. Direct instruction is characterized by increased opportunities to respond, maximum use of time-on-task, frequent measurement of progress, definite answers, and a developmental approach. Each curriculum chapter in this book endorses direct instruction and provides curricular modifications designed to help mainstream teachers assist behaviorally disordered and other students to succeed.

Childhood Psychosis

Because of the extreme nature and rare incidence of childhood psychosis problems in mainstream settings, educational implications are unwarranted here. Teachers should be aware of the signs of childhood psychosis and should seek special assistance when they detect relevant characteristics of childhood psychosis in students.

REFERENCES

American Psychiatric Association. (1980). *Diagnostic and statistical manual of mental disorders* (3rd ed.). Washington, DC: Author.

American Psychiatric Association. (1987). *Diagnostic and statistical manual of mental disorders: Manual of mental disorders: III—Revised.* Washington, DC: Author.

Barnett, W. S. (1986). Definition and classification of mental retardation: A reply to Zigler, Balla, and Hodapp. *American Journal of Mental Deficiency, 91,* 111–116.

Bryan, T. H., Pearl, R., Donahue, M., Bryan, J., & Pflaum, S. (1983). The Chicago Institute for the Study of Learning Disabilities. *Exceptional Education Quarterly, 4,* (1), 1–22.

Canter, L., & Canter, M. (1976). *Assertive discipline: A take charge approach for today's educator.* Seal Beach, CA: Canter and Associates.

Deshler, D. D., Alley, G. R., Warner, M. M., & Schumaker, J. B. (1981). Instructional practices for promoting skill acquisition in severely learning disabled adolescents. *Learning Disability Quarterly, 4,* 415–421.

Deshler, D. D., & Graham, S. (1980). Tape recording educational material for secondary handicapped students. *Teaching Exceptional Children, 12,* (2), 52–54.

Deshler, D. D., & Schumaker, J. B. (1983). Social skills of learning disabled adolescents: Characteristics and interventions. *Topics in Learning and Learning Disabilities, 3,* (2), 15–23.

Dougherty, J. M., & Morgan, J. D. (1983). The relationship of Piagetian stages to mental retardation. *Education and Training of the Mentally Retarded, 18,* 260–265.

Drew, C. J., Logan, D. R. & Hardman, M. L. (1988). *Mental retardation: A life cycle approach* (4th ed.). Columbus, OH: Merrill.

Duane, D. D. (1988). The classroom clinician's role in finding the cause of ADD/LD. *Learning Disabilities Focus, 4,* (1), 6–8.

Ellis, N. R. (1963). The stimulus trace and behavioral inadequacy. In N. R. Ellis (Ed.), *Handbook of mental deficiency* (pp. 135–158). New York: McGraw-Hill.

Ellis, N. R. (1970). Memory processes in retardates and normals. In N. R. Ellis (Ed.), *International review of research in mental retardation* (Vol. 4) (pp. 134–158). New York: Academic.

Federal Register. (1977). Washington, DC: U.S. Government Printing Office.

Forness, S. R., & Kavale, K. A. (1984). Education of the mentally retarded: A note on policy. *Education and Training of the Mentally Retarded, 19,* (4), 239–245.

Gresham, F. N. (1985). Behavior disorder assessment: Conceptual, definitional and practical considerations. *School Psychology Review, 14,* 495–509.

Grossman, H. J. (1973). *Manual on terminology and classification in mental retardation.* Washington, DC: American Association on Mental Deficiency.

Grossman, H. J. (Ed.). (1983). *Classification in mental retardation.* Washington, DC: American Association on Mental Deficiency.

Haring, N. G., & Schiefelbusch, R. L. (Eds.) (1976). *Teaching special children.* New York: McGraw-Hill.

Hazel, J. S., Schumaker, J. B., Sherman, J. A., & Sheldon-Wildgen, J. (1981). The development and evaluation of a group skills training program for court-adjudicated youths. In D. Upper & S. Ross (Eds.), *Behavioral group therapy 1981: An Annual Review* (pp. 113–152). Champaign, IL: Research Press.

Heward, W. L., & Orlansky, M. D. (1988). *Exceptional children* (3rd ed.). Columbus, OH: Merrill.

Huntze, S. L. (1985). A position paper of the Council for Children with Behavioral Disorders. *Behavioral Disorders, 10,* 167–174.

Information for Authors. (1988). *American Journal on Mental Retardation, 92,* (6), p. 554.

Kauffman, J. M. (1985). *Characteristics of children's behavior disorders* (3rd ed.). Columbus, OH: Merrill.

Langone, J. (1986). *Teaching retarded learners.* Boston: Allyn and Bacon.

Lerner, J. W. (1989). *Learning disabilities: Theories, diagnosis, and teaching strategies* (5th ed.). Boston: Houghton Mifflin.

Mastropieri, M. A., Jenkins, V., & Scruggs, T. E. (1985). Academic and intellectual characteristics of behaviorally disordered children and youth. In R. B. Rutherford (Ed.), *Monograph in behavioral disorders: Severe behavior disorders of children and youth.* Reston, VA: Council for Children with Behavioral Disorders.

Morgan, D. P., & Jenson, W. R. (1988). *Teaching behaviorally disordered students: Preferred practices.* Columbus, OH: Merrill.

Myers, P. I., & Hammill, D. D. (1976). *Methods for learning disorders.* New York: John Wiley and Sons.

National Joint Committee on Learning Disabilities (1987). Learning disabilities: Issue on definition. *Journal of Learning Disabilities, 10,* 107–108.

North Carolina State Department of Public Instruction. (1987). *Teaching new behaviors: A guide to curriculum development for teachers of the behaviorally/emotionally handicapped.* Raleigh: North Carolina State Department of Public Instruction, Division for Exceptional Children.

Paine, S. C., & Anderson-Inman, L. (1988). Teaching academic skills to behaviorally disordered students. In D. P. Morgan & W. R. Jenson, *Teaching behaviorally disordered students: Preferred practices* (pp. 195–241). Columbus, OH: Merrill.

Patton, J. R., Payne, J. S., & Beirne-Smith, M. (1986). *Mental retardation* (2nd ed.). Columbus, OH: Merrill.

Pearl, R., Donahue, M., & Bryan, T. (1986). Social relationships of learning disabled children. In J. K. Torgeson & B. Y. L. Wong (Eds.), *Psychological and educational perspectives on learning disabilities* (pp. 193–221). Orlando, FL: Academic.

Polloway, E. A., Payne, J. D., Patton, J. R., & Payne, R. A. (1985). *Strategies for teaching retarded and special needs learners* (3rd ed.). Columbus, OH: Merrill.

Polsgrove, L., & Nelson, C. M. (1982). Curriculum intervention according to the behavioral model. In R. L. McDowell, G. W. Adamson, & F. H. Wood (Eds.), *Teaching emotionally disturbed children* (pp. 196–205). Boston: Little, Brown.

Raiser, L., & Van Nagel, C. B. (1980). The loophole in PL 94–142. *Exceptional Children, 46,* 516–520.

Robinson, N. M., & Robinson, H. B. (1976). *The mentally retarded child: A psychological approach* (2nd ed.). New York: McGraw-Hill.

Schloss, P. J., & Sedlak, R. A. (1986). *Instructional methods for students with learning and behavior problems.* Boston: Allyn and Bacon.

Schumaker, J. B., Denton, P. H., & Deshler, D. D. (1984). *The paraphrasing strategy.* Lawrence: University of Kansas.

U.S. Department of Education. (1988). *Tenth annual report to Congress on the implementation of the Education of the Handicapped Act.* Washington, DC: U.S. Department of Education, U.S. Office of Special Education and Rehabilitative Services.

Utley, C. A., Lowitzer, A. C., & Baumeister, A. A. (1987). A comparison of the AAMD's definition, eligibility criteria, and classification schemes with state departments of education guidelines. *Education and Training in Mental Retardation, 22,* 35–43.

Wallace, G., & McLoughlin, J. A. (1988). *Learning disabilities: Concepts and characteristics* (3rd ed.). Columbus, OH: Merrill.

Yard, G. J. (1977). Definition and interpretation of PL 94–142. Is behavior disorders a question of semantics? *Behavioral Disorders, 24,* 252–254.

Ysseldyke, J. E., & Algozzine, B. (1984). *Introduction to special education.* Boston: Houghton Mifflin.

Zigler, E., Balla, D., & Hodapp, R. (1984). On the definition and classification of mental retardation. *American Journal of Mental Deficiency, 89,* 215–230.

5

Students with Exceptional Gifts and Talents

Case Study: Academically Gifted Student

For me, the AG (Academically Gifted) program is a very enjoyable and rewarding experience. As an AG student, I have found many more learning opportunities than in a normal classroom. I have been in AG since third grade and I have been exposed to various types of thinking and a wide range of opinions. Students cover more material in the AG classroom, but it is expected of us.

I think the AG student has been stereotyped as the kid with horn-rimmed glasses who invented the computer. Actually, in my class, most of the students are physically, as well as academically, gifted. One fellow student is active in football and baseball while being ranked near the top of his class academically.

Some people have a negative attitude towards the gifted student when they discover his or her abilities.

"She's in AG? What a nerd!" That kind of reaction hurts and causes anger, but fortunately these sharp-tongued few are a minority. Other classmates constantly ask you for assistance, which is very rewarding.

The Academically Gifted Program has many advantages and opportunities for the creative student.

Robin Nations
Smoky Mountain High School
Sylva, North Carolina

The humanitarian movement of the 1960s and the resulting legislation of the 1970s brought about widespread changes in the education of children and young people with handicaps. Unfortunately, this movement did not respond to the needs of children and youth with exceptional gifts and talents. The groups that fought desegregation and disenfranchisement were not sympathetic with those who appeared to have it all.

A renewed interest and educational focus on high achievement in the nation's schools were stimulated in the 1980s by criticism of scholastic standards and expectations (*A Nation at Risk,* 1983). Parents and educators have insisted on a reexamination of programs to encourage gifted students to realize their potential and to become productive citizens and leaders. Education of students with exceptional gifts and talents has again achieved prominent status. This position can be defended as follows:

> The set of principles and procedures for evaluating and educating gifted and talented children can . . . no longer be considered the stepchild of special

121

education. Support for them has become an educational imperative and a national priority. (Cohn, Cohn, & Kanevsky, 1988, p. 458)

Justification for educating gifted and talented children and young people has been established: gifted and talented students are a vital natural resource that should not be squandered (Davis & Rimm, 1989).

Many gifted and talented children and adolescents remain in the nation's schools with their abilities unrecognized and their needs unmet. The National Commission on Excellence in Education reported that more than half the population of gifted students do not match their tested ability with comparable achievement in school (*A Nation at Risk*, 1983).

The response to such allegations has been encouraging. Although gifted children are not included in the provisions of PL 94–142, all 50 states have adopted definitions of giftedness, most states have legislated that gifted students receive special services, and many states have allocated funds for gifted programs (Davis & Rimm, 1989). Institutions of higher education have responded to teacher training needs; 134 colleges and universities in 42 states and the District of Columbia offer professional training programs in the education of gifted children (Parker & Karnes, 1987).

Two of the greatest challenges in planning programs have been to define the concept of giftedness and to identify children and young people who fall within the definition.

DEFINITIONS

There is no one theory-based definition of gifted and talented that will fit all programs and situations (Davis & Rimm, 1989). Although it is common and acceptable to use the terms interchangeably, academic ability may be referred to as *giftedness* and artistic ability as *talent*, resulting in the terms *academically gifted* and *artistically talented*.

Gifted and Talented

Originally conceptualized as a single-dimensional trait identified by a high intelligence quotient (IQ), the term *gifted* has come to mean multiple abilities and intelligence, inferred in the addition of the term *talented*. The most commonly used definition of *gifted and talented* was provided by the U.S. Office of Education:

> Gifted and talented children are those identified by professionally qualified persons who, by virtue of outstanding abilities, are capable of high perfor-

mance. These are children who require differentiated educational programs in order to realize their contribution to self and society. Children capable of high performance include those with demonstrated achievement and/or potential ability in any of the following areas, singly or in combination.

1. General intellectual ability
2. Specific academic aptitude
3. Creative or productive thinking
4. Leadership ability
5. Visual and performing arts
6. Psychomotor ability (Marland, 1972, p. 2)

This definition was later revised to delete the area of psychomotor performance, which has been recognized and developed through other programs. A number of states have adopted this definition or amended it for their purposes.

One of the most recent definitions appears in a bill passed by Congress in 1988 (Title IV–H.R.5):

> The term *gifted and talented children and youth* means children and youth who give evidence of high performance capability in areas such as intellectual, creative, artistic, or leadership capacity, or in specific academic fields, and who require services or activities not ordinarily provided by the school in order to fully develop such capabilities. (Kirk & Gallagher, 1989, p. 85)

This definition, like the definition from the Office of Education, does not restrict giftedness to the cognitive domain; it recognizes the many areas in which a student might display gifts and talents. It also recognizes, through the words "give evidence of high capability," that all gifted students do not achieve to the fullest and may not be gifted in all areas.

Academically Gifted

On the other hand, a more restrictive definition can be adopted. North Carolina, among other states, refers to this category as "academically gifted" and defines the population in the following manner:

> Academically gifted students are defined as those who demonstrate or have the potential to demonstrate outstanding intellectual aptitude and specific academic ability. In order to develop their abilities, these students may require differentiated educational services beyond those ordinarily provided by the regular school program. (Division for Exceptional Children, 1986, p. 1)

Gifted Behavior

A different approach to the concept of giftedness is suggested by Renzulli (1986), who bases his definition on descriptions of gifted persons who have made valuable contributions to society. His research indicates that gifted-ness is a condition that can be developed—a concept that calls attention to potentially gifted students. He hopes that emphasis will be shifted from the present concept of "being gifted" to a concern about developing gifted behaviors in students who have the highest potential for benefiting from special services. Renzulli defines gifted behavior as follows:

> Gifted behavior consists of behaviors that reflect an interaction among three basic clusters of human traits—these clusters being above average general and/or specific abilities, high levels of task commitment, and high levels of creativity. Gifted and talented children are those possessing or capable of developing this composite set of traits and applying them to any potentially valuable area of human performance.[1]

A graphic representation of this definition is presented in Figure 5.1

The definition adopted by a particular state or school system serves a number of important purposes. It may have a profound influence on (1) the number of students who are selected for a program, (2) the types of instruments and selection procedures used, (3) the scores required in order to qualify for a particular program or specialized instruction, (4) the types of differentiated education provided, (5) the amount of funding required to provide services, and (6) the types of training individuals need to teach students who are gifted and/or talented (Hardman, Drew, & Egan, 1987). The most immediate concern is the identification of students who are to be served in programs for gifted and/or talented students.

Identification

It is important to determine who the gifted and talented students are in a particular school or school system in order to design programs that are appropriate for their interests and needs. The determination of a student's eligibility requires two steps: screening and evaluation.

Screening
Through screening procedures, students who show unusual ability in any area may become part of a talent pool. This pool can then be drawn on to find candidates for differentiated programming. One state has adopted the following guidelines for screening:

> Local education agencies shall develop a local screening procedure in order to establish a pool of students who are possibly qualified for and in need of

---

[1]From "A Definition of Gifted Behavior" by J. S. Renzulli in *Conceptions of Giftedness* (p. 73) by R. J. Sternberg and J. E. Davidson, 1986. New York: Cambridge University Press. Copyright 1986 by Cambridge University Press. Reprinted with the permission of Cambridge University Press.

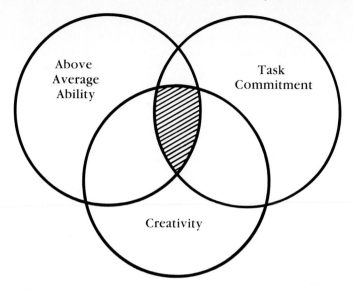

FIGURE 5.1 Renzulli's Three-Ring Conception of
Giftedness

Source: From J. S. Renzulli (1986). "The Three-Ring Conception
of Giftedness: A Developmental Model for Creative Productivity" by J.
S. Renzulli in *Conceptions of Giftedness* by R. J. Sternberg and J. E.
Davidson, 1986. New York: Cambridge University Press. Copyright
1986 by Cambridge University Press. Reprinted by permission.

differentiated instruction. Initial screening of the pool will determine students for whom formal referrals will be made. Suggested screening procedures may include checklists/behavioral scales of characteristics of the
gifted; scores obtained on system-wide standardized tests of intelligence and/
or achievement; teacher/parent/peer/self nomination; scores obtained on
screening instruments; and a listing of students from high, middle, and low
income levels who have demonstrated outstanding ability in the classroom,
school or community. (Division for Exceptional Children, 1986, p. 21)

Clark (1983) suggests screening for children "who show need for a
different quality of educational experience" (p. 117) and cites the following
screens:

1. teacher selection and nomination for testing;
2. group achievement tests;
3. group intelligence tests;
4. parent interviews;
5. peer identification;
6. pupil's work and achievements awards. (p. 117)

She stipulates that none of the screens mentioned should be used alone, but in combination and never as identification. Screening should be done as early as possible in the child's school career to enable the child to have appropriate education and to prevent the waste of talent that frequently occurs.

The purposes of screening are to gather broad information about the strengths and weaknesses of students and to find general indicators of ability. The purpose of evaluation is to distinguish which students in the talent pool meet the criteria for any given program (Parke, 1989). Following screening procedures, students who receive scores and ratings above a certain percentile or cut-off point are individually evaluated to determine if they qualify for specialized educational programs.

Evaluation
Techniques of evaluation should be closely related to the definition used by the school system and the nature of the program envisioned for the students. For example, some programs base identification entirely on intelligence test scores, admitting all students who score above a certain cut-off point or selecting the top 3 to 5 percent regardless of the particular scores (Davis & Rimm, 1989). In other programs measures of mathematical and verbal reasoning may be the only admission criteria.

In planning evaluation strategies, programs that use the multidimensional approach frequently use the five components of the Office of Education definition: general intellectual ability, specific academic talent, creativity, leadership, or talent in the visual or performing arts. Most states have adopted definitions of giftedness and assessment instruments that are consistent with this approach (Cassidy & Johnson, 1986).

Davidson (1986) expresses frustration with all formal testing, rating, and nomination procedures, contending that these procedures do not allow students to demonstrate their abilities in areas in which they are interested and talented. The proposed solution includes (1) setting a liberal selection quota of about 15 to 20 percent of the school, (2) selecting students who score in the 90th percentile or above on intelligence, achievement, or creativity tests, and (3) increasing the use of informal parent and teacher nominations, based on observations of creativity, critical thinking, problem solving, or motivation.

A number of gifted and talented students are difficult to identify. Although most children who have participated in educational programs for the gifted have come from advantaged backgrounds, many others are disadvantaged or have a disability (Klein, 1989). Many of these students are not being identified by traditional methods. Inasmuch as culturally different learners tend to score, on the average, lower than middle-class students on standardized intelligence tests, a multidimensional approach is essential for identifying minority students who are gifted and talented.

Young gifted children may also be difficult to identify. Many questions remain unresolved about the utility and validity of traditional test instruments for children in preschool and early grades as well as for minority children. In the absence of adequate screening and evaluation instruments, teachers find informal checklists useful for identifying potentially gifted children in their classrooms (Kitano, 1982).

Regardless of the identification measures used in a given school system, teachers' first indication of giftedness in students depends on the recognition of characteristics observable in children who are gifted and talented.

CHARACTERISTICS OF GIFTED AND TALENTED STUDENTS

The first longitudinal study of giftedness was conducted by Lewis Terman, who investigated physical characteristics, personality attributes and psychological adjustment, educational attainment, and career achievement of more than 1,500 intellectually gifted students. This study, which began in 1922 and covered a 50-year period, dispelled many of the prevailing but erroneous beliefs about brilliant individuals who were perceived as so-called reclusive bookworms. Researchers since that time have helped achieve a comprehensive picture of gifted people and their characteristics (Hardman, Drew, & Egan, 1987). A majority of the research indicates that children who are gifted are, in general, healthy, popular, and emotionally well adjusted (Klein, 1989).

The multifaceted definitions of giftedness suggest that members of this group would form a heterogeneous population of individuals. Clark (1983) states that the more gifted a person becomes, the more unique that person appears. There are, however, many characteristics that recur in groups of people who are gifted. She groups these characteristics into the following categories: differential cognitive (thinking), differential affective (feeling), differential physical (sensation), differential intuitive, and differential societal characteristics. Clark's work is important in suggesting examples of related needs and possible concomitant problems accompanying the differentiating characteristics.

To get a brief overview of characteristics of students who are gifted and talented, this discussion focuses on the cognitive domain, the affective domain, and creativity.

Cognitive Domain

Most children who are gifted function at a high intellectual level. This level may be reflected in typical academic skills, but it often extends beyond traditional skills to include more abstract processes. The teacher may find that gifted students are far ahead of the group and may not be content to leave facts alone. Klein (1989) suggests abilities that fall within the cognitive domain; the gifted student

- asks many questions; is often not satisfied with "simple" answers
- has a good memory; is often exceptionally facile at retaining numbers and other symbols
- begins to read at an early age and is often several grade levels above age-mates
- likes to experiment, hypothesize, test out new ideas
- has good reasoning ability; understands quickly
- has a strong vocabulary

Parke (1989) adds that gifted students may evidence uneven cognitive and physical abilities. This discrepancy causes frustration in students whose unusual capacity to think does not correspond with their abilities to write, draw, act, or speak.

Affective Characteristics

Clark (1983) states that "high levels of cognitive development do not necessarily imply high levels of affective development. The same heightened sensitivities that underlie gifted intelligence can contribute to an accumulation of information about emotions that the student needs to process" (p. 26). Some of the affective characteristics displayed by gifted students include

- sensitivity to themselves, others, and their environment
- preference to be with adults or older children
- intensity of concentration, perseverance, and commitment to the task
- perfectionism—an inner motivation to be perfect, resulting in high performance levels or inability to perform for fear of failure
- leadership ability
- moralistic—strong sense of right and wrong; deep sense of conviction
- resourcefulness
- advanced sense of humor (Parke, 1989, pp. 20–21)

Although gifted people demonstrate the abilities to make friends and to adapt well, they may encounter some difficulties that stem from their exceptionality (Kirk & Gallagher, 1989). They may have unrealistic expectations placed on them and may have difficulty finding people who share their interests. Gifted students frequently have to deal with boredom from being in classes that are below their intellectual level. The following poem expresses a 9-year-old girl's frustration with boredom:

> Oh what a bore to sit and listen,
> To stuff we already know,
> Do everything we've done and done again,
> But we still must sit and listen.
> Over and over read one more page.
> Oh bore,
> Oh bore,
> Oh bore.
> Sometimes I feel if we do one more page
> My head will explode with boreness rage
> I wish I could get up right there
> and march right out the door.[2]

Creativity

Many children who score high on intelligence tests also show high performance in creativity; there also appears to be a distinctive group of children who have aptitude for creativity (Gallagher, 1985). Although there is no universally accepted definition of creativity, it can be defined as

> a process of becoming sensitive to or aware of problems, deficiencies, and gaps in knowledge for which there is no learned solution; bringing together existing information from the memory storage or external resources; defining the difficulty or identifying the missing elements; searching for solutions, making guesses and producing alternatives; perfecting them and finally communicating the results. (Torrance, 1978, p. 146)

Guilford (1959) discusses four dimensions of creative behavior:

1. *Fluency.* Many words, associations, phrases and/or sentences, and ideas are produced.
2. *Flexibility.* A wide variety of ideas, unusual ideas, and alternative solutions are offered.
3. *Originality.* Low probability, unique words and responses are used.
4. *Elaboration.* The ability to provide details is evidenced.

Students who are creative may or may not have many of the characteristics demonstrated by other gifted students. They may be quite different and not as well liked by teachers as are students who are more conventional in their thinking and behaviors (Parke, 1989).

SPECIAL GROUPS

There are many subgroups within the category of gifted and talented; groups whose characteristics may be different from those described above. These groups include girls, culturally different students, gifted under-achievers, and handicapped students who are gifted.

Girls who are gifted represent one of the largest groups of untapped intellectual potential in the United States (Kirk & Gallagher, 1989). In spite of the strong movement toward women's liberation in this century, there are still different expectations for girls than for boys in school, home, and career situations.

In the school environment, girls generally receive little encouragement from counselors to pursue careers in mathematics or science. Teachers are likely to expect more from males than from females, especially in mathematics and science classes. Textbooks used in schools offer few appropriate female role models for bright girls, with males portrayed as being active, earning money, and participating in sports while females are portrayed as passive (Fox & Tobin, 1988). Many studies of gifted females show a pattern of declining career aspirations, declining intellectual achievement, and disappointing career achievements. Increasingly, educators are becoming aware of the need for specialized guidance strategies to prevent the underachievement of gifted girls and women (Kerr, 1985).

Culturally different gifted children may express their characteristics in ways different from children of majority groups. The following behaviors have been attributed to the gifted minority child:

- rapidly acquires English skills, given exposure
- exhibits leadership ability, sometimes in an unobtrusive manner
- enjoys intelligent risk taking
- keeps busy and entertained, especially by imaginative games designed from simple toys
- accepts responsibility, reserved for older children, such as supervising younger children or helping with homework
- is street-wise (Kitano, 1982, pp. 16–17)

As mentioned previously, culturally different students are at a great disadvantage in the identification and evaluation process. Once culturally different gifted students are identified, educational plans for their special needs and circumstances must be developed. Kirk and Gallagher (1989) issue the challenge of this task:

As minority groups gradually assimilate into the larger community, educational programs carry the difficult task of encouraging youngsters to respect their cultural heritage and, at the same time, to take on those characteristics of the larger society that can help them succeed within that society. The balance is a delicate one. (p. 100)

Gifted underachievers are students who indicate exceptional potential on intelligence tests and yet do not achieve the level of performance predicted for them. Although these students may not fail in school, they do not perform at the level that would place them in programs for gifted students.

Whitmore (1980) describes the personality and behavioral traits of the gifted underachiever:

> A negative self-concept, low self-esteem, expectations of academic and social failure, a sense of inability to control or determine outcomes of his efforts, and behaviors that serve as mechanisms for coping with the tension produced by conflict for the child in school. (p. 189)

Whitmore has shown that carefully designed programs can make a positive difference in the academic and social performance of underachievers. Kirk and Gallagher (1989) suggest that very few school systems offer such programs because gifted underachievers do not often come to the attention of special educators.

Students with handicaps may also be gifted. Obvious examples include violinist Itzak Perlman, Thomas Edison, and Ludwig von Beethoven. There are also a number of students whose handicaps and gifts are more subtle. Categories of gifted/sensorily handicapped, gifted/mobility impaired, gifted/socially-emotionally disturbed, and gifted/learning disabled have been recognized (Weill, 1987). Of increasing concern to educators are the gifted/learning disabled students—students achieving near grade level whose strengths and weaknesses remain undetected due to their compensating skills. Some of these students learn to use their high intellectual abilities to compensate for their learning disabilities, permitting them to perform near grade level but preventing their needs for specialized services from being identified.

Teachers need to be made aware of shared characteristics of learning disabled and gifted students. The psychometrist needs to focus on a breakdown of subtest information and an analysis of strengths as well as deficits in the learning-disabled student. All professionals and parents should observe any student in question and note compensatory techniques that may indicate a high degree of intelligence. Although the population of gifted/learning-disabled students involves a very small number, it is a group that needs attention and deserves assistance in reaching full potential (Gunderson, Maesch, & Rees, 1987).

EDUCATIONAL IMPLICATIONS

The definition of giftedness states the necessity for specialized educational services for students who are gifted and/or talented. Davis and Rimm (1989) state the goals for such services:

1. To provide programs designed to help meet the psychological, social, educational, and career needs of gifted and talented students.
2. To assist students in becoming individuals who are able to take self-initiated action . . . and who are capable of intelligent choice, independent learning, and problem solving.
3. To develop problem solving abilities and creative thinking skills; develop research skills; strengthen individual interests; develop independent study skills; strengthen communication skills; receive intellectual stimulation from contact with other highly motivated students; and expand their learning activities to include resources available in the entire community.
4. To maximize learning and individual development and to minimize boredom, confusion, and frustration.
5. To enable them to realize their contributions to self and society. (p. xi)

Although these goals are generally accepted, the manner of reaching them is debatable. In describing the regular classroom, Clark (1983) states that this arrangement is "not adequate for gifted education. These classrooms rely on group instruction and a set curriculum. The instruction is by subject, with similar experiences for everyone" (p. 140). On the other hand, Reynolds and Birch (1988) declare that "instruction for gifted and talented pupils should be conducted in adaptive regular classes" (p. 165).

To provide for various professional preferences and the wide variability in the abilities of gifted and talented students, a number of alternatives are available in most school systems. Traditional methods include ability grouping, student acceleration, and program enrichment.

Ability Grouping

Ability grouping refers to ways in which the learning environment can be arranged to accommodate the gifted students. Placements vary from cluster groups within the regular class to special schools, from total mainstreaming to complete segregation. Table 5.1 depicts ways of individualizing instruction.

TABLE 5.1   Ways of Organizing for Instruction

Full Mainstreaming	*Complete Segregation*

- Special schools
- Special summer programs
- Clustered special classes in regular schools
- Limited enrollment seminars and courses
- Resource rooms and clinical centers
- Limited participation field trips and events on school time
- Cluster groups within the regular class
- Limited participation before and after school groups
- Tutoring carried on in regular class
- Independent and individualized study in the context of the regular class

Source: From *Adaptive Mainstreaming: A Primer for Teachers and Principals* by Maynard C. Reynolds and Jack W. Birch. Copyright © 1988 by Longman, Inc. Reprinted by permission of Longman Publishing, New York.

Acceleration

The process of acceleration passes students through the educational system as quickly as possible. This technique has the advantage of saving years of schooling for students who will probably pursue careers requiring advanced and prolonged education. Stanley (1979) describes different ways of accelerating students. They can be summarized as follows:

Early school admission. The intellectually and socially mature child is allowed to enter kindergarten at a younger-than-normal age.

Skipping grades. The child is accelerated by completely eliminating one semester or grade in school. The primary drawback here is the potential for temporary adjustment problems for the gifted student.

Telescoping grades. The child covers the standard material, but in less time. For example, a 3-year junior high program would be taught over 2 years.

Advanced placement. The student takes courses for college credit while still in high school, shortening the college program.

Dual enrollment in high school and college. The student takes college courses while still in high school.

Early college admission. An extraordinarily advanced student may enter college at 13, 14, or 15 years of age.

Although many parents, teachers, and administrators have strong negative feelings about acceleration, research studies invariably report that children who have been accelerated have adjusted as well as or better than those who have not been accelerated (Kirk & Gallagher, 1989).

Enrichment

Enrichment refers to the addition of disciplines or areas of learning not normally found in the regular curriculum. This technique can be used in a traditional classroom to meet the needs of advanced learners without separating them from the typical learners at their grade level (Clark, 1983). The purpose of enrichment is to provide an extensive range of additional experiences so the students' mastery of important ideas embedded in the standard curriculum is strengthened (Gallagher, 1985).

Enrichment can also be provided through summer, vacation, and Saturday programs designed to provide activities and experiences new to the student. One example is the Cullowhee Experience, a summer enrichment program for gifted students conducted on the campus of Western Carolina University in the mountains of western North Carolina. Typical themes revolve around mountain music and unusual instruments, geological field trips and investigation, crafts, Indian lore, and topics based on the students' interests.

Regardless of the program options available in a particular school system, the students' abilities and interests should be the primary concern. There are guidelines that should direct every program to insure that the students' development is fostered.

The following ten principles should be considered in planning the curriculum for gifted and talented students:

1. Teachers and principals should be sure that all gifted and talented pupils acquire the basic skills and content of the standard curriculum and that they do so thoroughly. This means checking to see that there are no gaps in their knowledge or skills. Sometimes gifted students advance so rapidly on the basis of incidental learning (that is, without formal instruction) that assumptions are made about thoroughness of learning. Such assumptions should be checked.

2. Students should be encouraged to move ahead in the standard curriculum (reading, motor development, writing, sciences, mathematics, languages, music, art, literature, etc.) as rapidly as fits each pupil's individual pace. Advanced books, materials, and instruction should be readily available in a systematic and orderly fashion, and a child's efforts at curriculum acceleration should be reinforced. The policy of holding, say, all fourth-graders to fourth-grade books, still common in too many schools, is totally inexcusable.

3. The scope of curricular offerings should be extended for students who master the regular curriculum in less than the usual time. For example, typing, foreign languages, art, and various specialized studies should be added at the times that gifted and talented students can schedule them, provided that interest is high and they promise to contribute to the students' general pattern of development.

4. Teachers and counselors should encourage particularly able students to reach beyond the usual curriculum. In such cases, parents should be involved in planning. If a 10-year-old wishes to pursue content areas like astronomy, animal husbandry, ethics, epistemology, morality, Moslem culture, paper making, or population control, there must be understanding and cooperation between home and school. Such prearrangement gives parents a voice in what is going on and ensures that their values relating to the relevance and propriety of particular studies are respected. At the secondary school level, this reaching beyond may well take the form of registering for specialized advanced placement courses, working with a mentor, or special summer studies.

5. Teachers should provide opportunities for gifted students to connect whatever they are studying to what they already know and to collateral areas of study. Such opportunities might mean extending the curriculum to include exploring the history of ideas more thoroughly than is common for other students or learning how skills and knowledge relate to various professions and advanced fields of scholarship. These adaptations encourage the transfer or generalization of knowledge and the search for deeper meanings.

6. Gifted students should be encouraged and assisted to undertake independent study and to polish skills in self-directed learning. The activities should include special efforts to create awareness of their own awareness (metacognition) as an aspect of discovering their personal best strategies for independent study, solving problems, and constructing meaning from reading and other activities. Activities should also include using data on their own performance as a basis for planning.

7. Gifted students should be given opportunities to explore, experiment, and create in environments that provide rich resources and guidance, along with large measures of freedom. The combination permits students to discover that they can discover and create and to experience the surge of motivation that usually accompanies such self-discovery.

8. Students should be pressed to carry issues and discussions all the way to culminating activities, such as decision making, policy formation, and moral or ethical analysis, and to engage in com-

munication activities by making reports to or holding discussions with other people.

9. Gifted students should be encouraged and assisted to develop leadership skills and to exercise them in the school and community. Often the activities entail studies in social psychology, formal and informal procedures for group process (e.g., Roberts's rules of order), understanding oneself as a social agent, and acquiring respect for all other humans, whatever their characteristic.

10. Gifted students need to build positive expectations for careers and adult living that will optimize their talents and gifts. More than other students, they may need special help in understanding how to accomplish advanced and very complex learning in pursuit of high goals.[3]

It is important to provide a diverse range of school programs that match the diversity of gifted students. Different types and levels of giftedness require differential programs. The needs of the intellectually gifted will not be adequately met by a program suited to the student with special artistic talents (Thompson, 1987). The identification and differential education of gifted and talented students depends on the attitudes that parents, teachers, and administrators have toward the students and toward gifted education.

Attitudes of parents toward their gifted child vary; in some cases the identification of their child as gifted enhances the child's status in the family. When both parents agree that the child is gifted, they have a positive reaction. When parents disagree, the label is not perceived as positive (Colangelo & Brower, 1987).

Teachers and administrators may perceive gifted students as aggressive or obnoxious. Teachers of gifted programs need high energy, flexibility, strong acceptance and understanding of differences, high tolerance for ambiguity with great curiosity, imagination, and originality.

It is essential to change attitudes of parents, teachers, and administrators toward gifted children and programs for them. Parents need help at home for better understanding; teachers need help in school for guiding and sustaining the talents of their gifted students (Williams, 1988).

Although the labels of *gifted* and *talented* are associated with high status, especially in the eyes of parents and teachers, they contain the risk of separating individuals from their natural peer groups both physically, as in the case of segregated programming, and psychologically, by designating them as different (Guskin, Okolo, Zimmerman, & Peng, 1986).

[3]From *Adaptive Mainstreaming: A Primer for Teachers and Principals,* Third Edition by Maynard C. Reynolds and Jack W. Birch. Copyright © 1988 by Longman, Inc. Reprinted by permission of Longman Publishing.

Teachers need to develop strategies to mainstream their gifted and talented students successfully. A fourth-grade teacher suggests several techniques that have worked well in her classroom:

> *The learning environment must be open so the students can digress from usual procedures. The teacher has to stay in the background and be available if needed. Teachers have to realize that gifted students may require extra patience.*
>
> *Students who are gifted can be definite assets to the class. For example, Melody is always finished with her assignments before anyone else and helps other students with their work. This is a good way for the others in the class to interact with someone besides the teacher and gives Melody an opportunity to practice leadership qualities and to interact with those who aren't as gifted as she is. The students in the classroom are in no way intimidated by Melody. (Taylor, 1988, n.p.)*

The following chapters give examples of a teacher who encourages a student to share an outside interest with his classmates, a teacher who has the brightest students tutor other children in difficult word problems, and a teacher who allows an impulsive and precocious student to prepare lesson summaries to present to classmates. Teaching gifted students requires a respect for individual talent and the flexibility to allow students to go beyond minimum requirements.

REFERENCES

A nation at risk. (1983). The National Committee on Excellence in Teaching. Washington, DC: U.S. Government Printing Office.

Cassidy, J., & Johnson, N. (1986). Federal and state definitions of giftedness: Then and now. *Gifted Child Today, 9,* (6), 15–21.

Clark, B. (1983). *Growing up gifted* (2nd ed.). Columbus, OH: Merrill.

Cohn, S. J., Cohn, C. M. G., & Kanevsky, L. S. (1989). Giftedness and talent. In E. W. Lynch & R. B. Lewis (Eds.), *Exceptional children and adults* (pp. 456–501). Glenview, IL: Scott, Foresman.

Colangelo, N., & Brower, P. (1987). Labeling gifted youngsters: Long-term impact on families, *Gifted Child Quarterly, 31,* (2), 75–78.

Davidson, K. (1986). The case against formal identification. *Gifted Child Today, 9,* (6), 7–11.

Davis, G. A., & Rimm, S. B. (1989). *Education of the gifted and talented* (2nd ed.). Englewood Cliffs, NJ: Prentice-Hall.

Delisle, J. R. (1987). *Gifted kids speak out.* Minneapolis: Free Spirit.

Division for Exceptional Children. (1986). *Procedures governing programs and services for children with special needs.* Raleigh, NC: State Department of Public Instruction.

Fox, L., & Tobin, D. (1988). Broadening career horizons for gifted girls. *Gifted Child Today, 11,* (1), 9–12.

Gallagher, J. J. (1985). *Teaching the gifted child.* Boston: Allyn and Bacon.

Guilford, J. P. (1959). Traits of creativity. In H. H. Anderson (Ed.), *Creativity and its cultivation* (pp. 142–161). New York: Harper & Brothers.

Gunderson, C. W., Maesch, C., & Rees, J. W. (1987). The gifted/learning disabled student. *Gifted Child Quarterly, 31,* (4), 158–160.

Guskin. S. L., Okolo, C., Zimmerman, E., & Peng, C. Y. J. (1986). Being labeled gifted or talented: Meanings and effects perceived by students in special programs. *Gifted Child Quarterly, 30,* (2), 61–65.

Hardman, M. L., Drew, C. J., & Egan, M. W. (1987). *Human exceptionality* (2nd ed.). Boston: Allyn and Bacon.

Kerr, B. A. (1985). Smart girls, gifted women: Special guidance concerns. *Roeper Review, 8,* (1), 30–33.

Kirk, S. A., & Gallagher, J. J. (1989). *Educating exceptional children* (6th ed.). Boston: Houghton Mifflin.

Kitano, M. (1982). Young gifted children: Strategies for preschool teachers. *Young Children, 37,* (4), 14–23.

Klein, E. (1989). Gifted and talented. In G. P. Cartwright, C. A. Cartwright, & M. W. Ward (Eds.), *Educating special learners* (3rd ed.) (pp. 316–341). Belmont, CA: Wadsworth.

Marland, S. (1972). *Education of the gifted and talented.* Washington, DC: U.S. Government Printing Office.

Parke, B. N. (1989). *Gifted students in regular classrooms.* Boston: Allyn and Bacon.

Parker, J. P. (1989). *Instructional strategies for teaching the gifted.* Boston: Allyn and Bacon.

Parker, J. P., & Karnes, F. A. (1987). A current report on graduate degree programs in gifted and talented education. *Gifted Child Quarterly, 31,* (3), 116–117.

Renzulli, J. S. (1986). The three-ring conception of giftedness: A developmental model for creative productivity. In R. J. Sternberg & J. E. Davidson (Eds.), *Conceptions of giftedness* (pp. 53–92). New York: Cambridge University Press.

Reynolds, M. C., & Birch, J. W. (1988). *Adaptive mainstreaming* (3rd ed.). New York: Longman.

Rinderle, S. (1987). The gift. *Roeper Review, 10,* (1), 9.

Stanley, J. (1979). Identifying and nurturing the intellectually gifted. In W. George, S. Cohn, & J. Stanley (Eds.), *Educating the gifted: Acceleration and enrichment* (pp. 172–180). Baltimore: Johns Hopkins University Press.

Taylor, G. (1988). Class assignment: Teaching the Exceptional Child. Cullowhee, NC: Western Carolina University.

Thompson, G. B. (1987). An experimental program for highly gifted children in the early primary grades. *Gifted Child Quarterly, 31,* (1), 35–36.

Torrance, E. P. (1978). Healing qualities of creative behavior. *Creative Child and Adult Quarterly, 3,* 146–158.

Weill, M. P. (1987). Gifted/learning disabled students. *Clearing House, 60,* (8), 341–343.

Whitmore, J. (1980). *Giftedness, conflict, and underachievement.* Boston: Allyn and Bacon.

Williams. F. E. (1988). A magic circle. *Gifted Child Today, 12,* (1), 2–5.

PART TWO

Educational Strategies

—6—

Developing Individualized Education Programs

The IEP document is the written plan that specifies the nature of each handicapped student's instructional program and the degree to which it is specially designed. This chapter provides an overview of the components that comprise the IEP and offers guidelines to classroom teachers for participating with educators, parents, and the handicapped student in the meeting to develop the IEP. An IEP is mandated by PL 94–142 for students who are handicapped and therefore eligible for special education services. PL 94–142 does not include pupils who are gifted and talented, and an IEP is not required for gifted and talented pupils who have no identified handicap. In order to understand IEP development, however, it is important to recognize the steps in the special education planning process that must occur before the point of planning the IEP. The total sequence of the special education planning process is outlined in Figure 6.1.

The special education planning process is coordinated within each school by a committee of persons responsible for insuring that appropriate procedures are used to refer, evaluate, and provide special education programs for handicapped students. In different states this committee goes by different names, including the special services committee, school-based committee, placement team, and child study team. In this chapter, it is referred to as the special services committee. The standing members of the

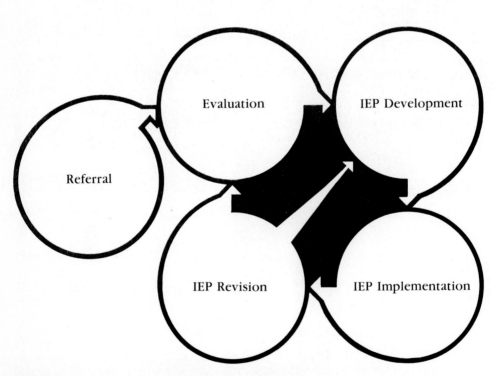

FIGURE 6.1 Special Education Planning Process

special services committee typically include the principal, special education teachers, school psychologist, guidance counselor, and therapists. Classroom teachers are frequently asked to meet with the special services committee when a student they teach is being evaluated for special education programming.

The first two steps of the special education process coordinated by the special services committee are referral and evaluation. In addition, prereferral is a much needed step that is sometimes a part of the special education process determined by state regulation and sometimes a responsibility of regular education. The next three sections focus on prereferral, referral, and evaluation before focusing on the mechanics of IEP development.

PREREFERRAL

Prereferral activities are implemented by an individual teacher or by a group of educators to address the needs of any student who is not progressing as expected before the student is referred for possible special education placement. These activities try to individualize or personalize instruction so that it matches the student's current developmental capabilities and motivation (Adelman & Taylor, 1983). Prereferral activities typically involve some adaptation of the curriculum or usual instructional methodology to accommodate the student's learning mode, level, and rate. Examples of such adaptations include:

1. selecting fewer objectives for the student to learn,
2. using an aide, parent volunteer, or peer to tutor the student individually,
3. changing the student's seat in the classroom,
4. changing the reinforcer or reinforcement schedule for the student, or
5. changing the student's group.

Almost any adaptation that does not include special education and related services can be thought of as prereferral activity.

The prereferral intervention model has been highly recommended. Several advantages have been identified (Kerr, Nelson, & Lambert, 1987).

1. Pre-referral intervention reduces the number of referrals to special education, many of which may be inappropriate.
2. This model provides assessment information without labeling the student.

3. It reduces the delay between referral and intervention (by shortening the diagnostic process).
4. This approach takes advantage of existing (and often overlooked) data on the student's progress.
5. It relies on the expertise of classroom teachers who know the student best (p. 11).

Prereferral is a suggested approach not mandated by PL 94–142 but endorsed by experts and by the U.S. Department of Education (Chalfant, 1985). In a recent survey, 23 states indicated that prereferral interventions were required for students suspected of having a handicap (Carter & Sugai, 1989). The National Task Force report, *Identifying Learning-Disabled Students: Guideline for Decision Making* (1985), includes strong recommendations for a prereferral plan. The report promotes initial teacher intervention, stating that the classroom teacher can use "alternative learning situations or instructional methods to help students progress through the curriculum" (Chalfant, 1985, p. 14). Also recognized are teacher consultants, who can consult with teachers rather than provide direct instruction to students. In addition, in team teaching, teacher teams assume common responsibility for coordinating instruction for a specific group of students. The report also endorses teacher support teams.

According to the National Task Force report, 16 states use building-based teacher support teams to

1. Clarify the nature of learning and behavior problems.
2. Generate instructional alternatives for the classroom.
3. Monitor the implementation of the recommendations.
4. Refer students for individual testing. (Chalfant, 1985, p. 15)

These teams can be composed of regular educators, special educators, administrators, counselors, and other people in a variety of ways, but usually they include only individuals working at one particular school (Stokes, 1982).

According to Stokes (1982), a building-based staff support team is a "problem-solving group whose purpose is to provide a vehicle for discussion of issues related to specific needs of teachers or students and to offer consultation and follow-up assistance to staff" (p. 3). Although no single model has been found to be most effective, the results can be impressive, including more appropriate special education referrals, expanded instructional alternatives, and improved school climate.

North Carolina is one state that mandates prereferral interventions for students who are suspected of being eligible for special education in the categories of learning disabilities and behavioral disorders (called behavioral-emotional handicapped). A 9-month investigation of the effectiveness of prereferral procedures compared to standard procedures used previously yielded impressive results (North Carolina Department of Public Instruction, 1987). Some of these results are summarized here.

1. The prereferral model provided teachers assistance in an average of 8 days as opposed to the 69 school-day average between previous referrals and teacher assistance.
2. Assessment costs in personnel time were reduced by more than $80,000 compared to the previous procedures.
3. Teachers who were trained in prereferral intervention strategies used a greater array of intervention strategies than did teachers who were not trained.
4. Trained teachers submitted a higher proportion of referrals that led to special education placement than did those not trained. Untrained teachers submitted more referrals that did not lead to special education placement. Thus, trained teachers made more appropriate referrals.
5. Prereferral submissions during the 9 months of the study were distributed in the following manner: 60 percent were kindergarten through grade 6; 17 percent were in grades 7 through 9; and 23 percent were submitted in grades 9 through 12.

REFERRAL

A referral represents the initial indication that a student has special needs that may be disadvantageous for achieving school success. At this point, a student may be experiencing problems in the classroom but has not yet been formally identified as handicapped and in need of special education programming. Based on an awareness that professional assistance is needed to document whether students are handicapped and the extent of their special needs, a referral form is completed for the purpose of requesting formal evaluation. This form can be completed by any member of the school's faculty or by persons outside the school, including parents, physicians, psychologists, or anyone else concerned with the educational welfare of the student. Classroom teachers play a major role in the referral process, because they have more direct contact with the students in their classes than any other person in the school.

Federal guidelines for the referral process are not specified by PL 94–142; however, guidelines are provided in each state's legislation and regulations and in the operating policies of local school systems. Thus, teachers are advised to discuss the specific referral guidelines and their associated responsibilities with their principal or the chairperson of the special services committee. Copies of the actual referral form used in the school should be obtained at that time.

Classroom teachers should be acquainted with general referral guidelines that can be applied to the specific procedures in each school. These guidelines are in the areas of identifying, verifying, and reporting the special needs of students.

Identifying Special Needs

Classroom teachers have the responsibility to identify the special needs of students. The characteristics of handicapped students discussed in chapters 2 through 4 represent the types of special needs that teachers should identify when such characteristics are manifested by an individual student. Remember that the severity of these characteristics and the number of different characteristics representing special needs will vary from student to student. The major criterion teachers use should be whether the special needs of students adversely affect their educational performance to the point at which they are placed at a disadvantage for achieving success. To make this determination, teachers should compile information from a variety of sources, including observation of classroom performance, analysis of classroom assignments, review of performance on teacher-made tests and standardized achievement tests, and reports from parents. A careful analysis of this comprehensive information can help insure that special needs are accurately identified.

Verifying Special Needs

Once teachers have compiled and analyzed comprehensive information and have documented their own concern that the special needs of a particular student are interfering with educational performance, it can be helpful to obtain an independent opinion about the concern from a member of the special services committee. Such an independent opinion could be established by having a committee member observe the student in the classroom, review the information compiled by the teacher, and discuss concerns with the teacher. The purpose of this independent opinion is to verify that the degree of the student's special needs warrants the action of a formal referral for evaluation. Such a verification can possibly provide new insights for the teacher in understanding the nature of the referral concerns and can also minimize the possibility that referral is initiated when it is actually not warranted. Some states require a third-party verification before referring a student for evaluation. There are three possible outcomes of verification: (1) referral to the special services committee for evaluation, (2) adaptation of classroom procedures to deal with the problem without referral, and (3) referral to resources outside the school, such as law enforcement agencies or vocational rehabilitation agencies (Turnbull, Strickland, & Brantley, 1982).

Reporting Special Needs

When the decision is made to refer the student to the special services committee, the specific referral guidelines of each school must be followed. Again, teachers are advised to discuss these guidelines with the principal or chairperson of the special services committee. Such reporting typically involves completing a referral form.

It is important to complete referral forms as thoroughly as possible, since the tests and procedures used to evaluate the student will be selected on the basis of this information

In many states and local school systems, policy requires that the student's parents be notified that a referral is being made to the special services committee. Because many parents are unaware of the purpose and function of referrals and evaluations, this process needs to be explained to them. Frequently, the special services committee assumes responsibility for parent notification.

Teachers should recognize that referring students for evaluation to determine whether a handicapping condition exists is a critical step in the special education planning process. Unless special needs are identified, the student may never receive the specially designed instruction needed for optimal progress. Referring students for an evaluation is *not* an indication of a teaching weakness or of an inability to individualize instruction. Rather, it represents the fulfillment of an important responsibility of classroom teachers, which is the identification of students with handicaps so that specially designed instruction can be provided to meet their special needs. Once the referral form is completed and forwarded to the special services committee, the second step in the special education planning process—evaluation—is initiated.

EVALUATION

According to PL 94-142, the two major purposes of evaluation are:

1. to determine whether or not a student has a handicapping condition (according to the definitions included in chapters 2 through 4).
2. to identify the student's strengths and weaknesses as a basis for instructional planning.

Students must receive a comprehensive evaluation before they can be classified as handicapped. In some cases, the results of the evaluation confirm that fact that students are not handicapped, and that their educational problems that initiated the referral must be handled in ways other than special education programming. When students are found to be handicapped, the evaluation information collected on strengths and weaknesses serves as the basis for planning the IEP.

As stated in chapter 1, PL 94–142 includes many regulations on the nature of conducting evaluations to insure that procedures are fairly administered and interpreted. Thus, federal guidelines exist that pertain to the evaluation process; however, state and local policies must also be followed. Just as teachers should inquire about the referral process in their local schools, they should also investigate state and local evaluation requirements that exceed federal ones. In analyzing federal evaluation requirements from the perspective of classroom teachers, the major areas of concern are personnel responsible for evaluation, type of evaluation procedures, administration of evaluation procedures, and interpretation of evaluation procedures.

Personnel Responsible for Evaluation

As stated earlier, the special services committee in each school is responsible for coordinating the entire special education planning process, including the important step of evaluation. The typical procedure used by special service committees is to appoint a multidisciplinary team of persons to plan, administer, and interpret the evaluation procedures. PL 94–142 requires that the team include at least one teacher or specialist in the area of the student's suspected disability. Frequently, this team is comprised of a special education teacher, school psychologist, therapists (e.g., speech therapists, physical therapists) related to the student's needs as specified on the referral form, and a guidance counselor. Because the composition of the team depends on the nature of the student's special needs, membership can vary widely in individual situations. For example, a school nurse would be an appropriate member of an evaluation team for a student with a health impairment, whereas a mobility specialist would be needed for a blind student. It is the responsibility of the special services committee to appoint the appropriate persons to serve on the multidisciplinary evaluation team, based on the areas of concern documented on the referral form.

Classroom teachers are sometimes asked to assist the evaluation team in collecting information on their students. The sources of this information could be tests, class assignments, and/or observation. Another important role for teachers who initially refer students is to specify the particular questions they would like the multidisciplinary evaluation team to address. Sample questions include:

- What reading level of textbooks would be most appropriate to use in the content areas?
- What concepts has the student currently mastered in mathematics?
- To what extent does the student's difficulty in hearing interfere with the ability to comprehend classroom lectures?
- How long should the student be expected to attend to classroom assignments without a break?
- What classroom management procedures are likely to be successful in decreasing the student's disruptive behavior?

The identification of specific questions increases the probability that the evaluation procedures are appropriately planned and result in relevant, functional findings. Thus, a critical role for classroom teachers is to identify the areas of needed information.

Parents also have responsibilities associated with the evaluation process. Before evaluating the student, the special services committee is responsible for informing parents, through a written notice, why a formal evaluation is being considered. When a student is initially being evaluated to determine whether a handicap exists, parents must give their written consent for the evaluation. The only way an evaluation can proceed without parental consent is for school personnel to override the parents' refusal through the proceedings of a due process hearing (see chapter 1).

Parents can also be asked to contribute information to the evaluation process on such topics as the student's adaptive behavior, language skills, cultural background, social and emotional status, and health needs. Obviously, many parents have a wealth of information on their child's past and current functioning that can be extremely helpful to the evaluation team. Although parents are required members of the committee to plan the IEP, their involvement in contributing information during the evaluation process is optional.

Identifying Types of Evaluation Procedures

The multidisciplinary evaluation team is responsible for identifying tests and procedures to determine whether a student is handicapped and the nature of specially designed instruction tailored to the student's strengths and weaknesses. As stated earlier, the referral information is carefully considered by the evaluation team as they identify appropriate tests and procedures, as well as legal guidelines.

The evaluation team can choose from among a large number of tests and procedures those most suited to the student's particular areas of concern. The major types of instruments and procedures that are used fall into the general categories of standardized tests, criterion-referenced tests, and observations.

Administering Evaluation Procedures

Once the tests and evaluation procedures have been identified, the multidisciplinary evaluation team begins administering them to the student. The testing should be spread over a minimum of several days to insure that the student is not fatigued by the testing demands and that a variety of testing situations are used to gather a comprehensive view of student functioning. Situational factors, such as time of day, length of sessions, characteristics of the testing materials, and distractions in the environment (e.g., noise, lighting) can influence student performance (Turnbull, Strickland, & Brantley, 1982). Other important considerations include whether the student is anxious, the student's motivational level, and the rapport between the examiner and the student.

Classroom teachers can play an extremely important role in helping to prepare students for the evaluation by explaining to them the purpose of evaluation and the procedures that will be followed, as well as helping to build rapport between the student and the evaluation team members.

The day before Phillip was to be evaluated, his teacher, Mrs. Henderson, explained to him that he was going to be asked to do some special work as soon as he arrived at school the following morning. The work, she explained, would involve some tests in the areas of reading, language arts, and math. Mrs. Henderson told Phillip that he should try to do his best on these tests, but he would not get a grade on them that would count for his report card. Rather, the tests would be used to help her and his parents decide on how to plan the best possible school program for him. She told Phillip that Mr. Williams, who would be giving him the test, is a really nice person who likes to do many of the same things he likes to do—play basketball, soccer, and softball. She told Phillip that he might like to bring some of his basketball autographs to show Mr. Williams.

Interpreting Evaluation Data

The interpretation of evaluation data is an extremely important responsibility of the multidisciplinary evaluation team. General guidelines include the following:

1. Consider test results and observational information from a variety of sources;
2. Recognize that test scores are estimates of performance under a specified, and rather limited, set of circumstances;

3. Consider alternative interpretations of test scores;
4. Recognize and document the limitations of the tests and procedures used;
5. Identify whether more information is needed before final decisions are reached and gather more information if necessary;
6. Adhere to the definitional criteria of handicapping conditions to insure that classifications are accurately made; and
7. Identify trends of performance in an effort to determine the student's strengths and weaknesses as a basis for instructional planning.

As stated earlier, classroom teachers can help insure the relevance of test interpretation by giving team members a list of questions for what information is needed. When team members meet as a group to analyze and interpret the evaluation data, these questions can direct the attention of team members to functional classroom implications.

The purpose of this interpretation process is to determine the existence of a handicapping condition. If the student is found not to be handicapped, recommendations need to be formulated by the team on strategies for addressing the referral concerns that do not involve special education placement and services. On the other hand, if the student is classified as having a particular handicapping condition, the next step in the planning process is the development of the IEP. The student's strengths and weaknesses as identified by the evaluation team form the foundation for planning the IEP. The team is responsible for preparing a written report describing the evaluation procedures, results, and the recommendations for programming. PL 94–142 and state legislation require that a copy of this report be sent to the student's parents. Classroom teachers responsible for teaching the student should also have access to the report, either by reading the copy placed in the student's permanent file or asking for their own copy. Each school system has policies for maintaining evaluation reports on students; thus, teachers need to be aware of these policies and to abide by them.

INDIVIDUALIZED EDUCATION PROGRAMS

An IEP must be developed for each student who is classified as handicapped and in need of special education programming and placement. The development of the IEP is the focal point for planning the student's program and coordinating instruction among the classroom teacher, special education teachers, related services providers (e.g., speech therapist), and parents. As stated in chapter 1, IEP development can be viewed in two parts: the IEP document and the IEP meeting.

IEP Document

The components of the IEP required by federal law are reviewed in chapter 1. Also, the legislation of some states requires additional information on IEPs, such as the person responsible for teaching each objective and the special methods and materials that will be used to teach objectives. Although components of the IEP are specified by federal and state legislation, local school systems are free to develop their own forms according to preferred formats. Because there is a tremendous range of formats, teachers are advised to ask for a blank copy of the form used in their system.

This section discusses each required component of the IEP. Readers interested in sample IEPs at preschool, elementary, and secondary levels are referred to Turnbull, Strickland, and Brantley (1982). This source also provides an in-depth guide to IEP development.

Current Levels of Performance

Stating the student's current levels of performance provides documentation of entry level skills and concepts and establishes the starting point for planning goals and objectives. The evaluation information can readily be translated into performance level statements. Teachers also need to collect current information on the student's performance. This can be done by reviewing the student's mastery of objectives on the previous year's IEP, administering classroom tests, and observing the student's progress in academic as well as behavioral areas.

A major decision to be made when reviewing evaluation information is the determination of *all* subjects and skill areas (e.g., adaptive behavior) requiring specially designed instruction. These subjects and skill areas need to be addressed on the IEP. A student who has an orthopedic handicap and mobility impairments only in the lower body and has no academic problems will likely need an IEP only in physical education; a student with mental retardation may need to have all curriculum areas covered by the IEP. Once subject and skill areas have been identified, the student's current levels of performance should be specified for each area. Performance statements should be written by the IEP committee according to the following criteria:

- use of current information,
- use of concise and clear language, and
- identification of specific skills. (Turnbull, Strickland, & Brantley, 1982, p. 137)

Annual Goals

An annual goal is a statement of the student's expected achievement over a period of 1 calendar year. Annual goals must be written for every subject or skill area included on the IEP. Because it is impossible for the IEP committee to know in advance exactly how much progress a handicapped student will make, an annual goal represents an estimate of accomplishments.

The National Association of State Directors of Special Education (1976) suggests critical areas to consider in formulating goals:

- What are the priority parental concerns? What are the priority teacher concerns?
- What are the appropriate developmental sequences of tasks or behaviors that the child would be expected to move through?
- What behaviors appear to be the most modifiable, as determined from baseline assessment data including the child's strengths, weaknesses, and learning style?
- Are there any other crucial considerations one needs to make in selecting areas of educational need, such as any problem areas that are truly dangerous for the child, injurious to his or her health, or others? (p. 30)

Annual goals are broad, global statements and should not be confused with more specific instructional objectives. An example of an annual goal is "Sabrina will demonstrate skills in applying for jobs." The short-term objectives would address the particular application skills to be covered and the criteria of mastery to be demonstrated for each. Although there is no set standard, typically IEPs include three or four annual goals per subject or skill area (*To assure the free appropriate public education for all handicapped children*, 1980).

Short-Term Objectives
Short-term objectives are measurable statements outlining the intermediate steps between the student's current levels of performance and the projected annual goals. Objectives should be sequential, specific in stating desired behavior and criteria, and manageable for both the student and the teacher.

As with goals, the number of objectives is not set by law. Morgan (1981) recommends that at least quarterly objectives be written, which would be three or four objectives per year. These quarterly objectives could then be broken down into smaller units as teachers develop monthly, weekly, and daily instructional plans. This process of breaking down objectives is referred to as task analysis and is discussed in the section on curriculum adaptations in chapter 7. IEP objectives represent benchmarks of progress and are not expected to include every skill and concept the student will be taught throughout the school year.

If criterion-referenced tests have been used to evaluate the student, a list of sequenced objectives is already available for the IEP committee to consider. Other sources of objectives are contained in curriculum guides and in the teacher's manual of many commercial materials.

Some school systems are using computer banks to store objectives. Teachers are given a master copy of objectives for each subject area, and they select by number objectives appropriate for the student. These numbers are typed into the computer, and the computer provides a printout of the selected objectives, saving a great deal of the teacher's time.

Evaluation Procedures, Criteria, and Schedules

A required component of the IEP is the specification of evaluation procedures, criteria, and schedules to be used at least annually to evaluate student achievement of the short-term objectives. Evaluation procedures refer to the type of measures to be used and include any measure that is appropriate for assessing the specified objectives—standardized tests, criterion-referenced tests, observation, teacher-made tests, and a review of classroom assignments.

The criterion for evaluation is the degree of accuracy that the student must demonstrate. If objectives are appropriately written, they will include the necessary criteria. Thus, once the criteria are specified in the objective, they do not have to be restated on the IEP form in the evaluation section.

The third required dimension of evaluation is the schedule that refers to the frequency of student assessment. PL 94–142 requires that the student's progress in meeting objectives be evaluated at least annually. Some states and local school systems require a more frequent schedule of evaluations. It is preferable for evaluations to be conducted on a short-term basis—daily, weekly, and monthly—so that teachers have current information on the student's progress and on the effectiveness of the methods and materials they are using. In this way, problems the student encounters can be identified quickly and changes in the instructional program can be made. Also, student success can be readily identified and reinforced, which can be an impetus for motivation. The IEP committee must determine the appropriate evaluation schedule and specify that schedule on the IEP.

This evaluation component of the IEP is extremely important because it relates to the difficult task teachers face in grading handicapped students. A more detailed discussion of evaluation procedures, criteria, and schedules is included in chapter 7, with suggestions of how this information can be used to devise individualized approaches for assigning and reporting grades.

*Documentation of Special Education Placement and Related
Services*

Decisions pertaining to the particular special education placement and related services that are appropriate to student needs are based on current levels of performance, annual goals, and short-term objectives. Thus, the determination of placement and related services is made *after* these curriculum-related decisions are made. As discussed in chapter 1, special education placements can include a variety of educational environments—regular classrooms, resource rooms, special classes, special schools, residential facilities, and hospital/homebound instruction. The placement decision is made based on the environment that will best provide the needed support for the handicapped student in accordance with the guidelines of the least restrictive environment principle of PL 94–142.

Related services are defined as developmental, corrective, or supportive services necessary to enable a student to benefit from special education. Definitions of related services are included in chapter 1. In addition to specifying the type of service needed by the student, it is desirable to document the extent of service (e.g., two 30-minute speech therapy sessions per week) and the person responsible for providing the related service. When school systems do not have needed related services available in their program, they can contract with other programs, including neighboring school systems, other public agencies (e.g., mental health clinics), or private service providers (e.g., physical therapists in private practice).

Extent of Time in Regular Education Programs
Because of the legal preference for placing handicapped children in regular classes when appropriate in light of their educational needs, a required component of the IEP is the specification of the extent of time the student will participate in the regular program. Extent of participation can be expressed in a percentage of instructional time or in the actual number of hours spent in the regular classroom on a daily or weekly basis.

This requirement should not be interpreted to mean that all handicapped students must be in the regular classroom for at least some portion of the school day. To the contrary, placement decisions must be made individually on the basis of the educational environment in which the student's IEP goals and objectives can most successfully be taught. Thus, if a student is in a special class for the entire school day, the extent of participation in the regular class would be documented as zero on the IEP.

Dates of Services
The final components of the IEP are the specifications of the dates for initiating services and the anticipated duration of services. As previously discussed, school systems are legally required to provide the related services needed by the handicapped student. In some cases, however, there may be an unavoidable delay when the IEP committee must make arrangements to subcontract with other agencies for services. Thus, the initiation date recorded on the IEP should occur either immediately after the IEP is approved or shortly thereafter when necessary arrangements have been made.

The anticipated duration of the service is determined based on the student's individual needs. A student with a mild articulation problem may need only 6 months of speech therapy, whereas more severe problems may require much more time. Although some services, such as transportation, may be needed throughout a student's total school career, services on the IEP are typically not documented for more than 1 year. Because the IEP must be reviewed and revised on an annual basis, extensions of service from one year to the next can be made when the updated IEP is planned.

IEP Meeting

A meeting must be held to develop the initial IEP after a student has been classified as handicapped, and the IEP must then be reviewed and revised on an annual basis. The IEP meeting is discussed here in terms of the participants and the components of the meeting.

IEP Meeting Participants

The legally required participants in the IEP meeting, according to PL 94–142, are identified in chapter 1. As with other legal regulations, some states and local school systems require that additional persons attend the IEP meeting (e.g., related service providers). In a national survey of special education directors conducted by one of the authors, the typical number of participants at IEP meetings was found to be five persons.

More than one representative of the school system may attend the IEP meeting, including the principal, director of special education, psychologist, or a special education teacher other than the student's teacher. Particularly when the student for whom an IEP is being planned needs a variety of related services, a system representative attending the meeting should have the authority to commit resources without the concern that this decision will be reversed at a higher administrative level (*Federal Register*, 1981; Morgan, 1981).

Although only one teacher is required to be present, the special education teacher, classroom teacher, or both may attend. Research on IEP meetings has revealed a pattern of minimal to moderate attendance and participation by classroom teachers (Goldstein, Strickland, Turnbull, & Curry, 1980; Pugach, 1982). In a study involving 33 regular classroom teachers, Pugach found that 52 percent had attended the most recent IEP meeting for a student in their class. The teachers reported that their most frequent types of involvement were conferring with the special education teachers and reporting current levels of performance. Low levels of involvement were indicated in participation in decisions related to goals, objectives, and related services. A particularly troublesome finding of this study was that 67 percent of the teachers reported that no goals and objectives were written on the IEP for the subjects the handicapped students were taught in the regular classroom. The lack of IEP coverage of the regular program is a major barrier to the delivery of specially designed instruction, since the majority of mildly handicapped students spend a substantial portion of their school day in the regular class.

There are three primary reasons that the involvement of classroom teachers in IEP meetings has been low and the coverage of the IEP devoted mostly to time a handicapped student spends in a resource room or special class. First, more than 10 years since the instigation of the IEP process in 1977, many classroom teachers still do not have sufficient knowledge of the IEP's purpose and of their important role in its development and implementation. Second, administrators and special educators have not involved classroom teachers in the IEP process in a meaningful way. Third, special educators have had the primary responsibility for educating handicapped students. These situations are changing and should continue to do so because of local, state, and federal initiatives.

One major recent force for change is the U.S. Department of Education. Madeleine Will, former assistant secretary for the Office of Special Education and Rehabilitative Services, called for more integration of regular and special education (Will, 1986). She addressed the need for classroom teachers to take a larger part in our "shared responsibility" (p. 411) for educating all students, including the handicapped. If this Regular Education Initiative (REI) is a continuing force, then classroom teachers in greater numbers will be significantly involved in IEP development.

The involvement of classroom teachers is needed in all phases of education for handicapped students. Prereferral interventions have resulted in significant involvement of classroom teachers in the referral process and subsequently in IEP meetings.

The involvement of classroom teachers can insure that the IEP is appropriate to the needs of the handicapped student and that it guarantees that teachers will receive the assistance they need. It is important to remember that anything seems possible to those with no responsibility for implementation. If classroom teachers are required to provide specially designed instruction to handicapped students, they have both the right and responsibility to share in decisions regarding the nature of the student's program.

Parents are other important members of the IEP committee. The intent of PL 94–142 is for parents to be equal participants in shared decision making with school personnel (*Federal Register*, 1981). Parents have a wealth of information on their child's educational and health history, ways to adapt daily procedures to enhance the success of their child, levels of adaptive behavior, strategies for discipline, likes and dislikes, and the nature of peer interaction outside school. Parents can be extremely helpful in helping educators understand the special needs of their child, and teachers are encouraged to take advantage of the parents' knowledge and perspective.

Although the legal intent was for parents to be equal participants in decision making, research has shown a rather minimal level of parental participation (Goldstein, Strickland, Turnbull, & Curry, 1980; Lynch & Stein, 1982; Morgan, 1982). Some parents of handicapped children are intimidated by the idea of shared decision making in conferences and believe that educators are experts and know what is best for their child. Accordingly, teachers are encouraged to provide a conference atmosphere that will enable parents to relax, to ask questions that elicit parental perspectives, and to provide feedback to parents that their contributions are helpful and appreciated (Goldstein & Turnbull, 1982; Schulz, 1987; Turnbull, Strickland, & Brantley, 1982).

The student's involvement in the conference is extremely important as well. Too frequently, we talk *about* handicapped students and fail to talk *with* them. In interviews with adolescent students who had been classified as learning disabled, educable mentally handicapped, seriously emotionally disturbed, and orthopedically handicapped, Gillespie and Turnbull (1983) reported that 75 percent of the students were unaware of their right to participate in the development of their IEP. These students, however, strongly agreed with the concept of student participation and expressed a desire to be included. They stated that they thought they would benefit from participation, in terms of gaining information about themselves and their school program and sharing information about their preferences and their desire to cooperate with teachers and parents. Sample responses of students to the question, Why do you think it is a good idea for you to go to your own IEP meeting? indicate the viewpoints of these students:

> The teachers and parents get everything out and students have feelings and want to get them out too. (*12-year-old, emotionally handicapped student*)
> I could learn more about why I'm in a special class. (*14-year-old, educable mentally retarded student*)

One source for teaching students how to prepare for and participate in an education-planning conference, including an IEP, is *The Education Planning Strategy* (Van Reusen, Bos, Schumaker, & Deshler, 1987). This strategy shows students how to inventory their strengths and weaknesses and contribute effectively to an education-planning conference.

IEP Meeting Components

Because there is no one standard procedure for conducting IEP meetings, formats vary among school systems. Despite the differences that exist, there are certain components of IEP meetings with which all teachers should be familiar. These components are:

1. *Preconference preparation*—advanced planning on the part of participants to insure that necessary information is gathered, the meeting is scheduled at a convenient time, and special concerns to be discussed are identified;
2. *Initial conference proceedings*—creating an atmosphere for open communication and a plan for decision making;
3. *Interpretation of evaluation results*—reporting formal and informal evaluation information as a basis for establishing the student's current levels of performance and the subject areas to be covered in the IEP;
4. *Development of goals, objectives, and evaluation methods*—specifying the skills and concepts appropriate to the needs of the handicapped student and the methods to be used to evaluate the student's progress;
5. *Decision of special education placement and related services*—specifying the particular classroom placement for the student, the percentage of time in the regular class, the nature and extent of related services, the dates for initiating services, and the anticipated duration of services; and
6. *Conclusion of the meeting*—synthesizing decisions that have been made and outlining future actions, such as communication with parents and timelines for reviewing and revising the IEP.

Table 6.1 includes a summary of suggestions for classroom teachers related to enhancing their active decision-making role in each of these six components.

IEP development is a major step in meeting the educational needs of handicapped students, although it is a hollow accomplishment unless the IEP is effectively implemented. Thus, the IEP is a means rather than an end—it is a means of providing systematic instruction. Readers interested in further information on IEPs are referred to Larsen and Poplin (1980); Morgan (1981); Strickland and Turnbull (1990); Turnbull (1986); Turnbull, Strickland, and Brantley (1982); and Weiner (1978). The remaining chapters in this book focus on strategies for effectively implementing IEPs through the provision of specially designed instruction.

TABLE 6.1 Suggestions to Enhance the Active Participation of Classroom Teachers in IEP Meetings

1. *Preconference Preparation*
   a. Tell the chairperson of the special services committee that you would like to attend the IEP meeting for a handicapped student who is presently in your class or who is being considered for placement in your class.
   b. Insure that the time of the meeting is convenient in light of your schedule.
   c. Reschedule the meeting if the time suggested is inconvenient.
   d. Collect any information that you believe will be helpful at the meeting, such as samples of the student's classroom work, anecdotal records on performance, and/or test papers.
   e. Develop a *draft* list of subjects that you believe require specially designed instruction and any tentative ideas you have on goals and objectives. Take these draft notes to the IEP meeting.
   f. Make notes in advance of potential problems that could arise with the student with which you would like assistance from the IEP committee.

2. *Initial Conference Proceedings*
   a. If you are not introduced at the meeting to any persons you do not know, introduce yourself to all committee members—especially the student's parents.
   b. Ask questions to clarify the particular role of other committee members, if this is unclear to you.
   c. If you have a time limit for the meeting, let other committee members know.
   d. Ask the chairperson to review the agenda for the meeting, if this is not done. If you have concerns that are not already included on the agenda, ask that these concerns be included.

3. *Interpretation of Evaluation Results*
   a. Insure that the resource teacher or psychologist states all tests that were administered and the specific results of each.
   b. You may make notes of evaluation results or ask for a written copy of the student's evaluation report.
   c. Insure that the classroom implications of the evaluation results are identified. Ask questions, if necessary, to insure your understanding.
   d. If any professional jargon is used that you do not understand, ask for clarification. If you do not understand the jargon, it is likely that the parents and student do not understand it.
   e. If you disagree with the evaluation findings in light of the student's previous performance in your classroom, state your disagreement and provide rationale for your perspective.
   f. Insure that the student's current levels of performance are clearly identified.
   g. State the subjects and skill areas that you believe require specially designed instruction. Insure that performance levels are specified for each one.

4. *Development of the Goals, Objectives, and Evaluation Methods*
   a. Contribute your own ideas for goals and objectives. If you question the goals and objectives suggested by others at the meeting, ask for justification. Remember that you may be assigned major responsibility for teaching the student.
   b. Insure that goals, objectives, and evaluation methods for *all* subjects requiring specially designed instruction are included in the IEP.

   c. Insure that the evaluation methods can be translated into procedures for grading the handicapped student. Discuss criteria for assigning grades and strategies for reporting grades to the student and parent.

   d. Insure that you understand the nature of the specially designed instruction needed by the student.

5. *Placement Decision and Related Services*

   a. Suggest the placement (e.g., regular classroom, resource program, special class) that you believe is most appropriate for the student.

   b. Be sure all necessary related services (e.g., speech therapy, physical therapy, transportation) that you believe the student needs are included. Remember that the school is not obligated to provide related services that are not written into the IEP.

   c. If the student is to receive instruction from both you and the resource teacher, clarify the manner in which the responsibility for teaching the objectives will be shared.

   d. Insure that the student has appropriate opportunities to interact with nonhandicapped children (placement in the least restrictive setting).

   e. If the student is to be placed in your class, clarify with all committee members whether you believe you can effectively implement the IEP. Ask for whatever help and support of the committee members or other school personnel you believe you will need.

6. *Conclusion of the Meeting*

   a. If the chairperson does not initiate it, ask for a summary of the meeting to review major decisions and follow-up responsibility. You may want to make a written record of this summary.

   b. If follow-up responsibility has not been specified (e.g., locating or purchasing specialized materials), ask who is going to be responsible for each task.

   c. Insure that a tentative date is set for reviewing the IEP on at least an annual basis and preferably more often.

   d. State in what ways and how frequently you would like to keep in touch with the student's special education resource teacher, related service provider(s), and parents. Discuss mutually preferred strategies for maintaining ongoing communication.

   e. State your desire and intent to work in close cooperation with IEP committee members to insure that an appropriate education is provided to the student.

   f. Express appreciation for the opportunity to share in decision making.

REFERENCES

Adelman, H. S., & Taylor, L. (1983). *Learning disabilities in perspective.* Glenview, IL: Scott, Foresman.

Carter, J., & Sugai, G. (1989). Survey on pre-referral practices: Responses from state department of education. *Exceptional Children, 55,* 298–302.

Chalfant, J. C. (1985). Identifying learning disabled students: A summary of the natural task force report. *Learning Disabilities Focus, 1,* (1), 9–20.

Federal Register. (1981). Washington, DC: U.S. Government Printing Office.

Gillespie, E. B., & Turnbull, A. P. (1983). Involving special education students in planning the IEP. *Teaching Exceptional Students, 16,* 26–29.

Goldstein, S., Strickland, B., Turnbull, A. P., & Curry, L. (1980). An observational analysis of the IEP conference. *Exceptional Children, 46,* (4), 278–286.

Goldstein, S., & Turnbull, A. P. (1982). The use of two strategies to increase parent participation in IEP conferences. *Exceptional Children, 48,* (4), 360–361.

Kerr, M. M., Nelson, C. M., & Lambert, D. I. (1987). Helping adolescents with learning and behavior problems. Columbus, OH: Merrill.

Larsen, S. C., & Poplin, M. S. (1980). *Methods for educating the handicapped: An individualized education program approach.* Boston: Allyn and Bacon.

Lynch, E., & Stein, R. (1982). Perspectives on parent participation in special education. *Exceptional Education Quarterly, 3,* (2), 73–84.

Morgan, D. P. (1981). *A primer on individualized education programs for exceptional children: Preferred strategies and practices.* Reston, VA: Foundation for Exceptional Children.

Morgan, D. P. (1982). Parent participation in the IEP process: Does it enhance appropriate education? *Exceptional Education Quarterly, 3,* (2), 33–40.

National Association of State Director of Special Education. (1976). *Functions of the placement committee in special education.* Washington, DC: Author.

North Carolina Department of Public Instruction. (1987). An investigation into the effectiveness of the North Carolina Pre-Referral (and Intervention model in terms of cost, time, referral appropriateness, and impact of training models). Raleigh, North Carolina State Department of Public Instruction, Division for Exceptional Children and U.S. Department of Education.

Pugach, M. (1982). Regular classroom teacher involvement on the development and utilization of IEPs. *Exceptional Children, 48,* (4), 371–374.

Schulz, J. B. (1987). *Parents and professionals in special education.* Boston: Allyn and Bacon.

Stokes, S. (Ed.). (1982). School based staff support teams: A blueprint for action. Reston, VA: Council for Exceptional Children, ERIC Clearinghouse on Handicapped and Gifted Children.

Strickland, B. B., & Turnbull, A. P. (1990). *Developing and implementing individualized education programs* (3rd ed.). Columbus, OH: Merrill.

To assure the free appropriate public education of all handicapped children, Second Annual Report to Congress on the Implementation of Public Law 94–142: The Education for All Handicapped Children Act (1980). Washington, DC: U.S. Department of Education.

Turnbull, A. P., Strickland, B., & Brantley, J. C. (1982). *Developing and implementing individualized education programs.* Columbus, OH: Merrill.

Turnbull, H. R. (1986). *Free appropriate public education: The law and children with disabilities.* Denver: Love.

Van Reusen, A. K., Bos, C. S., Schumaker, J. B., & Deshler, D. D. (1987). The education planning strategy. Lawrence, KS: Excellent Enterprises.

Weiner, B. B. (Ed.). (1978). *Periscope: Views of the individualized education program.* Reston, VA: Council for Exceptional Children.

Will, M. (1986). Educating children with learning problems: A shared responsibility. *Exceptional Children, 52,* 411–415.

7

Implementing Individualized Education Programs

Individualized instruction involves the process of tailoring instruction to the educational needs of each student. Such instruction does not require the teacher always to work with a student in a one-to-one situation. Rather, individualized instruction can be delivered in many ways, including large groups and small groups as well as individual formats.

As stated in chapter 1, special education is defined as specially designed instruction. Such instruction is specially designed to meet the unique needs of each student. That is also the essence of individualized approaches—to design instruction specifically according to the performance levels and special needs of the handicapped student.

The development of the IEP is the beginning point for delivering individualized instruction in the regular classroom. The IEP contains vital information for the classroom teacher to use in making instructional decisions. It should be remembered, however, that the IEP is a means to an end—it is a plan for the actual delivery of specially designed or individualized instruction on a daily basis. It is the teacher's responsibility to translate the IEP into daily and weekly lesson plans. To make this translation, teachers must make instructional decisions to answer the following questions:

1. What types of adaptations are needed to adjust the curriculum content to the goals and objectives that have been determined appropriate for the handicapped student?
2. What instructional strategies will be effective for the student and manageable for the teacher in delivering instruction?
3. What procedures will be the most effective in coordinating instruction between the classroom and resource room?
4. How can the evaluation procedures as specified on the IEP be implemented in regular classrooms, and how should grades be assigned?

This chapter addresses each of these questions by suggesting strategies that can realistically be implemented in regular classrooms.

Adaptations always require time, effort, and costs (either in human or material resources). The strategies presented here are realistic; some may be more reasonable than others given a specific situation. A continuum of reasonableness has been devised to gauge each suggested strategy (Fagan, Graves, Healy, & Tessier-Switlick, 1986).

Low Reasonableness—accommodations that require much extra time, much change in usual teaching practices, and much additional help.
Moderate Reasonableness—accommodations that require some extra time, some change in usual teaching practices, and some additional help.

High Reasonableness—accommodations that require little extra time, little change in usual teaching practices, and little additional help. (pp. 5–6)

Classroom teachers can judge each suggestion by these criteria.

ADAPTATIONS IN CURRICULUM CONTENT

A variety of adaptations can be made to adjust the content of the regular classroom curriculum to the particular needs of a handicapped student. Such adaptations are needed when the handicapped student's current levels of performance are below those of the majority of students. Thus, the goals and objectives as specified on the IEP are ones that most of the other students in the class have already mastered.

> *Kea is in the third grade and has been classified as learning disabled. Math is the subject with which she has the greatest difficulty. She has obtained about 75 percent accuracy on addition and subtraction facts, but she still needs more instruction on solving problems with regrouping. While most of her classmates are successfully mastering multiplication and division concepts, Kea needs more practice on addition and subtraction.*

Below grade-level achievement almost always occurs with students who are mentally retarded and often with students who are learning-disabled. Because of special learning needs, students with sensory handicaps may also have achievement deficiencies.

Determining the Need for Curriculum Adaptations

The first step in making curriculum adaptations is to review carefully the current levels of performance, annual goals, and short-term objectives on the IEP. This information will apprise the teacher of the extent of needed adaptations by comparing the goals and objectives considered appropriate for the handicapped student with the general goals and objectives that comprise the regular curriculum.

A second step in decision making concerning curriculum adaptations is to break down the IEP objectives into the subskills and concepts that are inherent in each. This process is referred to as task analysis. To analyze a task, ask questions such as: What must the learner be able to do to achieve the objective? What kinds of learning are involved? What prior skills are necessary? What specific knowledge is required? What concepts or meanings must be understood? What is prerequisite to ultimate success (Johnson & Johnson, 1970)? If objectives are not analyzed before teaching a student, a teacher is often unaware of which prerequisite skills the student has mastered.

> *A student teacher was observed attempting to teach a child to tell time. Her materials were carefully prepared, the child was well motivated, and still the child would respond to 12:15 sometimes as 15 minutes before 12 and sometimes as 15 minutes after 12. An experienced observer immediately identified the problem: the child did not have the concepts of "before" and "after," prerequisite skills to telling time. A similar problem was encountered when an experienced teacher attempted to offer typing instruction to a visually impaired child. In dictating simple sentences, she learned that the student had limited phonics and spelling skills. It was necessary, therefore, that he be instructed in basic word-attack skills before typing could be offered.*

The determination of how many steps are necessary to master a skill or concept is based on the complexity of the objective and the learner's current abilities. The method of completing a task analysis recommended by McCormack (1976) for a group of learners working toward the same objective, but functioning at different levels, is to construct the instructional sequence for those learners demonstrating the least competence. The task is analyzed into the simplest steps; the more capable learners simply skip steps.

Frank (1973) presents an example of a task analysis that leads to an informal test constructed from the steps. The objective is stated as follows: The child is able to count correctly a specified number of coins handed to him by the teacher. A partial task analysis includes:

1. Identifies a penny and nickel.
2. States that a nickel is equivalent to five pennies.
3. Counts a row of pennies placed in a straight line.
4. Counts pennies placed in scattered fashion.
5. Counts one nickel and several pennies which are placed in a straight line where the nickel is first.

The following items comprise a corresponding test:

Test Item Number	Test Item	Directions Given by Teacher
1	Coins or pictures of coins	Teacher asks child to name each coin as he points to it
2	Same	Teacher asks child how many pennies he can get for one nickel
3–5	Same	Teacher asks child to count the money

After administering the test to each child who will be learning about money, the teacher is able to determine which steps each student needs to master to reach the stated objective.

For some tasks, it is possible to determine the steps by observing and recording the sequential activities of a person performing the task. In most cases, the teacher decides what activities presented in what order will most assist the learner in acquiring the skill (McCormack, 1976).

Task analysis is an important aspect of adapting the content level of the curriculum. An ability to analyze tasks allows the teacher to determine pupil readiness, to teach groups of students with varying skills, and to produce alternatives to instructional failure. It identifies the demands that a task will make on students and allows the teacher to prepare them to meet each demand (Junkala, 1972). Task analysis is a tool that helps to teach the goals and objectives specified in the IEP.

After the IEP has been carefully reviewed and a task analysis of objectives has been completed, several curriculum alternatives are possible. First, the teacher may decide that the goals and objectives for a handicapped student are consistent with the goals and objectives for the majority of other students in the class. Thus, adaptations in content would not be needed. Rather, the student may require adaptations in instructional strategies (e.g., the methods and materials used to deliver the content), which is discussed in the next section. The other three alternatives include supplementing, simplifying, or changing the regular curriculum (Allen, Clark, Gallagher, & Scofield, 1982).

Supplementing the Regular Curriculum

The skills and concepts comprising the regular curriculum may be generally appropriate for a handicapped student; however, the student may need instruction on some prerequisite skills that most other students have already mastered. Another special need can arise when a handicapped student requires more practice than the rest of the class on the particular steps of a skill sequence.

Individualization can occur in these instances by supplementing the regular curriculum with special materials. The student would generally be taught the same curriculum as other students. The adaptation would include the insertion of additional materials to teach prerequisite skills, to allow for more intense instruction over a longer period of time, or to provide for more practice. Such materials could be acquired from the library or found in textbooks from a lower grade (in the case of prerequisite skills); or supplementary materials could be devised by the teachers, peer tutors, or classroom volunteers. Commercial kits graded and organized for practice according to specific skills also provide more practice at varied grade levels (Lambie, 1980).

Simplifying the Curriculum

The goals and objectives for handicapped students in certain curriculum areas may be substantially below those of their classmates. When such deviations occur, the IEP committee must decide the subjects that should be taught in the resource room by the special education teacher and the amount of time that is appropriate for the handicapped students to attend the resource program. For students who have substantial learning problems, it is likely that the instruction in the resource room will not cover all subjects requiring specially designed instruction. In these cases, the classroom teacher will need to simplify the regular curriculum to accommodate the goals and objectives that are appropriate for the student.

> *Sandy, a tenth-grade student who has been classified as mildly mentally handicapped, attends the resource program for 2 hours each day. During this time, he receives instruction in his areas of greatest needs, which are reading and spelling. The resource teacher also helps him with his homework in the subjects being taught in the regular classroom. These subjects include civics, business arithmetic, and vocational education. He particularly has trouble in these subjects when reading and written reports are required. His classroom teachers have found it necessary to simplify the curriculum in these subjects by task analyzing the objectives and teaching skills and concepts in small steps with special learning aids and materials.*

The skills and concepts in a particular subject area can be simplified by using alternative levels of task difficulty. Task requirements for students can be adapted to their level of cognitive thinking. Table 7.1 outlines levels of the cognitive domain based on the work of Bloom and described by Popham and Baker (1970). These levels can be used to formulate objectives and task requirements. The cognitive levels range from simpler ones (i.e., knowledge level) through increasing degrees of intellectual complexity (i.e., evaluation). This model of cognitive thinking is an example of curriculum simplification.

> *Mr. Sims taught the same units to all of the students in his eleventh-grade government class. A wide range of achievement and ability existed in the class. Mr. Sims was aware of the need to simplify his curriculum for the 2 students with learning disabilities. He also had students who were extremely gifted and needed to go beyond the requirements of the majority of the class. Mr. Sims adapted his instruction according to the level of cognitive functioning expected of the students. The students with learning disabilities worked primarily on unit tasks requiring them to perform at the* knowledge *and* comprehension *levels. For example, in a unit on the branches of the federal government, they were required to identify each of the branches and to*

TABLE 7.1 Levels of Cognitive Domain

Knowledge.   Knowledge involves the recall of specifics or universals, the recall of methods and processes, or the recall of a pattern, structure, or setting. It will be noted that the essential attribute at this level is recall. For assessment purposes, a recall situation involves little more than "bringing to mind" appropriate material.

Comprehension.   This level represents the lowest form of understanding and refers to a kind of apprehension that indicates that a student knows what is being communicated and can make use of the material or idea without necessarily relating it to other material or seeing it in its fullest implications.

Application.   Application involves the use of abstractions in particular or concrete situations. The abstractions used may be in the form of procedures, general ideas, or generalized methods. They may also be ideas, technical principles, or theories that must be remembered and applied.

Analysis.   Analysis involves the breakdown of a communication into its constituent parts such that the relative hierarchy within that communication is made clear, that the relations between the expressed ideas are made explicit, or both. Such analyses are intended to clarify the communication, to indicate how it is organized and the way in which the communication manages to convey its effects as well as its basis and arrangement.

Synthesis.   Synthesis represents the combining of elements and parts so that they form a whole. This operation involves the process of working with pieces, parts, elements, and so on, and arranging them so as to constitute a pattern or structure not clearly present before.

Evaluation.   Evaluation requires judgments about the value of material and methods for given purposes. Quantitative and qualitative judgments are made about the extent to which material and methods satisfy criteria. The criteria employed may be those determined by the learner or those given to him.

Source: From *Systematic Instruction* (pp. 32–33) by W. J. Popham and E. L. Baker, 1970. Englewood Cliffs, NJ: Prentice-Hall, Inc. Copyright 1970 by Prentice-Hall, Inc. Reprinted by permission.

state the contribution each of them makes to the establishment of federal policy. On the other end of the spectrum, gifted students contracted for an independent project involving the cognitive processes of analysis, synthesis, and evaluation. Each of these students selected a particular federal policy. They analyzed legislation related to the policy and the findings of at least two judicial cases that had provided interpretations of the policy. Mr. Sims found that every student in the class benefited by having options available for them to work on at their own individual level.

A curriculum model (Bailey & Leonard, 1977) using these levels of cognitive thinking has been developed for the target group of preschool children who have been classified as both handicapped (e.g., visually impaired, orthopedically handicapped) and gifted (e.g., intellectual ability or talents). The model is comprised of instructional units with activities at each of the cognitive levels depicted in Table 7.1.

Another strategy for simplifying the curriculum at the secondary level is to insure that the student's courses are carefully chosen each semester. After considering the student's strengths and weaknesses, caution should be taken to avoid an overload of heavy courses. In some instances, it may be necessary to reduce the total course load (Allen et al., 1982).

Changing the Curriculum

In some cases, the performance levels of handicapped students differ so markedly from those of their nonhandicapped peers that curriculum must be altered to the point of teaching different content. Rather than working on the same unit with other students, the handicapped student may need to work on a prerequisite unit already mastered by other students. As previously indicated, the teacher first needs to determine the student's entry level for instruction by reviewing the goals and objectives on the IEP and completing a task analysis on the objectives. If it is determined that the student's goals and objectives differ *substantially* from those of other students, a change in the regular curriculum will be needed to accommodate the delayed achievement level.

In such cases, the appropriateness of placing a particular handicapped student in the regular classes should be carefully reviewed. If the student's needs for specially designed instruction cannot be accomplished within the framework of the regular curriculum, a more specialized setting may be required. In some instances, it may be appropriate to keep the student in a regular class setting and to make substantial curriculum changes.

The instructional strategies discussed in the next section apply to all three levels of curriculum adaptation—supplementing, simplifying, and changing (Howell & Morehead, 1987). Because of the extent of specially designed instruction required to teach a modified curriculum, such instructional strategies are essential.

ADAPTATIONS IN INSTRUCTIONAL STRATEGIES

After the curriculum content of the handicapped student's program has been appropriately modified, the next major consideration is devising instructional strategies to package and teach the content specified by the goals and objectives. Instructional strategies, as used here, refer to methods and/or materials for delivering instruction. When mainstreaming handicapped students in the regular classroom, it is essential that the methods and materials used are not only effective for the handicapped student but also manageable for teachers, in the light of their responsibilities to the other students in the class.

This section discusses five instructional strategies, including changes in the format of materials discussed, changes in the input and output requirements of tasks, tutorial programs, contracts, and educational technology.

Changes in Format

The special needs of many students can be accommodated by changing the format of materials, directions, or assignments. This is one of the simplest adaptations to make. Examples of special needs that may require format changes are:

- Short attention span—student can maintain attention to task only for relatively short intervals;
- Distractibility—student is distracted or attention is diverted by an overload of stimuli on a worksheet;
- Hypoactivity—student is slow and lethargic, taking an excessive amount of time to complete an assignment;
- Memory problems—student has trouble remembering directions and frequently forgets important points.

To accommodate special needs associated with short attention spans, assignments can be divided into smaller units or reduced in length. This type of adaptation can also help students who are hypoactive. A secondary language arts teacher described the use of such an adaptation.

The note from the Learning Center teacher said, "Very slow worker. Ability higher than you might suppose, like vocabulary." "Very slow" is an understatement. Stephen speaks at about 60 words a minute and he writes correspondingly. My Reading Improvement class uses vocabulary tests as well as individual oral book reports. Stephen is in a class with 23 other students; time was clearly going to be a real problem. After several weeks of trying to give Stephen's vocabulary with the rest of his group, it became obvious that this would not work. So with Stephen, I gave him 10 words and then randomly selected 5 of them for him to use in sentences instead of all 10. I also explained the reason why his was being done differently. He had often come to me saying "I didn't have time to finish this" or "Can I finish this tomorrow?" By giving him 5 words, he was able to finish on time and feel successful with having finished his assignment. We still had the problem of Stephen's oral book reports. After one disastrous attempt with his giving me his report during the class hour as the usual procedure, he was embarrassed, waiting students were frustrated, and I was frantically trying to cope with all of this. Sometimes I wonder why it takes me so long to come up with a solution when it is so apparent. I have a study hall 5th hour. Stephen is in the Learning Center 5th hour. The two rooms are next door. Solution:

Stephen comes into my study hall and gives his book reports. We have all the time we need; he enjoys the lack of pressure, the other 23 students can have more of my attention during class.

Format adaptations can also be made by providing shorter work periods with more frequent activity changes than are typically used. Teachers can consider several types of work periods for students with short attention spans, such as:

1. warm-up activity—individual activity completed at a learning center;
2. main activity—usually teacher directed; and
3. cool-down—can be done alone or with peers.

Another strategy for breaking up work periods is to schedule preferred and less preferred activities alternatively. While working on less preferred activity, the student can eagerly anticipate completing a favorite activity. This strategy is called Premack's Principle (Premack, 1959) and can lead to improved academic behavior when properly used (Gallant, Sargeant, & Van Houten, 1980) (see chapter 10).

Misunderstanding or forgetting directions to tasks, or confusion over the sequence of steps to solve problems, can also be overcome through format changes. Some students benefit from simplified directions or cues that prompt them in a correct response. Such cues are an example of a correct response or an outline of the steps to follow in completing a task. A first-grade teacher finds the following format adaptation successful in insuring that directions are understood and tasks accurately completed.

A student who recently entered my classroom has extreme difficulty transferring work from the board onto paper. He copies what he sees but has no idea of placement. To aid this student, I have found it very helpful if I make a copy of the day's assignment on a piece of paper exactly the way I want it copied. He then can visualize it on paper and know exactly what I expect from him.

When practicing writing, he has difficulty with letter placement, size, and spacing. For this assignment, I use a colored marker to write the letters, words, or sentence on his writing paper. Again, he can see the correct way I want him to write.

Math is another difficult area for this child. When presenting a new concept, I always have a few students come to the board to insure that I have made myself clear. This student is always called on so I can clearly see if and where he is having difficulty. When giving a math assignment, I stand near his table and point out everything on his paper that I am explaining, step by step. After I have given the assignment, I work with him individually, making sure he fully understands what he is supposed to do. When I feel he does understand, I let him finish alone.

**Changes in Input or Output
Requirements**

All students, handicapped and nonhandicapped, have preferred modes of
receiving information (input) and expressing known information (output).
Alternative input and output modes are depicted in Table 7.2. Five input

TABLE 7.2 Alternative Input and Output Requirements

Input/Data Collection

View/Observe	Read	Listen
visuals	books	radio
bulletin boards	comic books	records
banners	pamphlets	TV
posters	posters	speeches
transparencies	newspapers	lectures
slides	bulletin boards	debates
films/filmstrips	flash cards	discussions
flashcards	reports	dramatics
TV	wall graffiti	interpretive readings
graphs	letter	concerts
community events		interviews
field trips	*Smell/Taste/Touch*	
dramatic presentations		*Try/Do/Use*
nature/animals	objects	
diorama	textures	games
collage	foods	experiments
scroll	temperatures	exercises
sand painting	chemicals	manipulative materials
diary		theme
pictograph	*Solve*	research paper
media presentations		report
maps	puzzles	workbook answers
models	mazes	blackboard problems
timelines	problems	poems
leaf prints	equations	essays
paintings	games	
food	riddles	*Perform*
clothing		
bulletin board		simulation
banner		role play
graph		sociodrama
work wall drawings		concert
		pantomime
		interpretive reading

Source: From *Facilitator Manual, Teacher Training Program. Mainstreaming Mildly Handicapped Students
in the Regular Classroom* by P. B. Smith and G. Bentley, 1975. Austin, TX: Copyright 1975 by Education
Service Center, Region XIII. Reprinted by permission.

methods are identified: view/observe, read, listen, smell/taste/touch, and try/do/use. The five output methods include make/construct, verbalize, write, solve, and perform. This model suggests that many different instructional strategies can be used to teach the same skill or concept. Table 7.3 uses this model to provide an example of alternative instructional strategies that can be used in a social studies class to teach the concept of democratic decision-making.

In reviewing Tables 7.2 and 7.3, it is obvious that certain input and output modes are more appropriate than others in meeting the special

TABLE 7.3   Alternative Input and Output Modes for Concept of Democratic Decision-Making

Input Modes

View/Observe	*Read*	*Listen*
Watch film on voting procedures	Read newspaper acount of committee meetings	Listen to tape of political speakers
Observe political candidates and visit their offices	Review results of elections	
	Read books on democracy	*Try/Do/Use*
Observe meetings of school committee, school board, and local government	*Smell/Taste/Touch*	Practice using voting machine; fill out ballot
		Conduct a mock election
		Participate in club and civic organizations
		Conduct a meeting with Robert's Rules of Order

Output Modes

Make/Construct	*Verbalize*	*Solve*
Make political posters	Make speeches in favor of or against a candidate or proposal	Compute the percentage of votes each candidate receives
Construct bulletin board displays	Prepare oral questions and answers for school elections	Conduct a poll and compute probability that a candidate will win
Make local voting maps of districts and precincts		
	Write	*Perform*
	Write campaign slogans	Set up and hold mock elections
	Write essay on previous elections	Role play committee decision-making process; deal with a classsroom problem and propose solution

needs of students with different handicaps. Blind students would need input modes other than viewing/observing or reading print; hearing-impaired students, however, could benefit from these modes. Mentally retarded or learning-disabled students may need the output mode of making/constructing; students with mobility impairments may require adaptations in these types of activities.

Much stress is typically placed on the reading, writing, and listening skills of students. From an observational analysis of secondary classes in the areas of language arts, science, and social studies, Moran (1980) found that the predominant input mode is lecture. Teachers rarely asked questions or provided opportunities for students to respond verbally in class. Student output was primarily obtained through written performance. From self-report data collected, it is interesting to learn that teachers perceived themselves as lecturing less and asking more questions of students.

One method to alter the format of materials for pupils with low reading ability is to provide cassette tapes of printed material. Verbatim recordings of printed text require excessive time to listen. Consequently, Deshler and Graham (1980) have suggested guidelines for tape-recording text for handicapped pupils, including organizing information for enhanced comprehension. A scheme for taping portions of text verbatim, paraphrasing some portions, and omitting some text is suggested. Printed text is marked so that students can follow which portions are read verbatim, paraphrased, or omitted. Additionally, text can be marked to indicate where oral directions for activities are provided on tape. An example of marking on text is illustrated in Figure 7.1.

One technique that can help both handicapped and nonhandicapped students use printed materials is the use of advance organizers. Advance organizers are activities at the beginning of the lesson or reading to help the student take advantage of the material. Lenz (1983) provides these examples:

> "Today we are going to continue to discuss American citizenship."
> "Before we start, I want to give you an overview of the lesson that will help you to follow the lesson better. I suggest you take some notes on my overview."
> "Two words you should know before we start are (write on board):
> *telethon*—a special fund raising program for TV
> *deduct*—this means to take away"
> "At the end of today's lesson you should be able to state the different ways candidates can get money from supporters, and how they can spend it." (p. 13)

These examples could be used together or individually. Lenz (1983) also has provided 10 steps in developing an advance organizer (see Table 7.4).

Many historians consider that James K. Polk, who became President in 1845, was uncommunicative, narrow-minded, and intensely partisan. Yet, few Presidents have been more successful. Polk knew what he wanted, and he was a hard worker. He was a friend and disciple of his fellow Tennessean Andrew Jackson, and Polk's followers liked to call him "Young Hickory." Polk shared both Jackson's political outlook and Jackson's belief in a strong Presidency.

On his first day in office, Polk told a member of his Cabinet that, as President, he had four great goals: 1) to lower the tariff, 2) to reestablish the Independent Treasury System abolished by the Whigs in 1842, 3) to annex California, and 4) to settle the Oregon question. ☆

In 1846, under the President's urging, Congress restored the Independent Treasury System and passed the Walker tariff, which reduced duties on imported goods but did not entirely abandon protection. The acquisition of California and an

Oregon settlement proved much more difficult to achieve, though Polk was successful in these areas too.

The Question of California   In the 1840's, America's interest turned to California. New Englanders who had traded with California for 50 years described the region as "the richest, most beautiful, the healthiest country in the world." In the 1840's, after four rebellions it became clear that the unstable Mexican government could not govern this region effectively. Fearing that Great Britain, or France, might annex California to gain the great harbor of San Francisco, President Polk began to maneuver to acquire California.

Late in 1845 Polk sent John Slidell as his envoy to Mexico to discuss the question of the Texas border. He also told Slidell to buy both California and the area between it and Texas, known as New Mexico. However, Mexican officials were so angered at the loss of Texas that they refused to meet with Slidell, and he returned to Washington.

Source: From *Heritage of Freedom: History of the United States* (p. 324) by D. A. Ritchie, 1985. New York: Macmillan. Copyright 1985 by Macmillan Publishing Company, a division of Macmillan. Used by permission of Glencoe/McGraw-Hill, a Macmillan/McGraw-Hill Company.

Key: taped verbatim |
paraphrased 〈
omitted ⋮
added activity not in text   ☆

FIGURE 7.1   Example of Markings on Text That Has Been Taped

Advance organizers can be presented orally and in other ways. Brief outlines at the beginning of a selection are one kind of advance organizer. An illustration in the form of a diagram or a picture can aid in understanding and preparing for what will follow. Darch and Carnine (1986) used an overhead projector in a science class to present a visual spatial display of the relationships of various concepts in the units to students with learning

TABLE 7.4 Steps in Developing an Advance Organizer

Step 1: Inform students of advance organizers
    a. Announce advance organizer
    b. State benefits of advance organizer
    c. Suggest that students take notes on the advance organizer
Step 2: Identify topics of tasks
    a. Identify major topics or activities
    b. Identify subtopics or component activities
Step 3: Provide an organizational framework
    a. Present an outline, list, or narrative of the lesson's content
Step 4: Clarify action to be taken
    a. State teachers' actions
    b. State student's actions
Step 5: Provide background information
    a. Relate topic to the course or previous lesson
    b. Relate topic to new information
Step 6: State the concepts to be learned
    a. State specific concepts/ideas from the lesson
    b. State general concepts/ideas broader than the lesson's content
Step 7: Clarify the concepts to be learned
    a. Clarify by examples or analogies
    b. Clarify by nonexamples
    c. Caution students of possible misunderstandings
Step 8: Motivate students to learn
    a. Point out relevance to students
    b. Be specific, short-term, personalized, and believable
Step 9: Introduce vocabulary
    a. Identify the new terms and define
    b. Repeat difficult terms and define
Step 10: State the general outcome desired
    a. State objectives of instruction/learning
    b. Relate outcomes to test performance

Source: From "Using Advance Organizers" by B. K. Lenz, 1983, *The Pointer, 27,* p. 12. Copyright 1983 by B. K. Lenz. Reprinted by permission.

disabilities. The performance of students in this group was superior to that of students who did not have this advance organizer.

Using advance organizers can help low-achieving students who may be passive learners, who seldom use prior knowledge, or who have organizational problems. For example, previewing difficult reading material is an effective strategy. Previewing is a form of advance organizer (Graves, Cooke, & Laberge, 1983), and previews, written in paragraph form of from 300 to 600 words, allow learners to gain specific information that helps them understand new material.

Just as advance organizers help learners at the beginning of a lesson, postorganizers can help at the end of a lesson or reading activity. Postorganizers usually take the form of summaries or paraphrases (Hare & Borchardt, 1984; Reis & Leone, 1987).

Lovitt, Rudsit, Jenkins, Pious, and Benedetti (1986) have researched two adaptations of materials and methods in science—Precision Teaching and a Study Guide method. Used to teach science to seventh graders, including handicapped pupils, both methods helped all pupils achieve more than with traditional methods.

The Precision Teaching method involves the construction of worksheets on which major ideas, vocabulary words, and definitions are randomly printed and repeated several times. Students write in missing elements. Students practice until they can fill in blanks as quickly as more advanced students. Figure 7.2 shows an example.

The Study Guide method features a framed outline that has a sequenced listing of the chapter's main ideas with words or phrases left out. As the instructor lectures, students fill in the items on their outline. Figure 7.3 provides an example.

It is clear that many handicapped students can benefit greatly from instructional strategies that are individualized according to their special learning needs. Adapting input and output modes is an excellent strategy for meeting individual needs. As an example, many students with learning disabilities, mental retardation, and visual impairments benefit from using manipulative objects to supplement lessons that might otherwise be too abstract for them. It is possible for the handicapped student to deal initially with a concept in some concrete way and still participate in class discussions and group projects. A compact, simple way to provide manipulative materials is illustrated in Figure 7.4. Pockets attached to file folders can be used to store concrete learning materials that help in the development of concepts. Such folders can be prepared as supplements to regular textbook or group assignments.

If classroom teachers have questions about the ideal input and output modes to use with handicapped students, they should raise these questions at the IEP meeting and discuss appropriate alternatives with the committee members. It is important for classroom and resource teachers to share information throughout the school year on the success they are having with various input/output modes.

Tutorial Programs

Many different types of tutorial programs can be devised in the regular classroom to provide individualized instruction to handicapped students. Tutors can include peers, paraprofessionals, parents, and community volunteers.

Peer tutoring has become a popular and prevalent strategy in many regular classrooms. In comparing teacher preferences for peer, parent, or

Vocabulary Words
theory
kinetic-molecular theory
phlogiston
experimentalist
theorists
hypothesis
testing a theory

Chapter 4: Experimenting: Section: Why Do Experiments:
Student _____
Data _____
Teacher _____
Period _____

People used to believe that _____ had something to do with burning.	A _____ is an idea or principle that scientists believe to be true.
A _____ is an idea or principle that scientists believe to be true.	The idea that matter is made up of tiny, fast-moving particles is the _____.
Scientists who make observations and gather information from experiments are _____.	People used to believe that _____ had something to do with burning.
The idea that matter is made up of tiny, fast-moving particles is the _____.	Scientists who try to explain discoveries and observations are _____.
To find out if a prediction based on a theory works, or has to be thrown out, is called _____.	Scientists who make observations and gather information from experiments are _____.
A possible answer to a question is a _____.	A possible answer to a question is a _____.
	Scientists who try to explain discoveries and observations are _____.

FIGURE 7.2 Example of Worksheet Used in Precision Teaching

(continued)

To find out if a prediction based on a theory works, or has to be thrown out, is called ____.	A ____ is an idea or principle that scientists believe to be true.	A possible answer to a question is a ____.	Scientists who try to explain discoveries and observations are ____.	People used to believe that ____ had something to do with burning.
A possible answer to a question is a ____.	To find out if a prediction based on a theory works, or has to be thrown out, is called ____.	Scientists who make observations and gather information from experiments are ____.	The idea that matter is made up of tiny, fast-moving particles is the ____.	A ____ is an idea or principle that scientists believe to be true.

Source: From "Adapting Science Materials for Regular and Learning Disabled Seventh Graders" by T. Lovitt, J. Rudsit, J. Jenkins, C. Pious, & D. Benedetti, 1986, *Remedial and Special Education, 7,* p. 33. Copyright 1986 by Pro-Ed Journals. Reprinted with permission from *Remedial and Special Education,* 1986.

FIGURE 7.2 (continued)

Chapter 4   Framed Outline # 2   Pages 83–87
Student _____   Teacher _____
Data _____   Period _____

1. In experiments, we set up situations and make observations.
2. One kind of experiment is a control experiment. It has two parts: the test and the control.
3. The control experiment tests a variable by setting up a comparison between the test and the control.
4. The variable is the only difference in conditions between the test and the control, so your experiment tells you the effect of the variable.
5. Here is a control experiment:
   a. Make a hypothesis: If you add baking powder to a cake, then it will rise.
   b. Do the control experiment:
      Part one is the test. Bake a cake without baking powder.
      Part two is the control. Bake a cake with exactly the same ingredients, for exactly the same time, in exactly the same pan and oven, BUT add baking powder.
   c. Look at the results. Was your hypothesis right?
6. A theory is an idea that scientists believe to be true. It can explain something observed.
7. But how do we know whether the theory works?
8. We test the theory.
9. First, we develop a prediction based on the theory.
10. Remember, a prediction is a statement made in advance about how something will happen.
11. Next, we do an experiment to test whether the prediction is right.
12. Remember, in an experiment, we set up a situation and make observations.
13. If our prediction based on the theory is right, we can have confidence in the theory.

Source: From "Adapting Science Materials for Regular and Learning Disabled Seventh Graders" by T. Lovitt, J. Rudsit, J. Jenkins, C. Pious, and D. Benedetti, 1986, *Remedial and Special Education, 7,* p. 34. copyright 1986 by Pro-Ed Journals. Reprinted with permission from *Remedial and Special Education,* 1986.

FIGURE 7.3   Example of Study Guide

volunteer tutors, it has been reported that teachers prefer the use of student tutors (Semmel, Cohen, & Kandaswamy, 1980). Also, students find satisfaction in working together, recognizing that knowledge and skills can be shared in a profitable way. They soon realize that tutor and tutee learn from each other.

The integration of handicapped students into regular classrooms can be facilitated immeasurably by students teaching students. In any classroom, there is always a student asking for help and there is usually one giving it. When this occurrence is used systematically, it becomes a powerful instructional technique.

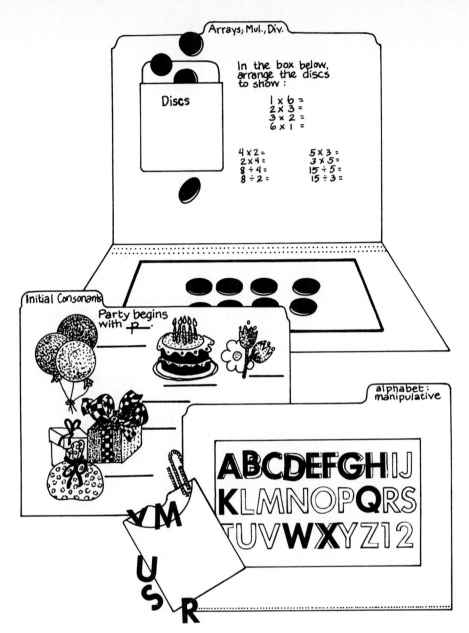

FIGURE 7.4   File Folders

Debbie, who receives help with math in the resource room, was reviewing multiplication tables. Kevin, who has severe emotional problems, was asked to help her. He used drill cards and became the "teacher." His self-image and Debbie's multiplication skills both improved.

Frequently, a nonhandicapped student will help a handicapped schoolmate. The process can and should work in reverse.

David, who is blind, has mastered the use of the Numberaid, a pocket-sized abacus. He was asked to demonstrate its use to a group of fourth graders who were having difficulty with the concepts of place value and regrouping.

Peer tutoring is a popular instructional arrangement. According to Scruggs and Richter (1988), who reviewed more than 20 studies of peer tutoring involving students with learning disabilities, no other approach equals peer tutoring in the enthusiasm it generates. The studies focused on the academic and social benefits to tutees and to tutors. Among the social benefits were on-task behavior, self-concept, attitude toward school, cooperation, and social behavior. Classroom teachers have used a variety of tutoring arrangements with a great likelihood of success primarily in reading and also spelling, math, social studies, and library skills.

Classwide peer tutoring has been used effectively with pupils with other kinds of handicaps (Delquadri, Greenwood, Whorton, Carta, & Hall, 1988). They cited peer tutoring programs involving students with learning disabilities, mental handicaps, behavioral disorders, hearing impairments, and autistic pupils, as well as young, high risk, and minority children. Delquadri et al. (1988) also used parents as tutors. The purposes of these tutoring programs have been to increase the students' opportunities to respond in instructional sessions and their key academic skills and also to improve key learning behaviors by such means as more frequent and direct reinforcement. One of the most important components of peer tutoring is the initial training of tutors using explanation, modeling, and practice with feedback. Tutor training is critical for successful classwide peer tutoring to work in the variety of settings, with the variety of students, and in the range of subject areas mentioned here.

Another approach involves the cooperative grouping of students as contrasted with the one-to-one tutoring model. Cooperative grouping involves structuring learning experiences for heterogeneous groups that include handicapped and nonhandicapped students. The group is given a task to complete and required to work together in sharing skills and giving assistance.

A junior high science teacher divided his class into cooperative groups (comprised of nonhandicapped and mentally handicapped students) to complete an array of projects and participate in curriculum-based games. One game involved the teacher's calling out questions for each group to answer. The first persons in the group to raise their hands and answer were not allowed to answer again until everyone else on the team had answered a question. Questions progressed from simple to hard. The outcomes of this game, according to the teacher's report, were very consistent: brighter students tended to coach the mentally handicapped students "for the sake of the team" and brighter students avoided answering easier questions that the handicapped students in the group could answer. The teacher enthusiastically cited a high level of cooperation among students and aid offered to the handicapped students, as well as an impressive percentage of correct responses.

Johnson and Johnson's research on the outcomes of cooperative learning (1980, 1984, 1986) indicates that cooperative learning situations promote higher achievement in all students, in addition to more social acceptance and friendships among handicapped and nonhandicapped students. This technique is discussed further in chapter 11.

Contracts

A contract is an agreement written for, by, or with the student. It provides opportunities for a student to learn independently and usually includes a variety of learning resources, such as tapes, records, books, films, pictures, loops, slides, and games (Dunn & Dunn, 1972). Contracts usually specify the type, amount, and quality of work to be completed by a student as well as the timeline. They cover academic as well as social behaviors and can be specially designed according to the individual needs of handicapped students. Contracts are particularly helpful for students with emotional problems who benefit from having contingencies clearly identified in advance. Students who are poorly motivated, or who are disorganized and frequently forget assignments, can also be aided by the use of contracts.

Contracts include behavioral objectives, a listing of many kinds of learning resources, and a series of activity alternatives that provide the student choices in applying and reporting gathered information. Contracts may be primarily determined and negotiated by teachers or by students. Blackburn and Powell (1976) define the following types of contracts:

- Structured contracts, in which all components are predetermined by the teacher. The student and the teacher negotiate a contract from these components.
- Partly structured contracts, in which some components are predetermined by the teacher and others are designed and developed by the teacher and the student.
- Mutually structured contracts, in which no components are predetermined; the teacher and the student cooperatively develop and negotiate the contract.
- Unstructured contracts, in which no components are predetermined; the student initiates and develops the parts and negotiates with the teacher.

Teachers should systematically encourage students to assume increasing responsibility for devising their own contracts. Many different forms can be used for contracts, including commercial forms produced by some publishers.

Contracts help remove the time variable from learning and permit students to work at their own pace. With the choices provided, they allow students to achieve independence and to assume responsibility for learning. Contracts also allow the teacher to prescribe activities on individual bases for many students. As students engage in contract activities, the teacher has time to spend with those students encountering difficulties or needing assistance. Figure 7.5 is an example of a contract.

Educational Technology

The rapid increase in educational technology has great potential for enhancing the degree of individualized instruction that can be provided to exceptional students. Some advances are currently being used extensively; others are emerging. The technologies include computer-assisted instruction (CAI), computer-based electronic games, computer simulations, adaptive devices, artificial intelligence applications, and robotics. These advances are discussed in order of most readily available and widely used. Of course, technology benefits all pupils, but it is discussed here as helping to implement individualized educational plans for handicapped pupils.

Objective and Activities:	Identify 15 plants in the chart below. You may use plants, labels, seed catalogs, and library reference books.
	1. Fill in the plant name.
	2. Draw a leaf.
	3. Draw the flower if there is one.
	4. Identify the plant type (annual, biennial, perennial).
	5. Give the use of the plant (potting plant, bedding plant, shrub, tree, etc.)
	6. Tell or show how the plant may be propagated (seed, leaf cutting, stem cutting, etc.)
Evaluation	100% of activities completed
	Criteria for grade include accuracy, neatness, and promptness of completion
Timeline:	Due one week after contract is signed
Date Signed: _____	
Student: _____	
Teacher: _____	
Date Contract Completed: _____	

Source: Adapted from Simulated Work Laboratory, J. P. Schulz, Unpublished program of instruction, 1972.

FIGURE 7.5 Responsibility Contract: Plant Identification

Computer Applications

Although the cost of computers has been prohibitive for many schools, the availability of computers has made computer-assisted instruction a reality for providing effective individualized instruction. The computer language LOGO, developed by Papert (1980) at MIT and based on the work of Piaget, teaches computer programming, problem solving, and mathematical thinking to students who are handicapped as well as to those who are gifted. This program has been successful with autistic, orthopedically handicapped, and learning-disabled students (Torgeson, 1986; Weir & Watt, 1981).

According to Wieck (1980) and Yeager (1977), evaluations of the computer program PLATO in teaching number concepts and reading skills (word attack, encoding, decoding, and comprehension) to exceptional students indicate successful applications.

Computers have made two other major contributions to instruction. They have made writing (called *word processing* when accomplished with computer assistance) much easier for many students because of the capabilities to edit and check such mechanical aspects as spelling, punctuation, and capitalization. Computers' other contribution has been in software programs, which provide direct instruction and drill and practice in a more individualized way without the traditional demands on the teacher's time.

Writing with word processors has helped exceptional students in several ways. Their written products are longer and easier to read than are handwritten pages and misspellings are fewer (Lerner, 1989; Outhred,

1989; Vacc, 1987). Even though the quality has not been shown to have improved (Daiute, 1986; MacArthur & Graham, 1987; Vacc, 1987), learners do seem to be more eager to write and revise and more confident (Lerner, 1989; MacArthur, 1988; Outhred, 1989; Rust, 1986). Writing with word processors may help children who have poor handwriting skills, but it also means that students must learn some basic computer keyboarding or typing skills in order to become computer literate (Cohen, Torgeson, & Torgeson, 1988; Eagan & Wilson, 1983).

The most frequent use of computers in schools is with commercial or public domain software programs that provide basic instruction, drill, and practice. When students need practice on a particular skill or concept, the computer program draws questions from the data bank, presents them to the student, and provides immediate feedback on the accuracy of the student's response. Frequently, handicapped students have a slower learning rate and thus require more practice. Computer-assisted instruction (CAI) in this area can increase student performance and decrease daily teacher responsibility for locating and correcting appropriate worksheets.

CAI in drill and practice applications includes math facts and operations, science and social studies information, and reading vocabulary. The advantages of such programs are that they can be presented individually, provide immediate feedback, and can be tailored for level of difficulty and rate. Most software programs also automatically record progress.

Basic instruction delivered with computer programs varies in kind and use of effective instructional principles. Many programs do not provide the specific direct instructional components that handicapped learners require and are unsuitable for use with them. However, some of these programs may be suitable for gifted learners, who need little explanation. Such programs allow gifted students to proceed with little or no teacher assistance.

Instructional courseware (computer software for instruction) used effectively with handicapped pupils includes commercial and teacher-made programs. Some programs developed by teachers assess spelling performance and provide minimal instruction in spelling (Hasselbring, 1984; Hasselbring & Crossland, 1982). Researchers in two studies have emphasized the need to adapt commercial educational software for use with handicapped pupils. Gersten, Carnine, and Woodward (1987) reported that a program to teach vocabulary words was devised to teach fewer words at a time and to provide more practice than a popular commercially available program. Handicapped pupils using the experimental program performed better than did those using the commercially produced program. In a similar vein, researchers studied the use of two versions of a program designed to increase the sight-word reading vocabulary of children with reading disabilities. Although both versions were equally effective in increasing vocabulary, students enjoyed the version that required no typing more than the one that required typing; they also learned words at a faster rate when typing was not required. (Cohen, Torgeson, & Torgeson, 1988). These results underscore the need for classroom teachers to choose computer software carefully.

The selection of software is a key factor in the effective use of computer-assisted instruction. When the goal is to individualize instruction for exceptional students, software selection must take into account the educational characteristics of these students (Taymans & Malouf, 1984). Lee (1987) has investigated courseware and proposed some of the first empirically derived guidelines for selecting courseware to be used with students with learning disabilities. These guidelines are presented in Table 7.5.

Computer technology has also contributed to the proliferation of electronic games used successfully in the individualization process. *Speak*

TABLE 7.5 Guidelines for Selecting Computer Software for Use with Students with Learning Disabilities

Essential Components

1. Directions the students most need should be simple and not interfere with the students' comprehension.
2. The courseware must provide alternate means of presenting the same concept if students do not comprehend the first presentation (recasting).
3. The screen must be uncluttered.
4. Students should be able to operate the program with minimal keyboard skills.
5. The program must provide praise/feedback regarding the correctness or incorrectness of response.
6. The courseware must provide adequate opportunities for students to review concepts.
7. The software must teach very basic skills that nonhandicapped students would learn incidentally.

Secondary Desired Components

8. The program requires students to respond in some manner before moving to the next frame.
9. Adequate prompts are embedded in the program to curtail the impulsive student and encourage the hesitant student.
10. Double spacing is used between lines of type.
11. The program provides for overlearning.
12. The program uses effective animation, color-cuing, and/or underlining to focus students' attention on relevant aspects to be learned.
13. Answers are multiple choice rather than requiring students to compose answers.
14. The type of lettering is conducive to preventing reversals.
15. The program provides for competition.
16. The program has a speech synthesizer (or the potential for a speech synthesizer).

Source: Adapted from Lee, 1987, p. 437.

and Read, Speak and Spell, and *The Little Professor* provide entertaining and intensive skill development and problem solving in the areas of reading, spelling, and mathematics. *Speak and Read* provides practice in phonics, sight words, and comprehension. Through the various games that can be played, students have an opportunity to hear, see, pronounce, and spell words by pressing letters. Students can also punch in the letters of unfamiliar words that they encounter during silent reading, and the machine will pronounce the word for them (if the word is in the *Speak and Read* bank). Such individual assistance can free teachers from having to identify words for students. Other electronic games also are timely, motivating, and filled with instructional possibilities. Drawbacks to some games are that the size and type of controls require fine manipulations and that the speed of play may be too fast for some handicapped students.

Computer simulation uses a computer-controlled sensory or motor experience that provides an individual with exposure to and involvement in an artificial environmental setting (Yin & Moore, 1987). For example, computer simulations are used for games that give the player the feeling of driving in an auto race or flying a plane. They are used in several kinds of instructional situations.

Videodisc technology, a burgeoning part of computer-simulation technology, uses an interactive format. Computer graphics, sound effects, highlights, and other techniques help provide vivid visual demonstrations for nearly every concept presented. According to Hofmeister (1989), several hundred videodiscs are being used in regular and special education classes covering such topics as fractions (Miller & Cooke, 1989), chemistry, earth science, and also decimals and word problems in mathematics. A recent study used videodisc technology in a course teaching basic fractions to handicapped pupils (Kelly, Carnine, Gersten, & Grossen, 1987). The videodisc group's performance exceeded that of a group using a basic textbook (Kelly et al., 1987).

> When used in a group setting, the disc addresses a fundamental question faced by virtually all teachers: How can the teacher provide dynamic, powerful presentations and demonstrations in front of the class and still maintain extensive, individual contact to ensure that instruction is consistently adapted to meet the needs of students? Most teachers address this problem by spending approximately half their time in front of the class and half on the classroom floor observing and contacting individuals. With the aid of videodisc players and well-designed videodiscs, teachers can spend the majority of their time in individual contact with their students and direct the presentations with remote control. (Hofmeister, 1989, p. 53)

Another advantage to schools is that videodiscs are more durable than are other media, such as audio cassette tapes and videotapes, because they are not subject to stretching and winding.

Adaptive Technology and Artificial Intelligence

Educational technology also has designed and manufactured such adaptive devices as language boards for students who cannot talk and switches to operate a variety of equipment, like tape players. These innovations have been most helpful for students with physical impairments.

Artificial intelligence involves the use of a computer to conduct the types of problem solving and decision making people face in dealing with the world (Yin & Moore, 1987). Artificial intelligence applications have not yet reached school classrooms from their medical practice and postsecondary settings.

Robotics involves the use of reprogrammable, multifunctional manipulators designed to move materials, parts, tools, or specialized devices through variable programmed motions. Robotics is a fast-emerging area for students with physical handicaps and promises to help students in mainstreamed settings. Unfortunately, the cost is high and the use of robotics technology in school settings appears rare (Yin & Moore, 1987).

COORDINATING INSTRUCTION BETWEEN THE CLASSROOM AND SPECIAL EDUCATION SERVICES

A misconception about mainstreaming is that classroom teachers will have to go it alone. Actually, the mainstreaming process requires a great deal of ancillary help from special education resource teachers, itinerant teachers, and related service providers, such as speech therapists, adaptive physical education teachers, and occupational therapists. Other support and advice will come from psychologists, social workers, parents, volunteers, college personnel and students, paraprofessionals, and peer tutors.

In order to achieve the optimum benefit from special education services provided by resource teachers and related service providers, it is essential to coordinate these services carefully with the regular classroom program. Two important issues of coordination involve scheduling and communication.

Scheduling

When direct services are provided by an itinerant or resource teacher or related service provider, scheduling student time away from the regular classroom may become difficult. Although proper scheduling requires time and attention, it is extremely important for smoother operation and good working relationships. The classroom teacher should consider several time blocks during which handicapped students could be away from the classroom without jeopardizing their instructional program. Generally, it is wise to schedule special student services during the period of the subject being remediated. For instance, if students are provided with special services in reading, they should be taken from the class during the regular reading period. Thus, they will be absent from class during a time when they do not usually experience success. Also, they will not miss instruction in other important subject areas.

Students typically should not be scheduled for direct services during physical education, music, art, or library classes. Handicapped students usually enjoy and need this instruction; the resource room should not be punitive.

Scheduling preferences of teachers and students can be discussed at the IEP meeting. It is important for classroom teachers to state their preferences and negotiate for a convenient arrangement. If the schedule is in the student's best interest and manageable for both the classroom and resource teachers, the program will be more likely to succeed. It is extremely important for all teachers to adhere to the determined schedule. From the resource teacher's point of view, every minute counts because students are usually scheduled in short, consecutive blocks. From the classroom teacher's point of view, lack of adherence to the schedule can mean interruptions in group activities. Handicapped students should be taught and expected to assume responsibility for leaving the regular classroom at the appropriate time in order to arrive punctually for their special services.

Communication

Communication among regular classroom teachers, resource teachers, and related service providers is an essential ingredient of successful mainstreaming programs. This communication should begin at the IEP meeting and continue throughout the school year as the IEP is implemented.

At the IEP meeting, the roles of the various persons responsible for the handicapped student's program should be clarified. It should be specified at that time which teacher or related service provider will be primarily responsible for teaching each objective, providing each service, and meeting the special needs identified as essential in providing the student with an appropriate education. Also, a plan can be devised at the IEP meeting to maintain communication throughout the year. Such a plan could schedule periodic review meetings for teachers to discuss the student's progress, or set up a notebook the student could take back and forth from the classroom teacher to the resource teacher. This notebook would include comments on the student's progress and any special concerns noted by either teacher.

Johnny completed his math quiz with 100 percent accuracy today. I am really proud of him. The use of manipulative objects and the practice sheets he has been completing at home seem to be a very successful strategy for him.

Maria had an argument with several of her friends at recess, which resulted in a great deal of anger and frustration. Her work is likely to be affected by her disposition.

Next week we will be starting a unit on erosion. Jason has a list of vocabulary words for this unit in his notebook. I would appreciate it if you would help him with the meaning and spelling of these words. It would give him a head start on keeping up with our unit work. Thanks very much. Your assistance is invaluable to him and to me.

As instructional strategies are planned and implemented throughout the year, ongoing communication and coordination are vitally important. Many resource programs have failed because the special educator and the classroom teacher did not have time to communicate and to coordinate services. Frequently, the result is that instruction provided in the resource room has no relation to that provided in the regular classroom. Classroom teachers and resource teachers do not have to use identical instructional approaches; however, their approaches should be complementary. It is essential that the classroom teacher and the special educator have established times, convenient for both, to talk, plan, and explore ways of mutually assisting handicapped students in achieving success.

EVALUATION PROCEDURES AND GRADING

A high school social studies teacher, who has been the recipient of several teaching awards during her 18 years of experience, recently commented, "I believe grading and grade reporting are the most difficult tasks for the classroom teacher." Most teachers would probably agree with her perspective. The evaluation dilemma is even more complex for handicapped students who require specially designed instruction in the regular classroom. The challenge for educators is to devise fair systems that accomplish the purpose of evaluation while considering the interests of both handicapped and nonhandicapped students.

Evaluation is a means of informing students, parents, and teachers of the students' achievement (both strengths and weaknesses) and the areas that need attention. This type of information should lead to appropriate decision making about the nature of the students' educational program and career choices. Thus, evaluating student progress and reporting grades should enhance the quality and appropriateness of educational and vocational decisions (Carpenter, Grantham, & Hardister, 1983).

Teachers should never underestimate the impact that grades have on both students and parents. They can strongly influence the student's self-concept, attitude toward school, peer relationships, development of hobbies, and level of motivation. For parents, grades can play a large role in shaping parental expectations, defining priorities for the use of time at home, and influencing the quality of the parent-child relationship. Evaluating student progress and reporting grades thus become major responsibilities for teachers.

This section focuses on two aspects of the evaluation process: the individualization of classroom evaluation procedures, criteria, and schedules and methods for assigning and reporting grades.

Individualization of Evaluation

Just as the curriculum should be adapted in light of the special needs of handicapped students, so should the evaluation procedures. The beginning point for planning such adaptations is the IEP conference. One required component of the IEP is the specification of evaluation procedures, criteria, and schedules. At the IEP conference, classroom teachers have an opportunity to work with the other committee members in planning for evaluation that reflects the particular student's special needs and the goals and objectives that have been determined appropriate for the student.

Clearly, there is no best evaluation system that can be applied to every mainstreamed student. There are, however, general principles and guidelines that can be helpful in making these evaluation decisions at the IEP conference and implementing them in the classroom.

Evaluation Procedures

Evaluation procedures refer to the types of assessment instruments used. There are two important guidelines to consider. The first is that students should be evaluated on the curriculum they have been taught. Thus, if the student's curriculum has been simplified or changed, evaluation procedures need to be adapted accordingly. Evaluation procedures should be tailored to the content (goals and objectives) of the student's program.

Criterion-referenced tests have a particular advantage because they include a listing of objectives the student is expected to learn, criteria for mastery of the objectives, and test questions keyed to the objectives. By using criterion-referenced tests, the progress of students is assessed in relation to their starting point rather than an arbitrary normative standard. Criterion-referenced tests also are readily transferable into checklists that can be used to report progress to parents, as discussed in the next section. In addition to criterion-referenced tests, other types of appropriate evaluation procedures include observation, teacher-made tests, review of assignments, and student self-reports.

The goals and objectives comprising the student's program constitute one basis for selecting evaluation procedures. Decisions must also be made on other areas of evaluation, such as the student's effort, social adjustment, work habits, and peer relationships. Most school districts have written policies on target areas for evaluation. The first step for teachers is to review these policies carefully. If the teacher believes that modifications in the policies are necessary in light of the needs of a handicapped student, such modifications should be discussed with the principal.

The second guideline is that some students will need adaptations in the way evaluation procedures are administered, just as they need adaptations in the way instruction is delivered. The earlier discussion in this chapter regarding changes in the format of materials and directions and changes to input or output requirements applies to evaluation as well as instruction. All the alternative output modes illustrated in Table 7.2 can be translated into evaluation procedures.

It is obvious from reviewing Table 7.2 that many evaluation procedures can be used as alternatives to tests. The performance of some students will increase according to the output mode used. Through a review of the student's performance, and discussion at the IEP meeting, teachers should identify the output mode best suited to the individual student's needs.

When traditional tests are administered, techniques can be used to insure that handicapped students are not at a disadvantage because of their special needs. Techniques in the areas of format considerations, test adaptations, technical aspects, and strategies for minimizing stress and strain are outlined by Regan (1979). Many of these suggestions are also highly appropriate for use with nonhandicapped students.

A secondary language arts teacher described adapted evaluation procedures that she found to be successful:

> Because of Michelle's cerebral palsy, handwriting is a very slow, deliberate effort. To compensate for this, I attempted to keep her writing tasks at a minimum on tests so that she would not be unfairly penalized.
>
> Those parts of tests which were essay in nature posed a particular problem. The best solution was to have her answer the questions orally. Sometimes she answered directly to me and other times she went into an adjoining work room and answered into a tape recorder. I could then play back her responses at a convenient time.
>
> When the tests involved theme writing, we again needed to make adjustments. One solution to the problem, which worked well, was to shorten the required length of her themes so that she could do all of the writing herself. She generally preferred to do the same work in the same manner as her classmates so this procedure was particularly effective. Another way we sometimes handled this was by having her use the tape recorder to record her thoughts. I would then write down what she had recorded and she would then go over it and finalize it before turning it in.

Evaluation Criteria

The evaluation criteria must be specified for each IEP objective. In making decisions pertaining to criteria, a major issue to consider is the referent for the criteria. Will the criteria be based on the norms for progress of nonhandicapped students at the same grade level or on the student's progress in relation to current level of performance? This fundamental decision involves specifying either a norm-referenced or criterion-referenced standard for setting criteria. Consistent with the philosophy of individualization, the criterion-referenced standard of evaluating students according to their progress on IEP goals and objectives is the most reasonable procedure. Particularly in the case of students whose achievement is significantly below grade level, expecting them to meet the standards of nonhandicapped students gives them no option but failure.

> *Don, a student identified as mentally retarded, was mainstreamed into a fourth-grade class for science, social studies, and music. His reading skills were at the first-grade level, and he had a great deal of difficulty with concept development. Don's teacher had ignored the IEP objectives and taught him on a fourth-grade level with no adaptations. His teacher used a norm-referenced standard of evaluation. Don tried very hard to do his assignments and worked far more diligently than most students in the class. But his achievement, as compared to others with normal ability, just didn't measure up. On his daily assignments and on his report card, he received an F in every subject. Is it Don who failed or was it really the teacher who failed?*

It is important to state the level of mastery that the student is expected to demonstrate on each objective. If an 80 percent criterion is agreed on for a given objective, then the teacher and student are clear about what constitutes an acceptable performance.

In addition to qualitative standards for criteria, quantitative standards can be set. In the development of contracts, as previously discussed, the teacher and student can agree on criteria for determining the successful completion of a project. Quantitative criteria could include the number of books read, worksheets completed, or problems solved. For handicapped students who work more slowly than other students, modifications can be made in quantitative criteria to adjust the level of expectation to their work pace.

Schedules

The schedule or frequency with which handicapped students are evaluated is an important consideration. Some handicapped students, particularly those who have experienced a high level of failure in the past, may benefit from more frequent evaluations to reassure them that they are making progress and to provide them with positive reinforcement. Also, some students who have learning and/or emotional problems may perform at an optimal level if given shorter quizzes on a smaller amount of material rather than longer exams covering an extensive amount of content. Thus, the schedule of evaluations may need to be specially designed to account for the strengths and weaknesses of a given student.

Assigning and Reporting Grades

Based on the classroom evaluations conducted on a daily, weekly, and monthly basis, teachers must formally assign grades to the students, report them to the students and parents, and record the grades in the students' permanent file. Again, there is no best system to handle the complexities of grading handicapped students, particularly those achieving significantly below grade level. As mentioned earlier, teachers need to familiarize themselves with the grading policies and forms of their school system. Some school systems have flexible policies; others have policies that place major restrictions on adaptive procedures. Thus, teachers need to be aware of the negotiable and nonnegotiable aspects in their own school system for individualizing grading procedures (Carpenter, 1985).

Another aspect of grading that is typically dictated by system policy is the schedule of reporting grades to parents. Schedules vary from a monthly to a quarterly basis.

This section presents two types of reporting systems—progress checklists and assignments of letter and number grades.

Progress Checklists

The use of progress checklists naturally follows if criterion-referenced assessment and instruction have been used. Based on IEP goals and objectives, this checklist would list skills and concepts taught in each subject area for the period of time covered by the reporting schedule. Columns can be provided for the teacher to check indicating whether each skill or concept has been "mastered" or "needs improvement." Figure 7.6 contains an example of a progress checklist. Space can be provided on the form for written comments pertaining to the student's strengths and weaknesses.

The advantage of using such a system is that grading is clearly based on the substance of the student's individualized curriculum. Additionally, parents and students are provided with specific information on skill development indicating the progress the student is making and the areas needing more concentrated effort. Such information can help parents select the skills and concepts to practice and reinforce at home.

Progress checklists also have disadvantages. Many school systems require the use of grades to compute grade-point averages. An alternative is to combine features of the checklist with the assignment of letter and number grades as discussed in the next section. Also, many handicapped students want to have report cards similar to those of their peers. Thus, if

		Objectives
Mastered	*Needs Improvement*	*Linear Measurement*
———	———	1. Identifies the number of inches in one foot with 100% accuracy.
———	———	2. Identifies the number of inches in one yard with 100% accuracy.
———	———	3. Identifies one inch with 100% accuracy.
———	———	4. Measures with 100% accuracy a 6-inch line drawn on paper, with 12-inch ruler.
———	———	5. Measures with 100% accuracy a $4^{1}/_{2}$-inch line drawn on paper, with 12-inch ruler.
———	———	6. Completes with 100% accuracy.
———	———	a. one foot = ———— inches.
———	———	b. one yard = ———— inches.
———	———	c. one yard = ———— feet.
———	———	7. Orders correctly from shortest to longest with 100% accuracy: 1 foot, 1 yard, 8 inches, and 24 inches.
———	———	8. Completes with 100% accuracy numerical problems in addition and subtraction involving inches, feet, and yards. No conversion required.
———	———	9. Completes with 100% accuracy word problems in addition and subtraction involving inches, feet, and yards. No conversion required.
———	———	10. Completes with 100% accuracy numerical problems in addition and subtraction involving inches, feet, and yards. Conversion required.
———	———	11. Completes with 100% accuracy word problems in addition and subtraction involving inches, feet, and yards. Conversion required.
———	———	12. Reads the following words with 100% accuracy.
———	———	a. foot
———	———	b. inch
———	———	c. yard

Source: From *Developing and Implementing Individualized Education Programs* (2nd ed.) (pp. 81–83) by A. P. Turnbull, B. Strickland, and J. C. Brantley, 1982. Columbus, OH: Merrill. Copyright 1982 by Charles E. Merrill Publishing Co. Adapted by permission.

FIGURE 7.6 Progress Checklist Based on Criterion-Referenced Assessment

nonhandicapped students do not receive progress checklists, many handicapped students may be embarrassed to receive such reports.

Letter and Number Grades
A combination of letters and numbers is probably the grading system used most frequently in schools. Two issues need to be resolved—the areas

around which letters and numbers are assigned and the criteria used to assign the grades.

The target areas around which grades are assigned and reported should depend on the areas that have been identified as vital to the student's educational program. The two areas routinely included on report cards include achievement and effort.

Achievement grades can be assigned in several ways:

1. Use criterion stated in IEP objective so that if a student masters an objective to 80 percent accuracy, a grade of B would be assigned. The subject grade would then be computed as an average of the objective grades.
2. A more global, IEP-based system could be used according to a scale such as:
   A——the student surpasses the expectations of the IEP
   B——the student meets IEP expectations
   C——the student performs somewhat below IEP standards and expectations
   D–F——the student performs significantly below IEP standards and expectations.
3. Letter grades can be used to indicate the extent of the student's progress in various subject areas.
   S——progress is satisfactory
   I——improving but not completely satisfactory
   N——needs to improve
   U——progress is unsatisfactory
   X——not being evaluated at this time

Reporting grades on the student's effort can also provide helpful information. This can be done using the satisfactory/unsatisfactory scale shown previously, or by using numbers. For example:

1——best effort
2——good effort but could work harder
3——poor effort——needs much improvement

Other areas that can be included in the grading system are social adjustment, work habits, and peer relationships.

An advantage of this system of letters and numbers is that it is likely to conform to the grading system used with nonhandicapped students. Thus, handicapped students would not have a different report card setting them apart from their peers or causing extra difficulty in the record-keeping system of the school. Also, the use of multiple grades helps insure that handicapped students are assessed over a broad spectrum of areas. Thus, they have the opportunity to receive feedback on their strengths as well as weaknesses.

A major disadvantage of letter and number grades that are criterion-referenced rather than norm-referenced is that the grades of handicapped students can be viewed as inflated compared to grades of nonhandicapped students (who have higher standards to meet in some subject areas in line with their higher ability). Some people argue that it is unfair for handicapped students to receive an A when their IEP objectives may be below grade-level expectations. One strategy for addressing this issue on a school district level is to devise a weighting system for academic credits as a basis for formulating grade-point averages. The following example of a weighting system uses a 4-point scale, so that for a given class:

1. Student 1, of average ability, does grade-level work and receives a grade of A and an assignment of 4 points;
2. Student 2, who is gifted, does accelerated work and receives a grade of A and an assignment of 5 points;
3. Student 3, a student who is learning disabled, does below grade-level work appropriate to his level of achievement and receives a grade of A and an assignment of 3 points.

Such a system enables students who meet grade-level or above expectations to be rewarded without depriving handicapped students of success.

These two strategies of progress checklists and assignment of letter and number grades primarily rely on a written reporting format. Both strategies, however, can be combined with a student and parent conference to explain the basis for grading, to highlight areas of the student's progress, and to pinpoint areas of needed improvement. Verbal communication can clarify areas of misunderstanding and can take into account the special needs of the student.

In summary, providing specially designed instruction to handicapped students requires individualization, and individualization requires creative teaching strategies. It is necessary for teachers to maintain perspective on both the challenge and reality of this task.

> Complete individualization is a goal for educators much as democracy is a goal for Americans or Christianity is a goal for Christians. Everyone in education should strive to reach the goal, knowing that complete individualization is rare, if not impossible. Anytime, however, that the school situation is focusing on the individual student in the teaching-learning process, another step is being made toward the ultimate goal. (Musgrave, 1975, p. x)

REFERENCES

Allen, J. B., Clark, F., Gallagher, P., & Scofield, F. (1982). *Classroom strategies for accommodating the exceptional learner.* Minneapolis: National Support Systems Project.

Bailey, D. B., & Leonard, J. (1977). A model for adapting Bloom's taxonomy to a preschool curriculum. *The Gifted Child Quarterly, 21,* (1), 97–103.

Blackburn, J. E., & Powell, W. C. (1976). *One at a time all at once: The creative teacher's guide to individualized instruction without anarchy.* Pacific Palisades, CA: Goodyear.

Carpenter, D. (1985). Grading handicapped pupils: Review and position statement. *Remedial and Special Education, 6,* (4), 54–59.

Carpenter, D., Grantham, L. B., & Hardister, M. P. (1983). Grading mainstreamed handicapped pupils: What are the issues? *Journal of Special Education, 17,* 183–188.

Cohen, A. L., Torgeson, J. K., & Torgeson, J. L. (1988). Improving speed and accuracy of word recognition in reading-disabled children: An evaluation of two computer program variations. *Learning Disability Quarterly, 11,* 333–341.

Cole, D. A., Vandercook, T., & Rynders, J. (1988). Comparison of two peer interaction programs: Children with and without severe disabilities. *American Educational Research Journal, 25,* 415–439.

Daiute, C. A. (1986). Physical and cognitive factors in revising: Insights from studies with computers. *Research in the Teaching of English, 20,* 141–159.

Delquadri, J., Greenwood, C. R., Whorton, D., Carta, J. J., & Hall, V. R. (1988). Classwide peer tutoring. *Exceptional Children, 52,* 535–542.

Deshler, D. D., & Graham, S. (1980). Tape recording educational materials for secondary handicapped students. *Teaching Exceptional Children, 12,* (2), 52–54.

Dunn, R., & Dunn, K. (1972). *Practical approaches to individualizing instruction: Contracts and other effective teaching strategies.* West Nyack, NY: Parker.

Eagan, A., & Wilson, M. A. (1983). Word processing with students: What does the teacher need to know? *The Pointer, 29,* (2), 27–31.

Fagen, S., Graves, D., Healy, S., & Tessier-Switlick, D. (1986). Reasonable mainstreaming accommodations for the classroom teacher. *The Pointer, 31,* (3), 4–7.

Frank, A. R. (1973). Breaking down learning tasks: A sequence approach. *Teaching Exceptional Children, 6,* (1), 16–19.

Gallant, J., Sargeant, M., & Van Houten, R. (1980). Teacher-determined and self-determined access to science activities as a reinforcer for task completion in other curriculum areas. *Education and Treatment of Children, 3,* 101–111.

Gersten, R., Carnine, D., & Woodward, J. (1987). Direct instruction research: The third decade. *Remedial and Special Education, 8,* (6), 48–56.

Graves, M. F., Cooke, C. L., & Laberge, M. J. (1983). Effects of previewing difficult short stories on low ability junior high school students' comprehension, recall, and attitudes. *Reading Research Quarterly, 18,* 262–276.

Hare, V. C., & Borchardt, K. M. (1984). Direct instruction of summarization skills. *Reading Research Quarterly, 20,* 62–78.

Hasselbring, T. S. (1984). Using a microcomputer for imitating student errors to improve spelling performance. *Computers, Reading, and Language Arts, 1*, (4), 12–14.

Hasselbring, T. S., & Crossland, C. L. (1982). Application of microcomputer technology to spelling assessment of learning disabled students. *Learning Disability Quarterly, 5*, 80–82.

Hofmeister, A. M. (1989). Teaching with videodiscs. *Teaching Exceptional Children, 21*, (3), 52–54.

Howell, K. W., & Morehead, M. K. (1987). *Curriculum-based evaluation for special and remedial education: A handbook for deciding what to teach*. Columbus, OH: Merrill.

Johnson, S., & Johnson, R. B. (1970). *Developing individualized instructional material*. Palo Alto: CA: Westinghouse Learning Press.

Junkala, J. B. (1972). Task analysis and instructional alternatives. *Academic Therapy, 8*, 33–40.

Kelly, B., Carnine, D., Gersten, R., & Grossen, B. (1987). The effectiveness of videodisc instruction in teaching fractions to learning handicapped and remedial high school students. *Journal of Special Education Technology, 8*, (2), 5–17.

Lambie, R. A. (1980). A systematic approach for changing materials, instruction and assignments to meet individual needs. *Focus on Exceptional Children, 13*, (1), 1–12.

Lee, W. W. (1987). Microcomputer courseware production and evaluation guidelines for students with learning disabilities. *Journal of Learning Disabilities, 20*, 436–438.

Lenz, B. K. (1983). Using advance organizers. *The Pointer, 27*, (2), 11–13.

Lerner, J. W. (1989). *Learning disabilities: Theories, diagnosis, and teaching strategies* (5th ed.). Boston: Houghton Mifflin.

Lovitt, T., Rudsit, J., Jenkins, J., Pious, C., & Benedetti, D. (1986). Adapting science materials for regular and learning disabled seventh graders. *Remedial and Special Education, 1*, (3), 31–39.

MacArthur, C., & Graham, S. (1987). Learning disabled students' composing under three methods of text production: Handwriting, word processing and dictation. *Journal of Special Education, 21*, 22–42.

MacArthur, C. A. (1988). The impact of computers on the writing process. *Exceptional Children, 54*, 536–542.

McCormick, J. E., Jr. (1976). The assessment tool that meets your needs: The one you construct. *Teaching Exceptional Children, 8*, 106–109.

Miller, S. C., & Cooke, N. L. (1989). Mainstreaming students with learning disabilities for videodisc math instruction. *Teaching Exceptional Children, 21*, (3), 57–60.

Moran, M. R. (1980). An investigation of the demands of oral language skills on learning disabled students in secondary classrooms (Research Report no. 1). Lawrence: The University of Kansas Institute for Research in Learning Disabilities.

Musgrave, G. R. (1975). *Individualized instruction*. Boston: Allyn and Bacon.

Outhred, L. (1989). Word processing: Its impact on children's writing. *Journal of Learning Disabilities, 22*, 262–263.

Papert, S. (1980). *Mindstorms: Children, computers, and powerful ideas*. New York: Basic Books.

Popham, W. J., & Baker, E. I. (1970). *Systematic instruction.* Englewood Cliffs, NJ: Prentice-Hall.

Premack, D. A. (1959). Toward empirical behavioral laws: 1. Positive reinforcement. *Psychological Review, 6,* 219–233.

Regan, M. K. (1979). *Vocational education inservice training: Training modules* (Vol. 1). Kansas City: Department of Special Education, University of Kansas.

Reis, R., & Leone, P. E. (1987). Teaching reading and study skills to mildly handicapped learners: Previewing and text summarization. *The Pointer, 31,* (2), 41–43.

Rust, K. (1986). Word processing: The missing key for writing. *The Reading Teacher, 39,* 611–612.

Schulz, J. P. (1972). Simulated work laboratory. Unpublished program of instruction. Columbus, GA.

Scruggs, T. E., & Richter, L. (1988). Tutoring learning disabled students: A critical review. *Learning Disability Quarterly, 11,* 274–286.

Semmel, M. I., Cohen, D. A., & Kandaswamy, S. (1980). Tutoring mainstreamed handicapped pupils in regular classrooms. *Education Unlimited, 2,* (4), 54–56.

Smith, P. B., & Bentley, G. (1975). *Facilitator manual, teacher training program. Mainstreaming mildly handicapped students in the regular classroom.* Austin, TX: Education Service Center, Region XIII.

Taymans, J., & Malouf, D. (1984). A hard look at software in computer assisted instruction in special education. *The Pointer, 29,* (2), 12–15.

Torgeson, J. K. (1986). Computer-assisted instruction with learning-disabled children. In J. K. Torgeson and B. Y. L. Wong (Eds). *Psychological and educational perspectives on learning disabilities* (pp. 417–435). Orlando, FL: Academic.

Turnbull, A. P., Strickland, B., & Brantley, J. C. (1982). *Developing and implementing individualized education programs* (2nd ed.). Columbus, OH: Merrill.

Vacc, N. N. (1987). Word processor versus handwriting: A comparative study of writing samples produced by mildly mentally handicapped students. *Exceptional Children, 54,* 156–165.

Weir, S., & Watt, D. (1981). Logo: A computer environment for learning-disabled students. *The Computing Teacher, 8,* (5), 11–17.

Wiek, C. (1980). Computer resources: Will educators accept, reject, or neglect in the future? *Education Unlimited, 2,* (3), 24–27.

Yeager, R. F. (1977). Lessons learned in the PLATO Elementary Reading Curriculum Project. Ed 139 966. Arlington, VA: ERIC Document Reproduction Service.

Yin, R. K., & Moore, G. B. (1987). The use of advanced technologies in special education: Prospects from robotics, artificial intelligence and computer simulation. *Journal of Learning Disabilities, 20,* 60–63.

__8__

Teaching Language Arts

The language arts are the communication arts. All aspects of a pupil's world are constantly interacting; communication is a vital part of that interaction. Thus, the language arts, or communication skills, are the fundamentals of learning (Wallace, Cohen, & Polloway, 1987).

The tools of communication are essential to social and academic development. Communication is related to every area of school and also to every area of life. The person who is deficient in communication skills is unable to follow directions in school (or on the job), is unable to gain information from textbooks (or from news media), and is limited in interacting with other children (or adults).

A hierarchy of development helps explain the relationships among the elements of the language arts (see Figure 8.1). It is necessary to identify commonalities among these elements in order to develop an instructional program that is oriented toward total communication skill development (Cohen & Plaskon, 1980).

One difficulty in teaching language arts involves the variety of skills that, although taught independently, must be well integrated in language arts performance (Cohen, 1980). For example, writing includes the related skills of vocabulary, expression, spelling, and handwriting.

Another problem is associated with most people's natural use of the language arts. In normal development, one skill flows into another, with little awareness of the transition on the part of the child or the teacher. The integration may be more difficult with handicapped students; frequently, each step in the development process has to be taught separately. It may be necessary to examine each component to be sure a foundation exists for the next step.

LIFE EXPERIENCES

Communication is based on total, multisensory experiences. Through interaction with environment and people, students develop the ideas, concepts, and relationships on which language and other communication skills are built.

Many handicapped students may be limited in their life experiences. Students with sensory handicaps, for example, miss many visual and auditory stimuli that provide other students with information about their surroundings. Students who are physically impaired may have limited experiences in exploring their immediate environments through such motor activities as crawling, climbing, and exploring. And students who are intellectually handicapped may lack the ability to interpret the information and experiences to which they are exposed.

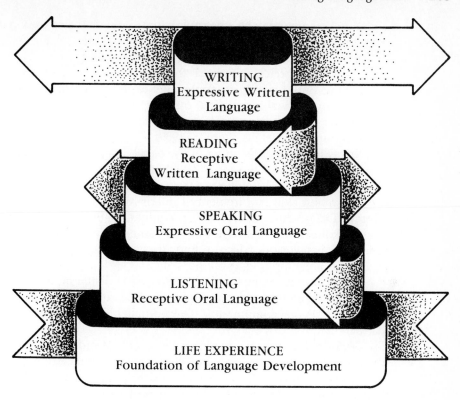

FIGURE 8.1   Relationship of the Elements of the Language Arts

Craig (1980) indicates two tasks required of the teacher in the experiential realm. Teachers must first familiarize themselves with the individual experiences of the students and use those experiences to plan basic thinking, talking, writing, and reading materials. They then must structure classes to enable students to begin their learning with concrete, direct, meaningful experiences. Direct experiences provide the background and the motivation to listen, talk, read, and write.

LISTENING

Fritz, a curly-haired, snaggled-toothed outdoor boy, had trouble controlling his indoor behavior. After a particularly rough day, Fritz's kindergarten teacher was talking to him about her expectations of him in the classroom. After serious talk, the teacher asked, "Now Fritz, do you have any questions?" "Yes, teacher. Why do you wear green on your eyes?"

Not listening may be a natural defense against the reception of undesirable or useless information that constantly assaults the ear, or it may be the result of limited auditory perception or training.

Although special concern for the instruction of speaking and reading is common, until recently students were expected to acquire the ability to listen without special instruction. And yet, listening is the foundation of all language growth; the pupil deficient in listening skills is handicapped in all the communication skills (Lerner, 1989).

Investigations of listening in the elementary classroom revealed that 57.5 percent of class time was spent in listening (Taylor, 1973). Other studies confirm that listening is a very important skill at other grade levels as it is a major skill requirement of junior high and high school students (Moran, 1980; Schumaker, Sheldon-Wildgen, & Sherman, 1980). Furthermore, Okolo (1988) reports that even some secondary vocational classes consist of a majority of lecture and discussion activities, placing a high burden on listening and speaking skills.

According to Robinson and Smith (1981), listening consists of input (message), listening, and output (observable response). Each portion is made up of several components. Conceptualizing listening in this way aids instruction.

Input is the message made up of words, sounds, and the nonverbal message conveyed. The input has the following characteristics: (1) clarity; (2) vocabulary level; (3) complicity, which is the conceptual level rather than vocabulary; (4) duration; (5) being informative or ambiguous; and (6) nonverbal emphases.

Listening involves the cognitive process of making sense of the input and includes comprehending and remembering. According to Robinson and Smith (1981), prerequisites for listening are attention, acoustic competence (hearing acuity), and language competence. Language competence means being able to perceive and discriminate sounds as well as having syntactic and semantic skills that allow for understanding.

Output is the listener's response, which is necessary to verify that acceptable listening occurs. Output can be in the form of verbal, physical, or written response.

Handicapped students can have deficits in any of these areas. Two recent studies documenting some of the listening problems of handicapped students indicate that these problems are not necessarily amenable to improvement as the result of maturation (Bowen & Hynd, 1988; Wood, Buckhalt & Tomlin, 1988). Other problems reviewed by Norton (1989) include attention, perception (such as discrimination), main idea comprehension, and ability to generalize and conceptualize. Robinson and Smith (1981) offer specific suggestions to modify input and listening behavior to help solve some of these problems (see Tables 8.1 and 8.2).

Lerner (1989) identifies the seven skills that contribute to the listening process:

TABLE 8.1   Strategies to Modify Input (the Message)

Input	Interventions
Attention—Focusing the listener's attention on the speaker	1. Give direct instruction (Example: "Listen to what I'm going to say"). 2. Shorten input. 3. Use visual aid. 4. Reduce extraneous stimuli. 5. Increase proximity of speaker to listener.
Language	1. Simplify vocabulary. 2. Restate message. 3. Simplify syntax.
Memory—The speaker's facilitating listener recall	1. Use high frequency words. 2. Disseminate group information in easily associated categories. 3. Use groupings categorized by semantic membership (what they are) rather than where or when. 4. Control message length. 5. Control linguistic (or surface) structure. 6. Control restatements—should be exact or will confuse. 7. Control serial position of information—information given last is remembered best, information given in the middle is forgotten most easily. 8. Use careful phrasing—can group words or elements for listener. 9. Increase relevance of material to listener—increases recall
Comprehension	Provide practice at all levels of literal, critical, and appreciative comprehension.

Source: From "Listening skills: Teaching Learning Disabled Students to Be Better Listeners" by S. Robinson and D. D. Smith, 1981, *Focus on Exceptional Children, 13,* p. 8. Copyright 1981 by *Focus on Exceptional Children.* Reprinted by permission.

1. Auditory perception of non-language sounds.
2. Auditory perception and discrimination of isolated single language sounds.
3. Understanding of words and concepts, and building of a listening vocabulary.
4. Understanding sentences and other linguistic elements of language.
5. Auditory memory.
6. Auding or listening comprehension:
   a. Following directions.
   b. Understanding a sequence of events through listening.
   c. Recalling details.

TABLE 8.2 Strategies to Modify Listening Behavior

Input	Interventions
Attention	1. Peer modeling. 2. Teacher modeling. 3. Verbal rehearsal. 4. Reinforcement. 5. Physical guidance.
Language	1. Increase in vocabulary. 2. Increase in knowledge of multiple word meanings. 3. Increase in syntactic skills.
Memory	1. Rehearsal during listening. 2. Clustering or chunking information. 3. Coding information (POP for people, organizations, populations; etc.). 4. Visualization. 5. Question asking. 6. Identifying organizational cues (First . . . , second . . . , etc.) 7. Rehearsal after listening. 8. Summarizing message after listening. 9. Comparing information received to develop categories.
Comprehension	1. Practice at all levels of literal, critical, and appreciative comprehension. 2. Practice in identifying nonverbal messages.

Source: From "Listening skills: Teaching Learning Disabled Students to Be Better Listeners" by S. Robinson and D. D. Smith, 1981, *Focus on Exceptional Children, 13,* p. 11. Copyright 1981 by *Focus on Exceptional Children.* Reprinted by permission.

> **d.** Getting the main idea.
> **e.** Making inferences and drawing conclusions.
> **7.** Critical listening. (pp. 331–332)

She claims that listening is a basic skill that can be improved through training and suggests teaching strategies for each level of listening.

Listening as a skill is particularly valuable for handicapped students. The use of audiovisual materials is frequently necessary for poor readers. The ability to listen and to comprehend is vital if such materials are substituted for reading.

Obviously, students who are deaf or hard of hearing cannot develop speech and language through avenues of casual hearing or listening. Specific auditory training is necessary to help develop limited hearing into listening skills.

Students with visual impairments depend on listening to a greater extent than do any other students. Their education as well as their safety and existence depend on their ability to listen to sounds in their environment.

If listening is to be learned, it must be taught. The objectives of a listening program include helping students use listening for varied purposes, increasing the efficient use of listening as a mode of learning, understanding the interdependence of the listener and speaker, and increasing awareness of listening as an active skill (Tiedt & Tiedt, 1978).

Assessment of Listening Skills

Several areas of listening can cause deficiencies: not paying attention, thinking about how to respond while attempting to concentrate on what is being said, and neglecting to ask questions when clarification is needed (Otto & Smith, 1980). Specific areas of difficulty can be evaluated by using formal and informal tests. Three selected standardized tests are:

1. Detroit Tests of Learning Aptitude–2. (Hamill, 1985). This test is designed for students 6 to 18 years old and has listening components. It is administered individually. (Pro-Ed)
2. Goldman-Fristoe-Woodcock Test of Auditory Discrimination. (Goldman, Fristoe, & Woodcock, 1970). This instrument can be used with individuals from age 3 years–6 months through adults. It measures auditory discrimination in quiet and noisy contexts and is administered individually. (American Guidance Service)
3. Peabody Picture Vocabulary Test–Revised. (Dunn & Dunn, 1981). This is an individually administered instrument designed for students aged 2 years–6 months to 40 years; it measures receptive vocabulary. (American Guidance Service)

In addition, the instruments listed in the section on speaking have listening subtests and yield factor scores for listening. Other tests also have listening components.

Teacher-made listening tests, close observation by the teacher, and self-checking by the student are likely to produce the best assessment of listening skills and habits. Two facets of the listening process should be evaluated constantly. The student's ability and motivation to listen should be determined, and the teacher's responsibility for evaluating and teaching listening skills should be established.

The procedure for assessing the student should examine the categories of auditory short-term memory, auditory discrimination, auditory recognition, and auditory comprehension. The following activities suggested by Cohen and Plaskon (1980) provide information in each area:

- *Short-term auditory memory:* Have the child listen, eyes closed, to the sound that the teacher makes (clapping hands, tapping foot, or humming a short tune) and repeat the pattern and sound.

- *Auditory sensitivity:* Play a sound-effects record and ask the child to identify as many sounds as possible.
- *Auditory discrimination:* Present two sounds in sequence and ask the child to distinguish between them. Tap a pencil on a desk top, then a pen, and ask the child which sound was the pen and which was the pencil.
- *Auditory recognition:* Identify for a child a particular sound, such as the sound that /s/ makes in /snake/. Present a series of sounds that include the /s/ sound. Each time the child hears the /s/ sound, an object can be placed in a container. At the end of the session, the objects can be counted to determine the degree of recognition.
- *Auditory comprehension:* Ask the pupil to follow a specific set of directions, such as completing a puzzle, coloring a picture, or designing an art project.

If no specific problems are found and there still seems to be an attention deficit, an informal checklist to help determine the student's overall listening behavior may be of value (see Figure 8.2).

Improving Listening Skills

Listening skills can be taught, and listening instruction produces improvement in reading and in language use. Because learning depends on listening and because most students are not accomplished listeners, many educators recommend a developmental listening improvement program.

Listening is a process that is learned in conjunction with experiences. Unless students learn to listen and attend to the activities in their environment, they cannot learn maximally from that environment. Temple and Gillet (1984) suggest that two guidelines should be followed when developing listening skills and habits:

1. The teacher should make sure that the children can understand the language structures—sentence forms, functions of language, and school subject registers—that are necessary for productive learning at their grade level.
2. The teacher should show the children ways to listen actively, ways to respond both overtly and covertly to what they are listening to. (pp. 36–37)

The following activities help the younger child to listen, to retain, and to recall auditory information.

Name _____		*Yes*	*No*

1. Does the child consistently request to have directions repeated? ____ ____
2. Does the child appear to be easily distracted when presentations are being made in class? ____ ____
3. Does the child appear to understand what is expected when assignments are given? ____ ____
4. Does the child frequently participate in class discussions? ____ ____
5. Is the child able to pick out inconsistencies in the conversations of others? ____ ____
6. Does the child frequently complete the wrong pages in the workbook, or do inappropriate homework assignments? ____ ____
7. Are requests, messages, or informational items orally presented to the child frequently misinterpreted resulting in misinformed parents or guardians? ____ ____
8. Does the child not hear you so often that it has become annoying? ____ ____
9. Are the other children in class complaining about the child's behavior in small group activities because the child does not seem to "listen"? ____ ____
10. Does the child consistently have problems on the playground with peers because of misinformation regarding the rules for a particular game? ____ ____

Source: From *Language Arts for the Mildly Handicapped* (pp. 179–180) by S. Cohen and S. Plaskon, 1980. Columbus, OH: Merrill. Copyright 1980 by Charles E. Merrill Publishing Co. Reprinted by permission.

FIGURE 8.2 A Simple Checklist of Listening Behavior

Learning to Listen

1. Several times a day, play a game of being quiet and relaxed with eyes shut. The voice and the whole body should be quiet so that not a sound is made.
2. Once the children can maintain reasonable quiet for 30 seconds or more, whisper children's names and have them rise gently and come to you. As the child's listening ability improves, give simple directions in the same whispered voice and move to different areas of the room.
3. To encourage children to listen and to prevent them from shouting, make a habit of using a low, quiet tone of voice when presenting tasks or play items that the children really enjoy.

Actions Performed from Auditory Clues

1. Give simple one-sentence, one-action commands.
2. Increase the number of words in each command and the number of commands.
3. Use clues other than words for starting and stopping an activity. The activity may be a simple motor movement, a game, or a task. The task may be as simple as sitting still until a buzzer sounds.

Developing Auditory Memory

1. Have the child repeat unrelated words.
2. Have the child repeat digits and/or letters after you.
3. Increase the length of time between naming of the digits, words, or sounds, as the child demonstrates competency.
4. Read or tell a short, simple story containing two or more elements in a sequence.
   a. Ask the child to retell the story.
   b. Ask the child, "What did I say first . . . last?" (adapted from Chaney & Kephart, 1968, pp. 69–74)

As educators have become more aware of the importance of auditory training for many children, commercial programs have become available. The following programs are designed to improve listening skills (Robinson & Smith, 1981).

- *Listening to the World.* The material is intended for children in kindergarten through primary grades and is designed to teach five listening skills: (1) auditory discrimination (environmental as well as speech sounds), (2) selective auditory attention (listening for important sounds and ignoring distracting sounds), (3) auditory vigilance (listening for particular words or sounds), (4) hypothesis testing (identifying words obscured or absent from sentences and then filling in by context clues), and (5) auditory memory skills (including visualization, rehearsal, grouping, and linking). (American Guidance Service)
- *Auditory Perception Training II: Listening Skills.* The program is intended for middle school and junior high students and is modeled after DLM Auditory Perception Training Program. It is designed to train the following four listening skills: (1) figure-ground (attending to instruction while ignoring background noise), (2) memory (including practice in remembering sequence and fact recall), (3) imagery (forming a visual image from verbal information), and (4) motor responding (following verbal directions with various motoric responses). (Developmental Learning Materials)
- *Auditory Perceptual Enhancement Program, Volumes I–IV.* The material is intended for elementary through senior high school students and is designed to aid the following skills. Volume I aids memory organizational skills of chunking by association and categorization. Volume II aids discrimination of words in isolation and in sentences. Volume III provides instruction in following directions. Volume IV aids alertness, evaluation of orally presented information, and retention of factual information. (Modern Education Corporation)

- *Scholastic Listening Skills. Unit I: Easy Ears. Unit II: Ear-power.* The materials are intended for first grade through upper elementary-age students and require reading with listening skills. Skills taught in Unit I are following directions, sequence, main idea, predicting outcome, understanding character, drawing conclusion, discrimination of selected sounds, and rhyming. Unit II includes some of the skills in Unit I as well as listening for significant details, finding proof, identifying supporting details, discriminating between fact and opinion, problem solving, and finding word meaning through context. (Scholastic Book Services)

Creating a Good Listening Climate

Many improvements can be made in the listening skills of all students by carefully inspecting the quality of the listening climate. A reevaluation of teaching methods may lead to a greater variety of listening situations, including independent activities, pupil-team learning, and greater use of audiovisual approaches.

SPEAKING

> We walked down the path to the well-house, attracted by the fragrance of the honeysuckle with which it was covered. Someone was drawing water and my teacher placed my hand under the spout. As the cool stream gushed over one hand she spelled into the other the word water, first slowly, then rapidly. I stood still, my whole attention fixed upon the motions of her fingers. Suddenly I felt a misty consciousness as of something forgotten—a thrill of returning thought; and somehow the mystery of language was revealed to me. I knew then that "w–a–t–e–r" meant the wonderful cool something that was flowing over my hand. That living word awakened my soul, gave it light, hope, joy, set it free! (Keller, 1954, p. 36)

Although oral language is identified as the primary form of language, instructional practices in both regular classrooms and special classes do not always reflect the relationship between oral and written language (Lerner, 1989). Language is used to communicate information and to influence other people (Wallace, Cohen, & Polloway, 1987). It is also directly related to cognitive processes that help us understand our world (Roberts & Schaefer, 1984).

Language acquisition is a special problem for many students. Most of the students referred to in chapter 4 on learning and behavior disorders have some language deficits. Therefore, language must be a critical part of their educational plan. Students' success in their social and academic environments depends largely on how they use language. Their ability to express language (speech) and to use language interpersonally (communication) must be increased through activities built into the educational program (Schiefelbusch, Ruder, & Bricker, 1976).

Norton (1989) found that pupils who are mildly learning disabled and mentally handicapped evidence the following deficiencies in oral language: (1) problems in thought development; (2) delayed language development; (3) using abstract language; and (4) use of only short, simple sentences. No developmental sequences have been established for retarded and other handicapped persons; the content for language training must be taken from the data available on language development in normal children.

Three major components are necessary for language development in children: cognitive-perceptual development, linguistic experience, and nonlinguistic experience. In order to acquire the language system, children must be capable of perceiving objects, events, and relationships in the environment; they must be exposed to the linguistic system used to express those recognized objects, events, and relationships; and they must have direct experience with those objects, events, and relationships in the environment (Bloom, 1970). Consequently, children who have cognitive, perceptual, physical, and/or emotional deficits frequently have difficulty achieving normal language development.

Students with language problems do not display consistency in the severity of their various deficiencies. A student with a mild problem may have good comprehension of language yet produce relatively unintelligible speech. Another student may possess all the tools for becoming a competent speaker and listener but lack the communicative skills to comprehend or to use language appropriately in a learning environment (Schiefelbusch, Ruder, & Bricker, 1976). Therefore, individual assessment is necessary for good program planning. Because language assessment is based on comparisons with normal children, teachers must understand normal language development.

Normal Language Development

Communication, an exchange of ideas and information, can be nonverbal (facial expressions or gestures) or verbal (spoken language). Speech is uniquely human and is a part of a larger system of symbols that carry meaning. Norton (1989) provides a general overview of oral language development (see Table 8.3).

Assessment of Language Development

Language is a complex process involving many skills, including the ability to receive (receptive language) and the ability to transmit (expressive

TABLE 8.3 A General Overview of Language Development

Age	General Language Characteristics
3 months	The young child starts with all possible language sounds and gradually eliminates those sounds that are not used around her.
1 year	Many children are speaking single words (e.g., "mama"). Infants use single words to express entire sentences. Complex meanings may underlie single words.
18 months	Many children are using two- or three-word phrases (e.g., "see baby"). Children are developing their own language rule systems. Children may have a vocabulary of about 300 words.
2–3 years	Children use such grammatical morphemes as plural suffix /s/, auxiliary verb "is," and past irregular. Simple and compound sentences are used. Understands tense and numerical concepts such as "many" and "few." A vocabulary of about 900 words is used.
3–4 years	The verb past tense appears, but children may overgeneralize the "ed" and "s" markers. Negative transformation appears. Children understand numerical concepts such as "one," "two," and "three." Speech is becoming more complex, with more adjectives, adverbs, pronouns, and prepositions. Vocabulary is about 1,500 words.
4–5 years	Language is more abstract and most basic rules of language are mastered. Children produce grammatically correct sentences. Vocabularies include approximately 2,500 words.
5–6 years	Most children use complex sentences quite frequently. They use correct pronouns and verbs in the present and past tense. The average number of words per oral sentence is 6.8. It has been estimated that the child understands approximately 6,000 words.
6–7 years	Children are speaking complex sentences that use adjectival clauses, and conditional clauses beginning with "if" are beginning to appear. Language is becoming more symbolic. Children begin to read and write and understand concepts of time and seasons. The average sentence length is 7.5 words.
7–8 years	Children use relative pronouns as objects in subordinate adjectival clauses. ("I have a cat which I feed every day.") Subordinate clauses beginning with "when," "if," and "because" appear frequently. The average number of words per oral sentence is 7.6.
8–10 years	Children begin to relate concepts to general ideas through use of such connectors as "meanwhile" and "unless." The subordinating connector "although" is used correctly by 50 percent of the children. Present participle active and perfect participle appear. The average number of words in an oral sentence is 9.0.
10–12 years	Children use complex sentences with subordinate clauses of concession introduced by "nevertheless" and "in spite of." The auxiliary verbs "might," "could," and "should" appear frequently. Children have difficulties distinguishing among past, past perfect, and present perfect tenses of the verb. The average number of words in an oral sentence is now 9.5.

Source: From *The Effective Teaching of Language Arts* (3rd ed.) (p. 30) by D. E. Norton, 1989. Columbus, OH: Merrill. Copyright 1989 by Charles E. Merrill Publishing Company. Reprinted by permission of the publisher.

language). In oral language, information is received by listening and expressed by speech; in written language, information is received by reading and expressed by writing (Mercer & Mercer, 1985).

Formal assessment

A series of three oral language standardized tests that may be helpful in the beginning stage of language assessment are:

> Test of Language Development–2: Primary. (Newcomer & Hammill, 1988a). This test is individually administered for ages 6 months to 12 years. (Pro-Ed)
>
> Test of Language Development–2: Intermediate. (Newcomer & Hammill, 1988b). This instrument is useful for students aged 4 to 12 years. (Pro-Ed)
>
> Test of Adolescent Language–2. (Hammill, Brown, Larsen, & Wiederholt, 1987). Portions of this instrument can be administered in a group setting. This test is normed on students in grades 6 through 12. (Pro-Ed)

One limitation of formal assessment is that it frequently indicates whether a child possesses a certain structure but gives little indication of where to begin training. To be maximally beneficial, the assessment instrument should have relevance for the development and implementation of the student's IEP.

Informal Assessment

Informal assessment is a valuable part of the total language evaluation. In its simplest form, it is the parents' or teacher's report of the student's language capacity or their impressions of the student's language problem (Ruder & Smith, 1974). A somewhat more structured assessment by the teacher may include the following features:

Receptive Language

1. Awareness or attention: include items that require observable responses to sound or speech (e.g., eye contact).
2. Discrimination: ability to respond differently to sound or speech sounds.
3. Understanding: speech accompanied by
   a. gestures
   b. situational clues (e.g., "Turn on water" while in bathroom)
   c. speech alone

Expressive Language

1. Imitating
2. Initiating
3. Responding

Samples can be taken of the pupil's interaction with other people and reactions to elicited speech, such as, "Tell me about the picture." Such language samples are useful in planning IEPs.

Black (1979) stresses the importance of informal observation, claiming there is more to evaluation than hearing students verbalize in formal settings. Communication can be seen and assessed by observing a student's use of language in a variety of social contexts.

Among the many difficulties teachers encounter in assessing oral language are realizing and understanding that background differences influence language, that the course of language development is uneven, that data collection and transcription are difficult, and that students respond to various listener characteristics (Cohen & Plaskon, 1980). To obtain and interpret useful information, the help of a speech therapist is valuable. Cooperative effort is necessary in determining the needs of handicapped students.

Assessment procedures built into language development programs will probably be most useful to the teacher. Such procedures provide for pupil placement in a particular phase of a training program. They also provide feedback concerning the relevance of a particular training sequence and the behaviors required to enter particular stages of a program (Ruder & Smith, 1974).

Speech and Language Problems

The purpose of assessing and identifying language and speech disorders is to plan relevant programs for students. In determining which students should be considered as having a communication disorder, McLean (1974) compares the pupil's language with the standard language form of the culture and with the language of other students at the same age level. He categorizes the most common problems as nonverbal children, language-disordered children, and speech-impaired children. McLean (1974) states that:

> because language is learned behavior, it can be affected by the factors which affect any learning. Factors like intellectual ability, motivation and/or good models of the behaviors to be learned can all affect language acquisition. Because language models are received in the auditory mode, the auditory sensory channel is critical to natural language learning. Because the natural language production mode is a motor behavior, disrupted or diminished motor systems can affect language acquisition. Because language is connected with the child's world and learned within relationships in that world, a child's emotional status can be a factor. Language carries the marks of whatever problems have affected the child. (p. 474)

The most critical factors in poor speech and language development are related to physical, sensory, intellectual, and environmental abilities of the student.

Orthopedic Handicaps

Students with orthopedic handicaps, particularly those with cerebral palsy, frequently have speech and language problems (see chapter 2). Molloy and Witt (1971) state that a child's speaking mechanism is usable for speech if the child is able to swallow, suck, maneuver the tongue by controlling its action, and use some speed in tongue action. Exercises for developing and strengthening the muscles involved can be prescribed and demonstrated by a speech clinician.

Sensory Deficits

Sensory deficits refer to hearing and visual problems. Hearing provides contact with the environment and with other people. It permits the learning of spoken language and plays a major role in the development of abstract concepts and temporal sequences. The student who is hard of hearing misses much of this association of sound with experience (Lowell & Pollack, 1974).

Students with intact hearing learn the sound, shape, and sense of their language through their auditory modality; the student with hearing impairments depends on vision to learn about language. Comparisons of the written language of the deaf and the hearing suggest that the students who are deaf are significantly inferior in all aspects of language development and facility (Moores, 1972). Adler (1964) suggests that when hearing is faulty, the development of speech is likely to be retarded or imperfect. The student learns faulty interpretations of sound or learns to substitute other senses for hearing. Gestures tend to replace speech as a method of communication.

Because of limited interaction with the environment, the child with a hearing impairment has difficulty acquiring concepts. A speech therapist described a sequence of steps necessary for a particular student who is hearing impaired to develop an understanding of the word *mammals:*

The student was asked to use a dictionary to find meanings of words she did not know and write a sentence with the words to demonstrate her understanding of their meaning. She found that the dictionary defined mammal as any class of animals that nourishes its young with milk. Her first sentence read "I don't want to go to mammal today." The therapist asked the student what the meaning of mammal was. The student replied that it was a class and that the sentence meant that the student didn't want to go to class today.

After discussing the entire meaning of the word with the student, the therapist asked her to write another sentence. The second sentence read, "The puppy is mammals its mother." The definition of the word was discussed again and again and examples given. When the student presented her third sentence, it read, "My kitten is a mammal."

The pupil who is hearing-impaired has a limited vocabulary and experiences difficulty with words that have more than one meaning. Prefixes and suffixes added to words may be confusing. Word order is often improper, prepositions and articles may be omitted from sentences, and syntax is generally poor.

The results of a study by Brenza, Kricos, and Lasky (1981) reveal a deficit in the comprehension of semantic concepts by students age 13 and 14 who are severely and profoundly hearing impaired. When mainstreaming students who are hearing impaired, teachers need to evaluate and teach basic concepts before moving on to more advanced concepts.

The pupil who is visually impaired suffers much of the same experiential deprivation as the pupil who is hearing impaired and has similar problems with concepts.

> *A child who is blind was in a language arts group playing the game* Password. *The word to be discovered was* room. *In giving a clue, the boy who was blind gave the word* box. *While he may have used models to help develop spatial concepts, he had a poor understanding of* room.

Intellectual Deficits

Intellectual deficits have a strong bearing on language acquisition because, as Bloom (1970) states, "the acquisition of language is a complex process that is crucially related to the child's cognitive-perceptual growth and his interaction in an environment of objects, events, and relations" (p. 1). The cognitive prerequisites for the development of grammar relate to the meanings and forms of language; the first linguistic forms to appear in a child's speech are those that express meanings consistent with the child's level of cognitive development. Miller and Yoder (1972) conclude that "children do not talk in the absence of something to talk about" (p. 9).

The student with mental retardation frequently exhibits delayed language. Data available on language development in normal children can be used to plan language training.

Children first learn aspects of language within the scope of their current cognitive development; as they develop cognitively, they gradually learn to use more complex linguistic formulations (Clark, 1974). Miller and Yoder (1972) suggest that children's target language behavior should have some functional relevance to their environment and to their personal and physical needs. Miller and Yoder present the following procedures and constructs that are essential in coordinating the implementation of content with teaching strategies in developing programs for language training:

- Before children become language users, they have to have something to say (concepts) and a way to say it (linguistic structure).

- Throughout the entire program the teacher works from comprehension to production.
- New words and syntactical relationships are best established by supplying the underlying concepts through environmental manipulation and experience.
- For the child who is mentally retarded, as for other children, language is acquired through interaction with the environment.
- Language is part of the child's mental development and should not be isolated. (p. 10)

Variant English Speakers

Variant English speakers use nonstandard speech patterns in approximately one-third or more of their conversation. Two difficulties for teachers are to distinguish handicapped students, particularly those with language or speech disorders, from variant speakers and to identify handicapped variant English speakers. According to Wallace, Cohen, and Polloway (1987), variant speech patterns can be the result of geographic location, social class, age, race, and/or national origin. These differences can be in (1) pronunciation (*De boy rode on de train*); (2) expression (*Mash the button* for *Press the button*); and (3) structure (*She be happy*).

It may not be easy to distinguish students who have a language disorder or handicap from those who use a different or variant language. Students who are language different fit into their own environment without any loss of communication efficiency. Their language is appropriate in the context of their environment, although it may not be appropriate in other environments and may hinder communication efficiency. Students who are language disordered have a communication difficulty in most environments. Problems include the inabilities to articulate sounds and/or to use words in coherent sentences, and/or dysfluency.

Gifted and Talented Students

Students who are gifted usually express themselves well, have an advanced vocabulary and fluency of speech, use a high level of sentence structure, and are original in expression (Wallace, Cohen, & Polloway, 1987). Approaches with gifted students should involve the students in setting goals, interacting frequently, and critically evaluating their own and others' work. Roleplaying, drama, and radio and television journalism are worthwhile activities (Robinson, 1986).

Promoting Language Use

An effective curriculum designed to promote language use has several purposes. As described by Klein (1979), the curriculum design consists of talk purposes, talk contexts, and talk planning. Talk purposes are to inform, to move to action, to inquire, to enjoy, and to conjoin. Talk contexts are settings or environments in which language use takes place. Talk planning refers to processes attended to while preparing to talk, while talking, while taking in the talk of others, and after talking. Talk opportunities should be consciously structured into the curriculum to encourage students to use talk in a wide variety of contexts and purposes.

Language is a tool to be used, not a subject to be studied. Experience and purpose are the key factors in language learning; they are guides for planning instruction aimed at promoting language (Winkeljohann, 1981).

For most students, language evolves naturally as they interact with their environment, family, and friends. For students who do not acquire language naturally, this interaction may have to be provided by the classroom teacher. The experiences provided will be most effective if they are related to each pupil's life—to the home background, to experiences in and out of school, and to past and future learning.

Activities for Language Development

Language develops as children become aware of their surroundings. Awareness of the environment can be developed through experiences that stimulate the senses.

Language is stimulated in a classroom in which experiences are encouraged and promoted. According to Pasamanick (1976), this means organizing and equipping the room with materials that stimulate language, drama, and thought. She suggests materials for a Language Center that will enrich the possibilities for dialogue. Such materials can include:

- A round table and perhaps one or two other tables to hold language games.
- Storage shelves and a comfortable chair, rug, or mats.
- A good supply of blank pages bound into books for students' original stories. Some of these might be precut into different animal and geometric shapes.
- A good stock of colorful magazines—*Woman's Day, Family Circle, Ebony, Sports Illustrated.*
- A picture file of interesting trigger pictures on various subjects chosen for the stimulation they offer to concept development and problem solving. Pictures evocative of emotional reaction are very valuable, too. Be sure to include pictures of many different people: black, white, Indian, oriental, and also young and old, urban and rural. All pictures could be trimmed, mounted on stiff bright paper, and covered with transparent paper to insure their longevity.

- Language games such as lottos, alphabet letters of various kinds (sandpaper, felt, wood), small and large flannelboards and felt pieces. Your ditto sheets and task cards (simple ones with more drawing than words) belong here, too, as do sequence cards and other homemade language materials.
- Crayons, felt markers, fat pencils, and scissors stored in attractively covered or painted cans should be placed beside stacks of paper for writing and drawing.
- Small treasures or doll figures (such as are often found in penny-candy machines); figures of animals, people, vehicles, and furniture are often stimulants to story making. Store them in transparent containers alongside trays for manipulation.
- And finally, the primer typewriter. This is a distinct asset to letter recognition and word building. If you can, get one and keep it, along with an abundant supply of paper.

Several software programs for microcomputers are interactive and include speech synthesizers that can help in language development. Pets in the classroom offer opportunities for observation and description. Gerbils, hamsters, rabbits, guinea pigs, snakes, lizards, and fish are attractive and provocative choices.

Language can be stimulated through play activities in which children enact pretend or real-life situations. Doll houses, puppets, household centers, and dress-up clothing facilitate such experiences.

Instructional Materials

Many of the materials suggested can be made from inexpensive products. For example, puppets can be made from wooden spoons, paper plates, popsicle sticks, and paper bags (Deen & Deen, 1977). Many commercial products also are available. The following list suggests some appropriate materials:

- Language Big Box. Designed to promote the acquisition of basic language skills, the materials reinforce auditory and conceptual skills by building on the student's existing language strengths. The Big Box includes 170 activity cards for lesson planning and 24 products to be used for language development. (Developmental Learning Materials)
- Caption Cards. Designed for creative writing and language development, the cards are cartoons without captions that form the basis for learning activities. All cards have a situation and a verbal action. The idea is to design verbal interaction displayed in the picture. (Educational Design Associates)

- Developmental Syntax Program. A programmed approach to the development of syntax, this program is designed to teach the child the grammatical and morphological structure of language. The most common syntactical structure errors have been selected and sequenced to reflect a developmental sequence. (Learning Concepts)
- Language Development Pak. Develops language skills, including word formation, contractions, phonics, classification, and dictionary skills. Includes open-ended, multilevel spirit masters and perforated worksheets. (Love Publishing Company)
- Peabody Language Development Kit. Designed to stimulate oral language development, the activities in the kit are highly motivating. The kits include lesson plans, stimulus cards, hand puppets, taped stories, transistorized, battery-operated intercommunication sets, and cards to stimulate imagination and continuity in story telling. The kits require no special training, can be used effectively in large or small groups, and are effective in promoting oral language expression. (American Guidance Service)
- Language Making Action Cards and Stickers. Sets of pictures designed to make teaching communication skills easier and more effective. The cards in the set are action-verb pictures and designs for teaching color, number, and plural concepts. Also included are pictures helpful in teaching prepositions, personal expression modifiers, polars, comparatives, and multiple attributes. Other cards contain sequence pictures for verb-tense illustration and story telling. (Word Making Productions, Inc.)
- Let's Talk: Developing Prosocial Communication Skills. Students learn effective ways to handle everyday social interaction through use of a communication card-game format and structured training activities designed for students aged 9 through adult. (Merrill)

READING

An eighth-grade student approached his teacher the first day of school with the declaration, "My dad says if I don't learn to read this year, I'm all washed up."

Parents, teachers, and people in general are concerned about the lack of literacy among the nation's students. Low reading ability is not a new problem; Wolfthal (1981) reports that in 1926 reading failure was the major cause of nonpromotion. Although progress has been made in identifying problems and developing successful strategies in reading, educators are still a long way from realizing the reading potential of every child.

The greatest concern in mainstreaming centers around reading—at the elementary and secondary levels, in subject matter areas, and in vocational training. Hargis (1982) describes students in intermediate, junior high, and high school who can barely read and claims that they usually do not survive secondary education programs. Frequently, these are students who have not benefited from reading instruction because of the disparity between the curriculum provided and their actual learning rate and readiness.

One example of the concern about reading is that many states require successful completion of a minimum competency test before a high school diploma is awarded. Reading is a major part of these tests. Unfortunately, the performance of handicapped students on such tests is often dismal (Crews, 1988).

Success in all academic areas depends on success in reading; all teachers are responsible for teaching reading. The first step in the process is assessment, an essential element that helps the learner and the teacher.

Assessment

There are five important purposes for reading assessment: (1) to determine when children are ready to begin reading instruction or to enter the next instructional level; (2) to identify students who have problems in reading; (3) to identify the causes of reading problems; (4) to derive information for instructional decisions; and (5) to determine accountability (Hargis, 1982).

The Diagnostic Process in Reading

The diagnostic process in reading can be organized into three levels: the survey level, the specific level, and the intensive level (Otto & Smith, 1980).

At the survey level, screening should include reading-related areas, such as vision, hearing, language development, and intelligence. Symptoms relating to these problems are discussed later in this chapter. Even though general health screening is conducted annually in many schools, it may be necessary for the teacher to request it from the school or from the local health department.

At the specific level, diagnosis is used to check a tentative diagnosis made at the survey level and to identify strengths and weaknesses as a basis for planning instruction. Intensive diagnosis is used to determine the causes of severe reading problems; it becomes necessary only when information gathered at the specific level does not result in reading success. Intensive diagnosis usually requires a multidisciplinary team approach.

The level and amount of assessment individual students require should be proportional to their needs; poor readers should receive more extensive assessment than better readers. Handicapped students will, in many cases, require intensive reading assessment. The resource teacher, who has a background in diagnostic testing, should work cooperatively with the classroom teacher to determine the needs of each student.

Classroom diagnosis relies on school records, teacher observation, interviews with students and parents, and test results (Wilson, 1981). The diagnostic process is facilitated by the use of standardized reading tests, criterion-referenced tests, and informal reading inventories. Increasingly, curriculum-based measurement is used (Choate, Bennett, Enright, Miller, Poteet, & Rakes, 1987; Howell & Morehead, 1987).

Standardized Reading Tests

In planning reading instruction for handicapped students, group testing has little value.

> *During a schoolwide testing program, Tommy was observed by a monitor, who noticed that his test booklet was closed. The monitor pointed out to him that his test booklet was closed. The monitor pointed out to him that his booklet should be in use. Tommy replied, "Oh, I don't need it; I was the first one through." Tommy, who does not read, scored a reading grade level of 3.5.*

Achievement tests, used for academic screening purposes, provide relatively global information about students' skill development. Diagnostic tests provide data to help teachers pinpoint skill development through strengths and weaknesses, leading to appropriate educational planning (Salvia & Ysseldyke, 1988).

The following are three selected standardized, diagnostic reading instruments that can be used.

> Stanford Diagnostic Reading Test. The instrument can be administered in a group setting, is appropriate for grade-1 students through those in community college, and assesses such skills as word recognition, comprehension, and reading rate. (Psychological Corporation)
>
> Test of Reading Comprehension. This is an individually administered test meant for students 7 to 18 years old and measures vocabulary and comprehension. (Pro-Ed)
>
> Woodcock Reading Mastery Tests–Revised. Individually administered, this instrument is normed on students age 5 through adult. It measures letter and word recognition, vocabulary, and comprehension. (American Guidance Service)

Diagnostic reading tests provide the classroom teacher with a systematic analysis of strengths and weaknesses in reading (Salvia & Ysseldyke, 1988). Although grade scores, stanines, and percentiles shown on standardized tests are of little value in program planning, careful analysis of performance on individual test items can provide useful information.

Informal Reading Inventories

An informal reading inventory (IRI) is a teacher-implemented testing procedure used to determine the student's reading level, specifically, the independent level, the instruction level, or the frustration level. The criteria in Table 8.4 are used to determine whether material is appropriate for instruction.

To build an IRI, the teacher chooses a well-graded series of readers that the child has not used. Two selections are chosen from the first part of each book, one for oral reading and the other for silent reading. Selections from the preprimer through the second readers should contain from 60 to 120 words; for grades 3 to 6, 100 to 200 words. The teacher then prepares three to five comprehension questions, avoiding those that can be answered yes or no. To check sight vocabulary, a word list can be prepared using every third or fourth word from the book's word list. A checking system similar to those used in standardized individual reading tests is useful (Gillespie-Silver, 1979).

TABLE 8.4 Informal Reading Inventory Scoring Criteria

Independent Level	Word Recognition	Comprehension	Fluency
A level at which a student reads with obvious ease as illustrated by reading accuracy.	97% or more accuracy	80% or more accuracy	Smooth
Instruction Level			
A level at which the student has some difficulties in one or more of the three areas. The difficulties supply the teacher with specific skills deficiences.	92%–96%	60%–70%	Lacking
Frustrational Level			
A level at which the student is unable to perform instructionally because of the lack of numerous skills.	91% and lower	50% or lower	Poor

Curriculum-Based Assessment

Curriculum-based assessment in the context of reading means evaluating how well the student reads in tasks and materials used in the classroom or similar to the reading required. This sort of assessment allows the teacher to pinpoint strengths and weaknesses relevant to planning for instruction. Curriculum-based assessment relies heavily on criterion-referenced tests. Howell and Morehead (1987) provide an outline for assessing curriculum-based reading by posing these sequential questions:

1. Is the student's oral reading (accuracy and rate) on grade-level passages acceptable?
2. Is the student's comprehension of grade-level passages acceptable?
3. Does the student improve reading rate when allowed to reread a passage?
4. Do more than half the student's reading errors violate the meaning of the passage?
5. Are decoding difficulties a result of poor phonics skills?
6. Are decoding difficulties a result of consistent error patterns?
7. Can specific causes of comprehension problems be identified? (p. 204)

Answering each question can require one or more specific procedures. This approach is consistent with the questions teachers ask and for which they need answers to plan effective instruction.

Goals and Objectives

The development of goals and objectives in teaching reading depends on the interpretation of the reading process itself. Common to recent definitions are the convictions that reading, thought, and language are closely related (Gillespie-Silver, 1979) and that reading is a communication process (May, 1982).

For years, educators have debated whether reading instruction should emphasize decoding or comprehension. May (1982) stresses that reading is not an either-or proposition and supports a rationale for teaching components:

1. For children who are first learning how to read there has to be more emphasis given to specific decoding and comprehension subskills than there needs to be given for children who have already jumped over the first hurdles.
2. At the same time, teachers who neglect to help children perceive "reading as communication" from the very first stage of reading

instruction will probably give them the wrong perception of reading and thereby risk slowing up their progress in becoming good readers.

3. A child who learns to read for the purpose of communicating with an author normally becomes a good reader. The teacher who attempts to help children read in this manner normally becomes a good teacher of reading.

4. A child who has learned all of the subskills involved in reading has not necessarily learned to read. (pp. 9–10)

For beginning or unsuccessful readers, reading as a communication process is a distant goal. The more immediate goal is to develop the concepts that (1) reading is a meaningful process, (2) a relationship exists between their own oral language and reading, and (3) ideas, when written, are built of words (Greenslade, 1980).

Basic reading objectives should include the development of these four elements:

1. A basic sight vocabulary based on the student's existing speaking and listening vocabulary.

2. Consistent methods for word attack appropriate for each student.

3. The ability and desire to read independently for information, pleasure, and personal satisfaction.

4. An adequate level of reading ability to permit effective social and vocational participation in society.

Approaches to meeting these objectives are discussed as they pertain to prereading skills, word recognition, comprehension, and functional reading.

Prerequisites

Prereading Skills
Reading readiness has frequently been reserved for 5- and 6-year-olds and has been the responsibility of kindergarten and first-grade teachers. Within the concept of individual differences, it is apparent that many older students will not have the skills necessary for reading. In order to read, the learner must integrate each of the following: (1) visual attention to print; (2) directional rules about position and movement; (3) talking like a book; and, (4) hearing sounds in words (Mass, 1982).

By definition, handicapped students lack many of the prerequisites considered essential to reading. Teaching them to read requires recognizing, assessing, and remediating or compensating for problems related to

vision, hearing, language, intelligence, emotional development, and physical factors.

VISUAL DISCRIMINATION   Wallace and Kauffman (1973) state that "many children who have normal visual acuity experience difficulties in differentiating, interpreting, or remembering different shapes, letters, or words" (p. 166). They suggest that students with visual skill deficiencies should learn to:

1. Discriminate sizes and shapes
2. Discriminate specific letters
3. Discriminate the directionality of specific letters
4. Remember letter names and words
5. Remember particular words learned mainly by sight
6. Recognize structural parts of words. (p. 166)

AUDITORY DISCRIMINATION   Auditory discrimination is the ability to discriminate between the sounds or phonemes of a language; this ability is essential to success in reading. Students who cannot hear sounds correctly usually cannot speak them correctly. If they confuse sounds in speech, it may be impossible for them to associate the correct sound with the visual symbol. If a weakness is detected in this area, the teacher should use exercises to strengthen it and should provide reading instruction that is not related to phonics until the auditory skills are developed.

LANGUAGE Even though oral communication skills for handicapped students are discussed in the previous sections of this chapter, their relationship to the reading process should also be emphasized here. Because reading is, as one child put it, "wrote-down talking," the skills of reading are based on the skills of speaking.

Evidences of delayed and immature speech can be seen in pupils who are deaf, blind, mentally handicapped, learning disabled, and culturally disadvantaged, as well as in the pupil whose primary difficulty is a speech problem. Therefore, any reading program designed for handicapped students must strongly emphasize language stimulation.

For students who are unable to speak clearly because of sensory, cognitive, or motor handicaps, reading and writing can accelerate speech and language growth (Geoffrion, 1982). Programs like the language-experience approach and related activities are particularly appropriate for nonvocal students.

INTELLIGENCE There is a cause-effect relationship between intellectual ability and reading ability. Although controversy exists on the extent of the relationship, the correlations between scores on intelligence tests and scores on reading tests are usually high (Savage & Mooney, 1979). The degree of the relationship varies with grade level and tests used. On the Wechsler Intelligence Scale for Children–Revised (Wechsler, 1974) there are few items requiring reading, but reading-related items, such as picture completion and picture arrangement, are included. Picture completion measures the abilities to visualize essential from nonessential detail and to identify familiar stimuli from school and home. Picture arrangement measures the ability to see a total situation based on visual comprehension and organization, as well as on environmental experiences.

Wilson (1981) claims that intelligence is related to causes of reading difficulties only in relation to the school's ability to adjust its program to meet the abilities of various types of students. Thus, it is not intelligence (or lack of it) that prevents students from reading to their potential, but the inadequacy of school programs.

The use of group readiness tests and group and individual IQ tests in the first grade makes it possible to identify the children whose rate of mental growth is below average. The reading program for such children can be adapted by prolonging the readiness program, extending the period of reading readiness activities, and gearing the pace of reading instruction to their learning rates.

Experience and maturation alone do not guarantee success in reading; the pupils need certain intellectual skills. Reading requires perceiving likenesses and differences, remembering word forms, and possessing thinking skills. It requires telling stories in proper sequence, interpreting pictures, making associations and inferences, and thinking on an abstract level. A review of the educational characteristics of students who are mentally handicapped (chapter 4) suggests that the absence of many of these intellectual and sensory skills impedes reading progress. Students with mental handicaps lack several learning characteristics particularly relevant to the reading process: memory, reasoning skills, language acquisition, perceptual development, and cultural factors.

EMOTIONAL DEVELOPMENT   Students who cannot read or who cannot read as well as their age group are marked as failures. They are reminded of their failure every day. Even the skilled classroom or corrective reading teacher often cannot restore their confidence in themselves, because their classmates and worried parents often magnify their deficiencies (Schiffman, 1966).

The incidence of maladjustment among poor readers is greater than among good readers. As indicated in chapter 4, however, it is difficult to establish a causal relationship; it is not known whether emotional maladjustment causes reading failure, or whether reading failure causes maladjustment. Not all pupils who are emotionally handicapped are poor readers, nor are all poor readers emotionally handicapped students.

PHYSICAL FACTORS   Learning to read begins when parents or other people read to young children and allow them to handle books. Children develop spatial relationships, discover that people begin at the front of the book and turn pages, hold the books and play with the books, and try out behaviors they have experienced while in a reading situation (Hoskisson, 1979). Reading does require some degree of physical ability. However, this seems to be less relevant than other factors.

Students who have health impairments (diabetes, glandular dysfunction, and nutritional and circulatory problems), who fatigue easily, and who are ill for prolonged periods of time may have difficulty with any academic skills.

SUMMARY   Students need prereading skills to serve as a foundation in learning to read. Prereading instruction is the responsibility of every teacher and should be carried out at all age and grade levels. Group instruction moves too quickly for poor readers (Speckels, 1980). For them, the reading process should be carefully analyzed and slowed down; often, they are beginners. Because reading readiness can be a function of vision, hearing, language, intelligence, and emotional and physical development, teachers should consider these factors in planning and implementing prereading activities.

Instructional Approaches

Word Recognition

Reading can be defined as a two-step process of translating the written medium to language and translating the language to thought. The translation of writing involves recognition; the translation of language to thought involves comprehension. Word recognition (decoding) skills enable a reader to translate printed letters into speech sounds (May, 1982). The four subskills of this process are sight vocabulary, phonetic analysis, structural analysis, and context clues. The following sections discuss instructional approaches for each subskill.

SIGHT VOCABULARY   Most children start school knowing many words. A problem occurs when they do not know the correct words. Such children do not know how to read for school; presumably, they have brought no prereading experiences with them.

> Billy's mother had been told that he would never learn to read, that his intellectual functioning would not permit it. One day in the grocery store, Billy went to a carton he had seen on television many times, pointed, and said, "Geritol." His surprised mother pointed out other items and heard the responses, "Colgate," "Dentyne," and "Bayer."

People in our culture are constantly exposed to the written word through billboards, television, packages, product labels, street signs, and graffiti. The beginning level of reading should incorporate what the learner knows informally and add other skills.

The successful classroom environment is conducive to sight recognition of words. Materials are available for every purpose and age level. Props for house play and dramatic play encourage exploration, spark interest, and feed an ongoing project or interest. Books of all kinds and levels are everywhere, including telephone books, magazines, recipe books, and books made by the students. Many things in the room require reading: a sign on the bathroom door indicating that it is vacant or in use; activity charts or lists of students' activity selections; experience charts recording shared activities; recipes used for cooking; records or graphs recording plant and animal growth or behavior or weather changes; and maps, reference books, and diagrams—all adapted to the particular needs of the pupils. Words on standardized lists, such as the Dolch Word List and Kucera-Francis List, are valuable both as diagnostic instruments and in content development. However, for handicapped students, these lists are formidable and do not offer much hope for total success.

Kolstoe (1976) claims that sight words should be taught in the context of meaningful activities. He suggests selecting words and listing them by categories, as in these lists:

Action Words

stand	come	bend	whisper	laugh
draw	kneel	sit	go	hop
wave	touch	clap	run	jump
skip	fly	walk	nod	scratch
cry	write			

Objects

chair	wagon	plate	cow	pencil
telephone	kettle	truck	knife	horse
table	crayon	basket	block	fork
book				
dog				

Prepositions (These were taught by pantomime)

up	out	behind	right	bottom
from	down	across	before	left
beside	beneath	in	around	on (p. 108)
top	under	between		

Using cards on which the words are written, games can be played that require students to act out or pantomime the words.

Students should be allowed to select words they want to learn from passages that interest them (Noble, 1981). When students select the words they want to learn, they are more apt to practice the words and remember them.

Many high-frequency structure words are difficult to remember because they cannot easily be represented by pictures. Houghton (1974) states that only 32 words make up one-third of the words used by a child (or adult). These words are *a, and, be, I, in, is, it, of, that, the, to, was, all, as, at, be, but, are, for, had, have, him, his, not, on, one, said, so, they, we, wish, you.* The list also should include *she, her,* and *hers.* These words should be used frequently in language experience stories, in captioning stories, and in classroom signs. Specific drill on them will help insure success in beginning reading.

For handicapped students who have limited reading and/or speaking vocabularies, survival words and phrases will comprise the sight vocabulary list. *Men, women, danger,* and other specific words that are essential to safety should be selected.

PHONETIC ANALYSIS   The process of analyzing unknown words on the basis of letter-sound relationships is called phonetic analysis (Wallace, Cohen, & Polloway, 1987). Auditory discrimination skills are essential to successful phonics instruction; do not assume prior learning in this area with handicapped readers. Phonics instruction is not for every student; some students do not seem to have the intact auditory perception skills necessary to benefit from phonics instruction.

Generally, students are ready for phonics instruction when they begin to notice word families and when they recognize that words consist of different letters and sounds that they see in other words. Phonics instruction should not be viewed as an end in itself (Wallace, Cohen, & Polloway, 1987). The optimum amount of phonics instruction for any learner is the minimum needed to become an independent reader (Heilman, Blair, & Rupley, 1986).

Some students seem to learn sound-letter correspondence and even phonics rules. They can sound out words letter by letter but are not able to blend the sounds. The letters *p–u–t* remain *p–u–t*. To help the student learn to blend sounds, the teacher can briefly present words of two or three letters, pronouncing them.

Word wheels can be used for drill in initial sounds, word families, final sounds, prefixes, and suffixes. Commercial word-building charts, flip cards, and word attack games are available at reasonable prices.

Children with poor auditory discrimination abilities should participate in a program that permits the use of visual and kinesthetic word attack skills. At the same time, efforts should be made to improve their auditory discrimination skills in a separate instructional program. A number of commercial programs available can help develop auditory discrimination, auditory sequencing, and auditory memory.

STRUCTURAL ANALYSIS   The process of identifying meaningful units in words is called structural analysis. It requires the ability to identify base words, plural and possessive forms, prefixes, suffixes, and syllables.

Although there is a continuing debate as to the advisability of teaching students to identify the syllables in printed words (Groff, 1981), the ability to break words into pronounceable bits is likely to help them deal with multisyllabic words (Otto & Smith, 1980). The use of this and other structural analysis skills, along with contextual clues, can greatly facilitate students' decoding of unknown words (Parks, 1982). Most reading material gives students the opportunity to apply structural analysis skills (Richek, List, & Lerner, 1989). A word-identification strategy developed by researchers at the University of Kansas Learning Disabilities Research Institute emphasizes structural analysis skills (Lenz, Schumaker, Deshler, & Beals, 1984). This strategy is remembered using the mnemonic aid DISSECT. The steps for decoding an unknown word are:

D–Discover the context
I–Isolate the prefix
S–Separate the suffix
S–Say the stem

E–Examine the stem
C–Check with someone
T–Try the dictionary

This strategy, originally intended for adolescents, has also been successfully used by upper-grade elementary pupils.

CONTEXT CLUES   Using the surrounding language to figure out what an unknown word may be is a useful word recognition skill. Reading a variety of materials is the best way to learn to use context clues.

All the word recognition skills operate together in the total act of reading. Even so, some students who possess the subskills have some difficulty using them. Wilson (1981) suggests teaching a strategy to be used consistently when approaching a new word:

1. Read on and look for clues.
2. Frame the word.
3. Try the first sound.
4. Divide the word into smaller parts.
5. Consult. (p. 300)

COMPREHENSION   During a reading workshop, the instructor asked teachers at different levels to state their main problem in teaching reading. The primary teachers indicated building a sight vocabulary; the intermediate teachers, word attack skills; and the secondary level teachers, comprehension. The instructor asked the teachers to consider the premise that if comprehension were given major consideration at all levels, perhaps it would not be a problem at the upper levels.

Reading programs may put too much emphasis on word recognition skills and neglect comprehension. Certainly, many students have reading problems because of difficulties in word attack sequences, which should be taught at every level. However, the ultimate goal of reading is comprehension; word recognition provides a means to this end.

Otto and Smith (1980) describe two characteristics of students who have trouble with comprehension. First, these students are usually able to comprehend oral communications; they have no disabilities that make them incapable of understanding. Second, their problems are not limited to complex passages; they also have problems with simple and straightforward structures. These characteristics suggest that the students' problem is a lack of a systematic approach to extracting meaning from printed materials.

To deal with this problem, teachers need to develop a repertoire of strategies that will help handicapped students improve their comprehension and organization of reading materials. The following techniques can be used before, during, and after silent reading:

Teacher actions before students read:

1. *Set goals:* Tell students to remember as much as possible about the passage and tell them why they are reading.
2. *Have students make predictions.* Teachers should ask questions eliciting student predictions, such as Who/what do you think the main character will be? What should the main character do?
3. *Activate prior knowledge.* Have readers write answers to teacher-prepared questions designed to help them relate their own background knowledge to the topic and to make predictions.
4. *Use advanced organizers.* Ask questions that help provide an overview of the passage such as What is the title? Discuss vocabulary. Survey any headings.
5. *Introduce key concepts and new vocabulary.* Use visual aids such as

chart or chalkboard to list and explain major concepts and related new vocabulary.

Teacher actions during and after student reading:

1. *Reinforce specific reading behaviors.* Two suggested practices are to teach students how to self-record their own reading behavior and to reward achievement in reading comprehension performance charted by students.
2. *Require repeated readings.* Teachers have found increased comprehension after requiring students to read passages three times.
3. *Insert questions into text.* Teachers asking at least one question before a paragraph or section have found increased comprehension by students over asking no questions until the end of passages.
4. *Focus students' attention on text structure.* Have students outline important elements of passage, such as (1) setting, (2) problem, (3) goal, (4) action, and (5) outcome.
5. *Focus students' attention on important information using charts and graphics.* Have students complete a teacher-prepared chart or graph to focus on important information.
6. *Ask postcomprehension questions.* Ask students questions and permit them to look back at text. (Graham & Johnson, 1989)

Because comprehension is built on the understanding of concepts, on memory, and on generalization and interpretation, it is particularly difficult for students who have deficits in these areas. Teachers working with handicapped students need to stress comprehension at every level.

Following directions is a valuable skill in itself; it also indicates sentence comprehension. With students who do not follow directions well, give one direction at a time: for example, "Open your book to page 30." After the direction has been followed, give another: "Read the title of the chapter." When students can follow one direction at a time, give them two to follow consecutively: "Open your book to page 30 and read the title of the chapter." The directions must be clearly stated and within the students' realm of understanding (Burmeister, 1974). Classroom teachers can use this technique to get the students to read more in such content areas as mathematics, social studies, and science. As skills develop, lists of directions to follow in these areas can be given.

Functional Reading

Functional reading skills enable students to use reading in adapting to societal demands. These skills are used to avoid danger; to understand symbols and abbreviations; to read maps, diagrams, and charts; to develop study skills; to develop living skills; and to enjoy reading as a recreational activity.

For handicapped students, the key to functional reading is relevance. Reading instruction should be relevant to their abilities, their interests, and their needs.

For some handicapped students, functional reading may be the primary goal of instruction. Reading in everyday, adult pursuits necessitates the ability to read newspapers, directions, and telephone books and to fill out forms (Wiseman & Hartwell, 1980). A relevant curriculum addresses the functional reading needs of handicapped students.

Functional reading achievement, as well as other reading skills, is part of the competency testing program in many states. Functional areas assessed are reading labels, store directions, signs, want ads, and schedules; following directions and completing forms and applications; recognizing the meaning of common abbreviations; and distinguishing fact from opinion.

Materials

Handicapped students, like other students, do not always respond to teacher-designed procedures. Some handicapped students will be able to use the same reading materials as other class members; others will need special materials and techniques to reach their full potential. Teachers should consider using informal materials, the language experience approach, and special reading programs.

Informal Materials

By using informal materials, students can relate more readily to their environment and therefore to printed materials. Kohl (1973) suggests such materials as the telephone book, *TV Guide,* bus and plane schedules, catalogs, menus, advertisements, instructions included with appliances, price lists in supermarkets, newspapers, campaign literature, posters, buttons, and how-to manuals. As teachers recognize their students' interests, they can put together packets of materials that will appeal to almost anyone.

One of the least expensive and most relevant materials is the local newspaper. Frequently, publishers furnish free newspapers for a specified time. Papers can be used to teach many areas besides reading and to focus on specific reading problems, such as sequencing, locating, and memorizing (Fenholt, 1980). The following activities are suggested and the possibilities are unlimited:

- Using pictures from the newspapers, have students discuss what they think is happening in the pictures, and then make up their own captions.
- Read a short article to the students; have them retell the story in the proper order.
- Introduce new words from the newspaper. Keep the list on the bulletin board. Have students learn the meaning and spelling of each word.
- Block out some well-chosen nouns, verbs, and adjectives from a story. See how effective your students are at selecting meaningful words to fill these slots.
- Write a news summary of the front page of today's newspaper.
- Use news stories or pictures to launch a discussion of the forces that change the earth's surface, such as flood damage, hurricanes, and earthquakes.
- Design a large calendar for each month. Clip and post news stories on the calendar for each day. At the end of the month, have the students choose the one item they think is most important and then include it on a yearly calendar.

The alert teacher will find many environmental items of interest to the student. Reading can be motivated and strengthened using baseball and football cards, greeting cards, joke books, bumper stickers, and cereal and other food boxes.

Local Chambers of Commerce can provide teachers with many materials describing local geographic areas, vacation points, and historical places, as well as with maps of the city/town and state. Many magazines provide addresses to which the teacher or students can write for materials about quarter horses, the trucking industry, or almost any topic of interest. Materials files can be built to hold materials for a number of reading levels and topics.

Special Reading Programs

In addition to the basal readers, programmed instruction, trade books, and other series, some unique programs have been designed for students with special problems. If other systems have failed, the teacher should investigate the following programs and others that are available.

Edmark Reading Program. The Edmark Reading Program teaches a vocabulary of 150 words and provides activities to use reading skills and to develop comprehension and language. Activities include word recognition lessons, direction books, picture-phrase matching, and storybooks. Pretest and review tests are provided throughout the program to confirm the student's progress. The program is designed for students with extremely limited skills.

Distar. The Distar program (Engelmann & Bruner, 1969) was designed to teach beginning reading to culturally deprived and slow-learning children. The program incorporates the teaching of skills considered necessary for beginning to read, such as sequencing, left-right progression, and association of sound with symbol (Gillespie-Silver, 1979). Lessons are highly structured, with teacher instructions for reinforcement, pacing, and correction.

The New Streamlined English Series. Developed by Dr. Frank C. Laubach (1945) to teach adults with no reading skills, this program is being used increasingly with students for whom other methods have been ineffective. The method uses pictures with letters superimposed on them. The lesson format guarantees success by eliciting the correct response from the student and reinforcing it. Each lesson includes phonics, reading sight words, comprehension checks, structural analysis, and vocabulary development.

High Interest-Low Vocabulary Materials. Many teachers find that books and reading materials with controlled vocabularies for limited readers appeal to students who are older than their reading ability would indicate, such as handicapped middle school or high school students, are very helpful. These materials are useful in reading and are increasingly available in content area materials. See Table 8.5 for a selected list.

Techniques

In evaluating reading instruction, a frequent question is, What reading program gets better results? The question should be, What is it that more successful teachers do that less successful teachers do not do? A number of studies indicate that more successful teachers individualize reading and spend more time in reading instruction (Cohen, 1971).

The integration of handicapped students into the reading program of the regular classroom requires individualization and a great deal of time. When reading programs are totally different for several students, specific techniques are helpful. The language experience approach, rewriting material, peer tutoring, tape recording, and using games are techniques that have been successful.

Language Experience Approach

The essential characteristic of the language experience approach is that students learn to read or to improve their reading by using material that they have dictated and the teacher has written down.

TABLE 8.5 High Interest–Low Vocabulary Materials

Title	Focus	Number in Series	Reading Grade Level*	Interest Grade Level	Publisher
Cowboys of Many Races	Racial/ethnics cowboys on frontier	7	pp-5	1-7	Benefic Press
Jim Hunter Books	Adventures of a secret agent	16	2-3	6-adult	Fearon
Deep Sea Adventure Series	Sea adventures and mysteries	12	2-5	3-8	Addison
Fastback Romance Books	Romantic adventures	10	4-5	7-adult	Fearon
Dan Frontier	Early pioneer life	10	pp-3	1-6	Benefic Press
Prime Time Adventures	Mystery and adventure tales	10	2	4-12	Children's Press
Cowboy Sam	Western content	15	pp-3	1-6	Benefic Press
Hi-Ho Paperbacks	Contemporary adventure and mystery	14	2-3	7-12	Bantam Books
Everyreader Series	Classics and short stories	20	4	6-8	Webster
Indians	Indian biographies	13	3	4-6	Garrard
Turning Point	Varied topics	30	2-6	5-10	McCormick
Mystery Adventure Series	Young adults solve mysteries	6	2-6	4-12	Benefic Press
Crisis Series	Teenagers facing crisis	6	2-4	6-adult	Fearon
Specter	Ghost Stories	8	2-3	6-adult	Fearon
Ready, Get Set, Go Books	Varied topics	24	1-3	1-6	Children's Press
Moonbeam Series	Adventures of a monkey	10	pp-3	1-6	Benefic Press
Mania Books	Varied topics	16	1	1-5	Children's Press
Space Police	Space-age police	6	2-3	6-adult	Fearon
Exploring and Understanding Series	Science processes	13	4	4-9	Benefic Press

(continued)

TABLE 8.5 (continued)

Title	Focus	Number in Series	Reading Grade Level*	Interest Grade Level	Publisher
Tom Logan Series	Old west adventures of boy growing to manhood	10	pp-1	1-6	Benefic Press
A Book About	Science	16	2	2-4	Raintree
Hiway Books	Mystery, racing and interpersonal relationships	17	2-4	7-12	Westminister
Emergency Series	Paramedic team adventures	6	2-4	2-9	Benefic Press
Pacemaker True Adventures	True stories of spies, pirates, etc.	11	2-3	5-adult	Fearon
Discovery	Biographies of different people	60	2-3	4-6	Garrard
Laura Brewster Books	Adventures of an insurance investigator	6	2-3	6-adult	Fearon
Landmark Books	Historical events and important people themes	65	4-6	5-9	Random
Famous Animal Stories	Animal stories	17	3	4-6	Garrard

*pp: Preprimer

Source: From Language Arts: Teaching Exceptional Children (pp. 204–205) by G. Wallace, S. B. Cohen, and E. A. Polloway, 1987. Austin, TX: Pro-Ed. Copyright 1987 by Pro-Ed, Inc. Reprinted by permission.

As a means of introducing young children to reading, this approach has three advantages:

1. The language experience approach uses the child's own experiences and oral language as the basis for development of reading behaviors.
2. The flexibility of the language experience approach is well-suited to the diverse needs and abilities of young children.
3. The language experience approach can be incorporated into most programs in a gradual, meaningful, and natural manner. (Jensen & Hanson, 1980, p. 61)

The language experience approach appeals to older students who have negative attitudes toward commercial reading materials. Secondary students with serious reading problems sometimes respond positively to stories, essays, plays, and commentaries of their own creation (Otto & Smith, 1980).

Peer Teaching

Reading instruction permits the good reader to help the poor reader and the poor reader to help the younger reader. The programs described in the previous section can be taught by students who have been instructed in the simple steps. Good readers can read to small groups of students and help them understand and react to the stories.

Cross-grade matching enables the poor reader to help younger children learn to read or learn to listen. Several children from a fourth grade were asked to read to a small group of kindergarten children. They had never been asked to read before; they wanted to be perfect. Practice sessions, tape recording, and prolonged preparation preceded the experience. Reading skills were improved; self-concepts were lifted!

Studies of cross-age tutoring at the high school level also have been encouraging. In addition to enhancing reading achievement, peer-assisted learning improved self-concept, frequency of social interaction, social adjustment, classroom behavior, and attitude toward school (King, 1982). This is a good option for the teacher concerned with providing as much individual help as possible to pupils with special needs.

Tape Recording

A great deal of material from the regular curriculum can be recorded. Passages from science, social studies, language arts, math, or any other material the student is expected to read can be taped and listened to at a learning station or with earphones. Books and articles of interest to the student can be taped and placed with the written material; the student can follow the print while listening. This amount of recording is time consuming, but the teacher can usually find help. Smitherman (1974) suggests asking a friend (perhaps one who is convalescing) to record. College and high school students, individually or through service clubs, also can help.

Deshler and Graham (1980) suggest not taping everything verbatim. Instead, they recommend paraphrasing some material and deleting some material. They also suggest putting directions for tasks at key places throughout long passages (see Figure 7.1 in chapter 7).

Computer-Assisted Instruction

Computer-assisted instruction (CAI) is not a separate approach to teaching reading; it can interface with any approach. Students can use computers for reading drill and practice, tutorial instruction, problem solving, and games and simulation (Thompson, 1980). Teachers can use the computer to help with diagnostic, prescriptive, and evaluative tasks related to reading.

Computer-assisted instruction is highly motivating and can be valuable in teaching reading to handicapped students. Some advantages of computer-assisted instruction in reading (Lerner, 1989) include these:

1. Poor readers have more time for learning in a one-to-one situation.
2. Computers help poor readers develop automaticity in basic reading.
3. Computers provide private instruction.
4. Computers allow poor readers opportunity and time to think about the reading passage.
5. Computers enhance the instructional connection between reading and writing.

Finding and selecting appropriate software is a key factor in assuring the success of computer-aided instruction.

Gifted and Talented Students

Most students who are gifted benefit from activities that develop critical reading skills. Reading a wide variety of materials should be encouraged, yet time given to in-depth reading on topics of interest. Gifted students should be taught to compare, contrast, analyze, and synthesize. Activities requiring students to respond to author intent and style are appropriate. The key adaptation should be an individualized reading program if it is not available for all students (Cooter & Alexander, 1984; Robinson, 1986).

WRITING

As indicated in Figure 8.1, writing is the most advanced of the language arts components. The goal in teaching written language skills is the ability to communicate thoughts that are legible and meaningful.

The three important aspects of written language are handwriting, spelling, and written expression. These areas are complicated because they involve many subskills, such as auditory and visual sequential memory, motor control of writing utensils, eye-hand coordination, phonetic knowledge, organization of thoughts, and application of grammatical rules (Piazza, 1979).

Even though the interactive nature of language arts skills can be an advantage in instructional planning, Reid and Hresko (1981) point out a disadvantage for handicapped students. Having had uncomfortable or failing experiences with reading, these students may not be enthusiastic about written compositions, spelling, and handwriting. However, just as students' oral language expression can be improved with appropriate experiences and instruction, their written communication can also be facilitated.

Handwriting

Handwriting is the most concrete of the language arts; it can be observed, evaluated, and used to provide a permanent record of the child's productive efforts. Although largely a motor skill, handwriting also requires visual ability.

Handwriting is not as important in the curriculum as it once was. Beautiful handwriting used to be the mark of a scholar; although the end product was admired, it was difficult to attain and left little room for individual expression (Hoffmeister, 1981). The present goal is the use of functional, efficient handwriting. Although it is viewed as a means of expression rather than an end in itself, instruction in the mechanics of writing should not be neglected.

Screening criteria are not as clear in handwriting as in other areas. Classroom teachers may not agree on the criteria because of differing emphases on the importance of speed, legibility, and form. Although individual differences in handwriting style are generally accepted, the primary criterion is the response to the question, Can it be read with ease?

The Zaner-Bloser Evaluation Scales (1979) provide a standard method of collecting and rating handwriting samples. The student's handwriting is judged for letter formation; vertical strokes in manuscript; slant in cursive; spacing, alignment, and proportion; and line quality.

The Test of Written Language (Hammill & Larsen, 1988) has a subtest that is scored only if the student has written in cursive. The most important consideration in this subtest is legibility; letter slant, spacing, and size are not stressed.

The Diagnosis and Remediation of Handwriting Problems (Stott, Moyes, & Henderson, 1985) is designed to assess handwriting deficits for instructional planning and can be particularly helpful with handicapped students.

Objectives

Beginning Instruction

Three groups of experiences lead to writing readiness. The first group, manipulative experiences, is designed to strengthen muscles needed for writing and to gain control over writing tools. The second group is designed to increase the pupil's oral use of language. Students must be able to express their ideas orally before learning to write. The third group of experiences is designed to give students practice in the basic movements of writing itself.

Students with learning problems may be unable to control their movements well enough to hold a pencil. They may need to do exercises to develop coordination and strengthen the muscles involved in grasping. Spring clothespins can be used for this purpose—the student squeezes the pins to open them and places them on the edge of a box. Strong tactile feedback may be needed to monitor movements. Such experience can be provided through tracing with finger paint or tracing letters made from sandpaper, felt, velvet, or clay. Frostig and Maslow (1973) suggest that kinesthetic feedback provided from tracing soft, warm materials may be more effective for many students than is tracing sandpaper letters because the materials feel better. The small muscles of the hands can be developed by playing with toys, dialing the telephone, setting the table, putting puzzles together, cutting with scissors, and modeling clay. The first writing exercise should be with chalk on the chalkboard or with crayons on large pieces of paper.

Practice in the basic movements of writing begins with variations of the circle, the curved line, and vertical, horizontal, and oblique lines. Verbal cues have been successful in teaching manuscript writing to mentally retarded students (Vacc & Vacc, 1979). These basic verbal cues provide a guide when making a writing stroke: touch, pull, touch, cross; touch, slant; touch, slide; and touch, dot. Used in a variety of combinations, the verbal cues strengthen the student's visual skill development.

Handicapped students can benefit from tracing exercises. Tracing paper or a plastic cover can be placed over the forms to be traced. Commercial vinyl overlays are available for this purpose, but inexpensive page covers or even the plastic inserts in bacon packages work just as well. The initial pattern may consist of lines and simple geometric forms oriented in different positions in space and drawn in a constantly varying assortment of colors. The primary purpose of this exercise is to supply practice in visual motor perception. The next step is to copy the pattern on paper without the aid of tracing.

Students who are left-handed require different instruction than their right-handed peers because their handwriting problems are more numerous and severe. Left-handed students suffer from a frequent lack of appropriate desks and models who are left-handed. Also, writing from left to right requires that left-handers position their writing hand in an awkward hook or they are unable to view letters because the letters are covered by the writing hand. The preferred right leaning slant of cursive writing is difficult to achieve. Suggestions for teaching left-handed students are to:

> Group left-handed children together for handwriting instruction. Provide them with a good left-handed model—a teacher, aide, parent, or another student.
>
> Give them readiness exercises to develop left to right directionality. Encourage a fuller movement of the writing area by having them practice at the chalkboard.
>
> Teach them to hold their pencils about 1-1/2 inches from the point, slant their papers to the right, and turn their bodies to the right when they write.
>
> Encourage them to eliminate excessive loops and flourishes in their writing.
>
> Teach them to write vertically or with a slight backhand slant; do not insist on a slant to the right.
>
> Provide each child with a model cursive alphabet showing left-handed writing. They can use this instead of the usual right-handed model to evaluate and self-correct their handwriting. (Harrison, 1981, p. 117)

Handwriting Problems

Handicapped students may be unable to perform the motor movements required for writing or copying; they may be unable to transfer visual information inputs to motor outputs; and activities requiring motor and spatial judgments may be difficult for them. The shortcomings that contribute to such problems are poor motor skills, unstable and erratic temperament, faulty visual perception of letters, and difficulty in retaining visual impressions (Lerner, 1989).

The student with poor motor skills due to orthopedic handicaps may have difficulty holding a pencil, pen, chalk, or crayon. A commercial pencil grip or a ball of clay or sponge modeled around the pencil (see Figure 8.3) can prevent the fingers from slipping; if the problem is severe, pencil holders or mechanical devices may be needed. Care must be taken to equip the person with adaptations to fit the specific functional problem (Bigge, 1976).

Because handwriting is a visual as well as a motor task, visually impaired students need special accommodations. Even if braille is used, the pupil needs some method of communicating with sighted persons in writing. Letters, spelling words, and signatures can be written with the aid of an APH signature guide (American Printing House for the Blind). The guide, which is made of metal or cord, provides tactile lines that fit over a

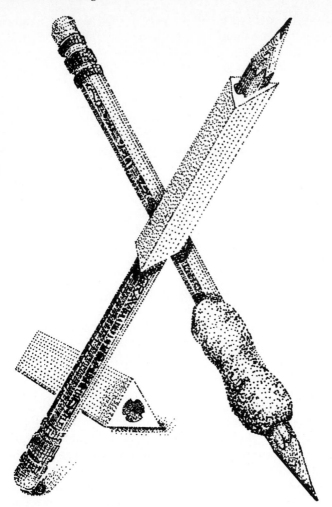

FIGURE 8.3 Pencil Grips

paper on a clip board. A small signature guide easily made from tagboard or plastic can be carried in the wallet (see Figure 8.4).

Pupils with visual impairments will need dark-line paper and may need to use large pencils past the primary grades. Writing in sand and in clay will help develop writing ability. The American Printing House for the Blind (see Appendix A for address) publishes many writing aids, including a raised-line checkbook, a cursive writing kit, script-letter sheets and boards, bold-line writing paper, and embossed pencil writing paper.

Students with handwriting difficulties due to visual impairments or orthopedic problems may be good candidates to learn typing or keyboarding skills for using a microcomputer word processor. In addition to hand-

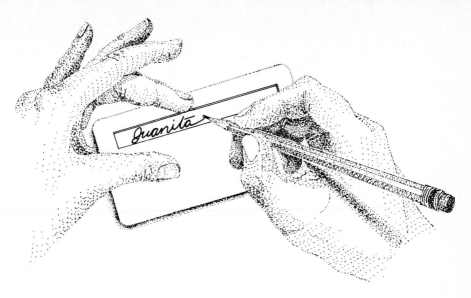

FIGURE 8.4 Signature Guide

writing, use of a word processor has advantages for spelling and composition (Lerner, 1989; Vacc, 1987). Typing skills cannot be learned, however, without deliberate instruction.

An additional problem in handwriting is poor instruction (Choate et al., 1987). Hoffmeister (1973) cites five common instructional errors in teaching writing: massed practice without supervision, no immediate feedback, emphasis on rote practice rather than on discrimination, failure to provide good models, and no differentiation between good and poor work. Frequently for students, the consequences of trying to improve their handwriting are the same as not trying when there is inadequate instruction and feedback. In addition, teacher-training programs have neglected handwriting (Graham, 1986; Milone, Wilhide & Wasylyk, 1984).

With knowledge of the developmental aspects of handwriting, regard for individual needs and differences, and skill in instructional procedures, the classroom teacher can provide activities to initiate and improve handwriting for handicapped as well as for nonhandicapped students.

Spelling

Spelling and handwriting have both been neglected in the development of innovative curriculum strategies. Consequently, teachers have little information to build on regarding types of spelling errors, kinds of instruction available, or strategies for task modifications (Reid & Hresko, 1981). This lack of help is especially critical because evidence indicates that poor spelling is increasing at the elementary, secondary, and college levels. In fact, some programs at the college level start out with the same words introduced at the elementary level (Rivers, 1974).

Many poor spellers are also deficient in other language abilities (Otto & Smith, 1980), especially reading (Carpenter & Miller, 1982). Therefore, special help in spelling should be given in conjunction with instruction in other language arts.

Proficient spellers use three kinds of knowledge when writing words. Language knowledge enables them to assign meaning to sounds to use prior knowledge in order to help determine word structures and to spell related words. Internalized rules enable them to predict and write the most probable spelling for words. And visual association helps in developing automatic spelling and in verifying written words (Nicholson & Schacter, 1979).

Lerner (1989) identifies the many subskills and abilities needed in the spelling process. Students must be able to read the word; they must be knowledgeable and skillful in certain relationships of phonics and structural analysis; and they must be able to apply the appropriate phonic generalizations, visualize the appearance of the word, and have the motor facility to write it.

Because handicapped students may have problems in visual and auditory discrimination, in making generalizations, and with motor skills, spelling success may be difficult to achieve. And yet, many handicapped students have become good spellers.

> *Larry, Libby, James, and David comprise a spelling group that comes to the resource room daily from the sixth grade. The resource teacher and the classroom teacher have worked out a weekly list of 10 words, taken from the sixth-grade spelling book, for this group to learn. After several months, this group became the best spellers in their class, sometimes even scoring well on the 20 words given to the whole class. Larry and Libby are mentally retarded, James is learning disabled, and David is blind.*
>
> *The resource teacher used a combination of discovery and drill. One of the most effective drill methods was to have one of the students dictate the words to David, who brailled them on cards. He could then drill the others orally, since they could not read his cards.*

Assessment

One commercially available and diagnostically useful spelling test is The Test of Written Spelling–2 (Larsen & Hammill, 1986), which can be used with students aged 6 through 18 years. It contains both phonetically regular and phonetically irregular words. Most standardized norm-referenced achievement batteries have spelling subtests that are of little use diagnostically.

Observation of students' written work offers the best assessment tool for the teacher, for the ability to spell in context is the ultimate goal of the spelling program. Because the purpose of assessment is remediation, the teacher should note the nature of spelling errors, determine any pattern presented, and plan a program to help students overcome the errors.

OBJECTIVES   The major goal of the spelling program for mildly handicapped students is to develop writers who can communicate without a number of spelling errors. Three major objectives for the student are:

1. To accurately spell the most frequently used words that the child needs to write now and in the future.
2. To develop self-correction skills for adjusting spelling errors.
3. To develop the ability to locate the correct spelling of unfamiliar words. (Cohen & Plaskon, 1980, p. 328)

INSTRUCTION IN SPELLING   According to research reviewed by Graham and Miller (1979), helpful spelling instructional techniques include:

1. The test-study-test method.
2. A synthetic spelling approach versus syllable-by-syllable.
3. Words presented in a list rather than in context.

In addition, they state that having students correcting their own spelling under the direction of the teacher is very effective.

Some authors advocate the development of spelling readiness through discrimination training, memory training, sound blending, and auditory closure (Lerner, 1989; Tiedt & Tiedt, 1978). Reid and Hresko (1981) claim that this type of prespelling instruction is inefficient. The best spelling readiness system is probably a broad language development program that integrates reading, writing, listening, and speaking skills.

Gentry (1981, 1987) suggests the "immersion of the speaker in a language environment" (p. 380) as a factor in learning to speak and to spell. Good spellers form a spelling consciousness through writing, augmented with formal spelling study.

Because of the overlearning feature, the cover-and-write method has been advocated for children who learn more slowly. This method includes the following 10 steps:

1. Look at the word; say it.
2. Write the word two times while looking at it.
3. Cover the word and write it one time.
4. Check your spelling by looking at the word.
5. Write the word two times while looking at it.
6. Cover the word and write it one time.
7. Check the word.
8. Write the word three times while looking at it.

9. Cover the word and write it one time.
10. Check the spelling.

This approach is useful in making an initial breakthrough with poor spellers, which is motivating in itself. However, it becomes dull if used too often.

Stowitschek and Jobes (1977) present a procedure that supports the importance of active teacher involvement during spelling instruction. Instruction is provided through a process of imitation training; teachers model spelling words, orally and in writing, for students to imitate. This direct, tutorial approach has been successful where previous spelling instruction has failed and would be useful if volunteer help or paraprofessionals were available.

One variation is the Imitation Plus Model approach reported by Kauffman, Hallahan, Hass, Brane, and Boren (1978) in which a teacher finds errors in a student's spelling. The teacher says, "Here is how you spelled the word," and imitates the student's spelling. The teacher then says, "Here is how the word should be spelled," and writes the word correctly in view of the student. The student rewrites the word. This effective technique has been duplicated by microcomputer (Hasselbring, 1984).

Activities

For children who need a multisensory approach to spelling, the Language Master is an effective tool. The Language Master, an audiovisual instructional system by Bell and Howell, provides visual, auditory, and some kinesthetic experiences for the child. Programmed cards are available, as are blank cards that the teacher can program. The blank cards can be reused if the top portion is laminated so that the spelling words can be erased or changed. The blank cards also permit the teacher to add clues, such as pictures or tactile stimulation (e.g., letters in yarn or sandpaper).

Additional activities for promoting spelling appear in teachers' magazines, children's weekly newspapers, and children's magazines. Of the many commercial games available for this purpose, some of the most successful have been created by children and teachers.

Remember that spelling is a tool for communication. It should be integrated with writing instruction and activities at all levels of instruction. The best motivation in spelling is the student's need to use particular words. Words identified as particularly useful for handicapped students are referred to as survival words.

Gifted and Talented Students

Spelling for students who are gifted is often linked to vocabulary study. Studying etymology and learning new words are appropriate activities, as are developing proofreading skills and studying anagrams. Selecting words from traditional spelling lists is probably inappropriate. On the other hand, gifted students are not automatically good spellers and should be given support in how to detect error and use aids such as spellers' dictionaries, which are designed for people who need to look up the correct spelling of words for which they do not have definitions.

Written Expression

It is apparent that students who have difficulty in one language arts area are at a disadvantage in related areas. The quality of student writing may be further limited by the scope of the students' ideas and the extent of their vocabulary. Their writing usually reflects the level of language they hear at home and at school. A wealth of language experience is needed to enrich the structure and purpose of spoken and written language.

Although once a neglected area, writing is now becoming an increasing focus of concern. Teachers are being held more accountable for the students' writing skills as written expression has become part of minimum competency tests, annual statewide testing programs, and criteria for gaining student employment and admission to postsecondary institutions.

Assessment

To evaluate a student's written performance, the teacher should be aware of the purpose of evaluation, the components of written language to be assessed, and the variety of assessment techniques available (Cohen & Plaskon, 1980). Two individually administered measures of written expression are:

1. Picture-Story Language Test–Revised for ages 7 to 17. (Grune & Stratton) The PSLT–R is an update of a popular individually administered measure of written expression using a writing sample.
2. Test of Written Language–2 for ages 7 to 17. (Pro-Ed) The TOWL–2 is a norm-referenced instrument measuring conventional, linguistic, and conceptual components of written language in individual or group administration. It measures a variety of writing skills using both a contrived and spontaneous format, including a writing sample.

Several other instruments include written expression components.

Work sample analysis is frequently used to evaluate written products for syntax, semantics, productivity, handwriting, spelling, and writing mechanics. Different skill areas can be analyzed to identify student strengths and weaknesses.

Informal assessment is valuable in providing diagnostic information and in determining appropriate instructional strategies. Before the informal assessment of written expression, the teacher should know the scope of necessary skills, the requirements of the specific writing task, and the characteristics of the student being assessed as they relate to the developmental nature of the student's language system (Poteet, 1980).

A number of checklists are available for assessing written language. One example is the Checklist of Written Expression (Poteet, 1980). Criterion-referenced tests, such as Brigance inventories (Brigance, 1977, 1978, 1981), are valuable in determining the needs of handicapped students. The Brigance instruments assess several written language skills. At the secondary level the Brigance Diagnostic Inventory of Essential Skills features survival skills, such as completing applications and tax forms and writing letters.

Objectives

Expressive writing is either functional or creative. Functional writing refers to letters, reports, and other means of relaying information in a structured form. Creative writing permits the author to express, through poetry or prose, personal thoughts, experiences, and observations in a unique fashion.

FUNCTIONAL WRITING   Letter writing is a valued social as well as business skill. As with handwriting, this is an area in which many students (including those who have not been successful academically) can excel.

> Robert, who is mentally retarded, has been writing thank-you notes since he was quite young. At first, he told his mother what he wanted to say; she wrote it and Robert copied it. As he acquired a small sight vocabulary, his mother put the words he used most frequently on small cards. With her help, he could form sentences from the cards and copy them into letter form. Last year, following his high school graduation, Robert wrote all his notes to thank friends and relatives for graduation gifts.

Classroom teachers can encourage letter writing in many ways. Noar (1972) suggests the use of individual mailboxes. They can be made from milk cartons, with the top cut off and a sign bearing the owner's name. The teacher can put into the mailboxes welcome back notes for absentees and notes to go home. Children can put in birthday cards, friendly notes to classmates, and notes to the teacher and to parents.

If the teacher wishes to plan a program in letter writing, a visit to the post office can be a starting point. The post office has a writing kit that the teacher can obtain for classroom use. Some teachers have a post office in the classroom. They may write to two or three students each evening and place the letters in the class post office. The students answer the letter with one of their own and drop their letters in the box the next day.

Forms of writing should be introduced as vehicles for conveying information rather than as rigid models or patterns to be imitated. Because writing is a very personal and individual production, the handicapped child should not be at a disadvantage. Leeson (1977) describes a project in which eighth-grade students assisted third-grade students in the composition, revision, and evaluation of their writing projects. Both groups improved their use of grammar and spelling, learned to proofread and read aloud clearly, and developed admiration for the other's accomplishments. A similar plan could improve the writing skills of handicapped students and their nonhandicapped peers.

Cooperation between the classroom teacher and the resource teacher helps the handicapped student achieve success in writing. Melissa, a second-grade student, was unable to complete a writing assignment in class. Assisted individually by the resource teacher, she produced her letter (see Figure 8.5).

The teaching of writing skills is an important aspect of mainstreaming mildly handicapped students in secondary English classes (Sargent, Swartzbaugh, & Sherman, 1981). Writing instruction can be applied to traditional language arts activities and to practical exercises, including letters of request, complaint letters, personal letters, telephone messages, descriptive essays, and note taking for other classes. The use of a combination of literature-related assignments and practical application assignments keeps instruction in line with requirements of the regular English curriculum and meets the needs of handicapped students.

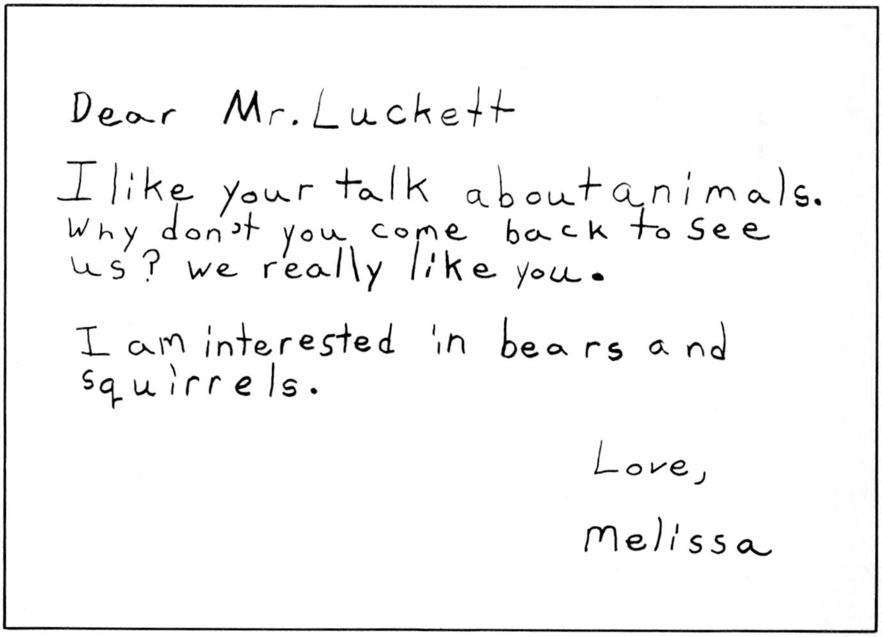

Dear Mr. Luckett

I like your talk about animals.
Why don't you come back to see
us? we really like you.

I am interested in bears and
squirrels.

Love,

melissa

FIGURE 8.5 Functional Letter Writing

Creative Writing

Writing is a threat to many people. For students who view reading, spelling, and school as areas in which they have failed, writing may seem impossible. Yet creative writing may be the vehicle for expression and growth vital to their intellectual and emotional development.

A program in creative writing for students with learning disabilities (Cady, 1976) demonstrated the value of writing and contributed some excellent techniques for teaching it to students whose reading skills were below the level at which written expression is usually introduced. The topic was introduced to the class by the teacher's reading aloud each day. In addition to such classics as *Charlotte's Web* and *The Story of My Life* by Helen Keller (1954), she read stories and poems written by students of all ages. The students were instructed to write as if they were talking and were provided with copies of *The Spelling Reference Book* (Developmental Learning Materials). Topics were chosen with or without the students' help, and they were free to write at any suitable time, provided a story was completed or a reasonable beginning was made on a particular day. On completion, the students shared their stories. Their pleasure in hearing each other's stories suggested that "real communication occurred and that some of the isolation of struggling with a learning disability was diminished" (Cady, 1976, p. 29).

In the early stages of writing, it is important not to restrict students by emphasizing the mechanics of writing. Even though editing is important, concern with punctuation may be inhibiting. The classroom climate should permit students to feel free to dare and to explore.

Students who have never written may feel less inhibited if they are granted privacy in their early endeavors. Kohl (1967) used this technique effectively in introducing writing to inner-city children. The students were encouraged to write about their lives and were assured that the teacher would see their products only if they wished. The results were moving experiences that helped the teacher understand the children and their problems.

INSTRUCTIONAL TECHNIQUES   Writing, like other language arts skills, is built on observation and experience. Schiff (1979) suggests that opportunities for prewriting observation should have a manipulative component, such as:

- field trips to museums where visitors can operate the exhibits;
- visits to farms where students may participate in the care of animals;
- tours of historical restorations where students can try out craft implements (spinning wheels, butter presses, blacksmithing equipment);

- school/neighborhood walks on which pupils can work the public address system or plant a flower at a nearby nursery;
- examination of objects with moving parts which students can touch, turn, prod, and pull (kitchen utensils, treadle sewing machines, typewriters). (p. 754)

The earliest expressive student writing originates from their little bits of news, their journals, their personal accounts of experiences, or a class activity. Early writing can begin with the teacher as a scribe, helping students attempt writing by themselves as soon as possible. Teachers who accept "invented" spelling find that students are willing writers (Clay, 1982). During the early stages of drafting, students should not be concerned with punctuation. In pointing out that learning to write takes a long time, Albert (1977) feels that as teachers

> We expect . . . students to spell perfectly before they grasp sound-letter relationships. We expect them to punctuate correctly before they tune into the pauses that commas and periods symbolize. We expect them to adhere to a flawless format before they find something worthwhile to say. (p. 48)

For students who lack adequate background experiences, story starters can stimulate ideas. Within the same classroom, students of varying ability can respond to the same starter. In a fifth-grade class, the teacher provided this starter: "I was sitting alone in my room last night when suddenly . . . ." She then asked the students to complete the story. The task was carried out differently by Cassi (Figure 8.6) and by Nathan (Figure 8.7).

For students who will not write, who do not have the skills to write, who are visually or physically impaired so they cannot write, and/or who still need to express themselves, the tape recorder is an excellent medium. The teacher can provide a list of topics or pictures from which to choose or students can select their own topics. When left alone, many students use the tape recorder with a great deal of creativity. One teacher placed the tape recorder on a table with a folder beside it and the following instructions written and recorded: "The pictures in this folder are illustrations for stories. Select one you like and write a story to go with it. You may use the tape recorder if you wish to tell your story. I will write it down later." A number of pictures cut from magazines were placed in the folder. As taped stories were written by the teacher and read to the class, the students began to read their own as well as others' stories.

Researchers of the University of Kansas have developed validated strategies to teach adolescents how to write sentences and themes and how to identify written errors. These strategies all follow a similar instructional pattern and are aimed at helping students to write better in mainstreamed classes.

Writing can develop in the same natural way as spoken language if

> I was sitting alone in my room
> last night when suddenly my cat came
> in and scolded me for not doing my
> homework. So I got up and finished
> my homework.
> When I was done I decided to
> read, but then 3 rotton eggs came in
> and told me to go to the kitchen to
> do the dishes. So I got up again and
> did the dishes.
> When I was done I was ready
> to go to bed but a robot came in
> and threw garlic and rotton tomatoes
> at me and said, "That's what you get for
> not taking a bath beep, beep." I decided
> to get up and take a bath.
> Now. I'm in bed waiting for
> something to happen, but I been
> thinking, Could I be watching
> too much T.V.?
>
> by Cassi

FIGURE 8.6 Expressive Writing

learning conditions are similar (Cohen, 1981). These conditions include a stimulating environment, encouragement, and a relaxed adult attitude.

THE LANGUAGE EXPERIENCE APPROACH   The communication skills of listening, speaking, reading, and writing are closely interrelated. In the language experience approach, students develop certain fundamental concepts about themselves and communication so that they have a framework on which to build the skills they find functional and meaningful.

the
Dream

I was sitting alone in my room last night when suddenly!! the door opened, my mom was standing there. Time to take your asprin. It was 12 o'clock, I had to take it because I had a cold. After that I fell asleep I had a dream I got on a sled went down a slide sharp curves that could nock you off. When you started you had 32,0000 feet to go. I went about 100 going down the whole thing. I went on, on, on I came to the bottom I landing Sand, Suddenly I woke up, I was on the floor. I got in to bed pulled the cover's to my neck I sigted..... Sunrise.

End

FIGURE 8.7 Expressive Writing

These principles are evident in classes in which the language experience approach is practiced. Children are eager to express and record their experiences.

> *A university teacher was visiting in a kindergarten class. She had just observed a little boy as he completed a building with blocks. She commented on the beauty of the production and was directed by the child, "Write it!" Since the teacher obviously did not understand, the boy took her by the hand and led her to a large tablet on an easel. Under his direction, the teacher wrote about the block building that had been constructed.*

At a very early age, students are aware of the importance of the written word. It is exciting for them to see their own experiences and words written down. The language experience approach has no age limits; it is as valuable to the high school student as it is to the young child. It may be especially effective for the student who has not learned to read and write by other methods.

> *Mike, a 15-year-old, was embarrassed because he could not read. Discovering Mike's interest in camping, his teacher brought in several camping magazines. She pasted several pictures on paper and asked Mike to tell a story about them. She wrote the stories beneath the pictures and Mike could read them; they contained words in his own vocabulary and were based on his interest.*

Language experience stories can be written by the whole class or by one person. A class experience may be interpreted in many different ways by the different participants. The important factor is the experience. Many students have a background of experiences to draw from, but some have to be provided with experience in school.

The language experience approach illustrates the interrelatedness of all the language arts. Based on the prerequisite skill of oral language expression, it adds the skills of spelling, writing, and reading to create total communication.

Microcomputers

The use of microcomputers in helping with students' written expression has been a boon in writing (Lerner, 1989; MacArthur, 1988), as in other language arts areas. Although the use of microcomputers does not seem to affect the overall quality of written products by handicapped learners or nonhandicapped learners (Daiute, 1986; MacArthur & Graham, 1987; Vacc, 1987), the length of written work has increased for some (Vacc, 1987), and other benefits also result. Rust (1986) mentions these benefits of word processing with microcomputers from recent research:

1. Word processing makes the physical act of composing easier.
2. Students whose handwriting is poor can have their work read more easily by other people.

3. Revision on computers is much easier than by handwriting.
4. Conferences are easier because revising and editing are easier. Students are less resistant to suggestions for change.
5. Making a final copy is easier.
6. Students write more.

Furthermore, spelling checkers, style analyzers, and outlining programs offer critical assistance for mechanical aspects of writing.

Gifted and Talented Students
For students who are gifted, writing should begin when reading instruction begins. Barbe and Milone (1985) suggest an instructional approach in which students begin with dictation followed by structured written expression and a writing center to support written expression efforts of students. Gifted students benefit from learning editing skills and from editing the work of other gifted students (Polette, 1982). Written expression instruction should emphasize drafting and should use sharing circles, where students read their own writing and give each other feedback. Other suggestions include emphasis on creative and technical writing (Robinson, 1986).

Chapter 8 is the first of content-specific chapters detailing key objectives and suggestions for teaching language arts to exceptional learners. Building on life experiences, language arts encompasses listening, speaking, reading, and writing. Integrating each component area with the others requires creativity and the use of all available resources. The following chapter on mathematics continues the focus of content-specific chapters.

REFERENCES

Adler, S. (1964). *The non-verbal child.* Springfield, IL: Charles C Thomas.

Albert, B. (1977). Are you giving writing its due? *Instructor, 87,* (3), 41–48.

Barbe, W. B., & Milone, M. N. (1985). Reading and writing. In R. H. Swassing, *Teaching gifted children and adolescents* (pp. 276–315). Columbus, OH: Merrill.

Bigge, J. L. (1976). *Teaching individuals with physical and multiple disabilities.* Columbus, OH: Merrill.

Black, J. K. (1979). There's more to language than meets the ear: Implications for evaluation. *Language Arts, 56,* 525–533.

Bloom, L. (1970). Language development: Form and function in emerging grammars. *Research Monograph No. 59.* Cambridge, MA: M.I.T. Press.

Bowen, S. M., & Hynd, G. W. (1988). Do children with learning disabilities outgrow deficits in selective auditory attention? Evidence from dichotic listening in adults with learning disabilities. *Journal of Learning Disabilities, 21,* 623–631.

Brenza, B. A., Kricos, P. B., & Lasky, E. Z. (1981). Comprehension and production of basic semantic concepts by older hearing-impaired children. *Journal of Speech and Hearing Research, 24,* 414–419.

Brigance, A. H. (1977). Brigance diagnostic inventory of basic skills (2nd ed.). N. Billerica, MA: Curriculum Associates.

Brigance, A. H. (1978). Brigance Diagnostic Inventory of Early Development. N. Billerica, MA: Curriculum Associates.

Brigance, A. H. (1981). Brigance Diagnostic Inventory of Essential Skills. N. Billerica, MA: Curriculum Associates.

Burmeister, L. E. (1974). *Reading strategies for secondary school teachers.* Reading, MA: Addison-Wesley.

Cady, J. L. (1976). Pretend you are . . . an author. *Teaching Exceptional Children, 9,* 26–31.

Carpenter, D., & Miller, L. J. (1982). Spelling ability of reading disabled LD students and able readers. *Learning Disability Quarterly, 5,* 65–70.

Chaney, C. M., & Kephart, N. C. (1968). *Motoric aids to perceptual training.* Columbus, OH: Merrill.

Choate, J. S., Bennett, T. Z., Enright, B. E., Miller, L. J., Poteet, J. A., & Rakes, T. A. (1987). *Assessing and programming basic skills.* Boston: Allyn and Bacon.

Clark, E. V. (1974). Some aspects of the conceptual basis for first language acquisition. In R. L. Schiefelbusch & L. L. Lloyd (Eds.), *Language perspectives— Acquisition, retardation, and intervention* (pp. 104–128). Baltimore: University Park Press.

Clay, M. M. (1982). Learning and teaching writing: A developmental perspective. *Language Arts, 59,* 65–70.

Cohen, S. A. (1971). Dyspedagogia as a cause of reading retardation: Definition and treatment. In B. Bateman (Ed.), *Learning disorders* (Vol. 4). Seattle: Special Child Publications.

Cohen, S. B. (1980). Using learning strategies to teach the language arts. *Exceptional Teacher, 1,* (7), 1–15.

Cohen, S. B., & Plaskon, S. P. (1980). *Language arts for the mildly handicapped.* Columbus, OH: Merrill.

Cohen, M. (1981). Observations of learning to read and write naturally. *Language Arts, 58,* 549–556.

Cooter, R. B., & Alexander, J. E. (1984). Interest and attitude: Affective connections for gifted and talented readers. *Reading World, 24,* (1), 97–102.

Craig, L. (1980). *Language experience approach.* Northbrook, IL: Hubbard Scientific Co.

Crews, W. B. (1988). Performance of students classified as educable mentally handicapped on Florida's State Student Assessment Test, Part II. *Education and Training in Mental Retardation, 23,* 186–191.

Daiute, C. A. (1986). Physical and cognitive factors in revising: Insights from studies with computers. *Research in Teaching of English, 20,* 141–159.

Deen, B., & Deen, F. (1977). Oral language development. *Elementary Teacher's Ideas and Materials Workshop,* March.

Deshler, D. D., & Graham, S. (1980). Tape recording educational materials for secondary handicapped students. *Teaching Exceptional Children, 12,* (2), 52–54.

Dunn, L. M., & Dunn, L. M. (1981). Peabody Picture Vocabulary Test–Revised. Circle Pines, MN: American Guidance Services.

Engelmann, S., & Bruner, E. C. (1969). *Distar reading: An instructional system.* Chicago: Science Research Associates.

Fenholt, J. (1980). Good news! *Exceptional Teacher, 1,* (7), 5.

Frostig, M., & Maslow, P. (1973). *Learning problems in the classroom.* New York: Grune & Stratton.

Gentry, J. R. (1981). Learning to spell developmentally. *The Reading Teacher, 34,* 378–381.

Gentry, J. R. (1987). *Spel . . . is a four-letter word.* New York: Scholastic.

Geoffrion, L. D. (1982). Reading and the nonvocal child. *The Reading Teacher, 35,* 662–669.

Gillespie-Silver, P. (1979). *Teaching reading to children with special needs.* Columbus, OH: Merrill.

Goldman, R., Fristoe, M., & Woodcock, R. (1970). Goldman–Fristoe–Woodcock Test of Auditory Discrimination. Circle Pines, MN: American Guidance Services.

Graham, S. (1986). A review of handwriting scales and factors that contribute to variability in handwriting scores. *Journal of School Psychology, 24,* 63–71.

Graham, S., & Harris, K. (1988). Instructional recommendations for teaching writing to exceptional students. *Exceptional Children, 54,* 506–512.

Graham, S., & Johnson, L. A. (1989). Teaching reading to learning disabled students: A review of research-supported procedures. *Focus on Exceptional Children, 21,* (6), 1–12.

Graham, S., & Miller, L. (1980). Handwriting research and practice: A unified approach. *Focus on Exceptional Children, 13,* (2), 1–16.

Graham, S., & Miller, L. J. (1979). Spelling research and practice: A unified approach. *Focus on Exceptional Children, 12,* (2), 1–16.

Greenslade, B. C. (1980). The basics in reading, from the perspective of the learner. *The Reading Teacher, 34,* 192–195.

Groff, P. (1981). Teaching reading by syllables. *The Reading Teacher, 35,* 659–664.

Hammill, D. D. (1985). Detroit Tests of Learning Aptitude, Revised-2. Austin, TX: Pro-Ed.

Hammill, D. D., Brown, V. L., Larsen, S. C., & Wiederholt, J. L. (1987). Test of Adolescent Language-2. Austin, TX: Pro-Ed.

Hammill, D. D. & Larsen, S. C. (1988). Test of Written Language-2. Austin, TX: Pro-Ed.

Hargis, C. H. (1982). *Teaching reading to handicapped children.* Denver: Love.

Harrison, S. (1981). Open letter from a left-handed teacher: Some sinistral ideas on the teaching of handwriting. *Teaching Exceptional Children, 13,* 116–120.

Hart, B. O. (1963). *Teaching reading to deaf children.* Washington, DC: Alexander Graham Bell Association for the Deaf.

Hasselbring, T. S. (1984). Using a microcomputer for imitating student errors to improve spelling performance. *Computers, Reading, and Language Arts, 1,* (4), 12–14.

Heilman, A. W., Blair, T. R., & Rupley, W. H. (1986). *Principles and practices of teaching reading* (6th ed.). Columbus, OH: Merrill.

Hoffmeister, A. M. (1981). *Handwriting resource book.* Allen, TX: Developmental Learning Materials.

Hoffmeister, A. M. (1973). Let's get it write. *Teaching Exceptional Children, 6,* (10), 30–33.

Hoskisson, K. (1979). Learning to read naturally. *Language Arts, 56,* 489–496.

Howell, K. W., & Morehead, M. K. (1987). *Curriculum-based evaluation for special and remedial education: A handbook for deciding what to teach.* Columbus, OH: Merrill.

Jensen, M. A., & Hanson, B. A. (1980). Helping young children learn to read: What research says to teachers. *The Reading Teacher, 35,* 61–71.

Kauffman, J. M., Hallahan, D. P., Hass, K., Brane, T., & Boren, R. (1978). Imitating children's errors to improve their spelling performance. *Journal of Learning Disabilities, 11,* 33–38.

Kean, M. J., & Personke, C. (1976). *The language arts.* New York: St. Martin's.

Keller, H. (1954). *The story of my life.* Garden City, NY: Doubleday.

King, R. T. (1982). Learning from a PAL. *The Reading Teacher, 35,* 582–685.

Klein, M. L. (1979). Designating a talk environment for the classroom. *Language Arts, 56,* 647–656.

Kohl, H. (1967). *36 children.* New York: New American Library.

Kohl, H. (1973). *Reading, how to.* New York: Dutton.

Kolstoe, O. P. (1976). *Teaching educable mentally retarded children* (2nd ed.). New York: Holt, Rinehart and Winston.

Larsen, S. C., & Hammill, D. D. (1986). The Test of Written Spelling–2. Austin, TX: Pro-Ed.

Laubach, F. C. (1945). *The silent billion speak.* New York: Friendship.

Leeson, J. (1977). Language arts: Story partners. *Teacher, 94,* (9), 68–69.

Lenz, B. K., Schumaker, J. B., Deshler, D. D., & Beals, V. B. (1984). *The word identification strategy.* Lawrence, KS: The University of Kansas.

Lerner, J. W. (1989). *Learning disabilities: Theories, diagnosis, and teaching strategies* (5th ed.). Boston: Houghton Mifflin.

Lowell, E. L., & Pollack, D. B. (1984). Remedial practices with the hearing impaired. In S. Dickson (Ed.), *Communication disorders* (2nd ed.) (pp. 446–496). Glenview, IL: Scott, Foresman.

MacArthur, C. A. (1988). The impact of computers on the writing process. *Exceptional Children, 54,* 536–542.

MacArthur, C., & Graham, S. (1987). Learning disabled students' composing under three methods of text production: Handwriting, word processing and dictation. *Journal of Special Education, 21,* 22–42.

Mass, L. N. (1982). Developing concepts of literacy in young children. *The Reading Teacher, 35,* 670–675.

May, F. B. (1982). *Reading as communication.* Columbus, OH: Merrill.

McLean, J. (1974). Language development and communication disorders. In N. G. Haring (Ed.), *Behavior of exceptional children* (pp. 449–491). Columbus, OH: Merrill.

Mercer, C. D., & Mercer, A. R. (1985). *Teaching students with learning problems* (2nd ed.). Columbus, OH: Merrill.

Miller, J. F., & Yoder, D. E. (1972). On developing the content for a language teaching program. *Mental Retardation, 10,* (2), 9–11.

Milone, M. N., Wilhide, J. A., & Wasylyk, T. M. (1984). Spelling and handwriting: Is there a relationship? In W. B. Barbe, V. G. Lucas, & T. M. Wasylyk (Eds.), *Handwriting: Basic skills for effective communication* (pp. 246–250). Columbus, OH: Zaner-Bloser.

Molloy, J. S., & Witt, B. T. (1971). Development of communication skills in retarded children. In J. H. Rothstuben (Ed.), *Mental retardation* (pp. 449–455). New York: Holt, Rinehart and Winston.

Moores, D. (1972). Language disabilities of hearing-impaired children. In J. V. Irwin and M. Marge (Eds.), *Principles of childhood language disabilities* (pp. 159–184). Englewood Cliffs: NJ: Prentice-Hall.

Moran, M. R. (1980). An investigation of the demands of oral language skills on learning disabled students in secondary classrooms (Research Report no. 1). Lawrence: University of Kansas, Institute for Research in Learning Disabilities.

Newcomer, P. L., & Hammill, D. D. (1988a). Test of Language Development–2, Primary. Austin, TX: Pro-Ed.

Newcomer, P. L., & Hammill, D. D. (1988b). Test of Language Development–2, Intermediate. Austin: TX: Pro-Ed.

Nicholson, T., & Schachter, S. (1979). Spelling skill and teaching practice – putting them back together again. *Language Arts, 56,* 804–809.

Noar, G. (1972). *Individualized Instruction: Every child a winner.* New York: John Wiley.

Noble, E. F. (1981). Self-selection: A remedial strategy for readers with a limited reading vocabulary. *The Reading Teacher, 34,* 386–388.

Norton, D. E. (1989). *The effective teaching of language arts* (3rd ed.). Columbus, OH: Merrill.

Norwood, M. J. (1976). Captioned films for the deaf. *Exceptional Children, 43,* 164–166.

Okolo, C. M. (1988). Instructional environments in secondary vocational education programs: Implications for LD adolescents. *Learning Disability Quarterly, 11,* 136–148.

Otto, W., & Smith, R. J. (1980). *Corrective and remedial teaching* (3rd ed.). Boston: Houghton Mifflin.

Parks, B. H. (1982). Acquiring syllabication skills: A simplified approach. *Teaching Exceptional Children, 14,* 186–187.

Piazza, R. (1979). *Language and writing disorders.* Guilford, CO: Special Learning Corp.

Polette, N. (1982). *3Rs for the gifted.* Littleton, CO: Libraries Unlimited.

Poteet, J. A. (1980). Informal assessment of written expression. *Learning Disability Quarterly, 3,* 88–98.

Reid, D. K., & Hresko, W. P. (1981). *A cognitive approach to learning disabilities.* New York: McGraw-Hill.

Richek, M. A., List, L. K., & Lerner, J. W. (1989). *Reading problems: Assessment and remediation.* Englewood Cliffs, NJ: Prentice-Hall.

Rivers, C. (1974). Spelling: Its tyme to do something. *Learning, 3,* (3), 72–78.

Roberts, K., & Schaefer, R. (1984). Cognitive abilities and infant language intervention. In D. F. Ruder and M. D. Smith (Eds.), *Developmental language interventions* (pp. 85–139). Baltimore: University Park Press.

Robinson, A. (1986). Elementary and language arts for the gifted: Assimilation and accommodation in the curriculum. *Gifted Child Quarterly, 30,* 178–181.

Robinson, S., & Smith, M. D. (1981). Listening skills: Teaching learning disabled students to be better listeners. *Focus on Exceptional Children, 13,* (8), 1–15.

Ruder, K. F., & Smith, M. D. (1974). Issues in language training. In R. L. Schiefelbusch & L. L. Lloyd (Eds.), *Language perspectives—acquisition, retardation, and intervention* (pp. 565–605). Baltimore: University Park Press.

Rust, K. (1986). Word processing: The missing key for writing. *The Reading Teacher, 39,* 611–612.

Salvia, J., & Ysseldyke, J. E. (1988). *Assessment in special and remedial education* (4th ed.). Boston: Houghton Mifflin.

Sargent, L. R., Swartzbaugh, T., & Sherman, P. (1981). Teaming up to mainstream in English: A successful secondary program. *Teaching Exceptional Children, 13,* 100–103.

Schiefelbusch, R. L., Ruder, K. F., & Bricker, W. A. (1976). Training strategies for language-deficient children: An overview. In N. G. Haring and R. L. Schiefelbusch (Eds.), *Teaching special children* (pp. 268–300). New York: McGraw-Hill.

Schiff, P. M. (1970). . . . Stand up, sit down, write, write, write! *Language Arts 56,* (7), 753–756.

Schiffman, G. G. (1966). Program administration within a school system. In J. Money (Ed.), *The disabled reader* (pp. 241–259). Baltimore: Johns Hopkins.

Shumaker, J. B., Sheldon-Wildgen, J., & Sherman, J. A. (1980). An observational study of the academic and social skills of learning disabled adolescents in the regular classroom (Research Report No. 22). Lawrence: University of Kansas Institute for Research in Learning Disabilities.

Smitherman, D. W. (1974). A hand-up for slow readers. *Learning, 3,* (3), 87.

Speakman, N. J., & Roth, F. P. (1984). Intervention strategies for learning disabled children with oral communication disorders. *Learning Disability Quarterly, 7,* 10–13.

Speckels, J. (1980). "Poor" readers can learn phonics. *The Reading Teacher, 34,* 22–26.

Stott, D. H., Moyes, F. A., & Henderson, S. E. (1985). *Diagnosis and remediation of handwriting problems.* Guelph, Ont: Brook Educational Publishing.

Stowitschek, E. E., & Jobes, N. K. (1977). Getting the bugs out of spelling. *Teaching Exceptional Children, 9,* (3), 74–76.

Strauss, A. A., & Lehtine, L. E. (1947). *Psychopathology and education of the brain-injured child.* New York: Grune & Stratton.

Taylor, S. E. (1973). *Listening.* Washington, DC: National Educational Association of the United States.

Temple, C., & Gillet, J. W. (1984). *Language arts: Learning processes and teaching practices.* Boston: Little, Brown.

Thompson, B. J. (1980). Computers in reading: A review of applications and implications. *Educational Technology, 20* (8), 38–41.

Tiedt, S. W., & Tiedt, I. M. (1978). *Language arts activities for the classroom.* Boston: Allyn and Bacon.

Vacc, N. N. (1987). Word processor versus handwriting: A comparative study of writing samples produced by mildly mentally handicapped students. *Exceptional Children, 54,* 156–165.

Vacc, N. N., & Vacc, N. A. (1979). Teaching manuscript writing to mentally retarded children. *Education and Training of the Mentally Retarded, 14,* 286–291.

Vallecorsa, A. L., Zigmond, N., & Henderson, L. M. (1985). Spelling instruction in special education classrooms: A survey of practices. *Exceptional Children, 52,* 19–24.

Wallace, G., Cohen, S. B., & Polloway, E. A. (1987). *Language arts: Teaching exceptional students.* Austin, TX: Pro-Ed.

Wallace, G., & Kauffman, J. M. (1973). *Teaching children with learning problems.* Columbus, OH: Merrill.

Wechsler, D. (1974). Wechsler intelligence scale for children–revised. New York: Psychological Corp.

Wiig, E. H., & Semel, E. (1984). *Language assessment and intervention for the learning disabled.* Columbus, OH: Merrill.

Wilson, R. M. (1981). *Diagnostic and remedial reading* (4th ed.). Columbus, OH: Merrill.

Winkeljohann, R. (1981). How can teachers promote language use? *Language Arts, 58,* 605–606.

Wiseman, D. E., & Hartwell, L. K. (1980). The poor reader in secondary schools. *The Education Digest, XLVI,* (2), 56–59.

Wolfthal, M. (1981). Reading scores revisited. *Phi Delta Kappa, 62,* 662–663.

Wood, T. A., Buckhalt, J. A., & Tomlin, J. G. (1988). A comparison of listening and reading performance with children in three educational placements. *Journal of Learning Disabilities, 21,* 493–496.

9
Teaching Mathematics

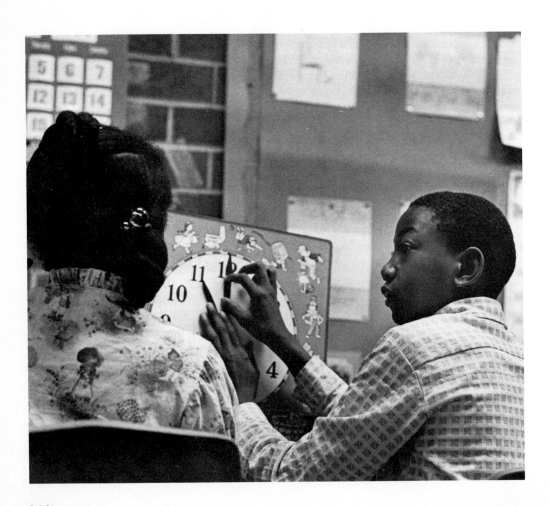

A knowledge of mathematics and the ability to apply it are essential to being able to function in society. Uses of mathematics principles vary from sorting objects in early childhood to applications in advanced scientific thinking. As valuable as the discipline is, teachers find many contradictions and discrepancies in how students learn (or fail to learn) basic mathematical processes.

Students experiencing difficulty with math range from those who are gifted in other areas to those with limited ability in all areas of learning. In addition to intellectual and sensory differences, disparities exist among cultural groups and between males and females in attitudes toward math and in development of math skills (Norman, 1988).

A regular math class may contain students specifically gifted in mathematics, students performing at an expected pace, and students unable to keep up with their peers. Assessment is the first step in determining which students require a differentiated program, which students will be comfortable with the prescribed curriculum, and which students will require modifications in the curriculum or in teaching strategies.

ASSESSMENT

Assessment can be used for several purposes. The most common questions to be considered are, What is the student's level of functioning in the sequence of math skills? and, What skills should the student learn next? In addition to gauging fact and skill achievement, these two other questions should be asked: What concepts or understanding does a student have? and, Does the student approach problems in a reasonable manner? These questions can be answered in several different ways.

Assessment usually proceeds from screening to diagnosis to remediation. Screening is the first step in determining a student's level of functioning in relation to peers. If screening indicates that the student is not functioning at grade level, diagnostic procedures are used to identify specific strengths and weaknesses in the student's performance. Once these factors are isolated, the in-depth assessment leading to remediation begins. Instruments traditionally used for these three purposes are classified as standardized tests, criterion-referenced tests, and error analysis.

Standardized Tests

The standardized math assessment tools are usually achievement tests and diagnostic tests. Achievement tests generally provide an overview of math achievement by sampling a variety of skills with a limited number of items per skill. The results of achievement tests are typically reported in the form of grade equivalent scores. For example, the Wide Range Achievement Test profile might indicate that a student in the fifth grade is on a 3.4 grade level in mathematics. This means that the student performs on math tasks similarly to the average student in the fourth month of the third grade. At first glance, this type of score seems to provide information to answer these two crucial assessment questions: What is the student's current level of functioning in the sequence of math skills? What skills should the student learn next?

However, when the meaning of a 3.4 grade level is analyzed, the precise sequence of skills that need to be introduced next is still not pinpointed. Two students scoring 3.4 are not at the same level, because they probably missed different items. An analysis of items on achievement tests will indicate the strengths and weaknesses of the class as a whole but produces limited information on an individual student's level of functioning. Teachers need to realize that quantitative scores do not provide the assessment information necessary to develop a systematic instructional program.

The second type of standardized assessment is the diagnostic test. Although diagnostic math tests vary widely, they tend to be more specific and precise than achievement tests. Usually, they provide more in-depth analysis of several components of math, such as computation, reasoning, fractions, and application. This type of profile is more likely to result in the identification of individual strengths and weaknesses. One math diagnostic test that is systematically and comprehensively constructed is the Key-Math, published by American Guidance Service, Inc. The Keymath is individually administered and requires only minimal writing responses. It is appropriate for use in kindergarten through sixth grade. The manual includes an instructional objective for each test item, which promotes the generalization of test results into the identification of specific skills for the IEP.

Norm-referenced tests, which compare students' performance to national norms, do not provide detailed views of students' strengths and weaknesses. They are not designed to be diagnostic instruments (Baroody, 1987). Norm-referenced tests can be used as the first step in identifying students who have high potential in mathematics. In the Search for Mathematically Precocious Youth at Johns Hopkins University, schools are asked to identify all students who scored in the 97th percentile or higher on measures of standard achievement in the last grade in which they have been tested (Gallagher, 1985). The second step is to invite these students to take the Scholastic Aptitude Test (SAT), which has been used to determine mathematics aptitude for eleventh- and twelfth-grade students prior to college entrance. The third step in this process is to place identified students in programs that match their capabilities. This process is used to identify students talented in math; competency tests are designed to insure that all students meet the minimum requirements.

The minimum competency tests implemented in the majority of states are diagnostic tests. Although items on the competency tests vary from state to state, a standard component of these programs is the inclusion of basic and functional math (Linde & Olsen, 1980).

The guidelines for competency test administration and scoring are developed by states and, in some cases, by local education agencies. Teachers should inquire about the policies and procedures for assessing math competencies in their schools. A major consideration for teachers is to insure that the student's math curriculum and vocabulary are consistent with the assessment questions and criteria on the minimum competency test. In many states, receiving a high school diploma is contingent on passing the competency test. Thus, high value is placed on a student's performance. In specifying goals and objectives for the student's IEP, consideration should be given to the state's minimum competency requirements.

Criterion-Referenced Tests

The two distinguishing characteristics of criterion-referenced tests are a sequential arrangement of tasks and the specification of criteria the student is expected to reach in order to attain proficiency. Teachers can develop criterion-referenced tests that insure a direct link between assessment and instruction in math. Teachers should adhere to the following procedure in developing these tests:

1. Specify which math skills the student should know;
2. State the desired criteria to indicate proficiency;
3. Develop test questions to assess the skill; and
4. Record student's performance.

An example of a teacher-constructed, criterion-referenced test in the area of multiplication processes is presented in Figure 9.1. In constructing criterion-referenced tests, it is important to include at least three test questions per item to help distinguish between random and substantive errors.

There are several ways to develop criterion-referenced tests for repeated use. One approach is to mimeograph skill sequences in checklist form and develop a laminated index card file of test items keyed by skill number to the checklist. Different students can follow the same sequence, and the mimeographed copies of skill checklists provide an individual record for each student. Skills can be dated as they are mastered. The laminated index cards enable the test items to be used repeatedly without any extra teacher preparation, beyond the initial organization. Test construction can be time consuming. The substantial benefit to the teacher is

Skills (Partial Listing)	Criteria		Sample Test Questions
1. Multiplies a 2-digit multiplicand with a 1-digit multiplier, involving no carrying in equations and word problems.	90%	1. (a) $\begin{array}{r}23\\ \times 2\end{array}$	(b) If there are 11 groups of people with 6 people in each group, how many people are in all the groups?
2. Multiplies a 3-digit multiplicand with a 1-digit multiplier, involving no carrying in equations and word problems.	90%	2. (a) $\begin{array}{r}123\\ \times 3\end{array}$	(b) A school has 123 classrooms with each having 3 erasers. How many erasers are in the whole school?
3. Multiplies a 4-digit multiplicand with a 1-digit multiplier, involving no carrying in equations and word problems.	90%	3. (a) $\begin{array}{r}2314\\ \times 2\end{array}$	(b) There are 4 schools in the district. Each school has 1021 children. How many children are in the school district?
4. Multiplies a 2-digit multiplicand with a 1-digit multiplier, involving carrying in equations and word problems.	90%	4. (a) $\begin{array}{r}35\\ \times 3\end{array}$	(b) If a car goes around a 25-mile track five times, how far has it traveled?
5. Multiplies a 3-digit multiplicand with a 1-digit multiplier, involving carrying to the ten's place in equations and word problems.	90%	5. (a) $\begin{array}{r}128\\ \times 2\end{array}$	(b) There are 4 piles with 217 rocks in each pile. How many rocks are in all the piles?
6. Multiplies a 3-digit multiplicand with a 1-digit multiplier, involving carrying to the hundred's place in equations and word problems.	90%	6. (a) $\begin{array}{r}384\\ \times 2\end{array}$	(b) If 5 trucks each have 141 boxes, how many boxes are in all the trucks?

FIGURE 9.1 Criterion-Referenced Test in Multiplication Processes

that the assessment sequence is the same as the instructional sequence. Behavioral objectives are the natural by-product of criterion-referenced tests. As teachers master the task of specifying skill sequences in math, this systematic approach to math programming will facilitate the progress of all students.

Some school systems are using microcomputers to generate criterion-referenced tests. These computers can print up to 10 or 15 test items for the objectives selected as appropriate for the assessment. Some computer programs are designed specifically to help teachers generate tests. The ideal test generator should accomplish the following seven tasks:

1. Allow the teacher to store and retrieve from the computer the same sort of items that the teacher would otherwise store in a test-item bank.
2. Generate tests at random from these electronic item banks, using the same selection strategies that the teacher would normally use, or better.
3. Permit entry of questions from a normal word processing program (such as AppleWorks).
4. Select items for test according to prescribed criteria (such as item format, level of difficulty, or instructional objectives).
5. Generate equivalent, alternate forms of the same test.
6. Permit the students to take tests interactively at the computer terminal, as well as in the normal printed format.
7. Provide statistical analyses (including item difficulty and item discrimination) that would enable the teacher to improve the quality of the test. (Vockell & Hall, 1989, p. 114)

When selecting a test-generating program, teachers should examine each program's strengths and weaknesses and select the package that comes closest to meeting the needs of their own situations.

Observation

In every math lesson, teachers have the opportunity to identify math strategies and activities that students appear to enjoy and use to achieve success. Seatwork, workbooks, games, large-group activities, and small-group activities, in addition to teacher-constructed tests, can provide a teacher with valuable assessment information on a continuous basis during the student's normal classroom routine. Although this type of observational assessment is more informal than are standardized or criterion-referenced tests, the insights available to teachers can be invaluable.

There are many children who at a very young age display unusual mathematical capabilities and interest in doing advanced mathematics.

Mathematically talented students do not seek to know whether math is useful, but enjoy doing it for its own sake; they enjoy challenges because they have an intense interest in ideas. They seek out difficult problems and dwell on them until the problems are solved. Such students are capable of harmonizing seemingly unrelated pieces of mathematics into a coherent structure that may escape the notice of many other students and even the teacher (Nichols & Behr, 1982). Close observation of approaches to problem-solving as well as of traditional math skills is important in identifying students who are gifted in this area.

Error Analysis

Standardized tests, criterion-referenced tests, and observation enable teachers to analyze students' errors in order to identify the types and causes of errors. Howell and Kaplan (1980) state that "errors are not just the opposite of corrects" (p. 245). They suggest three reasons for this:

1. There's more than one way to make an error.
2. The answer you get depends on the question you ask.
3. Nothing happens by accident. (p. 246)

Systematic error analysis involves the identification of response patterns and the student's rationale for the response as a basis for instructional planning. Examples of errors presented in Figure 9.2 illustrate this system of assessment.

Analysis of the subtraction test shows that student A either did not recognize the subtraction symbol or, not knowing how to regroup for

---

Subtraction Test

Student (A)					
	17	24	12	34	22
	−8	−5	−3	−9	−6
	25	29	15	43	28

Student (B)					
	17	24	12	34	22
	−8	−5	−3	−9	−6
	11	21	11	35	24

Division Test

Student (C) $3\overline{)269}$ (83) $7\overline{)426}$ (60) $9\overline{)294}$ (30)

FIGURE 9.2 Examples of Errors

subtraction, added the numerals. Student B apparently was not familiar with the process of regrouping for subtraction and subtracted the smaller numeral from the larger one. In both cases, the students relied on prior knowledge to solve the problems. In responding to the division test, student C apparently learned only part of the division process and relied on that part to solve the problem. Baroody (1987) concludes that

> when children encounter tasks they are not ready for or have not been given enough time to master, they often resort to invented, inappropriate, or partially incorrect procedures that produce systematic errors. Systematic errors, then, can provide an invaluable signal that instruction is out of synchrony with the psychology of the child—that external and internal factors are not meshing. (p. 56)

It is also possible to carry out error analysis in the area of math reasoning. In solving word problems, errors may be related to any of the following factors: lack of attention; poor reading comprehension; inability to recognize words; overlooking important cues, such as "how many all together," that indicate which computational process to use; inability to disregard irrelevant numbers included in the problem; writing down the problem incorrectly on paper; lack of knowledge of the correct computation process; lack of concept development; and general carelessness.

Fowler (1978) suggests that teachers sometimes need to go beyond written work and inquire into a student's thinking processes to pinpoint reasoning errors. She states:

> Granted, individual interviews take time; however, the results of two minutes of discussion can often provide insight into the cause of the difficulties. This is time better spent than time by the student in working problems incorrectly under the same misapprehension and time spent by the teacher in marking them as incorrect. (p. 24)

Error analysis enables teachers to determine what skills gifted students have and do not have. The missing skills can then be taught so students can move more rapidly into advanced areas of math. Sometimes systematic errors indicate that the concept is clear but that processes have not been learned. Errors can also show that the creative student has taken a unique approach to a problem.

Each type of error is different and therefore requires a different approach to correction. Error analysis is important for all students, but it is particularly relevant for assessing students handicapped by mental retardation, learning disabilities, or sensory impairments. Students who experience substantial difficulty in math make the most systematic progress when errors are consistently identified and then eliminated.

Carpenter (1982) suggests five guidelines for using error analysis:

1. Do not hypothesize with very few items. The more items measuring a specific skill, the more confident a teacher can be about the information derived.
2. Consider previous performances. Data from another administration of the same or a similar test should be used to increase confidence in findings.
3. If the items do not reflect classroom tasks or tasks common to functional life situations, be extremely cautious about making inferences from such items. Teachers must be careful not to overgeneralize from item performances.
4. Validate hypotheses with other criteria such as classroom assignments or other tests.
5. Use error analysis information with other diagnostic information.

Errors do not merely indicate a knowledge deficiency; they can also indicate what knowledge a student brings to the problem and how the student copes with it. Baroody (1987) declares that "Errors provide a window to children's internal thought processes and indicate how well these thought processes match up with a learning task" (p. 54).

Assessment should be an ongoing activity. Teachers must continue to evaluate the progress of all their students, including those who are exceptional.

The most widely used method of evaluating students' performance in math classes is the teacher-made test. Most students look on tests as a necessary evil; students with handicaps may view them with anxiety and apprehension. Although they may have mastered the information to be evaluated, the format of the test and the nature of their handicaps may prevent them from responding correctly.

Miederhoff and Wood (1988) suggest adaptations for three aspects of a test: test directions, test items, and test design.

Test Directions:

1. Define any unfamiliar or abstract words.
2. Give an example of how the student is to respond.
3. Avoid oral directions as the only means of making the purpose of the test known to students.

Test Items:

1. Provide manipulative objects that make the problems more concrete.
2. Avoid mixing different problem formats in the same section.
3. Supply visual prompts, such as

$$61\overline{)263}\;^{R}$$

4. Give formulas and meanings of symbols: < means less than
5. Give a set of written steps for applying algorithms:

Long Division:

1. Divide
2. Multiply
3. Subtract
4. Check
5. Bring down

Test Design:

1. Adjust the readability level of the test to meet the student's needs.
2. Prepare the test in short sections that can be administered individually if necessary.
3. Place one type of question on each page.
4. Use graph paper; the squares may help the students keep the figures aligned.
5. Avoid lengthy tests on the chalkboard for students with copying difficulties.
6. Use black ink rather than purple dittos for students with visual acuity and visual perception problems.

Close observation of students' behavior can indicate to teachers whether the students are learning. Many opportunities other than testing should be provided for students to demonstrate progress in mathematics.

GOALS AND OBJECTIVES

Knowing the student's level of functioning in the sequence of math skills and the skills the student should learn next leads directly to program planning and the development of the IEP. Goals and objectives for exceptional students in math are based on the sequence of skills prescribed for all students. Although some students with mild handicaps will be placed in secondary programs, basic skills outlined for the elementary grades become ultimate goals for many students with handicaps. The following outline includes the math topics and sequences usually taught in elementary school.

I. Sets
II. Numeration
   A. Counting and numbers
   B. Ordinal relationships

C. Vocabulary and symbols
III. Whole Number Operations
A. Addition
B. Subtraction
C. Multiplication
D. Division
IV. Fractions
V. Decimals
VI. Percentages and Ratios
VII. Relations
VIII. Measurement and Estimations
IX. Geometry
X. Problem Solving

Reisman and Kauffman (1980) approach the idea of goals and objectives in a hierarchy of arbitrary associations, relationships, concepts and generalizations. This hierarchy, which extends from prenumber relationships to statistics and vocational education, provides the structure for a developmental mathematics curriculum (see Figure 9.3). Within such a structure, which includes a screening checklist, assessment leads to the setting of goals and objectives.

In some instances, the standard goals and objectives do not meet the needs of exceptional students. For example, Parker (1989) sees a strong emphasis on problem solving as the primary objective for gifted students. The following course sequence is suggested for students gifted in mathematics:

Algebra I	Trigonometry
Algebra II	Analytic Geometry
Algebra III	Calculus
Geometry	

On the other hand, some educators believe that the goal of mathematical instruction for handicapped students should be restricted to the transmission of functional skills, such as the handling of money and simple budgeting, which are necessary for self-sufficient living (Halpern, 1981). An example of a lesson plan based on functional objectives is presented in Figure 9.4.

The establishment of goals and objectives depends on the student's ability; the student's needs as determined by the curriculum, the student, and the student's parents; and the student's placement.

Students with mild handicaps at the elementary level are frequently taught in the resource room. In an investigation of mathematics instruction in resource rooms, Carpenter (1985) found that one-third of resource room teachers' instructional time was spent on mathematics. Some of these

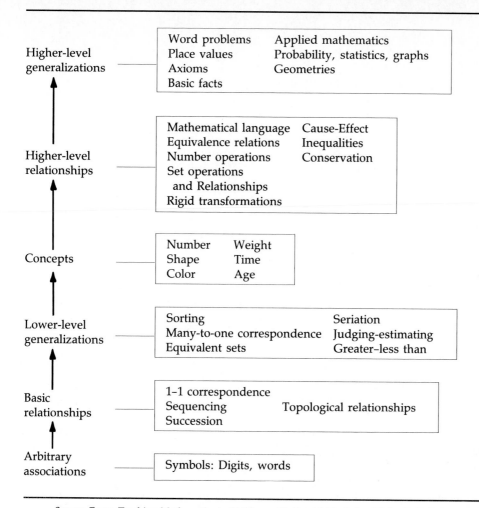

Higher-level generalizations
- Word problems
- Place values
- Axioms
- Basic facts
- Applied mathematics
- Probability, statistics, graphs
- Geometries

Higher-level relationships
- Mathematical language
- Equivalence relations
- Number operations
- Set operations and Relationships
- Rigid transformations
- Cause-Effect
- Inequalities
- Conservation

Concepts
- Number   Weight
- Shape   Time
- Color   Age

Lower-level generalizations
- Sorting
- Many-to-one correspondence
- Equivalent sets
- Seriation
- Judging-estimating
- Greater–less than

Basic relationships
- 1–1 correspondence
- Sequencing
- Succession
- Topological relationships

Arbitrary associations
- Symbols: Digits, words

Source: From *Teaching Mathematics to Children with Special Needs* (p. 11) by F. K. Reisman and S. H. Kauffman, 1980. Columbus, OH: Charles E. Merrill Publishing Co. Copyright 1980 by F. K. Reisman. Reprinted by permission.

FIGURE 9.3 Development of Arbitrary Associations, Relationships, Concepts, and Generalizations

students may have learned strategies to cope with their academic deficits through their elementary special education teachers.

At the secondary level, most mildly handicapped students will probably remain in the regular classes for prealgebra, algebra, and geometry. Although few modifications may be necessary with respect to the math curriculum offered in secondary schools, many modifications may have to be made with respect to how the content is taught (Burton & Meyers, 1987). The IEP reproduced in Figure 9.5 illustrates the types of adaptations

Domain: Daily Living Skills
Competency: 1. Managing Personal Finances
Subcompetency: 1. Identify Money and Make Correct Change

Objectives	Activities/Strategies	Adult/Peer Roles
a. Identify coins and bills less than or equal to $100 in value.	• Students practice with authentic money as much as possible. • Students quiz each other with money flash cards of coins and bills in values up to $100. • Students construct posters of different money values up to $100 using magazine cutouts and pictures.	• Parents and/or peers practice currency identification with student. • Parents and/or peers devise questions or games that allow the student to identify the varieties of currency from memory.
b. Count money in coin and bill denominations with sums less than or equal to $20.	• Students practice with authentic money as much as possible. • Students practice selecting different coin and bill denominations valuing $.01 to $20 from a box, and then count the money amounts aloud to each other. • Students devise buying/selling games using play money amounts up to $20. • Students play structured money games. • Students construct class bulletin board demonstrating money values up to $20.	• Parents and/or peers give the student different denominations of coins and bills up to $20 and ask the student to count out the combinations. Parents and/or peers allow the student, while shopping, to count out the necessary amounts for purchases equalling $20 or less. • Parents and/or peers allow the student, while shopping and making purchases equalling $20 or less, to receive the change and to count the change.

(continued)

c. Make correct change from both bills and coins for amounts less than or equal to $50.

- Students practice making change with large denomination bills ($10, $20, and $50), using department store items and their prices on flash cards.
- Students operate a "store" and "bank" to practice making correct change for amounts equalling $50.00 or less.
- Class role plays situations in which students must make change for purchases of amounts equalling $50.00 or less.
- Class identifies all possible situations where knowledge of making change would be important.

- Parents and/or peers allow the student while shopping to select the correct monetary denominations to give to the salesperson for a purchase amount equalling $50 or less, to receive the change, and to count the change and determine if the amount received is correct.
- Parents and/or peers role play "customer" while the student role plays "clerk" using monetary denominations equalling $50.00 or less.
- Parents and/or peers allow the student to make change from large denomination bills ($10, $20, and $50) for items listed in department store advertisement brochures or catalogs priced to $50.00.

Source: From D. E. Brolin (1989). Life Centered Career Education: A Competency Approach. Reston, VA: The Council for Exceptional Children, pp. 16–17. Used by permission.

FIGURE 9.4 Daily Living Skills

Short-Term Instructional Objectives

Student's Name Joe Steward

Annual Goal Perform basic algebraic computations dealing with concepts introduced in Algebra I.

Short-Term Objectives	Special Education Procedures	Measurement Procedures	Date Instruction Begun	Date Objective Achieved
1. Demonstrate the ability to manipulate numbers across the equality sign.	Flash cards for review and learning with peers and teacher	Successful mastery (80%) of 15 sample problems	1-10-90	2-5-90
2. Demonstrate what variables represent in equations, i.e. concept of their use.	Audiovisuals to help explain; filmstrip showing concrete examples	Work 20 problems successfully in front of teacher	2-5-90	2-15-90
3. Demonstrate the ability to factor out terms common throughout an equation.	Pamphlets, filmstrips, peer tutor, use of figures to show commonality	Work 20 problems successfully	2-15-90	2-25-90
4. Demonstrate the ability to factor a binomial equation.	Peer tutor, extra work with teacher after school, Math lab	Work 25 problems successfully	2-25-90	3-15-90
5. Demonstrate retention of the above objectives	Review of material in Math lab and also with peer tutor	Successful mastery (80%) of 50 sample problems on an untimed exam.	3-15-90	4-2-90

FIGURE 9.5 IEP for High School Math

that can be made within a common goal. Teachers working with mainstreamed students in mathematics programs will be better qualified to establish appropriate goals and to meet the varying needs of their students if they understand the nature of mathematics as well as the nature of the learner.

THE NATURE OF MATHEMATICS

In providing a framework for understanding children's learning of elementary mathematics, Baroody (1987) compares the absorption theory with the cognitive theory of learning. The absorption theory is based on the acquisition of knowledge (facts, skills, and associations) primarily by memorizing. In the cognitive theory, the essence of knowledge is structure—the elements of information connected by relationships to form an organized and meaningful whole.

The difference between these two theories in teaching mathematics is profound. The absorption theory defines math as a ready-made product that children must absorb, in contrast to the idea of the process of promoting understanding, reasoning, and problem solving.

In the framework of the cognitive theory, the teacher's tasks become translating the process into an understandable form, providing a variety of experiences, and creating opportunities to use the concepts developed. Teaching changes from group instruction at a single pace to the acknowledgment of individual readiness and ability; teaching and learning become problem-solving processes.

Mathematics is developmental in nature and should be taught in a sequential manner. Although the sequence is predetermined, students progress individually. The abilities to see relationships, to engage in abstract thinking, to use symbol systems, and to solve problems affect the student's acquisition of mathematics ideas (Reisman & Kauffman, 1980).

THE NATURE OF THE LEARNER

Even though characteristics of exceptional students are presented in Part One, a review of problem areas related to mathematics are discussed in this chapter. Because of the nature of mathematics, some types of handicapping conditions have a higher probability of interfering with achievement than do others. Students with mental retardation, learning disabilities, and sensory losses (visual and auditory) are likely to need adaptations in the math curriculum to enable them to perform at or near grade level. Difficulty might be experienced in the areas described in the following sections.

Discrimination

Discrimination is the ability to locate the relevant dimension or dimensions of a given stimulus. Students may be deficient in this skill as it applies to visual and auditory stimuli. Examples of poor visual discrimination include the inability to distinguish between math symbols, such as $+$, $-$, and $\times$, and to see similarities and differences in the size, shape, and number of objects.

With an auditory discrimination problem, the student may have difficulty distinguishing numbers in an auditory drill or understanding the teacher's oral presentation of a concept.

Generalization

Generalization, or transfer, involves locating the relevant dimension of similar stimuli or using a concept learned in one situation to apply to another similar situation. A student who learns that $6 + 1 = 7$ may not generalize that when 1 is added to a numeral the next highest numeral is the answer. This means that $7 + 1 = 8$ and $8 + 1 = 9$ would have to be learned as isolated facts.

A problem in generalization would also interfere with the practical application of numerical findings. For example, a student who could recite and write the multiplication tables without error would not be able to multiply when the teacher asked, "If each student in the class needs three pieces of paper, how much paper do we need?"

Attention and Distractibility

Students who have attention problems and who are easily distracted may not focus on one stimulus long enough to accomplish a task. Such students may lose track of the steps in long division or fail to follow directions for assignments or tests.

Students who are hyperactive may not be able to work for long periods of time. Shorter, more frequent lessons may be accomplished with success. They may need places to work that are not as distracting as a busy classroom.

Strategy

In order to generalize or transfer, it is necessary to develop some system with which to attack a new stimulus. Students who have learning or behavioral problems frequently fail to develop strategies for attacking new or novel problems and may not note clues to operations, such as the words *more* or *less*. Teaching strategies is a useful approach that is frequently used with students who have learning disabilities (see chapter 7).

Solving Abstract Problems

Students may be functioning at a concrete level beyond the developmental expectation based on age and grade level. Because math is highly abstract and deals with abstract symbols, this is a deterrent to progress for many students. Such students may be able to respond at a factual level but unable to see relationships and to deal with symbols and ideas.

Memory

Because memorization of basic number facts is essential to operation with large numbers and to efficiency in calculations, poor memory creates a problem for many students in math. They may overuse counting procedures and have difficulty with multiplication.

All students need to understand basic mathematical concepts before memorizing number facts. This background is particularly important for students who have poor memory skills. Memorization can be improved with a variety of drills, games, and practical applications.

Learning Set

Learning set is a frame of mind or attitude conducive to learning. It refers to attitudes toward math, motivation to practice, and probability of achievement based on experience. Because many students who have learning problems have not experienced success in math, they expect failure rather than success and do not attempt to solve tasks when they are presented. Such students do not display initiative and may refuse to participate. When a task is not attempted, it cannot be failed. A positive learning set develops with success.

Visual Deficits

Students who are visually impaired obviously need adaptations in their math program. This does not mean that they cannot be successful. David, the student with visual impairment described in chapter 3, was gifted in mathematics; he was beyond most of his classmates in problem-solving skills. His understanding of math was developed through manipulation of objects and through advanced thinking processes. He became proficient in using a talking calculator.

There are many more mildly handicapped students who have visual processing disorders than visual impairments. These students have trouble with visual discrimination, visual closure (difficulty understanding sets of groupings), visual motor tasks, visual memory tasks, spatial relationships, and directionality. Handouts and tests that are not clearly written and well-spaced are almost impossible for these students to deal with successfully.

Auditory Deficits

Students who are hearing impaired, like students who are visually impaired, do not necessarily have difficulty with math. However, because of difficulties in language, some concepts may develop slowly. Directions must be clearly written and demonstrated, and class lectures should have visual and manipulative components to insure understanding.

Adaptations made for students with visual deficits and hearing impairments may also be necessary for students who have auditory processing difficulties. Such students may have problems with auditory memory (retaining an auditory sequence of numerals), auditory discrimination, and auditory association (difficulty associating a numeral with its auditory referent).

Language Disorders

Mathematics as a discipline has a vocabulary of its own. Students who have language disorders may have difficulty understanding the words in story problems, the meaning of process signs, and words relating to time and space. These students may also have difficulty conceptualizing such directional words as *in between, within, beside, under,* and *next to.* Problems that contain lengthy, unnecessary data may be impossible for these students to follow.

Exceptional Ability

Students who are gifted in the area of mathematics learn more readily than their peers and transfer concepts to new challenges. Parker (1989) describes math abilities of gifted students:

> They are able to recognize patterns and relationships, and to draw valid conclusions from the results of their experimentation. Their ability to think in an openended, logical, and abstract manner enables them to solve more

complex problems and to generate new problems out of their solutions. Gifted students are intellectually curious and welcome new challenges that stimulate higher levels of thinking.[1]

Recognizing the problems and challenges presented by exceptional students is a start in planning to meet their needs. The general instructional strategies presented in chapter 7 will be of use to all teachers, and the math teacher will also find specific approaches to mathematics instruction helpful.

INSTRUCTIONAL APPROACHES

All children come to school with some mathematical knowledge. For example, if you break a cookie unevenly, and say, "Here is half a cookie for you," most children will know that the division was unfair. Many of them have acquired counting skills, and most identify with the ideas of two eyes, two ears, and ten fingers and toes. Such knowledge cannot be assumed with children who have learning problems, and informal observation is essential to planning from the beginning. Although the sequence of learning math is the same for all students, some general guidelines can help the teacher of students who have handicaps.

Building Basic Concepts

A significant component of math instruction for handicapped students is the development of concepts and problem-solving skills. Although teachers sometimes believe that these students are incapable of higher level conceptualization leading to problem solving, this is an unfounded assumption. Handicapped students can understand higher-order concepts and can solve problems if they are systematically taught these skills and provided with experiences to develop understanding. Handicapped students often have difficulties in math because computation and problem solving were taught before the students developed the foundation for understanding numbers (Hammill & Bartel, 1978) or because instruction was based on rote learning. Piaget (1952) has described concepts central to the development of understanding numbers. These concepts are briefly described in Table 9.1, with an example of an instructional activity for each concept.

[1]From *Instructional Strategies for Teaching the Gifted* (p. 220) by J. P. Parker, 1989. Boston: Allyn and Bacon. Copyright 1989 by Allyn and Bacon. Reprinted by permission.

TABLE 9.1 Piagetian Concepts and Instructional Activities

Concepts	Activity
1. Classification Grouping objects according to distinguishing characteristics.	1. Group objects of different shapes; verbally identifying the shape of each.
2. One-to-one correspondence Recognizing the relationship that one object in a given set is the same number as one object in a different set, regardless of dissimilar characteristics.	2. Match each ball in a set of three balls with a bat in a set of three bats.
3. Seriation Ordering objects according to a distinguishing characteristic, such as size, weight, or color.	3. Order Cuisenaire rods according to height.
4. Conservation The number of objects in a set remains constant regardless of the arrangement of the objects.	4. Make two identical balls of play dough. Have the student roll one out into a rope shape and state whether the objects contain the same amount of dough.
5. Reversibility Objects in a set, regardless of their rearrangement, can be returned to their original position without changing their relationship.	5. Pictorially depict the following equations with plastic chips. $4 + 2 = 6$ $6 - 4 = 2$ $4 + 2 = 6$
6. Developing number concepts Associated with numerals. Recognition of the number of objects corresponding to a particular numeral.	6. Place the number of clothespins, corresponding to the numerals, on tagboard cards.

Although some mathematicians claim that number is not dependent on the development of formal classification and serial-ordering skills as described by Piaget (Baroody, 1987), the Piagetian position does have important educational implications. The notion of "more than" is necessary for the development of number concept and meaningful counting; number has both ordering and classification meanings; and counting involves one-to-one correspondence.

Development of basic mathematical concepts occurs through experience with real objects. As children play, experiment, and verbalize their experiences, they form the foundation for being able to carry out more abstract processes.

As discussed, many students with learning problems have difficulty with abstract thinking. These students learn best through the manipulation of concrete objects before they proceed to other levels.

Using Manipulatives

Manipulative materials are objects that appeal to several senses and that students can touch, move about, rearrange, and otherwise handle (Kennedy, 1986). They can be objects from the environment, such as money or measuring instruments, or materials designed to teach mathematical concepts, such as base-ten blocks and balances.

In choosing manipulative materials, teachers should consider several criteria. Good manipulatives are adaptable, easy for students to use, safe, and inexpensive. In addition to physical criteria, several pedagogical criteria should be addressed (Hynes, 1986). Manipulatives should clearly represent the mathematical idea in question, appeal to the interest of the student, and be versatile enough to teach many mathematical concepts at various grade levels.

Manipulatives can be used for remediation as well as for development. Gifted students also benefit from the use of manipulatives in the initial stages of learning (Moser, 1986). Even though they pass through the concrete stages more rapidly than do other students, they still need these basic experiences.

Although usually associated with young children, manipulatives are effectively used with students of all ages and across a variety of topics. They are particularly effective in teaching counting, place value, multiplication, and fractions.

Counting

Children usually develop oral counting skills before they learn to assign a number to an object (one-to-one correspondence). However, this skill cannot be taken for granted in working with handicapped children. A great deal of practice is generally required, with the use of blocks or other manipulatives. As this practice becomes meaningful, the student learns to use the last number to name the set of objects.

Children themselves provide meaningful manipulatives. The questions, How many children make up the set of students in this room? and How many boys/girls make up a set within this set? provide the basis for set and subset development. Another question, How many elephants are in this class? leads to development of the concept of the empty set.

There are many opportunities for counting in the classroom. In addition to objects, motor activities, such as jumping, bouncing a ball, and clapping hands, can be counted. Games such as Jacks and those involving dice also provide counting experiences.

Sander (1981) suggests that the early introduction of numerals and number words may present an overload for students with learning problems. Written symbols should be introduced when the use of them is meaningful.

A system that has been used successfully involves counters (concrete level) and dots (semiconcrete level). Using these materials permits the student to progress from the concrete through the semiconcrete to the abstract numeral. This sequence is illustrated in Figure 9.6 and is referred to in the following sections.

Counting with concrete objects and with semiconcrete representations leads to learning simple addition and subtraction. Children who are visually handicapped can learn the same sequence of skills through the use of an abacus or with fingermath (Maddux, Cates, & Sowell, 1984).

Manipulative materials can be used to model operations and algorithms (Beattie, 1986). These materials clarify the concept or meaning of each operation, the language of each operation and algorithm, and the algorithm itself.

Place Value

The concept of place value, or regrouping, is basic to all mathematical operations. A student who can read the number 46 as "forty-six" may not be aware that the digit 4 represents four tens. Early manipulation to form groups (sets) of tens from ten ones helps establish this concept. As students are presented with addition and subtraction tasks, the concept of place value becomes more important.

Traditionally, teachers have used some confusing terms to teach the process of regrouping in addition and subtraction. Such terms as *borrow*

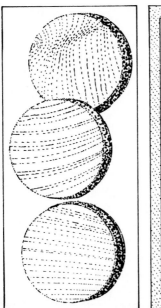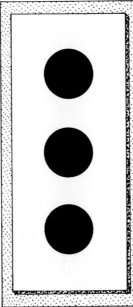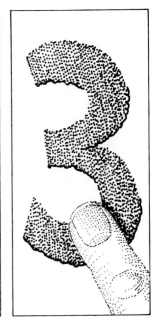

FIGURE 9.6 Concrete to Abstract

and *cross out and add* cloud the real purpose and understanding of regrouping. Because regrouping is a very abstract concept, it is important to use a concrete method to teach it to all students, especially to those who have learning problems.

The place-value chart, illustrated in Figure 9.7, is an excellent device to provide concrete experience in regrouping. In addition to a standard pocket chart, a supply of cards about 4 by 2 inches and some rubber bands are required.

In the example 19 + 9, all cards are spread out in the ones pocket. Two groups of ten cards are grouped and held with a rubber band, then placed in the tens chart. Eight cards remain in the ones chart, and 28 is concretely pictured. For subtraction, the following conversation would take place: "There are two groups of ten cards and eight ones. To subtract, you must regroup one set of tens, spread them out in the ones chart, and subtract nine. This leaves one set of tens and nine ones, or 19 cards." Practice with this system provides concrete evidence of the process and understanding of the concept. It is recommended that only the ones and tens charts be used; use of a hundreds chart and its accompanying cards becomes bulky and is not necessary for understanding the concept.

Multiplication

Multiplication seems to be especially difficult for handicapped students. Mainstreamed students are frequently expected to memorize multiplication tables without understanding that multiplication is repeated addition and that it can be represented concretely.

Using counters and dots, multiplication can be demonstrated clearly. For example, the problem 3 × 4 can be explained as three fours. Thus, three sets of four counters are displayed and later exchanged for three sets of dot pictures. Students can readily realize that adding the counters or dots will result in the same solution to the problem. It is important to use

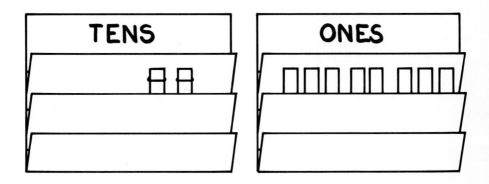

FIGURE 9.7 Place-Value Chart

realistic problems involving the same factors so the student will understand the practical applications of multiplication.

For students who have difficulty in learning multiplication facts, the teacher can develop a chart with the student so the student understands the rationale behind the chart. The chart can then be kept in the student's desk for reference if needed. A blank multiplication chart is illustrated in Figure 9.8.

The same materials used for teaching multiplication can be used to teach division. Teaching each operation along with its inverse reduces the difficulties students have with subtraction and division (Roseman, 1985).

Fractions
Many adolescents who have learning problems are still being drilled on basic multiplication and division while their peers are reviewing fractions,

X	0	1	2	3	4	5	6	7	8	9
0										
1										
2										
3										
4										
5										
6										
7										
8										
9										

FIGURE 9.8 Multiplication Chart

decimals, and percentages. Atkinson (1983) suggests that fractions can be used as the first step in remediation for these students. Overcoming the barrier of handling fractions provides motivation and allows the students to work with the same type of material their peers are learning.

Fractions should be introduced through demonstration as part of a unit and as a subset compared to the parent set. First experiences involve comparisons of a part to a unit; comparison of set to subset comes later.

Ordinary manipulatives can be used effectively to demonstrate the relationship between a whole and some portion of the whole. For example, cut an apple and ask what number could be used to name each piece. Place the parts together to form a whole, and reverse the process. Cutting a sandwich, a candy bar, or a pizza provides important experience. Using Cuisenaire rods, fraction kits, folding paper, and cutting string can provide similar examples.

The concept of fractions as part of a set can be developed with a number of counters, asking students to identify half of the set, one-third of the set, and so on. Illustrations in the environment can also be found, such as the four panes of a window.

Development of these two ideas may appeal to older students in contemplating a football field and two hockey teams (Prevost, 1984). A fraction as part of a whole can be illustrated with a football field, including the end zones. Into how many parts is the field divided by the yardline markers and goal lines? Each section is one-twelfth of the whole field. How many twelfths are there between the goalpost and the fifty-yard line? A number of such questions can be asked and answered with reference to this model.

In illustrating a fraction as part of a set, twelve players in a hockey game are examined. What fraction of the players are members of one team? What part of the players are goaltenders? This process can be repeated with other team sports of special interest to the class. Well-chosen models, a willingness to use manipulatives, and concerted efforts to appeal to the interest of students enable teachers to help handicapped learners acquire skills that have been considered almost impossible for them to master.

In general, handicapped learners benefit from a carefully structured, active approach to learning mathematics. Structured situations involving manipulatives help them organize their thinking so they begin to see relationships or follow a procedure involving computation. Thornton and Wilmot (1986) suggest four ways to provide this structure:

1. Vary the way you present manipulatives in a lesson to capitalize on students' learning strength. Stagger the presentation of visual, verbal, and tactile information.
2. Help students build important self-monitoring skills. Appropriate questions repeated during active instruction with materials elicit responses during initial instruction.

3. Provide for consistency. Special educators and classroom teachers must agree on ways to present content to students. This may require refining textbook suggestions in pre-book activities with manipulatives.
4. Carefully plan the use and the phasing out of manipulative materials both in concept and in skill learning. (pp. 38–39)

Using Manipulatives with Mathematically Gifted Students
As mentioned earlier in this chapter, gifted students need to have experiences at the concrete level. Usually the number of examples necessary is fewer than that needed for other students because these students can perceive relationships and make generalizations more readily.

In an enrichment curriculum for gifted students, concrete materials have an important place. The overriding purpose of the curriculum should be to extend the students' thinking to higher levels, using physical materials as tools. By working in small groups with manipulatives, students learn to brainstorm, analyze, cooperate, compromise, and evaluate their abilities. When used appropriately with gifted students, manipulatives have at least six functions. They can:

1. build concepts and related vocabulary;
2. improve spatial visualization;
3. allow discovery of patterns and relationships;
4. provide problem-solving experiences;
5. teach the essence of verification or proof; and
6. promote creativity. (Thornton & Wilmot, 1986, p. 40)

Manipulatives can be introduced in activities that are paced to meet each student's needs. Verbal instruction should be minimized and discovering maximized. The teacher does not need to know the answers to all questions and should include questions that have no answer.

Moving from Concrete to Abstract
Heddens (1986) emphasizes the importance of bridging the gap between concrete and abstract levels in math. The stage between concrete and abstract is usually referred to as the semiconcrete level. This level is a representation of a real situation in which pictures or representations of the real items are used rather than the items themselves. Helping students bridge this gap requires the teacher's assistance.

Teaching the step from concrete to abstract can be done in several ways. One way is through questioning, which guides children to think through the mathematical concepts being presented. Good questions can reveal new directions of thought, encourage children to continue their current line of thought, or provide clues that will stimulate thinking. Students also need opportunities to verbalize their thought processes;

verbal interaction with peers helps learners clarify their own thinking (Heddens, 1987).

The semiconcrete level can also be developed through activities. Such activities can involve pictures of objects, textbook illustrations, models on the overhead projector, and such semisymbolic representations as tallies, circles, squares, or triangles. This step is necessary before abstract numerals and ideas can be used and understood.

Teaching Basic Facts

Although the use of manipulatives and counting strategies is essential to understanding mathematical concepts, recent research suggests that the prolonged use of these procedures can interfere with learning higher-level math skills, such as multiple-digit addition and subtraction, long division, and fractions (Hasselbring, Goin, & Bransford, 1988). As basic skills become more practiced, their execution requires less attention and they become automatic. Students with learning handicaps are substantially less proficient than their nonhandicapped peers in retrieving answers to basic math facts.

Memorization of math facts should occur after the student demonstrates an understanding of the basic number concepts described. The beginning point of instruction in memorizing the basic facts is assessment. If the student is working on addition, the pretest should include all combinations of the basic facts. The pretest can be either written or oral, and the student should be instructed to answer only those problems known immediately. Each student's level of performance should be recorded, because the particular combination of facts mastered and not mastered will vary from student to student.

After the teacher has identified which facts are known and which must be learned, the student's rate of learning should be determined. Some handicapped students can learn five or six new facts a day; others have a rate of one or two facts per week. To establish learning rate, the teacher can use the following procedure:

1. Make an educated guess in assigning the student a certain number of facts to learn during a daily math lesson.
2. Use practice methods already identified as successful for the student. Remember that some students need more drill than others.
3. Evaluate the student on the assigned facts at the end of the day and at the end of the week. The number of basic facts learned per day, which the student successfully completes on the evaluation at the end of the week, becomes the student's daily learning rate.

When learning rate has been established, the student should be assigned that specified number of facts daily for practice and drill. The number of facts may have to be adjusted up or down based on the student's performance. The goal is for the handicapped student to master as many facts as possible while working at a success level. If the student consistently misses a number of problems on the weekly mastery test, then the learning rate is too high, the method of instruction is inadequate, or the student is not approaching the task conscientiously. Students can keep records of their progress, graphing the number of problems they learn each week and keeping charts of the particular combinations they learn. In this way, the reinforcement procedure (graphing and charting) for memorizing the basic facts provides an opportunity to learn different math skills.

The probability that handicapped students will learn the basic facts increases greatly when the instruction is geared to the student's level of achievement, preferred learning styles, and rate of learning. The students' awareness of their continuous and consistent progress often provides renewed impetus to master math skills. These same principles of programming the memorization of basic facts apply to other aspects of the math curriculum requiring memory skills, such as measurement tables and monetary relationships.

Teaching Problem Solving

Handicapped students should be taught verbal problem solving in conjunction with computational and process skills. Additionally, verbal problem solving should accompany skill development in the areas of money, time, and measurement. When problem solving is sequenced according to the skill hierarchy, it becomes an integral aspect of the math curriculum.

At the elementary level, students can roleplay problems to acquire skill in the problem-solving process. When problems are relevant to students' interests and needs, the students' motivation is higher than when they are dealing with nonrelated problems.

Montague and Bos (1986) have developed a strategy for verbal math problem solving that is useful at all levels. The following eight steps are suggested:

1. *Read the problem aloud.* The teacher will pronounce and provide meanings for any words the student needs pronounced or defined.
2. *Paraphrase the problem aloud.* State important information, giving close attention to the numbers in the problem. Repeat the question part aloud, asking such questions as, What is asked? or What am I looking for?
3. *Visualize.* Graphically display the information, drawing a representation of the problem.

4. *State the problem.* Complete statements aloud, such as I have . . . I want to find. . . . Underline the important information presented in the problem.
5. *Hypothesize.* Complete the following statements aloud. If I . . . Then . . . how many steps will I use to find the answer? Write the operation signs.
6. *Estimate.* Write the estimates: my answer should be around . . . or about. . . .
7. *Calculate.* Show the calculation and label the answer. Circle the answer. Use a self-questioning technique, such as, Is this answer in the correct form?
8. *Self-check.* Refer to the problem and check every step to determine accuracy of operation(s) selected and correctness of response and solution. Check computation for accuracy. Use the self-questioning technique by asking if the answer makes sense.

In addition to traditional techniques, special materials are available to promote skills in problem solving. Problem Solving in Mathematics (Pathescope Educational Media, 1981) is a sound-filmstrip package that includes worksheets and tests. The situations involve real problems that appeal to teenagers, including shopping, determining gas mileage, and loan payments. The skills developed involve whole-number operations, fractions, decimals, and percentages. This type of approach helps prepare students for competency testing and for solving problems that are related to life skills.

Calculators and microcomputers are excellent resources to use in teaching problem solving. Frequently, such technological aids are considered appropriate only to provide drill and practice for students; however, they can greatly assist students in developing problem-solving skills. Calculators allow students to solve problems they might otherwise avoid because of the computation demands. Some handicapped students may not have the computation skills to complete the problems; other students may have writing problems that interfere with their ability to complete long computations by hand.

Computers are valuable tools for developing problem-solving skills in handicapped students and in providing challenges to students who are mathematically gifted. The National Council of Teachers of Mathematics has recommended that the use of calculators and computers be "integrated into the core mathematics curriculum . . . [and] used in imaginative ways for exploring, discovering, and developing mathematical concepts and not merely for checking computational values or for drill and practice" (Parker, 1989, p. 233).

The National Council of Teachers of Mathematics has suggested that educators give attention to the following aspects of problem solving:

- Application of mathematics to solving real-world problems
- Methods of gathering, organizing, and interpreting information; drawing and testing inferences from data; and communicating results
- Use of problem-solving capacities of computers to extend traditional problem-solving approaches and to implement new strategies of interaction and simulation
- Use of imagery, visualization, and spatial concepts.[2]

Group problem-solving encourages cooperative learning and promotes effective mainstreaming. One teacher found that peer tutoring was particularly useful in problem-solving activities. He found that his gifted students who had finished their assignments were pleased to help students who were experiencing difficulty. The gifted students were particularly effective in helping other students develop strategies for dealing with word problems.

For handicapped students, problem-solving skills are particularly useful in dealing with money, time, and measurement.

Money

National Assessments of Educational Progress have documented that even though high school students are able to add, subtract, multiply, and divide, they often lack the ability to use these computational skills in problem-solving situations involving money (Edge & Burton, 1986).

Many students can identify coins and bills but are unable to pay for objects, receive change, or count a handful of coins. Handicapped children may not even have coin recognition skills. Beginning instruction is particularly difficult because the size of coins is not related to their value. For this reason, it is better to use real money than play money or pictures of coins.

Teachers who would not hesitate to spend $5.00 for instructional materials are frequently reluctant to use $5.00 in change to teach money concepts. Coins can be accounted for by having children count them as they are distributed, record the amount each child has, and count them when they are returned to the teacher. This method provides opportunities for counting as well as for insuring return of the money.

In teaching the value of money, the following sequence has been suggested:

1. Barter as an introduction to the medium of exchange.
2. Coin recognition activities involving coin boards, identifying coins by touch and size, and matching coins.

[2]From *Instructional Strategies for Teaching the Gifted* (p. 221) by J. P. Parker, 1989. Boston: Allyn and Bacon. Copyright 1989 by Allyn and Bacon. Reprinted by permission.

3. Learning to count money, including all appropriate equivalences such as one dime is equivalent to two nickels, to one nickel and five pennies, and to ten pennies.
4. Using money as a medium of exchange through the making of common purchases and the setting up of a playstore. (Note that the "classroom" store is not used to introduce the notions of money but is delayed until children already have some ability to recognize coins and to count money.)
5. Making change in an efficient manner. (Edge & Burton, 1986, p. 47)

As students mature, their interest in money and in purchasing increases. They can be asked to look for sales in newspapers, to plan budgets, to study local banking practices, or to simulate food purchases from local restaurant menus or markets. As consumers, students should be introduced to gaining the best value from their purchases, which gives practice in mathematical problem-solving and also provides students with a valuable skill for adult living.

A number of textbooks and materials deal with consumer skills in understanding installment purchasing, interest payments, balancing a checkbook, determining salary from rate of pay, identifying payroll deductions, and other topics necessary to earning a living and maintaining an acceptable life-style. Newspapers and advertising flyers, in addition to more formal material, are helpful in teaching consumer skills. However, the most valuable experience comes from students' spending their own money on items they need and want.

Time

Telling time is usually interpreted as using a clock accurately. However, understanding many concepts must precede the ability to tell time.

Many students have difficulty understanding and correctly using such temporal expressions as *in* _____ *minutes,* _____ *minutes ago, earlier,* and *later.* Being able to read from a clock and being able to interpret, predict, and plan, using one's ability to tell time, are different skills. Developing a sense of time or an awareness of time is an important concept that should precede telling time (Bley & Thornton, 1981).

Time concepts begin with such activities as observing a calendar and noting seasons and special events. Such questions as, When is my birthday? When do we go to lunch? and When is tomorrow? are relevant to children and their interests. The passing of time can become vivid and real through such conditioning strategies as learning to estimate the length of 1 minute and timing pleasant activities.

Teachers can assess their students' readiness to tell time by informal observation. A teacher in a resource room had the following experience:

Bryan was always late to the resource room. I noticed that he was wearing a watch and asked him one day, "Bryan, can you tell time?" He paused for a moment and responded, "Yes, when it's 12:00 I can." With that positive attitude, I knew he was ready. I made a paper clock face with his resource room time indicated and asked his teacher to tape it to his desk. He observed his watch, and when the appointed time came, left the classroom for the resource room. He was never late again, and soon was telling time accurately.

In learning to read a clock, children should be able to handle successfully the following skills:

- Skip count by 5s to 55.
- Count on from within this counting sequence, with visual reinforcement.
- Understand the meanings of before and after for clock times.
- Understand which hand moves most rapidly and, ideally, associate it with minutes.
- Identify the minute hand on the clock and realize that one counts on from this hand (the minute hand, not the hour hand) to determine "in ____ minutes" or "____ ago." (Bley & Thornton, 1981, p. 140)

In secondary programs for handicapped students, the focus is usually on time as it relates to employment. Being on time is critical to job performance and involves getting up on time, planning time to get ready for work, and pacing oneself on the job. Other time-related skills include signing in on a time clock, keeping a record of time worked, and understanding the basis for payment.

Measurement
Vocational education teachers may be frustrated because the students mainstreamed into their classes do not have appropriate measuring skills. Like other mathematical skills, measurement skills begin at the manipulative stage, with children measuring and pouring sand, water, or whatever materials are available to them. As the tasks become more difficult, children with learning problems frequently experience difficulty.

One area that is most difficult to teach and to learn concerns the basic measurement equivalencies needed for mathematical and vocational objectives. In introducing complex equivalencies, a starting point is the use of concrete objects used to develop the association between a measurement term and its size. Concrete illustrations of equivalencies include such activities as filling two pint milk containers and pouring the contents of both into a 1-quart container. This activity reinforces the concept that 2 pints equal 1 quart.

At the semiconcrete level, charts (class-size and individual) for each category of measurement can be made. Such charts can include linear measurement, liquid measurement, time, and bulk measurement. Equivalencies and illustrations can be presented on the charts, which can be used in solving problems. Students who have memory problems can keep the charts for referral when needed (Koons, 1984).

FIGURE 9.9 Adapted Cooking Material

Adaptations in materials can simplify the acquisition and use of measurement skills. In using the ruler, for example, the student can begin with a ruler marked only for 1-inch intervals. Following activities and problems using this beginning ruler, rulers marked at the half- and quarter-inch are gradually introduced until a conventional ruler can be used.

Measurement skills can be improved through cooking activities with the use of special cookbooks and utensils. As illustrated in Figure 9.9, directions, ingredients, and measurements can be presented graphically for students who do not read well. In addition, kits are available that include color-coded measuring spoons and cups. These colors can be included in the recipes to simplify cooking further. As important as measurement skills are for school achievement, they are even more critical in daily skills for living.

Mathematics is developmental; learning proceeds from basic mathematical concepts gained through experience to understanding and acquisition of process skills. The final achievements are the development of problem-solving skills and the functional use of mathematics in all areas of life. For students who are handicapped, adequate use of functional mathematics contributes to independence and fulfillment. For students who are gifted, mathematics opens doors to advanced technology and presents challenges to solve problems with insight and creativity.

REFERENCES

Atkinson, B. (1983). Arithmetic remediation and the learning disabled adolescent: Fractions and interest level. *Journal of Learning Disabilities, 16,* (7), 403–406.

Baroody, A. J. (1987). *Children's mathematical thinking.* New York: Teachers College Press.

Beattie, I. D. (1986). Modeling operations and algorithms. *Arithmetic Teacher, 33,* (6), 23–28.

Bley, N. S., & Thornton, C. A. (1981). *Teaching mathematics to the learning disabled.* Rockville, MD: Aspen Systems.

Brolin, D. E. (1989). *Life centered career education: A competency based approach* (3rd ed.). Reston, VA: Council for Exceptional Children.

Burton, G. M., & Meyers, M. J. (1987). Teaching mathematics to learning disabled students in the secondary classroom. *Mathematics Teacher, 80,* (9), 702–709.

Carpenter, D. (1982). Error analysis: Procedures and guidelines. *Diagnostique, 7,* 221–228.

Carpenter, R. L. (1985). Mathematics instruction in resource rooms: Instruction time and teacher competence. *Learning Disability Quarterly, 8,* (2), 95–100.

Edge, D., & Burton, G. (1986). Helping learning disabled middle school students learn about money. *Journal of Learning Disabilities, 19,* (1), 46–51.

Fowler, M. A. (1978). Why did he miss that problem? *Academic Therapy, 14,* (1), 23–33.

Gallagher, J. J. (1979). Minimum competency: The setting of educational standards. *Educational Evaluation and Policy Analysis, 1,* (1), 62–67.

Gallagher, J. J. (1985). *Teaching the gifted child* (3rd ed.). Boston: Allyn and Bacon.

Halpern, N. (1981). Mathematics for the learning disabled. *Journal of Learning Disabilities, 14,* (9), 505–506.

Hammill, D. D., & Bartel, N. R. (1978). *Teaching children with learning and behavior problems* (2nd ed.). Boston: Allyn and Bacon.

Hasselbring, T. S., Goin, L. I., & Bransford, J. D. (1988). Developing math automaticity in learning handicapped children: The role of computerized drill and practice. *Focus on Exceptional Children, 20,* (6), 1–7.

Heddens, J. W. (1986). Bridging the gap between the concrete and the abstract. *Arithmetic Teacher, 33,* (6), 14–17.

Hynes, M. C. (1986). Selection criteria. *Arithmetic Teacher, 33,* (6), 11–13.

Kennedy, L. M. (1986). A rationale. *Arithmetic Teacher, 33,* (6), 6–7.

Koons, T. L. (1984). Teach measurement equivalencies simply. *Academic Therapy, 19,* (5), 593–598.

Linde, J. L., & Olsen, K. R. (1980). *Minimum competency testing and handicapped students.* Washington, DC: Division of Media Services, Bureau of Education for the Handicapped.

Maddux, C. D., Cates, D., & Sowell, V. (1984). Fingermath for the visually impaired: An intrasubject design. *Journal of Visual Impairment & Blindness, 78,* (1), 7–9.

Miederhoff, J. W., & Wood, J. W. (1988). Adapting test construction for mainstreamed mathematics students. *Mathematics Teacher, 81,* (5), 388–392.

Montague, M., & Bos, C. S. (1986). The effect of cognitive strategy training on verbal math problem solving of learning disabled adolescents. *Journal of Learning Disabilities, 19,* 26–33.

Moser, J. M. (1986). Curricular issues. *Arithmetic Teacher, 33,* (6), 8–10.

Nichols, E. D., & Behr, M. J. (1982). *Elementary school mathematics and how to teach it.* New York: Holt, Rinehart and Winston.

Norman, C. (1988). Math education: A mixed picture. *Science, 241,* 408–409.

Parker, J. P. (1989). *Instructional strategies for teaching the gifted.* Boston: Allyn and Bacon.

Pathescope Educational Media. (1981). *Problem solving in mathematics.* New Rochelle, NY: Pathescope Educational Media.

Piaget, J. (1952). *The child's conception of numbers.* London: Routledge & Kegan Paul.

Prevost, F. J. (1984). Teaching rational numbers—junior high school. *Arithmetic Teacher, 31,* (6), 43–46.

Reisman, F. K., & Kauffman, S. H. (1980). *Teaching mathematics to children with special needs.* Columbus, OH: Merrill.

Roseman, L. (1985). Ten essential concepts for remediation in mathematics. *Mathematics Teacher, 78,* (7), 502–507.

Sander, M. (1981). Getting ready for arithmetic: Prerequisites for learning to add. *Teaching Exceptional Children, 13,* (2) 54–57.

Thornton, C. A., & Wilmot, B. (1986). Special learners. *Arithmetic Teacher, 33,* (6), 38–41.

Vockell, E. L., & Hall, J. (1989). Computerized test construction. *The Social Studies, 80,* (3), 114–121.

10

Teaching Social Studies and Science

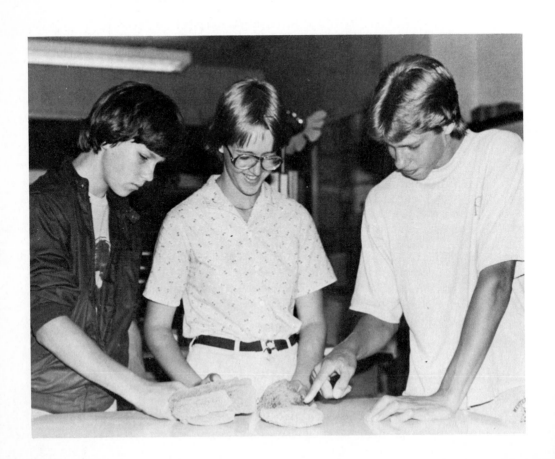

A professor in elementary education expressed the opinion that most handicapped students have not experienced failure in science because "most elementary teachers don't teach science." The back-to-basics emphasis on reading skills has resulted in a trend to diminish the amount of time devoted to social studies and science instruction for all children. In interviews with elementary teachers, Schug (1989) found that teachers were in agreement that the most important subject in the curriculum is reading. When asked what subject they considered to be least important, the responses were not in accord, but they frequently included social studies and science.

Teachers of handicapped students, in particular, have emphasized skill development in the language arts and mathematics areas. There is evidence that other skills, such as social and work skills, are improved through the social studies and science curricula. Another rationale for teaching these subjects is the opportunity for successful participation by handicapped students. The broad scope of these two fields provides a wide choice of goals, activities, methods, and materials to accommodate all learners.

The inclusion of social studies and science in the curriculum for gifted students is equally important (Parker, 1989). As potential leaders, gifted students must be prepared to deal effectively with technology and to be productive members of society.

At the elementary level, social studies and science are usually taught by the classroom teacher, and the topics can be interrelated with other curricular studies. At the secondary level, however, these disciplines are specialized, and the integration of exceptional students is difficult and frustrating for the content teachers. In an effort to provide practical approaches for teachers at all levels, social studies and science are discussed separately, with a summary presenting problems and techniques common to the two curriculum areas.

SOCIAL STUDIES

Social studies is often associated with the fields of history, geography, economics, and civics. More fundamentally, social studies education concerns itself with human beings. Although the entire school curriculum shares the responsibility for citizenship education, social studies occupies a unique role in contributing to the process (Jarolimek, 1986).

The National Council for the Social Studies (1984) defines social studies as an important component of the school curriculum:

Social studies is a basic subject of the K–12 curriculum that (1) derives its goals from the nature of citizenship in a democratic society that is closely linked to other nations and peoples of the world; (2) draws its content primarily from history, the social sciences, and, in some respects, from the humanities and science; and (3) is taught in ways that reflect an awareness of the personal, social, and cultural experiences and developmental levels of learners. (p. 251)

Social studies is an important part of the education that all students need if they are to understand their world and lead productive lives in it.

Assessment

The first step in educational planning for exceptional students is the development of the IEP (see chapter 6). The teacher responsible for social studies instruction should develop an IEP in cooperation with the special education resource teacher, the student's parents, and any other members of the committee responsible for devising the program. Each handicapped student who requires specially designed instruction in order to progress successfully will have an IEP; students who are gifted may have individual IEPs or group IEPs, depending on state regulations.

The foundation of the IEP is assessment, which must be completed to identify the student's level of performance in the content area. Stephens, Blackhurst, and Magliocca (1988) identify four sources of information that can be of planning and instructional value to the teacher: students' records, test results, permanent products, and direct observation.

Students' Records
Students' records provide basic demographic data, a history of school advancement and retention, and indications of erratic standardized test performance. This information contributes more to understanding the student than to planning for the student.

Tests
Tests are the most widely available sources of student assessment information. Assessment of academic achievement is routine practice in schools, with standardized group measures used on regular bases. Two of the most frequently used group achievement tests are the Metropolitan Achievement Test Series or MAT (Balow, Farr, Hogan, & Prescott, 1979) and the Stanford Achievement Test or SAT (Madden, Gardner, Rudman, Darlsen, & Merwin, 1973). The MAT extends from grades K.0 to 12.9 and includes norm-referenced survey tests in Reading Comprehension, Mathematics, Language, Social Studies, and Science. The SAT is available for grades 1.5 to 9.9. It includes norm-referenced tests in Reading, Language, Social Studies, and Science. Many other group tests of academic performance are used extensively in the public schools. They include the California

Achievement Tests (Tiegs & Clark, 1979), Comprehensive Tests of Basic Skills (1978), Iowa Tests of Basic Skills (Hieronymous & Lindquist, 1974), and the SRA Achievement Series (Naslund, Thorpe, & Lefever, 1981).

In addition to commercial tests, teachers often construct their own assessment tools. One method is to specify the major concepts and skills to be covered throughout the year. Many state- and/or system-adopted curriculum guides provide a comprehensive analysis of the component skills and concepts in the various topical areas the teacher plans to cover. Teachers might consider collecting curriculum guides in social studies from various sources to help with skill and concept specification. Textbooks are also helpful.

After the teacher has identified the general curriculum, which will serve as the core of the social studies program, a test sampling readiness for the content can be given to handicapped students. These tests can be administered orally by a volunteer or teacher aide. The purpose is not to ask every possible question on every topic, but rather to probe the student's level of knowledge in order to determine whether the student is ready to progress according to grade level expectations. For example, in the topical area of geography, a major objective might be map-reading skills. The teacher who plans to use a map of the United States may find that a student with learning problems cannot read a map of the United States and, moreover, has no map-reading skills at all. In such a situation, a teacher clearly learns that instruction must start on a much lower level than might have been anticipated. Planning sound instruction means identifying whether a student has the necessary prerequisite skills. If the student does not have these skills, they can be incorporated into the student's IEP.

An important assessment is the documentation of the student's reading level in content texts. Johnson and Vardian (1973) analyzed 68 social studies texts from grades 1 through 6 to pinpoint readability levels. A startling finding was that intermediate texts had a readability range from 2 to 12 years. Generally, their findings suggested that many elementary social studies texts have readability levels above grade level expectations. The assessment implication is that the reading level specified in the student's records might not reflect the student's capability to read social studies texts. For example, a student's reading level might be recorded at the low fourth-grade level; however, the fourth-grade social studies text could have a readability level of sixth grade. Based on the student's reading level, the teacher would expect the student to be able to read the text, unless the teacher was aware of the readability level of the book. To assess the student, the teacher can administer an informal reading inventory, using content from the social studies text (Turner, 1976). The procedure for constructing the inventory is identical to that described in chapter 8. The documentation of the student's reading level correlated to the available texts can guide the teacher in planning appropriate instruction.

Permanent Products
Students' products consist of written examinations, audio and visual recordings, completed tasks such as models, and art projects related to social studies. A series of products over time is particularly effective in documenting the progress students have made. Some mainstreamed students do not show measurable gains on standardized tests or do not appear to be learning. When data are collected systematically from their daily efforts, their rate of learning can be impressive (Stephens et al., 1988). Products collected from advanced students may indicate superior writing potential, artistic talent, and/or the ability to synthesize information in a creative way.

Direct Observation
As in other curriculum areas, observation is a valuable tool in planning for social studies instruction. Discussions of current events, for example, can reveal students' awareness of their environment and relevant issues, their ability to grasp ideas, and their interest in the community and worldwide activities. In simulated activities (discussed later in this chapter) teachers can readily observe students' abilities to relate to others in group situations, to use their imaginations to create specified conditions, and to work toward logical conclusions. Observation of such behaviors enables the teacher to determine which students are lacking in basic communication skills and which students should be stimulated to pursue more complex topics.

Goals and Objectives

Jarolimek (1986) presents three goals for social studies: knowledge and information goals, attitude and value goals, and skills goals.

Knowledge and Information
This goal refers to acquiring information and concepts. It includes learning about the world, its people and their cultures; the history and growth of the United States; community life; legal and political systems; career orientation; and basic human institutions and social functions that characterize all societies.

Attitudes and Values
Positive attitudes toward oneself and others are particularly relevant in a class containing handicapped students. The social studies curriculum presents an ideal opportunity to deal with the concept of handicapism, developed later in this chapter. It also provides the setting for handicapped students to understand themselves.

Skills
The third goal deals with the development of skills associated with social studies. Jarolimek (1986) delineates four categories of skills: social skills, study skills and work habits, group work skills, and intellectual skills. Because the responsibility for teaching many of these skills overlaps other curriculum areas, social studies can reinforce such skills and provide practical opportunities to use these skills and show pupils how general skills can be applied to a specific subject area. For example, listening, speaking, reading, and writing skills learned in the language arts curriculum are used and developed through discussion and reporting assignments in the social studies.

Instructional approaches in the three categories of social studies goals are presented in the following section.

Instructional Approaches

In planning social studies curricula to include handicapped students, the following considerations are important:

1. Some handicapped students will be able to handle the same curricular content as the non-handicapped students, with specialized materials/arrangements. For instance, visually handicapped students have access to illumination/magnification devices to read standard texts and texts with enlarged type, as well as the use of tactile devices, such as specially developed relief maps. The auditorily handicapped have available to them amplification of sound devices, or special seating, or hearing aids.
2. Many handicapped students and non-handicapped students will learn the same course content and be more motivated to learn if the content is presented in a manner, or through material, that indicates a more relevant or integrated relationship to standard course content. For example, the development of concepts, as a central core of the social studies curriculum, can be effected with an emphasis on project work or thematic learning centers.
3. A number of handicapped students (mildly mentally handicapped and some learning disabled students) may benefit from a prioritization of the standard social studies content at a particular level that may involve the modification of some course content for some individuals. (Herlihy & Herlihy, 1980, p. 45)

Knowledge and Information
Based on the needs and abilities of each handicapped student, the teacher must decide what to teach, what to emphasize, and in what sequence. Herlihy and Herlihy (1980) claim that an emphasis on memorizing informa-

tion and facts, as opposed to teaching understandings and concepts, is a problem in social studies programs for all students, especially handicapped children and youth. They suggest the use of an essential content checklist so that broad content areas or topics can be broken down into sequential topics or tasks.

In making decisions concerning the amount and kind of content to teach, priorities will be established in developing the student's IEP. Specific objectives are illustrated in Figure 10.1.

Attitudes and Values

Even though there seems to be little doubt that values should be taught, there is a great deal of controversy about how they should be taught. One viewpoint, called values clarification, states that the process of valuing rather than the values themselves should be taught. A second opinion holds that students should be encouraged to develop skills necessary to make rational value judgments. A third perspective emphasizes the importance of teaching specific moral education.

The most popular approach is that of values clarification. It is important for teachers to remember that valuing as a process may be new to many handicapped students. For those who operate at a concrete level of cognition, this abstract concept may be difficult. For others, protective parents and environments may have provided extremely structured guidelines for "right and wrong." Teachers need to be alert to ways of eliciting values consistently. An activity suggested in *Life Skills for Health* (1974) is the use of "thought sheets." This method requires students to turn in, once a week, single sheets or 4-by-6 cards on which they have written some thoughts of importance to them. Each thought is written after reflection and indicates something of the quality of living or thinking in the preceding week. In reacting to these thoughts and others, teachers should refrain from making judgmental statements, such as "I don't agree," "This is a terrible idea," or "What would your parents think?" Rather, comments should be accepting and thought provoking, such as "This would be a good topic for class discussion," or "If you were President, what would you do about this situation?" Seif (1977) states that children and adults are aware of many conflicting values and that questions about values and value issues have become important tools for organizing learning in the social studies.

Skills

Social skills can be defined as "those behaviors which involve interaction between the child and his peers or adults where the primary intent is the achievement of the child's or adult's goals through positive interactions" (Cartledge & Milburn, 1980). Once social deficiencies are identified, teaching procedures can be structured and implemented. A social skills training program designed to assess children in developing peer relationships

Current Performance Level	General Student-Centered Goals	Priority Number	Teaching Approach and Methodology; Monitoring and Evaluation Techniques; Specialized Equipment and Materials
Has completed a ninth-grade Social Studies class with minimal success. Reading is presently measured at the fourth-grade level, and writing skills are marginal.	Will demonstrate a basic understanding of the social characteristics of the American Nation (Sophomore Curriculum).	3	Team Teaching/varied groupings and materials/ adaptions as needed by resource room staff/ point system/informal and formal testing/class grade.

Goal Number	Objective Number	Specific Student-Centered Objectives	Quarters During Which Objectives Will Be Addressed 1	2	3	4
3	1	Will identify the six categories of culture (economics, family, religion, education, government, and language/art).	X	X		
3	2	Will describe contemporary American culture based on six characteristics.	X	X		
3	3	Will identify the sources of American immigrant groups and Black Americans and Native Americans.		X		
3	4	Will identify the reasons for immigration to America.	X			
3	5	Will identify immigrant settlement locations.	X			
3	6	Will describe the experiences of the immigrant crossing.	X			
3	7	Will describe the early experiences of the immigrants upon arrival.	X			

(continued)

FIGURE 10.1 Partial IEP—Social Studies Section—One semester

Goal Number	Objective Number	Specific Student-Centered Objectives	Quarters During Which Objectives Will Be Addressed 1	2	3	4
3	8	Will identify the impact of America on the immigrants.	X			
3	9	Will identify the impact of the immigrants on America.	X			
3	10	Will compare and contrast recent American immigrants with past groups.		X		
3	11	Will identify reasons for existence of racism.	X			
3	12	Will actively participate in a small group.	X	X		
3	13	Will complete Social Studies readings at a mid-fourth grade level.	X	X		
3	14	Will answer test questions utilizing complete sentences.	X	X		
3	15	Will answer essay questions by listing major points.	X	X		
3	16	Will demonstrate auditory attentive ability by completing guide sheets for listening activities.	X	X		
3	17	Will demonstrate ability to organize work by maintaining a student class folder.	X	X		
3	18	Will improve note-taking skills by copying outlines from teacher transparencies.	X	X		

(continued)

3	19	Will demonstrate ability to utilize charts and graphs.	X	X
3	20	Will be able to identify continents and oceans and locate 50% of the American states.	X	X
3	21	Will be able to gain meaning and make inferences from Social Studies-related pictures.	X	X
3	22	Will be able to construct and draw implications from a time line.	X	X
3	23	Will be able to list and describe required Social Studies evidence and data.	X	X
3	24	Will draw inferences from 25% of the data and evidence used in class.	X	X
3	25	Will identify positive and negative feelings on the social concepts presented.	X	X
3	26	Will begin to develop critically a humanistic value system.	X	X
3	27	Will demonstrate ability to rationally control her own life and her environment.	X	X

Source: From *Mainstreaming in the Social Studies* (pp. 26–27) by J. G. Herlihy and M. T. Herlily (Eds.), 1980. Washington, DC: National Council for the Social Studies. Copyright 1980 by the National Council for the Social Studies. Reprinted with permission of the National Council for the Social Studies.

FIGURE 10.1 (continued)

has identified nine important areas (Mesibov & LaGreca, 1981). These areas are: smiling, greeting others, joining ongoing peer activities, extending invitations to others, conversing, sharing and cooperating, complimenting others, physical appearance/grooming, and play skills. The social studies curriculum, with an emphasis on group participation and interaction, provides children with an excellent opportunity to develop such skills.

Another approach to teaching social skills is to develop a course in human relations. Dewey (1978) claims that the study of human relations is almost a survival course for special students in helping them find jobs, keep jobs, stay out of trouble with the law, defend themselves against exploitation, and win and keep friends.

Kelly (1979) claims that teachers have an obligation to teach the attitudes and behaviors fundamental to social living. Strategies suggested include the use of appropriate adult models, children's literature reflecting basic social ideals, and simulation games, sociodrama, and roleplaying.

The development of social skills can take place in a number of curriculum areas: vocational training, home economics, communication, and social studies. In this textbook, additional discussion is found in the chapters concerned with behavior management and social integration (see chapters 12 and 13).

Study skills, such as map reading, are a particular component of social studies. Observing, listening, reading, and writing are necessary skills in all subjects. Students can obtain information in a variety of ways: hear it from the teacher, read it, see it happen, or look for it in many sources (Oliner, 1976).

The problem presented by poor readers is discussed later in this chapter, as it is shared in the science curriculum. In the area of social studies, textbooks can be taped by volunteers or peer tutors to circumvent the reading problem. In one fifth-grade classroom where a college student recorded the social studies textbook for children with learning problems, it was found that many of the nonhandicapped students also appreciated a different approach to the textbook assignments.

Some students who do not read well are good conversationalists. Teachers alert to this strength can use it as a teaching evaluative tool and as a means of instructional and social integration.

In teaching conversational skills, children are encouraged to ask open-ended questions that require more than a one-word response (Mesibov & LaGreca, 1981). For example, "Do you like to play football after school?" is a closed-ended question, whereas "What do you like to do after school?" stimulates conversation.

Group discussion is one of the most important techniques that social studies teachers at all levels can use. Schug and Beery (1987) suggest four techniques that emphasize the importance of student thought, ideas, and thinking during classroom discussions:

1. Seating arrangements that maximize opportunities for all children to see one another during discussions are especially helpful in centering attention on the person contributing at a particular time and to promote group thought.

2. If thinking will require a fresh mind and serious attention, it is wise to schedule the discussion at a time of day when students will be best able to respond fully. The end of the day or immediately after lunch are poor times for extended social studies discussions. There is no educational reason why students need to have their social studies, science, or reading at the same time every day. While the school day is never completely open for teacher re-scheduling, there are some times that are better than others for difficult or serious group thought.

3. The reality of the interruptions in the school day also suggests another scheduling issue. If group thinking, whether it be whole class or small group, is an important process and if the skills in that process should be experienced, then it is important that thinking discussions take place when all students can be a part of that process, practicing necessary skills and benefiting from student modeling of complex thinking. These discussions should not be scheduled when some will be leaving the room.

4. For older students, study guides or worksheets should be designed to prepare them for thinking discussions or to guide follow-up application of concepts in new situations. This is different from a sheet on which facts are listed, where the emphasis is on being able to recall what you have put down on your study guide or worksheet. (pp. 166–167)

Carefully prepared questions can help students develop thinking and generalizing skills. Such questions also provide opportunities for expression within the group at different ability levels. A sequence of questions starting from a low level of fact and leading to relationships and problem solving can involve slow learners as well as gifted students. The use of Bloom's Taxonomy provides guidelines for developing questions at varying levels (see chapter 7).

Students' questions are also important to the development of their thinking skills. Questioning is an aid to retention, because it provides an opportunity to apply facts and principles, offers an opportunity for oral expression, provides for individual differences, and is an evaluative tool for teachers and students. Students feel free to raise questions in a non-threatening environment, where every question is acknowledged and respected.

Social Studies and Handicapism
Schuncke (1988) identifies three goals for social studies education:

1. To know about the world.
2. To be able to do something about present and future problems.
3. To care about one's fellow humans. (p. vii)

Within these goals, and other goals previously referred to, is the need to learn about groups of people who have not always been accorded full citizenship and whose causes have been embraced by people with a social conscience.

Shaver and Curtis (1981) make a strong point for including a study of handicapism in the social studies curriculum. Social studies teachers, in particular, have realized the need to deal with the denial to some groups of full participation in the political, economic, and social life of society.

Because people who are handicapped have been denied the opportunity of full participation, the study of handicapism is as vital as the study of racism and sexism. The negative effects of handicapism are equally important for handicapped and nonhandicapped people. These effects can be viewed in economic, political, and humane terms. A major citizenship goal in including education about handicapped citizens in social studies is "to help students understand the issues raised by handicapism so that they will be better prepared to think about and act on those issues as citizens— not just as adults, but in their daily lives in and out of school" (Shaver & Curtis, 1981, p. 6).

Individualizing Instruction

A number of techniques for meeting the needs of individual students have been used in the social studies content. These techniques include individualized inquiry, learning centers, learning activity packages, simulations, and microcomputers.

Individualized Inquiry
Individualized inquiry provides an opportunity for teachers to involve students who are responsible, motivated, and intellectually capable of inquiry-oriented investigations on an individual basis. Wilen and McKenrick (1989) suggest a proposition that might be offered to a student in a typical social studies class:

> *Andy, you're one of my best students in this class. I think you would appreciate a challenge. I would like you to think about doing a project related to what we have been studying—something that really interests you. This would be completely voluntary, of course. If you are interested, I could make arrangements for you to report to the learning resources center instead of coming to class for an extended period of time so that you could work on your inquiry project. Also, the credit and grade you would receive for your work could be substituted for the test and other written assignments*

you would normally complete. Take some time to think about it. Then, if this appeals to you, let's discuss it further. (p. 36)

Individualized inquiry can be particularly satisfying for the teacher who wishes to challenge and extend capable students' potential. This method is also discussed in relation to science in this chapter.

Learning Centers

Learning centers can be used for exploration, skill building, and reinforcement. In a classroom in which learning centers are used, a social studies center can contain maps, books, newspapers, filmstrips, and construction materials to provide exploration of a specific topic. Learning centers are particularly useful in individualizing instruction because they provide entrance at different levels and permit students to work at various speeds.

Learning Activity Packages

Learning activity packages (LAPs) provide the material for an individual to accomplish a single objective. Schuncke (1988) gives the following example of a LAP that a fifth-grade teacher used to teach simple measurement of distance using scale on a community map:

> *Objective:* At the end of this activity you will be able to measure the distance from place to place on a map using a ruler.
>
> *Directions:* Included in this packet are three items: a map, a ruler, and a cassette tape. Check to see if you have all three. You will also need a tape recorder and headphones and a pencil and paper.
>
> After you have gotten these, put the cassette into the recorder and follow all directions. (p. 303)

LAPs are useful for all students who want to work independently. They are particularly useful for students who have learning problems because the students can proceed at their own pace, work with a teacher aide or another student, and be engaged in a learning task that is more appropriate than the one the class as a whole is pursuing.

Simulations

A simulation is a learning experience that allows students to participate in a simplified representation of the social world (Schug & Beery, 1987). Simulation games are popular in social studies programs. Because they provide realistic approaches to life situations, simulations can help slow learners in concept development and generalizations. Particularly at the secondary level, players can develop decision-making strategies and can begin to feel that they have some control over their environment.

Although simulations have not been found to facilitate content learning, they do influence student attitudes. Simulations are also powerful tools for motivation when they contain a challenge and an element of fantasy and when they arouse curiosity (Schug & Beery, 1987).

Microcomputers

One major difference between the computer and other instructional media is that the computer has the capacity to interact with the student. (See the discussion of the use of microcomputers with mainstreamed students in chapter 6.) Jarolimek (1986) identifies four categories in which computer-assisted instruction can contribute to social studies:

1. Using the computer to obtain needed information (data) or to retrieve information stored in the computer. There is a growing number of collections of data, known as *data bases,* many of which are relevant to social studies. . . . Being able to access information from data bases through the computer, as well as being able to use the Computer Catalog Service in the library, are essential social studies skills in this "high tech" era.
2. Using the computer to practice and apply social studies skills such as map reading, graph reading, chart interpretation, thinking, and problem solving. Computer programs of this kind are referred to as "drill and practice."
3. Using the computer for tutorial assistance in providing a sequential program for the development and elaboration of concepts and knowledge that all students are expected to learn. These are essentially courses of study that have been programmed for the computer.
4. Using the computer for specialized presentations such as simulations, decision-making situations, analysis of given data, interpreting information needed to solve a problem or a series of related problems. (pp. 97–98)

The National Council for the Social Studies has published guidelines for evaluating social studies microcomputer courseware in the November–December 1984 issue of *Social Education.*

Media, pictures, and charts are used frequently in social studies. They are effective in providing variety, overlearning, and retention, but adaptations are necessary for students with visual and hearing handicaps. A number of geographic aids for students who are visually impaired are available, including braille atlases, relief maps made of molded plastic, dissected and undissected maps of continents and countries, relief globes and mileage scales, and large-type outline maps and land-form models featuring three-dimensional tactile maps (Herlihy & Herlihy, 1980) (see Figure 10.2).

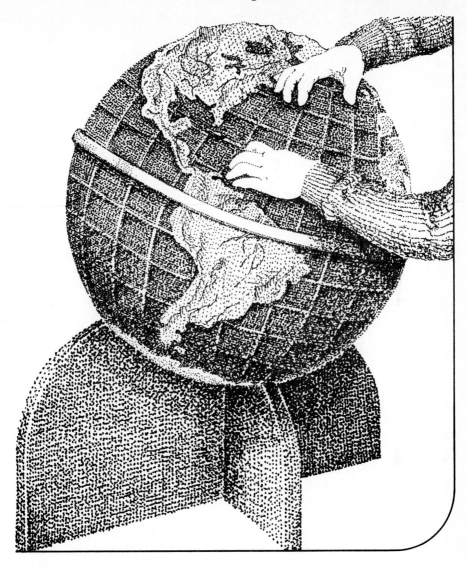

FIGURE 10.2 Tactile Globe

Manuel's favorite subject is social studies. He listens to the news regularly and is politically aware. Although he is visually impaired, he has acquired excellent geographic concepts through listening, class discussion, and the use of materials from the American Printing House for the Blind. Relief maps and globes have been of particular value to him in following world events. Manuel's teachers find that other students also benefit from the tactile input of these materials and enjoy having a new dimension to their learning.

Captioned films and filmstrips are available on loan for students who are hearing impaired. Information can be obtained from the Special Office for Materials Distribution at Indiana University.

Activities in social studies should be varied enough to appeal to a broad range of interests and abilities, including those of handicapped and gifted students. The social studies curriculum provides many opportunities for individual and group activities. Because of its relevance to community awareness and living, to the acquisition of skills related to decision making, to values clarification, and to cooperative working, social studies is an important part of every student's learning.

SCIENCE

One of my fondest memories as a parent is that of a science fair in which three of my children participated. Tom, a student in high school, displayed a maze in which he had charted the progress of earthworms. Mary, an elementary school scientist, exhibited a study of the nesting habits of hamsters. Billy, a member of a special education class, showed a chart and description of poisonous plants. Operating on vastly different maturity and ability levels, all three were actively involved in appropriate, relevant, and important scientific investigations.

Science is for all children. In science experiences, students have a chance to handle, manipulate, and experiment with magnets and wire, air and water, and many other concrete materials and objects. In science they deal with materials and activities to which words and symbols refer and also have experiences that are the foundations of logical thought (Jacobson & Bergman, 1987). Such experiences are particularly important for students who have not had success in other areas of learning and who profit most from hands-on experiences. Science is equally important for students who are able to go beyond this level and who need additional challenges.

In spite of the relevance of science for all students, research on a national level shows that the quantity and quality of science education are decreasing because science education has a low status in this country. In elementary school less time is spent on science than on any other subject area, and in secondary school, science education for many students usually ends after the tenth grade (Stefanich & Kelsey, 1989).

If science programs in general are inadequate, then science for handicapped students is especially meager. Frequently, students are sent to resource rooms or to special service areas during science classes; even if they remain in class they may not participate in science activities. Also, handicapped students may have been deprived of science in their curriculum because most educators assumed that they were not interested in science, that it was too difficult for them, and that they could not manipulate or would break laboratory equipment (Menhusen & Gromme, 1976).

Gifted students may also be victims of inadequate science programs and emphasis. They may not want to take science in high school because they found it boring in elementary school. Parker (1989) makes a strong statement that "unless we give them experiences of value beginning in the early grades, our gifted students will be won over to other areas, and our scientific superiority will be lost to other nations in the future" (p. 241).

In the past, handicapped children have not been encouraged to consider science as a career. There has been a movement, however, to provide role models and a directory of disabled scientists for children to consult (Redden, 1979). This effort was reinforced by the United States Postal Service in 1981 with the circulation of a stamp depicting a scientist in a wheelchair (see Figure 10.3).

The American Association for the Advancement of Science (AAAS) Project on the Handicapped in Science concluded from a 1975 survey that most handicapped students, whether in special schools or public schools, receive little science education. At a more advanced level, a National Science Board report (Coleman & Selby, 1982) noted that fewer than one-third of the 21,000 U.S. high schools offer physics courses taught by qualified physics teachers. The AAAS project is addressing two problems basic to the improvement of science education for handicapped students: (1) the improvement of preservice and inservice teacher training in science to prepare teachers to include the exceptional student in mainstream situations, and (2) the preparation and dissemination of inventories of human and material resources (Redden & Malcolm, 1976).

Wolfinger (1984) finds that students who are academically gifted can profit from a science program in four areas. First, a science program can contribute to the development of abstract reasoning ability, including the abilities to hypothesize, to reason from a premise, to make multiple inferences, and to test those inferences. Second, a science program can help the gifted student develop problem-solving skills and an objective viewpoint. Third, the science program can develop research skills that will permit the gifted student to pursue topics of interest and to create an individualized program based on the student's interests and needs. Fourth, for the student who is particularly gifted in science, a science program should permit the development of interests leading to a career in the sciences.

This rationale is reinforced by Parker (1989), who points out the value of inquiry education for the gifted. There is a need to teach gifted students

FIGURE 10.3 United States Postage Stamp: "Disabled doesn't mean Unable."

the research methods used by professionals in the various fields of endeavor; the abilities to identify a problem and solve it are part of inquiry training encountered in the science curriculum.

Assessment

Children are bombarded with stimuli from the environment. For some children, the stimuli are jumbled together. The science teacher might ask how children sort these stimuli in a meaningful way, how they make decisions, how they gain mastery of their environment, and how they distinguish between fantasy and reality, cause and effect (Hadary & Cohen, 1978).

Such questions are the beginning of the continuous evaluation of exceptional students in science programs. Evaluation techniques can be developed based on the type and severity of the handicap, the skill level of the student, and the adopted curriculum of the school system.

Frequently, the scope and sequence of the program will determine the assessment and entry level for the student. In a traditional, discipline-oriented program, students are expected to have acquired specified amounts of basic information prior to entering certain programs of study. Programs based on process skills present performance items. In a program devoted to concept development the level of understanding can be assessed.

It is essential that science teachers be involved in developing IEPs for their exceptional pupils. For even though the special education teacher and other personnel are familiar with the characteristics of the students, it is the science teachers who know the curriculum, the skills required, and the methods for assessing this information.

Reading is a concern in science as in other curriculum areas. Science teachers need to know which students will have difficulty reading the textbook and other written materials.

In testing for content, achievement tests referred to in assessment of social studies knowledge are applicable to science. To diagnose a student's level of understanding, standardized tests, such as the Nelson Biology Test or one of the Cooperative Tests in science, can be used (Simpson & Anderson, 1981). Tests accompanying textbooks are also useful as pretests.

Criterion-referenced tests are probably more valuable in determining the skills of students who have learning problems, because norm-referenced tests tend to accentuate differences in students' abilities. In a given set of instructional objectives, student performance and teacher observation can predict the appropriate entry level for the handicapped or gifted student.

There are many assessment methods other than tests. Discussion, when properly conducted, can be useful in appraising the student's knowledge of science content, scientific attitudes, and other behaviors. Observation is another valuable method for evaluating the student's comprehension of science concepts, performance of key operations of science and the scientist, and acquisition of desirable behavioral outcomes (Victor, 1980).

Goals and Objectives

Science can be defined as a search for understanding. In this search for understanding, science develops a body of knowledge, which is the result of certain attitudes and the product of human activity. Science, then, is usually considered to consist of three aspects: content, process, and attitude (Wolfinger, 1984).

Some educators feel that this is a restrictive scope of science, and that there are five domains of science education: knowing and understanding, exploring and discovering, imagining and creating, feeling and valuing, and using and applying. All of these domains are necessary to help students attain the level of scientific literacy demanded by today's society and tomorrow's needs (McCormack & Yager, 1989).

Because of the scientific nature of our society and the individualized needs of its members, each person should be scientifically literate. Scientific literacy, then, is the primary goal for teaching science in elementary and secondary schools. The scientifically literate person

- Has knowledge of the major concepts, principles, laws and theories of science and applies these in appropriate ways;
- Uses the processes of science in solving problems, making decisions, and other suitable ways;
- Understands the nature of science and the scientific enterprise;
- Understands the partnership of science and technology and its interaction with society;
- Has developed science-related skills that enable him or her to function effectively in careers, leisure activities, and other roles;
- Possesses attitudes and values that are in harmony with those of science and a free society; and
- Has developed interests that will lead to a richer and more satisfying life and a life that will include science and life-long learning. (Simpson & Anderson, 1981, pp. 6, 7)

Objectives derived from these goals are grouped into three areas: to learn science concepts and conceptual schemes—the content of science; to become familiar with the key operations of science and the scientist—the process of science; and to develop such desirable outcomes as scientific skills, attitudes, appreciations, and interests.

Although the goals and objectives for exceptional students are the same as those for all students, Menhusen and Gromme (1976) see particular benefits for students with learning problems. Science can serve as a vehicle for developing the basic skills of observing, describing, identifying, comparing, associating, inferring, applying, and predicting that lead to problem-solving skills. It can be useful in meeting the physical, psychological, and social needs of handicapped students and can help develop a more positive self-image, identity, and desirable work habits. Development of these skills is discussed in the following section.

There is considerable evidence that science is a viable tool in teaching basic and life skills to handicapped students. The nature of science itself demands many modes of learning and thus provides for sensory and physical input. Science also calls for experiences related to life experiences, providing opportunities for concrete learning. Hands-on experiences help develop abstract thinking, language, and quantitative skills. When activity choices are provided, interest and motivation are likely to be higher.

McConnell (1978) claims that the Human Sciences Program contributes rich resources for skill development. Reading skills include reading for general information, developing and using vocabulary meanings, reading to follow directions, and using verbal reasoning to comprehend and infer. The program also emphasizes listening, speaking, and writing skills. Opportunities are provided to develop quantitative and measurement skills through collecting quantitative observations, organizing data for use, displaying data, interpreting data, and manipulating data.

Research studies cited by the Science Curriculum Improvement Study investigate the contention that there is a positive carryover from innovative science programs to other academic areas. In one study, first-grade students using the SCIS program outperformed the control group in word meaning, listening, matching, alphabet, and numbers. A second study investigated SCIS and achievement in reading, mathematics, and social studies. In using SCIS with fifth graders, improvement was demonstrated in mathematics applications, social studies skills, and paragraph meaning (Renner, Stafford, Weber, Coffia, & Kellog, 1972).

One study specific to handicapped students involved 307 educable mentally handicapped students, aged 6 to 19, who received science instruction (Menhusen & Gromme, 1976). These pupils demonstrated improvement in science skills and a higher level of verbal ability.

Hurd (1970) offers an explanation for the high degree of success and skill development in science programs:

- Laboratory and field experiences get pupils involved; because of the low verbal load, these experiences are less threatening as a means of learning.
- Experiences provided are concrete.
- Experiences and the meaning of observation provide something to talk about.

- Discussions help build verbal mediators to improve the ability to discriminate, classify, label, and generalize.
- Field trips increase the students' ranges of experience and thus their potential for generating desirable science concepts.

Along with the basic skills mentioned, other survival skills are necessary for a person to be an effective jobholder, family member, citizen, and consumer (McConnell, 1978). Such skills include the ability to be self-directed in searching for knowledge; the ability to think rationally and to interpose evidence, reason, and judgment between impulse and action; and the ability to interrelate effectively with other humans.

Skills development occurs functionally in an experience-based curriculum. Science study provides the format for handicapped and nonhandicapped students to acquire skills because they are needed and important. Science programs developed specifically for handicapped students focus on skills related to the students' interests and needs.

Instructional Approaches

In an adaptation of the Science Curriculum Improvement Study, Linn (1972) demonstrated that by investing a comparatively small amount of time and money, existing curricula can be adapted for special groups of learners. Three underlying themes in science appear to apply to curriculum adaptation and instructional methods: (1) the foundation of all learning in science is firsthand experience with real things; (2) science experiences need not involve unusual, elaborate, or expensive apparatus and materials; and (3) investigating one's environment is an interesting and integral part of an education (Schmidt & Rockcastle, 1968). Science is taught most effectively when it relates directly to the world in which students live.

Many sets of science curriculum modules have been developed around hands-on experiences. A number of science curriculum books and articles are available to help science teachers use materials at hand. Many current projects and products are devoted to developing strategies for teaching science to handicapped students.

The development of Adapting Science Materials for the Blind (ASMB) is a step in giving students who are visually handicapped hands-on, concrete experiences in science (Schatz, Franks, Thier, & Linn, 1976). An adaptation of SCIS, the program is a sequential, ungraded, physical and life science curriculum consisting of thirteen units for children 5 to 13 years old. The following adaptation exemplifies techniques that can be used with any program.

> The SCIS Energy Sources unit (level 5) begins with the children making and flying paper airplanes. Although other mechanical systems such as the stop-

per popper and rotoplane have been adapted rather successfully for the visually impaired, there did not seem to be a meaningful way to give a sightless child real experiences with flying paper airplanes. This raised the important question: Why are we flying paper airplanes at this point anyway? Since the answer was to review and reintroduce the specifying and controlling of variables, the project designed an alternate activity using "Hot Wheel" tracks to accomplish the same educational objectives. Visually impaired children explore how far the cars roll on a straight track when one end is raised different amounts. Other variables they can explore and control are type of car, weight of car (adding small weights), surface characteristics of the track (adding cloth, sand, etc.), and multiple humps in the track. (Thier & Hadary, 1973, p. 9)

Science Activities for the Visually Impaired (SAVI) introduces physical and life sciences to students who are visually impaired in a multisensory way (DeLucchi, Malone, & Thier, 1980). Activities are developed to remediate and stimulate learning; materials are designed for able as well as limited students. The multisensory approach designed for students who are visually impaired is also appropriate for nonhandicapped students. The activities are compatible with standard science curricula and can be readily incorporated into most science programs.

The Biological Sciences Curriculum Study has developed three programs that have been used successfully with special students. *Me Now*, a program in science and health, was designed for students between the ages of 10 and 13. *Me and My Environment* is an environmental science program for students from ages 13 to 16. *Me in the Future* deals with careers and decision-making processes relative to the future. The programs are designed for teachers who have limited backgrounds in science; and they include teacher's guides, slides, posters and pictures, filmloops, worksheets, models, laboratory supplies, and evaluation materials. Six principles of presentation are used as a guide for developing a curriculum:

1. The tasks should be uncomplicated.
2. The tasks should be brief.
3. The tasks should be presented sequentially.
4. Each learning task should allow for success.
5. Overlearning must be built into the lesson.
6. Learning tasks should be applied to objects, problems, and situations.

The *Me Now* program has also been used successfully in classes for students who are hearing impaired and have low verbal skills (Egelston & Mercaldo, 1975). This program is particularly attractive for such students because it is (1) a commercially available course that needs very little adaptation for use with deaf students, (2) a teacher-directed program that allows control of verbally presented information, and (3) a valid science course feasible for use with deaf children.

In using the standard science curriculum, adaptations in activities may need to be made for students who are hearing impaired. For example, when description of sounds of objects is required, the child who is hearing impaired can concentrate instead on physical characteristics that are apparent visually or on the texture of the objects. When working with young children, teachers should use pictures to define words, concepts, or actions. Opportunities should be provided for students to explore materials freely before formal directions are given. The classroom should abound with concrete materials and opportunities to work with paints, clay, crafts, printing, and other expressive activities. In classes in which children with hearing impairments are integrated with hearing students, pairing of students is effective (Jacobson & Bergman, 1987).

Another approach to teaching science to handicapped students is described in the Laboratory Science and Art Curriculum for Blind, Deaf and Emotionally Disturbed Children (Hadary & Cohen, 1978). In a laboratory science, art, and music program, the science curriculum is combined with a program of individualized experiences in which children learn through interacting and by expressing themselves creatively. The program directors feel that science and art stimulate creativity by interaction with natural phenomena. Crafts techniques are adapted for the child who is blind, and lessons are designed to enable exceptional children to use the same techniques as their peers.

This philosophy can be used effectively with students who have various handicaps. In a lesson entitled "Creating the Structure of a Flower," the following science objectives are stated:

- To examine a flower and discover its structure—pistil, stamen, anthers, petals, stem.
- To relate the structures of a flower to the functions.
- To discover the similarities among flowers of different plants. (Hadary & Cohen, 1978, p. 205)

The development of an art project to reinforce the science lesson is presented in Figure 10.4. Such interrelated activities provide tactile stimulation and concrete experience and help students perceive natural form and order.

For students who are academically gifted, science has been viewed as a way to teach the use of the scientific method. The scientific method is defined as "the systematic pursuit of knowledge involving the recognition and formulation of a problem, the collection of data through observation and experimentation (the experiential element), the formulation of a hypothesis, and the testing and confirmation (or rejection) of that hypothesis" (Fields, 1989, p. 15). Fields suggests that teachers can and should

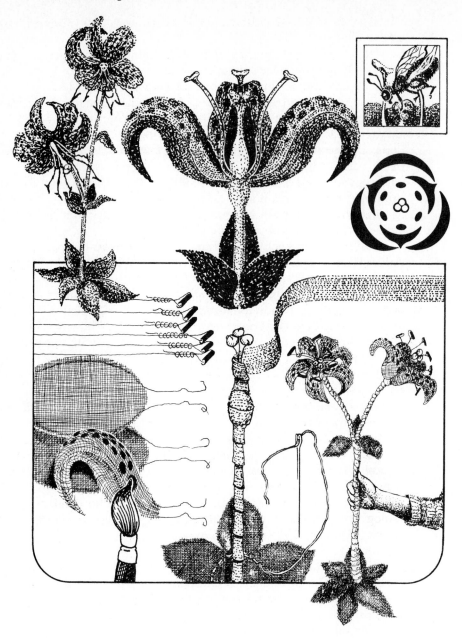

FIGURE 10.4   Science and Art

introduce the scientific method to upper elementary and middle school students. The scientific method as a teaching strategy involves guiding students through the following five steps:

1. Students conclude that experimentation will best answer the question.
2. In formulating their question, students must make it clear that they're seeking a specific answer.
3. Students brainstorm ways to answer the question.
4. Students follow the identified procedures, culminating in an answer to their question.
5. After testing and interpreting, students apply the newly learned concept. (Fields, 1989, pp. 15–16)

Cronin (1989) claims that even though the application of the scientific method is appropriate in many cases, creative thinking should also receive a significant emphasis. Techniques to develop creative thinking include brainstorming, the visualization of rich and colorful images, the development of fantasy scenarios (e.g., "just imagine"), and encouraging students to see things from different perspectives.

Individualizing Instruction

It has been said that individualized science teaching is more than methods of teaching. It is a *philosophy* of teaching in which *all* children's education is matched to their unique needs and/or special circumstances. (Carin & Sund, 1989, p. 241)

Special equipment can be used effectively in science programs. The computer has been used in many ways to individualize instruction for handicapped students. It is also useful in stimulating imagination and critical thinking for academically gifted students. One example of computer use is a research and development project aimed at building an intelligent computer called MENDEL. Gifted high school or university biology students can use this computer as a tool for learning concepts and problem-solving strategies in transmission genetics (Stewart, Streibel, Collins, & Jungck, 1989).

The light sensor, produced by the American Printing House for the Blind, affords students who are blind opportunities for direct observation, experimentation, and discovery. By focusing the light sensor on apparatus used in many basic science experiments, students receive immediate auditory feedback (Franks & Sanford, 1976).

In adapting laboratory equipment used in *Science—A Process Approach* for students who are blind, the tape recorder was used extensively (Eichenberger, 1974). It was used for laboratory competency quizzes, instructions, and for recording part of the periodic table of the elements. Mathematical problems can be worked with a braille abacus.

Classroom management for the laboratory is suggested by Hadary and Cohen (1978) for successful integration of handicapped students:

- *Laboratory stations* of groups of four are set up in the classroom, with handicapped students intermingled. This provides for individualized instruction, peer teaching, and social interaction.
- *Laboratory materials* for examination and exploration are distributed to each station. Materials are labeled and brailled. Stations and distribution centers remain in the same place all year.
- *Questioning and discussions* should take place in small groups in which students can see and hear each other. Demonstrations and introductions to problems are necessary. While the same problem is presented to all students, stations may be engaged in different activities. Example: half of the class (without blind students) is exploring the properties of light with the optics experiments, while the other half (with blind students) is investigating the properties of light with the light sensor.

In the science class referred to above, there are 6 handicapped children and 24 nonhandicapped children. In describing this particular class, Redden (1979, p. 46) observes that "the handicapped children learn to ask for the help they need, that the other children learn to help but not to help too much, and that there is a great feeling of sharing."

One of the most logical approaches to teaching exceptional students in the content areas is the integrated approach, which allows students to delve into aspects of specific topics that interest them. This technique helps teachers cover a wide range of information, exercise more flexibility, and develop essential academic, research, and critical thinking skills. Because it is flexible, integrated programming is appropriate for gifted students and for handicapped students. An example suggested by Kataoka and Patton (1989) uses the science topic "Ants and Interdependence" to incorporate math, social studies, arts, computer application, life skills, and language arts into an integrated approach matrix.

SOCIAL STUDIES AND SCIENCE

Common Problems and Techniques

According to the *Science Education Databook* (1981), kindergarten through twelfth-grade science teachers perceive problem areas as inadequate facilities, insufficient funds for purchasing equipment and supplies, and lack of materials for individualizing instruction. In the same databook, social studies teachers perceive problem areas as insufficient funds for purchasing supplies and equipment, lack of materials for individualizing instruction, out-of-date teaching materials, lack of student interest in subject, inadequate student reading abilities, and the belief that the subject is less important than other subjects.

Experiences with teaching social studies and science to handicapped students indicate that sensitive and creative teachers can overcome these problems. There are, however, several issues that relate to all subject areas, particularly social studies and science. They are content, timing, instructional methods, and reading.

Content

Content is a particularly crucial issue in science and social studies curricula when planning for students whose achievement is significantly below grade and age level expectations. These students typically lack many of the prerequisites necessary to proceed in higher order concept development; however, they are capable of advancing in the hierarchy of concept development when those prerequisites are in place. Sequencing of the content is a major consideration in developing the IEPs for science and social studies. At that time, the sequence of short-term objectives, which will serve as stepping stones to mastery of the annual goals, must be specified. The central concern affecting the sequential introduction of various concepts is that students have the necessary prerequisites to succeed at the new learning task. It is virtually impossible to meet the unique needs of every student in the class during every class period, but teachers have to work on foundation skills with students who are achieving substantially below grade level.

Another content consideration is that some students with learning problems will never catch up entirely with their peers. This means that they may never learn some skills and concepts in the general social studies and science curricula. Therefore, decisions must be made about what is most relevant and most necessary for adult adjustment and community living skills. Sometimes the issue of relevant curriculum decisions regarding adult adjustment and community living is postponed until the senior high years. By that time, some handicapped students have wasted inordinate amounts of time on topics that have no personal value. Science and social studies instruction, even at the early elementary levels, prepares the student for lifelong adjustment. Students handicapped by mental retardation, for example, need the most careful use of instructional time. In almost every case, they are going to learn less than their chronological age peers, and they will probably have lower problem-solving abilities as adults. These factors place a high premium on the value of every instructional hour spent in school.

Relevance to concept development is a central curriculum concern. For every topic the teacher considers including in the science and social studies curricula, these three questions should be asked: Will it help the student be more independent in the community, employment setting, and/or at home? What is the jeopardy of the student's not knowing this information? Will the student be receiving this information from other sources? As the responses to these questions are analyzed, teachers, parents, and students can identify the long-range goals and short-term objectives necessary to develop and implement the IEP effectively.

One strategy for systematically identifying the most relevant content is to have committees of science or social studies teachers in the school system decide jointly on the most essential skills and concepts that should comprise the basic curriculum. This relevant core could be drawn from the state or system-adopted curriculum guide. When the scope and sequence of relevant skills are specified by a systemwide committee, the probability of sequential concept development from grade to grade is increased.

There has been a significant attempt to bring more complex scientific ideas and practices into the school program for gifted children earlier in their school experience. The diversity of the social studies curriculum makes it less likely that content acceleration will be a recommended strategy for differentiated programming. However, many related fields of study, such as economics, can be presented earlier to gifted students. Gallagher (1985) suggests four principles that guide content development for students who are academically gifted:

1. Teach to the highest cognitive level possible.
2. Teach gifted children to utilize all their thinking processes.
3. Teach important ideas about all aspects of their life and times.
4. Teach methods by which the gifted children can discover knowledge for themselves. (p. 176)

Gifted and talented students can explore extensively into more sophisticated topic areas and gain additional understanding of how various discoveries or developments have influenced our lives and culture.

Timing

Handicapped students often require more instructional and practice time before a new skill or concept is mastered. Students with mental retardation typically have a slower learning rate; students who are hearing impaired may require more time to learn the technical vocabulary associated with science and social studies content. The problems associated with learning disabilities warrant careful consideration.

Joe has been diagnosed as having a learning disability. Science seems to be his most difficult class. It's the last period of the afternoon, when Joe usually is feeling tired and "hassled." It seems to take him most of the period to settle down and get to work. He wanders around the room, sharpens his pencil over and over, and tries to involve his peers in conversation. That is the reason Joe rarely completes his assignments by the end of class. He is falling farther and farther behind his peers.

The implication of arranging the curriculum so that handicapped students are afforded appropriate amounts of time to master concepts is that often the rest of the class is ready to move ahead whereas the handicapped student needs additional practice. Again, more individualization is required to manage this situation in the classroom. Some portions of the general curriculum can be deleted for students who are achieving substantially below grade level. Leaving out some concepts allows time to concentrate more intensively on more relevant concepts.

In addition to providing more extensive content for students who are academically gifted, teachers need to realize that these students will work more rapidly and therefore require more planned activities in social studies and science. As stated in chapter 5, gifted students frequently become bored and may present behavior problems. A fifth-grade teacher uses the following strategy:

> *Jamie is very impulsive. When I ask a question to the class, he is quick to respond. He continues to ignore the rule that students should not yell out answers until they are called on. To deal with this problem, I ask him to summarize in an outline form the material to be presented on a test. This benefits the class and gives Jamie the opportunity to talk in front of the class. (Taylor, 1988)*

To prevent gifted students from becoming bored and restless when they complete work, teachers may find it useful to maintain a list of supplementary activities that can be coordinated with topics the class is studying, have task cards handy, pose challenging questions, and convey an attitude that encourages further investigation (Jacobson & Bergman, 1987).

Instructional Methods

Language delays, which can interfere with lecture and discussion approaches to instruction, may be directly related to delayed vocabulary development and language problems associated with hearing impairment. The technical language of science and social studies may be difficult for students with delayed vocabularies to understand. In addition, some students who do not understand the technical word itself may not comprehend the words that the teacher uses to explain the technical term. It can be difficult, for example, to explain the terms *photosynthesis* or *electromagnet* to students with significant delays in vocabulary development. It is often helpful to introduce new vocabulary to these students before the vocabulary is used in the context of a lesson. If the students have dictionary skills, they might look up the new words and write the definitions on index cards. Also on the card, they might write the word in a sentence and either draw or find a picture to illustrate the word. All the cards can be kept in a file box. Reviewing the word cards could be done as an assignment or a free-time activity. Students who have not yet mastered dictionary skills will need guidance in initially defining the new vocabulary. This can be done by a teacher, teacher aide, special education resource teacher, volunteer, or peer tutor.

Media (visual and audiovisual), such as pictures, charts, films, filmstrips, maps, and graphs, can be effective instructional materials for many handicapped persons. Students with disadvantages associated with mental retardation and learning disabilities can benefit from experiences and activities that do not penalize them for a lower level of reading achievement. Additionally, these students often associate visual and audiovisual materials with higher motivational appeal.

Teachers must remember that students who are visually impaired are unable to take advantage of the typical visual media used in social studies and science classes. In addition to adaptations suggested in previous sections, many adaptations enable the student who is blind to participate in class activities related to visual methods of instruction. When the class is examining and discussing a map of the United States, the student who is blind can work with the relief map. Thus, audiotactile rather than audiovisual instruction is employed.

Many students who are hearing impaired are unable to hear the audio portion of films, filmstrips, or videotapes. In some cases, being seated close to the machine will help. For students with extremely limited residual hearing, teachers should consider ordering captioned films. These films and filmstrips provide a written statement on each frame or in each sequence that is correlated with the verbal content, thus enabling hearing-impaired students to read what other students are hearing. For information on ordering captioned films, teachers should write to the Special Office for Materials Distribution at Indiana University. Many films are loaned free of charge.

Students who are gifted seek out activities and hobbies in science and social studies areas; they enjoy puzzles and games of an open-ended type (e.g., Rubik's Cube), electronic games, and computers. There are many ways to challenge them by providing meaningful enrichment activities. The following suggestions may be useful:

- *Fear not: learn with and from your gifted and talented students.* You can truly become a teacher/facilitator/arranger of the learning environment, an adult questioner, and a constant positive critic.
- *Encourage gifted students to more open-ended activities.* Gifted students should be challenged to do simple, unstructured experiments to find answers which are not easily available from texts or encyclopedias.
- *Gifted students should use mathematics and technology frequently.*

Whenever possible, ask students to quantify their findings, and encourage them to use graphing in their communications to other students and you. With the increased availability of microcomputers, television, and videorecorders, gifted children especially are drawn to these challenging electronic learning devices.

- *Coordinate home/school learning with gifted children's parents.* Encourage parents of gifted students to obtain books, magazines, and science kits and materials and to discuss science [and social studies issues] with their children.
- *Provide leadership experiences for gifted/talented students.* Ask gifted students to be assistants to help with preparing materials, dispensing and collecting equipment and supplies, collecting information about experiments, and assisting less able classmates with some aspect of their work.
- *Encourage gifted/talented students in your mainstream classroom.* Your challenge is to help your gifted and talented students modify, adapt, and learn how to discover new skills and concepts for themselves. (Carin & Sund, 1989, pp. 264–266)

Reading

Karlin (1969) has estimated that 25 percent of the high school population does not possess the reading skills necessary to read the materials and textbooks they are expected to comprehend. The reading problem at the elementary and junior high levels is also very severe. Reading deficiencies can significantly interfere with successful performance in social studies and science unless instructional adaptations are made. Techniques for adapting reading materials are discussed in chapter 8.

Handicapped students, particularly those with learning problems, often have disadvantages associated with reading achievement. Reading problems occur in the areas of word recognition, comprehension, and study skills (reading tables, using the index, scanning, paraphrasing). The following are suggestions for minimizing reading problems while working to improve reading performance.

- Have a peer tutor and a student with a reading problem complete the reading assignment together. Both students might read orally, with the tutor helping to identify words that have not yet been learned. When this strategy is used with students who are blind, the peer tutor must do all the reading.
- Have students who excel in reading make summaries of chapters for less able readers. The less able reader might participate in the overall development by illustrating the summary with pictures from old textbooks or magazines or by binding several summaries to make booklets. Summaries can be laminated or covered with clear contact paper for repeated use (Turner, 1976).

- The teacher, volunteers, or a peer tutor can underline or highlight the key concepts on each page of the text. Slow readers overwhelmed by the length of the chapter are more likely to read the most important concepts if they are emphasized.

- Volunteers or peer tutors can tape-record the textbook for students who read significantly below grade level. Introductory organizers can be included on the tape. For example, a student can be told in advance which points to listen for or the main idea of the selection. Study questions can also be included after paragraphs to check the student's comprehension. This strategy is also helpful for students who are blind, although the introductory organizers and study questions may be superfluous for students who comprehend information easily.

- The language experience approach to reading instruction (see chapter 8) can be used to promote concept development in science and social studies. After information has been presented (through discussion, media, textbook, inquiry experiences), have students summarize the major points in their own words. If they are unable to write or spell adequately, a peer tutor or the teacher can assist them. They can find pictures in magazines or draw pictures that "visually paraphrase" (Turner, 1976, p. 40) the concepts they are learning. A similar approach is to write stories about the concepts rather than more objective summaries. This method helps students increase their reading skills while mastering science and social studies concepts. Learning centers with textbooks, reference books, and activities can be developed. Turner (1976) describes a center in which students plan learning activities and experiences for their peers based on a section of a chapter. These experiences can take the form of questions, inquiry activities, an oral report, a group project, or various alternatives. Both the students planning and completing the activities have the opportunity to expand their skills.

- Some children who are partially sighted need large-print textbooks. Teachers can sometimes borrow these from the State Library for the Blind and Physically Handicapped. If books are not available on loan, magnification equipment might be used or portions of the basic text could be retyped with a primary typewriter. Before retyping material, teachers should make sure that primary type print is large enough for the particular students. If it is, then perhaps a volunteer could be located to do the typing (the high school typing teacher might know of willing students) or the Lion's Club might be contacted about providing financial help. Another reading alternative to consider is the use of a textbook on a lower grade level for students with severe reading delays. It is also possible to acquire multilevel editions of the same text.

Even though poor reading skills present a problem, it is possible that more students would develop a greater interest in reading if they explored the topics offered by science and social studies.

The gifted student tends to have a large vocabulary and to use that vocabulary well. However, it cannot be assumed that the student has the experiential basis on which to build concepts. In writing reports, the gifted student should have a great deal of opportunity for creativity, speculation, hypothesizing, and development of argument. A wide variety of books, magazines, and newspapers should be available; the school library should be available at all times rather than only at a strictly scheduled time. For the gifted child who is conducting independent research in a particular area, the teacher should encourage the presentation of the research results to the rest of the class. The student gains the ability to speak before a group, and the rest of the class gains the benefit of the research (Wolfinger, 1984).

The academically gifted student can also share skills with other students. A seventh-grade teacher provides this example:

> *Johnny is an academically gifted student who is in my seventh-grade biology class. We are beginning a chapter on the microscope and Johnny has told me that he has a microscope at home. His mother has taught him how to make slides of different substances and to observe the slides through the microscope. I asked Johnny if he would be interested in bringing his microscope to class with some of his slides. He could explain the basic parts of the microscope, let the other students look at some of the slides, and even show the students how to make slides. I think Johnny will enjoy showing the other students something he is interested in and that they will listen to Johnny more closely than if I taught the information from the textbook. Johnny's interest in this aspect of biology may even arouse an interest in some of the other students. (Schulhofer, 1988)*

Conclusion

The goals and content of social studies and science are appropriate and essential for exceptional students. Social studies is based on interaction with the people around us; science has influenced everything we do. Teachers of students who are handicapped and those who are gifted must work closely with social studies and science teachers to insure that these areas of learning are not neglected. With cooperative effort, these areas can make a positive difference in the education of exceptional students.

REFERENCES

Balow, I. H., Farr, R., Hogan, T. P., & Prescott, G. A. (1978). Metropolitan Achievement Tests. New York: Psychological Corp.

Carin, A. A., & Sund, R. B. (1989). *Teaching science through discovery* (6th ed.). Columbus, OH: Merrill.

Cartledge, G., & Milburn, J. F. (1980). *Teaching social skills to children.* New York: Pergamon Press.

Coleman, W., & Selby, C. (1982). *Today's problems: Tomorrow's crises.* Washington, DC: National Science Board, National Science Foundation.

Cronin, L. L. (1989). Creativity in the science classroom. *The Science Teacher, 56,* (2), 35–36.

DeLucchi, L., Malone, L., & Thier, H. D. (1980). Science activities for the visually impaired: Developing a model. *Exceptional Children, 46,* (4), 287–288.

Dewey, M. (1978). *Teaching human relations to special students.* Portland, ME: Walch.

Egelston, J. C., & Mercaldo, D. (1975). Science education for the handicapped: Implementation for the hearing-impaired. *Science Education, 59,* (2), 257–261.

Eichenberger, R. J. (1974). Teaching science to the blind student. *The Science Teacher,* Dec., 53–54.

Fields, S. (1989). The scientific teaching method. *Science and Children, 26,* (7), 15–17.

Franks, F. L., & Sanford, L. (1976). Using the light sensor to introduce laboratory science. *Science and Children,* March, 48–49.

Gallagher, J. J. (1985). *Teaching the gifted child* (3rd ed.). Boston: Allyn and Bacon.

Hadary, D. E., & Cohen, S. H. (1978). *Laboratory and art for blind, deaf, and emotionally disturbed children.* Baltimore: University Park Press.

Herlihy, J. G., & Herlihy, M. T. (1980). Mainstreaming in the social studies. *National Council for the Social Studies,* Bulletin 62.

Hieronymus, A. N., & Lindquist, E. F. (1974). Iowa Tests of Basic Skills. Boston: Houghton Mifflin.

Hurd, P. D. (1970). *New curriculum perspectives for junior high school science.* Belmont, CA: Wadsworth.

Jacobson, W. J., & Bergman, A. B. (1987). *Science for children.* Englewood Cliffs, NJ: Prentice-Hall.

Jarolimek, J. (1986). *Social studies in elementary education* (7th ed.). New York: Macmillan.

Johnson, R., & Vardian, E. R. (1973). Reading, readability, and the social studies. *The Reading Teacher, 26,* (5), 483–488.

Karlin, R. (1969). What does education research reveal about reading and the high school student? *The English Journal, 58,* 386–395.

Kataoka, J., & Patton, J. R. (1989). Teaching exceptional learners: An integrated approach. *Science and Children, 27,* (1), 48–50.

Kelly, E. J. (1979). *Elementary school social studies instruction: A basic approach.* Denver: Love.

Life skills for health. (1974). Division of Health, Safety and Physical Education. Raleigh: North Carolina Department of Public Instruction.

Linn, M. C. (1972). An experiential science curriculum for the visually impaired. *Exceptional Children, 39,* (1), 37–43.

Madden, R., Gardner, E. F., Rudman, H. C., Darlsen, B., & Merwin, J. C. (1973). Stanford Achievement Test. New York: Psychological Corp.

McConnell, M. C. (1978). Basics . . . and the human sciences program. *The Biological Sciences Curriculum Study Journal,* April, 10–15.

McCormack, A. J., & Yager, R. E. (1989). A new taxonomy of science education. *The Science Teacher, 56,* (2), 47–50.

Menhusen, B. R., & Gromme, R. O. (1976). Science for handicapped children— why? *Science and Children,* March, 35–38.

Mesibov, G. B., & LaGreca, A. M. (1981). A social skills instructional module. *The Directive Teacher, 3*, (1), 6–7.

Naslund, R. A., Thorpe, L. P., & Lefever, D. W. (1981). SRA Achievement Series. Chicago: Science Research Assoc.

National Council for the Social Studies Task Force on Scope and Sequence. (1984). In search of a scope and sequence for social studies. *Social Education, 48*, 251.

Oliner, P. M. (1976). *Teaching elementary social studies.* New York: Harcourt Brace Jovanovich.

Parker, J. P. (1989). *Instructional strategies for teaching the gifted.* Boston: Allyn and Bacon.

Redden, M. R. (1979). Science education for handicapped children. *Education Unlimited, 1*, (4), 44–46.

Redden, M. R., & Malcolm, S. M. (1976). A move toward the mainstream. *Science and Children*, March, 14.

Renner, J. W., Stafford, D. G., Weber, M. C., Coffia, W. J., & Kellog, D. H. (1972). *Research studies of SCIS success in the classroom.* Chicago: Rand McNally.

Schatz, D., Franks, F., Thier, H. D., & Linn, M. C. (1976). Hands-on science for the blind. *Science and Children*, March, 21–23.

Schmidt, V. E., & Rockcastle, V. N. (1968). *Teaching science with everyday things.* New York: McGraw-Hill.

Schug, M. C. (1989). Why teach social studies? *The Social Studies, 80*, (2), 73–77.

Schug, M. C., & Beery, R. (1987). *Teaching social studies in the elementary school.* Glenview, IL: Scott, Foresman.

Schulhofer, S. (1988). Class assignment. Teaching exceptional children. Cullowhee, NC: Western Carolina University.

Schuncke, G. M. (1988). *Elementary social studies.* New York: Macmillan.

Science Education Databook. (1981). Washington, DC: National Science Foundation.

Self, E. (1977). *Teaching significant social studies in the elementary school.* Chicago: Rand McNally.

Shaver, J. K., & Curtis, C. K. (1981). *Handicapism and equal opportunity: Teaching about the disabled in social studies.* Reston, VA: Foundation for Exceptional Children.

Simpson, R. D., & Anderson, N. D. (1981). *Science, students and schools: A guide for the middle and secondary school teacher.* New York: John Wiley and Sons.

Stefanich, G. P., & Kelsey, K. W. (1989). Improving science attitudes of preservice elementary teachers. *Science Education, 73*, (2), 187–194.

Stephens, T. M., Blackhurst, A. E., & Magliocca, L. A. (1988). *Teaching mainstreamed students* (2nd ed). Oxford: Pergamon Press.

Stewart, J., Streibel, M., Collins, A., & Jungck, J. (1989). Computers as tutors: MENDEL as an example. *Science Education, 73*, (2), 225–242.

Taylor, G. (1988). Class assignment. Teaching exceptional children. Cullowhee, NC: Western Carolina University.

Thier, H. D., & Hadary, D. E. (1973). We can do it too. *Science and Children, II*, (4), 7–9.

Tiegs, E. W., & Clark, W. W. (1979). California Achievement Test. Monterey, CA: CIB/McGraw-Hill.

Turner, T. N. (1976). Making the social studies textbook a more effective tool for less able readers. *Social Education, 41*, 38–41.

Victor, E. (1980). *Science for the elementary school* (4th ed.). New York: Macmillan.

Wilen, W. W., & McKenrick, P. (1989). Individualized inquiry. *The Social Studies, 80*, (1), 36–39.

Wolfinger, D. M. (1984). *Teaching science in the elementary school*. Boston: Little, Brown.

—11—

Teaching Physical Education, Music, and Art

When asked to identify what would be the major issue in education in the near future, Samuel Hope, executive director, National Association of Schools of Music (1987), referred to the conflict over the relative importance of therapeutic versus intellectual emphases in education and learning. The conflict focuses on this question: To what extent should schooling focus on emotional adjustment and socialization as opposed to disciplinary content, intellectual and physical skills, and an orientation to civilization?

As mentioned in the previous chapter, there is an emphasis on getting back to basics for all students, and particularly for those who are handicapped and culturally deprived. Sava (1987) contends that for many children struggling with reading, writing, and arithmetic, this may be precisely the wrong approach. Learning has its emotional and psychological aspects as well as its strictly rational ones, and what many students who are handicapped and culturally deprived need above all is success—proof that they can perform well in a school-related endeavor. Physical education, music, and art offer such students another chance to succeed.

Some students who have not experienced success in academic areas have been successful in physical education and the arts, and success in these areas has contributed to the acceptance and self-esteem of students with handicaps. The mother of a student who had learning disabilities described an exciting experience:

> Paul tried out for basketball this year. At 6'1" before his thirteenth birthday, he had height in his favor but not much else. He had never played on a team, and since we live in a rural area he had not had much neighborhood experience either. At the first session I explained this to the coach, and he was very understanding. I could see that he made special efforts to teach Paul the basics of the game.
>
> After weeks of practice sessions, it became time to choose ten boys. Paul barely made the team, but he made it! His desire to play and improve and his regular and prompt attendance at practice had made a difference. In addition, the coach was a caring individual who wanted to give Paul a chance.
>
> Since this team was community sponsored, there was a provision that each player participate in at least one full quarter of each game. This was a definite benefit for Paul and two other inexperienced players on his team.
>
> As the season progressed, Paul played on the starting line-up in most games. Instead of playing just the required one quarter of each game, he played two, three, or even four quarters.
>
> At the end of the season, the coach said that if he had to choose the most improved player on the team, it would be Paul. He also said that Paul was one of three players on the team who had a future in basketball. He encouraged Paul to play again next year and gave him some tips on improving himself over the summer.
>
> Basketball has helped Paul be a part of something he wanted to do. It required self-discipline and hard work. It was a maturing, confidence-building experience for Paul, who now has at least one long range goal: improving and participating in basketball next year.

FIGURE 11.1 Basketball Player

I am grateful to both his coach and the community program for giving Paul a chance to play. It is so important to feel part of something worthwhile and to be able to participate, not just sit on the bench and watch the "stars" perform. (Barbara Schulz, letter to the author, 1981. Used by permission)

Other important factors of physical education, music, and art for exceptional students are the contributions such programs can make as they influence the cognitive, affective, and psychomotor growth of these students. This chapter discusses physical education, music, and art in relation to concept development, mobility, academic progress, and peer relationships.

PHYSICAL EDUCATION

Physical education is the only curricular area specifically mentioned in PL 94–142. The law requires that students with handicapping conditions have opportunities comparable to those of nonhandicapped students in extracurricular activities, including interscholastic sports.

The IEP must include the student's current level of performance as well as annual goals and short-term objectives. Three types of decisions must be made from assessment data: (1) whether the student is to be placed into a special class or specially designed program; (2) if placed, what should constitute the curriculum to meet the student's identified needs in the best way; and (3) if the student can be kept in a regular class with modifications (Seaman, 1988).

Students who are not able to participate safely or successfully in the regular physical education program should be served in adapted physical education programs. Adapted physical education is a specifically designed physical education program based on competency goals and performance indicators. Such programs can be especially beneficial to students who have orthopedic or health impairments. For example, students who have severe cerebral palsy may need a program designed with the help of the physical therapist to insure that activities are not counterproductive to goals of physical therapy (Miller & Schaumberg, 1988). Also, students who have asthma can profit greatly from sound physical activity, but there are basic guidelines that should be followed (Karper, 1986).

Concept Development

Many people associate concept development in physical education strictly with the psychomotor domain; however, physical education incorporates a much broader array of concepts and skills. Sherrill (1986) suggests a model to illustrate the interrelationships of the affective, psychomotor, and cognitive domains as they relate to the goals of physical education (see Table 11.1).

Many of these goals are reached by nonhandicapped students through normal development and in informal physical activities in the neighborhood. Students with handicaps, on the other hand, frequently have special needs that require alternative instructional strategies to enhance the probability of their success in learning the underlying concepts and behaviors comprising well-balanced physical development. Many students who are handicapped can function in regular physical education programs, whereas students with moderate and severe handicaps will require adapted programs.

Stein (1979) claims that 90 to 95 percent of those students with handicapping conditions can be successfully integrated into regular physical education programs. He suggests that they can be accommodated by making facilities accessible, by adapting methods and approaches, and by increasing the emphasis on and attention to class organization and class management.

Making Facilities Accessible

Schools need to modify such facilities as pools, locker rooms, and gyms so that students who are handicapped have access to them (Aufsesser, 1981). In addition to major accommodations, facilities can be altered or affected by temporary or portable ramps, class schedules, peer tutors, and other common-sense approaches.

The provision of adaptive devices and equipment makes it possible for students with handicaps to participate in regular physical education programs. This equipment includes ambulatory devices, such as crutches, walkers, wheelchairs, and scooter boards; leg and arm prostheses; and back braces (Fait, 1978). In addition, there are bowling rails, pushers, and special handle balls; beeper calls and other sound devices that enable students who are visually impaired to participate in many activities; special wheelchairs for basketball, track events, and marathons; and batting tees and swivel parts on golf carts for paraplegics (Stein, 1979).

Adapting Methods and Approaches

In order to open activities to students with handicaps, it may be necessary to adapt methods, approaches, and/or content. Physical education content can be adapted for students who are handicapped by using differentiated objectives. The decision as to which objectives constitute an appropriate curriculum for a particular student should be based on an evaluation of the student's skill level in physical development and motor performance.

Winnick (1988) suggests the use of classifications for physical fitness testing to make competition equitable and thus to encourage participation. Classifications in selected physical fitness tests are reflected in Table 11.2.

TABLE 11.1 Goals of Adapted Physical Education Classified According to Domains

Affective Domain Goals

Positive self-concept. To strengthen self-concept and body image through activity involvement; to increase understanding and appreciation of the body and its capacity for movement; to accept limitations that cannot be changed and to learn to adapt environment so as to make the most of strengths (i.e., to work toward self-actualization).

Social competency. To reduce social isolation, to learn how to deveop and maintain friendships, to demonstrate good sportsmanship and self-discipline in winning and losing, and to develop other skills necessary for success in the mainstream, including appropriate social behaviors (i.e., how to interact with others — sharing, taking turns, following, and leading).

Fun/tension release. To improve attitude toward exercise, physical activity, and sports, dance, and aquatics so that involvement represents fun, recreation, and happiness; to improve mental health through activity involvement; to learn to release tensions in a healthy, socially acceptable manner; to reduce hyperactivity and to learn to relax.

Psychomotor Domain Goals

Motor skills and patterns. To learn fundamental motor skills and patterns; to master the motor skills indigenous to games, sports, dance, and aquatics participation; to improve fine and gross motor coordination for self-care, school, work, and play activities.

Physical and motor fitness. To develop the cardiovascular system, promote ideal weight, increase muscular strength, endurance, and flexibility, and improve posture.

Leisure time skills. To learn to transfer physical education learnings into habits of lifetime sports, dance, and aquatics; to become acquainted with community resources for recreation; to expand repertoire of and/or to refine skills in individual and group games and sports and dance and aquatic activities.

Cognitive Domain Goals

Play and game behaviors. To learn to play spontaneously; to progress through developmental play stages from solitary and parallel play behaviors up through appropriate cooperative and competitive game behaviors. To promote contact and interaction behaviors with toys, play apparatus, and persons; to learn basic game formations and mental operations needed for play; to master rules and strategies of simple games.

Perceptual motor function and sensory integration. To enhance visual, auditory, tactile, vestibular, and kinesthetic functioning; to reinforce academic learnings through games and perceptual-motor activities; to improve cognitive, language, and motor function through increased sensory integration.

Creative expression. To increase creativity in movement and thought. When posed a movement problem, to generate *many* responses, *different* responses, *original* responses. To learn to imagine, to embellish and add on, to risk experimentation, to devise appropriate game strategy, and to create new games, dances, and movement sequences.

Source: From Claudine Sherrill, *Adapted Physical Education and Recreation*, 3rd ed. Copyright © 1986 Wm. C. Brown Publishers, Dubuque, Iowa. All Rights Reserved. Reprinted by permission.

TABLE 11.2 Classifications in Selected Physical Fitness Tests

Test	Classification
Special Physical Fitness (AAHPERD, 1986)	Age, gender, type and severity of condition (mild mental retardation)
Project ACTIVE (Vodola, 1978)	Chronological and mental age, gender, type of condition (mental, emotional, learning disability)
Buell Adaptation of the AAHPERD Health and Youth Fitness Test (1982)	Age, gender, type and severity of condition (blind and partially sighted)
Motor Fitness Test for the Moderately Mentally Retarded (Johnson & Londeree, 1976)	Age, gender, type and severity of condition (moderate mental retardation)
UNIQUE Physical Fitness Test (Winnick & Short, 1985)	
Visual	Age, gender, type of condition (visual), severity of condition (blind, partially sighted), level of assistance (unassisted, guidewire or rope assisted, partner-assisted)
Auditory	Age, gender, type of condition (auditory)
Orthopedic	Age, gender, type of condition (cerebral palsy, spinal neuromuscular, congenital anomaly/amputee), site of amputation or anomaly; mode of ambulation (unassisted; cane, crutch or other assistive device; wheelchair), wheelchair propulsion (moved with arms, moved with feet forward or backward)

Source: From "Classifying Individuals with Handicapping Conditions for Testing" by J. P. Winnick, 1988, *Journal of Physical Education, Recreation & Dance, 59,* p. 36. Copyright 1988 by the *Journal of Physical Education, Recreation & Dance.* Reprinted by permission.

Whether the student is in an adapted program or the regular physical education program, each student's movement and fitness must be placed along a continuum. The ability levels of each student in physical education class will vary along this developmental continuum; modifications will be needed to accommodate the different developmental levels of each student (Arbogast & Lavay, 1986).

Individualizing instruction in physical education varies from loose to tightly knit approaches (Zakrajsek & Carnes, 1986). Some programs allow students to select from a list of offerings and at some level of difficulty (such as swimming, where the choice ranges from beginning swimming to water safety instructor). Another approach provides the group with a core of information, followed by optional activity choices for the rest of the unit (such as a 6-week tennis unit, in which the main skills are covered in group instruction during the first 3 weeks). Another method, particularly effective for students who are physically and intellectually gifted, provides individualized learning opportunities through independent study. Students are excused from regular class and permitted to complete a unit of study or to perform at a level not offered in the school curriculum. Other methods include contractual agreements for a single day or a unit of activity and supervised task programming, which sets objectives and tasks and promotes the sharing of the teaching-learning process.

Mastery learning provides an excellent structure for physical education activities. A model used with students who are handicapped is based on seven steps:

1. *Physical Demonstration*—the presentation of a psychomotor learning task (by the instructor or teacher aide) in its entirety. The purpose is to provide the students with a visual picture.
2. *Verbal Explanation*—an explanation of a learning task accompanying the physical demonstration which is enthusiastic and animated. (Students often request a repetition of the demonstration and explanation and such requests are granted.)
3. *Manual Manipulation*—actual manipulation of the student through each segment of the psychomotor learning task by the teacher or teacher aide.
4. *Minimal Physical Assistance*—limited physical contact between teacher and student.
5. *Verbal Prompt*—no physical contact between teacher and students. Each student receives verbal instruction and reinforcement as needed.
6. *Upon Request*—implies student mastery of the psychomotor learning task and the ability to perform the task when requested.
7. *Mastery Demonstration*—the incorporation of a variety of psychomotor learning tasks into a single combination or routine. The mastery demonstration is conducted before an audience composed of other students, teachers, teacher aides, parents. (Chambless, Anderson, & Poole, 1981, p. 21)

A Schedule of Instruction, illustrated in Figure 11.2, enables the teacher to identify and evaluate components of each psychomotor task to be learned. The organization of curriculum data in this manner facilitates the preparation and implementation of meaningful IEPs.

Adaptations may include starting at more basic entry points, taking more steps in the teaching process, and using a variety of ways to reach the same goal or objective. Contract techniques (chapter 7) and behavior management strategies (chapter 12) can be used to meet individual needs.

Another consideration is the learning rate of students who are handicapped. All students differ in the rate at which they learn physical education skills and concepts. Some handicapping conditions impede learning

1. Manual Manipulation	2. Minimum Physical Assistance	3. Verbal Prompt	4. Upon Request
Date Initiated	Skill and Stunt		Date Mastered
1 2 3 4			1 2 3 4

Date Initiated	Skill and Stunt	Date Mastered
1 2 3 4	1. Line Walking according to given directions	1 2 3 4
	The student will be able to:	
	1.1 Stand with the weight evenly distributed on two feet	
	1.2 Step forward and maintain erect body posture while transferring weight from one foot to the other	
	1.3 Transfer his/her weight from heel to toe with arms in opposition to the legs	
	Comments: The instructor should provide verbal cues allowing students to change direction on command. Alternative Method: Many gymnasiums have color-coded boundary lines for various courts which can be used for determining changes in direction.	

Source: From "IEP's and Mastery Learning Applied to Psychomotor Activities" by J. R. Chambless, E. Anderson, and J. H. Poole in Teaching Handicapped Students Physical Education (p. 22) by G. R. Roice (Ed.), 1981. Washington, DC: National Education Association. Copyright 1981 by the National Education Association. Reprinted by permission.

FIGURE 11.2 Schedule of Instruction

rate more than others; even the same handicapping conditions will impede some persons more than others. Many students with orthopedic handicaps and other health impairments experience muscle weakness and become fatigued fairly quickly in a physical education class. It may also be more difficult for them to develop coordination. Because they can engage only in short periods of exertion, their learning rate may be slower than that of other students. On the other hand, students with learning problems might take longer to master the scoring system of tennis or the rules of football. Consideration of learning rate in the development of physical skills and concepts is essential for successful mainstreaming.

Experienced physical education teachers are aware that many individuals learn and train in unique ways. They also recognize similarities in specific methods that may, on the surface, appear to be different.

Stein (1979) suggests specific adaptations of methods and approaches to students with handicaps:

> Substitute walking, wheeling, rolling for running, skipping, hopping; use scooter boards, crawling, creeping, or moving in wheelchairs or on leg stumps in place of traditional and conventional means of locomotion; use bounce, roll or underhand toss to replace throwing, catching, batting; use crutches, wheelchair foot rests or prosthetic devices as implements to hit objects such as balls or pucks; substitute sitting, kneeling, lying down for standing; decrease distances as in horseshoes, ring toss, softball; reduce size of playing fields, courts, or areas; restrict players to definite places or positions; substitute lighter, larger, and more easily controlled equipment; add a bell, portable radio, or hand clapping for sound; adjust the number of tries a player is given to hit a ball; use a batting tee or let an individual hit a ball from his/her head; use hands, feet, arms, legs, head, ears, eyes, tongue, and whatever else is unique to the individual. (p. 9)

One appropriate teaching method for all students, regardless of their ability levels, is movement exploration. Sherrill (1986) advocates this approach to physical education instruction, particularly for students with physical handicaps, low fitness, and poor coordination. This approach capitalizes on a process of discovery and inquiry in encouraging students to assume responsibility for identifying problems and developing a plan to solve them. A student who is visually impaired may discover the most advantageous method of learning to bowl accurately by establishing individual objectives and instructional strategies. In testing out the instructional strategies, students can learn their own strengths and weaknesses and perhaps discover appropriate adaptations that never occurred to the teacher. This type of instruction can help teach the student a problem-solving process that can be used throughout life as physical or motor adaptations must be made.

Movement education is based on a foundation of fundamental patterns and skills. A system of abstract symbols can be used to enable students who are hearing impaired to follow directions (Schmidt & Dunn, 1980). When placed on cards, the symbols can be used to reinforce verbal directions for all children.

Class Organization

Class organization and management are crucial to the successful integration of students with handicaps into physical education classes. Consideration should be given to one-to-one instruction with a peer tutor or volunteer, small-group instruction, large-group instruction, learning centers, and independent work. To prevent the exclusion of handicapped students, teams should be chosen by the teacher rather than by having the students choose sides.

One classroom management model, RAID, is based on these principles:

- R = Rules. Rules in the physical education classroom are established with help from students, thus allowing them to know and to help formulate clear statements of expected behavior. Rules are stated in positive terms (e.g., "Put equipment away" instead of "Don't leave equipment out").
- A = Approval. Approve or reward those students who follow the rules. Approval may be signaled by nonverbal gestures, verbal praise, or special treats such as free time or individual choice of activities.
- I = Ignore. Students who do not follow the rules are ignored. This technique, in order to be most successful, must be paired with the preceding principle of rewarding those who do follow the rules.
- D = Disapprove. Disapproval is shown when student behavior disrupts the learning process for the group. Disapproval is shown by removing rewards or by temporarily removing the student from the activity. (Folio & Norman, 1981, p. 114)

When the teacher and students are concerned with involving everyone, the class emphasis is on playing rather than on winning. In such a class, the physical education teacher asked, "Who won?" The students yelled, "We did!"

Mobility

Mobility training is important for many students who are handicapped and essential for students who are visually impaired and those with restrictive orthopedic handicaps. Mobility evaluation must consider the locus of involvements (e.g., legs, arms), the nature of involvement (e.g., paralysis, lack of coordination, loss of limbs), and the rate of stability of motion (e.g., agility, endurance). After evaluating the student's skill level and specifying appropriate objectives, the teacher, with the help of special education resource teachers and a physical therapist (if available), should proceed to adapt or develop physical education activities for the student. A rule of thumb is that games and sports should be changed to the minimum extent necessary to insure the handicapped student's success and safety.

A common misconception is that students with epilepsy should not engage in physical education. On the contrary, physical activity is recommended for many epileptics. The American Medical Association has endorsed the participation of students with epilepsy in physical education programs, except for long periods of underwater swimming, body contact sports that may produce head injuries, and gymnastic and diving activities where heights could be dangerous in the event of a fall (AMA, 1968). Students with cardiac conditions, asthma, and allergies can also benefit from physical education programs. Working with their physicians and parents, the teacher can plan a program alternating short activity periods and rest.

Mobility training for students who are visually impaired includes simple map reading and tactile exploration of the environment. Mobility training in the physical education program could involve the following activities:

1. Practice walking a straight line. All sightless persons tend to veer about 1.25 inches per step or walk a spiral-shaped pathway when attempting to traverse a straight line. The 10-year-old, however, should not veer more than 10 feet when attempting to walk forward for 50 feet nor more than 30 feet when moving forward 150 feet.

2. Practice facing sounds or following instructions to make quarter, half, three-quarter, and full turns. Blind adults tend to turn too much (100–105 degrees). Full turns are the most difficult with the average person moving only 320–325 degrees.

3. Practice reproducing the exact distance and pathway just taken with a partner.

4. Take a short walk with a partner and practice finding the way back to the starting point alone.

5. Outside, where the rays of the sun can be felt, practice facing north, south, east, west. Relate these to goal cages and the direction of play in various games.

6. Practice determining whether the walking surface is uphill or downhill or tilted to the left or right; relate this to the principles of stability and efficient movement.

7. Practice walking different floor patterns. Originate novel patterns and then try to reproduce the same movement. (Sherrill, 1986, pp. 587–588)

Mobility training also involves instruction in the long-cane technique by persons trained in the education of people who are blind and in mobility training specifically (Cratty, 1980).

Mobility considerations must also be examined in light of the special needs of students who are hearing impaired. Because the semicircular ear canals are damaged, some students who are deaf have problems associated with balance and coordination. The multidisciplinary team should assess these students carefully. If a problem exists, balance and coordination exercises, such as dancing and gymnastics, might be added to develop greater skill. Precautions should be taken in climbing activities so that students with balance deficiencies are not placed in dangerous situations.

Some students who are learning disabled exhibit inadequate or inappropriate motor behavior and are often referred to as uncoordinated, awkward, or clumsy (Haubenstricker, 1982). Many students with such problems benefit from basic movement experiences involving activities with the balance beam, trampoline, dance, and rhythm.

High activity levels sometimes interfere with success in physical education programs. To help students control their level of activity, teachers might provide a quiet period after periods of intensive stimulation; restricted boundary areas limiting the space in which activity takes place; and reduced choices in activities and schedules. A structured lesson can contribute to a successful experience for these students.

Many students with learning disabilities are extremely sensitive to their low motor performance. Teachers can help to reduce these feelings by teaching less competitive games and sports, such as swimming, jogging, and bike riding.

The physical development and motor performance of students who are mildly mentally retarded is generally equal to chronological age expectations. Many of these students compete very successfully in interscholastic athletics. Although there are no unique mobility considerations for this population, it is worth noting that many retarded persons rely more heavily on motor skills than on intellectual skills in adult vocational endeavors. For this reason, the physical education program can be an integral part of their vocational training.

Relevance to Academics

Many handicapped students experiencing academic difficulty can improve their academic, as well as motor, skills in a well-balanced physical education program. Mathematical skills related to counting, number facts, and processes can be taught by having students learn to keep score in various games and sports. Laying out a volleyball or tennis court offers an excellent opportunity to teach and reinforce measurement skills. Many opportunities exist to work on time concepts, such as keeping up with the regulation time of a basketball or football game and clocking the time for track events. Some students who do not respond to more traditional approaches might benefit from learning mathematical skills in the meaningful context of physical activities.

Language arts is another curriculum area that can be closely related to physical education. Students might learn to read the rules of games and sports they particularly enjoy and improve their writing skills if given the opportunity to order special material and equipment. Library books, newspapers, and magazines related to sports might motivate students to learn to read.

Every academic subject has possible ties to physical education. When students find their greatest motivation and interest in physical education experiences, teachers should seize the opportunity to improve the students' academic performance as well. This does not require the physical education instructor to teach all subjects; rather, the classroom teacher can plan units of instruction and lesson plans around physical education themes. The coordination of objectives and strategies is essential to maximum student gain.

Peer Relationships

Physical education activities can provide a foundation for facilitating positive peer relationships of handicapped students. The nature of physical activities often involves groups, as in basketball and volleyball teams; interaction can be a natural by-product. Teachers should try to structure opportunities for handicapped students to contribute successfully to group goals.

Physical education programs have been used successfully to increase the social adjustment of students who are mentally retarded as well as peer relationships with students who are not retarded. In addition, it has been noted that students who acquired cooperative behavior in the physical education setting demonstrated a significant increase in overall social interaction (Marlowe, 1979; Santomier & Kopczuk, 1981).

Peer teaching can help the physical education teacher increase the amount of individual attention handicapped students receive. Peer teachers can be used for demonstrating skills, assisting with equipment, keeping records, and working individually with students who have adapted programs (Folio & Norman, 1981).

Peer relationships are improved as positive attitudes develop in all class members. Peer expectations increase as nonhandicapped students broaden their perceptions of the abilities of handicapped students.

The concept of reverse mainstreaming has been suggested to physical education teachers. One way of defining reverse mainstreaming is as a process of using able-bodied students to serve as aides in a special education setting. Another technique is suggested in which one or two new units within the regular physical education curriculum are introduced to emphasize sports for handicapped people, such as wheelchair basketball and blind wrestling. Simulations of handicaps using special equipment precede the entrance of handicapped students into the class. This procedure enables physical education teachers to be more comfortable when handicapped students do enter their classes (Davis, Woolley, & French, 1986).

MUSIC

Futrell (1987) presents two strong reasons for the inclusion of music in the curriculum for all students:

> Music is among the keys that open world history, and offers us access to the souls of civilizations past and civilizations still in the making. It is the language of the emotions.
>
> Perhaps more than any other discipline, music reflects our nation's cultural diversity. The student of music learns to cherish that diversity. (p. 52)

Because music is a multisensory experience, it can be a means for handicapped students to develop sensory perception and discrimination, rhythm, tonality, and other skills that contribute to cognitive and affective learning. Music plays an important part in the lives of exceptional children, youth, and adults, contributing to the total growth of the individual.

Placement in a mainstreamed music class, however, means a different approach to learning for the handicapped student. The emphasis is on group instruction, and individual progress is not monitored as regularly as it would be in a special setting (Coates, 1985). There is every evidence, however, that with more systematic planning and individualized instruction, most of the mild-to-moderately handicapped students in school can be mainstreamed into music classes (Graham, 1988).

Concept Development

Music classes are frequently expected to perform in unison, with students beginning and ending the musical selection together, singing each word at the same time, or playing an instrument in a precise rhythm dictated by the music (Beer, Bellows, & Frederick, 1982). Such expectations do not take into account the different learning rates and modalities that handicapped students bring to music classes. Music educators agree, however, that music is just as important to handicapped students as it is to nonhandicapped students. Thompson (1982) suggests that music education can be

FIGURE 11.3 Music Group

provided for handicapped learners by clarifying goals, conferring with other teachers, and modifying teaching strategies.

Clarifying Goals
The School Music Program: Description and Standards (1986) recommends the active involvement of music educators in placement decisions regarding handicapped students, with placement determined primarily on the basis of musical achievement. This document emphasizes the importance of instruction leading to specific musical skills and knowledge as well as enjoyment. Gfeller and Darrow (1987) pose this question: To what extent are these areas of musical achievement realistic for the handicapped student with serious mental or physical disabilities?

The final report of the Special Projects Committee of the Music Educators National Conference and the National Committee, Arts for the Handicapped, stated that

> the goals for music education for handicapped learners do not differ significantly from the goals for music education for all learners. The process of learning to perform, create, and respond to music makes a significant contribution to the development of that part of every being which is uniquely human. Although various handicapping conditions may limit the means through which individuals can make music and respond to music, the potential for enhancing the human experiences through musical learning does not change. (Thompson, 1982, p. 26)

In addition to the development of aesthetic responsiveness, there is considerable emphasis by music and classroom teachers on the development of motor skills, perceptual skills, social skills, and other nonmusical behaviors.

Conferring with Other Teachers

The special education teacher, the classroom teacher, and the music teacher need to share information and ideas. Communication can be facilitated by participating in the IEP meeting, observing students in various situations, and discussing the strengths and weaknesses of individual students as they relate to music.

Modifying Teaching Strategies

There are music curricular considerations that can help students progress in concept development. The teacher should use music that is meaningful to and valued by students. When concepts are introduced, the selected music should clearly illustrate the concept. The lesson plan should move gradually toward using many different music examples, requiring finer degrees of discrimination and understanding, so that mastery is possible. Some students learn more efficiently through one sensory channel than another, or from responding to music through one form or another. Generally, it is educationally sound to provide practice on music concepts in various ways, using diverse materials. Welsbacher (1972) advocates the multisensory approach when teaching upward movement of melody by having students *move* their hands up as the music portrays upward movement; *sing* sequences that move upward; *play* instruments, such as the xylophone, to depict upward movement; and *look* at pictures illustrating upward movement. By approaching concept development through different experiences and providing sufficient practice for mastery, teachers can help handicapped students to progress in the quality and rate of their concept formation.

For some handicapped students, only minor musical adaptations are necessary. Students with emotional problems will probably need adaptations only in the area of behavior management. Students with learning disabilities may lack the gross and fine motor coordination appropriate for their age or may have perceptual problems that result in impaired visual or aural reception of music (White, 1982). Students who are orthopedically handicapped encounter problems with the physical manipulation of instruments and with classroom organization for maximum mobility. It is necessary, therefore, to pinpoint the sensory, physical, and behavioral problems to be considered.

Students who are hearing impaired require adapted instructional approaches in music to develop musical concepts. As discussed in chapter 3, hearing impairment must be considered according to each student's hearing pattern as related to frequency (pitch) and intensity (loudness). Students who are hearing impaired vary in the pitch range of their handicap. Thus, some of these students might be less handicapped in learning musical concepts when examples are used at a high rather than low pitch level, or vice versa. Also, some students benefit from amplification more than others in minimizing intensity disadvantages. Developing residual hearing through auditory awareness and auditory discrimination activities is of special benefit to the student who is hearing impaired, as well as to the student with severe visual impairment who must rely on acute hearing for safety and space orientation.

Even students with severe hearing impairments can successfully develop musical concepts. Students who are deaf can experience music through touch and vision and can learn concepts through those sensory channels. These students can associate the sounds of instruments through feeling the vibrations. Fahey and Birkenshaw (1972) suggest that large drums or the timpani, bass xylophones, and base metallophones have been found most helpful in training students who are deaf to distinguish the vibrations of musical instruments from other environmental sounds. Students can also feel the vibrations of the piano and rhythm band instruments. By having students feel the instrument and indicate when the music starts and stops, teachers can reinforce the tactile perception of sound. Rhythmic visual clues can be provided to deaf students by using a metronome so that they can see fast and slow tempos. They can observe another student dancing to a musical selection and then go through the steps of the dance themselves.

Often teachers have assumed that the ear is the most essential factor in successful musical experiences. It must be remembered that all handicaps can be minimized with adapted instructional approaches. Epley (1972) describes her personal experience of playing the bass drum and cymbals in the university band following an accident that resulted in her becoming deaf. She stated that "alert eyes, strict counting, and self-confidence" enabled her to play successfully and find enjoyment with the rest of the band.

Why did I ask to join the band and risk the work of the other band members and the director? Why did I decide to make participation in music an aspect of my whole life? Aaron Copeland once said that to stop the flow of music would be like the stopping of time itself, incredible and inconceivable. In my opinion he is absolutely correct. Music can provide a feeling of achievement, give a personal pleasure as well as pleasure to other people, and in general, furnish an individual with a way to express himself. For these reasons, I want to continue taking part in soundless musical activities. This can only be possible, however, if musicians will open up their world to me and the thousands of other handicapped persons and let us join in their music-making. (p. 39).

Steps developed to teach music to students who are deaf can be used with students who have varying degrees of hearing loss. Perkins (1979) suggests starting with the young student sitting on the piano while the teacher plays. The student hears the music through a hearing aid, sees the teacher striking the keys, and feels the music through vibrations of the piano. As students focus on music, they begin to respond to it, to discriminate between sounds, and to substitute visual and auditory stimulation for the tactile stimulation.

In integrating the student who is visually impaired with sighted students, the usual visual approach must be modified. Auditory and tactile stimuli can be used for all students. Lam and Wang (1982) suggest the introduction of braille and conventional printed symbols to the student who is visually impaired. Because it is impossible to provide raised printed music scores, a knowledge of printed music symbols and braille music symbols helps the student understand the teacher in a mainstreamed situation. Some students may have the opportunity to use an optacon, an electronic device that converts the image of printed letters or symbols into a tactile form.

Very little adjustment is needed for students who are visually impaired in activities based on auditory input, such as clapping or rhythmic pattern recognition. In teaching notational skills, raised symbols can be constructed from pipe cleaners or felt, or by drawing with a crayon on a piece of window screen mounted on cardboard (Lam & Wang, 1982).

Students might also learn concepts through verbal instruction and physical guidance. For example, a student who is blind learning to play a guitar might be given a verbal explanation of finger positioning for a particular chord and then guided into the particular position by the teacher's placing the student's fingers correctly. Because students who are blind typically develop keen auditory abilities, they might learn to play instruments or sing musical selections by ear. To capitalize on this approach, the teacher can tape selections for them to listen to or model over and over. The American Printing House for the Blind and the Division of the Blind and Physically Handicapped of the Library of Congress (see Appendix B) have a wealth of resources available to music teachers. Some of these include slow taping of instrumental music, large-print and braille music, books explaining the braille music code, and records and tapes of music periodicals (Mooney, 1972).

Gifted students also have special needs related to music (Kenny, 1987). The need to be creative and innovative and a need for order can be met through music. Gifted students should have the option of participating actively or passively as musician, composer, or listener. Because many gifted students are creative, they may bring to the classroom a background of technical training in music that can contribute to the advancement of other students and also can provide means of self-discovery to the gifted student. Like most young people, gifted students are interested in music and share universal responses to it with all young people.

Mobility

Portions of the music curriculum, such as singing, dancing, rhythmic development, and instrumental instruction, require movement of one type or another. Each music curriculum subcomponent incorporates different types of mobility requirements focused on various body parts, including the oral cavity, lower trunk, arms, hands, and fingers. Some music experiences, such as playing a flute, require fine motor control, whereas clapping to keep time with rhythm is a gross motor activity. Mobility rate and stability are also important factors to consider as related to music. The rhythm of group music activities typically sets the rate at which students should perform or participate in the activity. Students who have slow rates of mobility may have a difficult time keeping up with a fast tempo, whether singing, playing instruments, or engaging in any other type of music experience. Finally, stability of motion is an important consideration when activities require physical endurance because of extended lengths of movement. These activities include participation in the marching band, frequent and extended practice and performance sessions of the school orchestra, and dancing classes. Mobility adaptations can be made in the music curriculum to minimize the disadvantages of blindness, deafness, and orthopedic handicaps.

On the whole, visual impairment is less of a handicap in music than in some other areas of learning. However, one subcomponent of the music curriculum that warrants special consideration is rhythmic movement, particularly when a child who is visually impaired is young and just learning skills related to orientation and mobility. Some students who are visually impaired may not be as secure or coordinated in rhythmic movement as their peers, due possibly to previous limited opportunities to explore the endless variations of movement. Rhythmic activities can aid the development of mobility skills. Visually impaired students may begin with large free movements, with gradual emphasis on the refinement of the movements. In helping to structure rhythmic activities for the student who is visually impaired, the teacher can use verbal directions and physical guidance, which involves helping to move the student's limbs or body in the desired manner.

Rhythmic movements can be valuable in teaching the student who is visually impaired concepts related to motion, such as a wheel rolling, trees swaying in the wind, and an elephant walking. Special emphasis might also be given to teaching students who are visually impaired popular dance steps to enhance their social acceptance, participation, and self-confidence at school social functions.

Children who are deaf can use movement to learn rhythms they cannot hear. They can observe a particular rhythmic sequence done in different meters and then reproduce the pattern by clapping or playing rhythm instruments. This kinesthetic approach to teaching rhythm can be a valuable teaching strategy. Movement exercises combined with music can improve all students' agility, posture, and physical fitness.

Adaptations in the music program should be considered for students who are orthopedically handicapped. Students unable to walk might crawl, roll over, clap their hands, or engage in some other response when rhythmic experiences are being shared by the class. Students with physical handicaps might learn rhythm by observing dance or gymnastics activities or by combining rhythmic activities with their physical therapy sessions. Playing instruments is another music experience that can be adapted for students with mobility disadvantages. Teachers should analyze the various degrees of coordination and types of movement required to play different instruments.

Relation to Academics

For students who are particularly interested in music, a more academic approach can be included in the curriculum. For example, a study of musical history and music theory could provide topics for individualized study. Through this pursuit of interest in music, gifted students can refine their skills of writing, reading, and using resources. Other activities could include interviewing local musicians, reporting to the class on biographies of famous musicians, and critiquing concerts.

Although music educators disclaim the central purpose of music education as a catalyst or reinforcer for other areas of study, this is an important purpose in music for handicapped students (Reichard & Blackburn, 1973). In the language arts curriculum, music is an appropriate tool in teaching many skills, including listening and reading. In developing oral communication skills, music is invaluable.

Music activities provide excellent opportunities for helping students with communication handicaps. Many students who have stuttering problems are more fluent when singing than when talking. Singing provides a structured rhythm that can be an excellent therapeutic tool. Instructional strategies need to be carefully coordinated among the music teacher, classroom teacher, and speech therapist to maximize the overall benefit of music experiences for students with communication handicaps. The speech therapist can suggest ways to help students who stutter minimize this handicap through music, which might generalize to other communication experiences. Additionally, if music poses no problems for these students, they should have the opportunity to sing in the school chorus or to join in similar experiences to gain recognition for their strengths in this area.

Articulation problems lend themselves to possible remediation activities in music. Teachers and students can make up songs that incorporate the particular sounds the student is working on in speech therapy. Such an example using the *M* sound is:

> Miles away there is a man
> Who makes the children happy.
> Miles away this merry man
> Sings songs to make them happy.[1]

While the student is being provided practice in speech, instruction on music concepts, such as melody, harmony, and rhythm, can be built into the experiences with song writing. Another opportunity for improving articulation is to provide vocal warm-up drills to exercise the lips, tongue, and larynx. Students can also be taught particular positioning of the parts of their oral cavity. This can help students learn to produce sounds correctly and can carry over to lipreading training for hearing-impaired students.

Music is an excellent vehicle for helping students disadvantaged by voice problems related to pitch, intensity, quality, and flexibility (chapter 3 includes an explanation of these communication handicaps). For example, students can be taught rhythm, which is necessary for appropriate flexibility in speaking, by clapping the accents of words or phrases, walking the rhythmic sequence, or illustrating it by playing percussion instruments (Fahey & Birkenshaw, 1972). Practice should be structured to insure generalization to speech patterns. Activities can also be provided to help students identify various instrumental pitch levels and experiment with matching their speech with the range in levels. Students with speech problems associated with pitch will be helped best if music teachers coordinate their program with that of the speech therapist. In order to provide appropriate practice for students with voice problems and to promote

---

[1]From *The Big Book of Sounds* (3rd ed.) (p. 139) by A. M. Flowers, 1980. Austin, TX: Pro-Ed, Inc. Copyright 1980 by Pro-Ed, Inc. Reprinted by permission.

generalization of communication skills learned through music to other speech and language experiences, teachers should pick songs and experiences that emphasize natural rhythmic accents, tonal inflections, and pitch.

Students who are disadvantaged by very low reading levels might learn concepts through music that they fail to master from reading their textbooks. One reading program, Hits (ModuLearn, Inc.), uses popular hit songs to teach phonetics, structural analysis, vocabulary, and comprehension skills. Skills in arithmetic, social studies, physical education, socialization, and all other curriculum areas can be reinforced through music experiences.

The development of perceptual skills can be facilitated by the use of motor skills (laterality, directionality, and regular pulse response); sequential memory (songs, chants, and movement); intellectual organization (study of form); and listening (following directions, mood sensitivity, and similarities and differences in sound). Science lessons could include a study of acoustics, and social studies could use songs that chronicle historical events. The social aspects of music are reinforced in folk dancing, games, and ensemble work (McCoy, 1982).

Peer Relationships

Music activities can provide opportunities for handicapped students to share experiences with their nonhandicapped peers, develop hobbies that promote peer relationships outside of school, and receive positive recognition accentuating their strengths, which could result in heightened classroom status. The group nature of many music activities provides an excellent setting for student interaction, and teachers should try to insure that handicapped students have the skills to make positive contributions to the group. For example, if several students are writing a song together and the handicapped member has severe language delays and poor penmanship, this student probably will not be able to participate effectively in this assignment. Positive peer relationships involve both giving and receiving. Teachers should structure situations in which the handicapped student can contribute to and draw from the group resources. The student with language and writing problems may be very successful in a group activity aimed at devising a folk dance. Handicapped students should be considered for the school chorus, orchestra, and other music activities on the same basis as other students. They should not be automatically ruled out because they are handicapped.

Hobbies related to music can be enjoyable leisure activities throughout one's life. Hobbies can also be socializing catalysts in neighborhoods and the community. Students who have special difficulty forming friendships might be aided by developing hobbies that provide natural ties with other persons. In music, these hobbies might include playing in a rock or folk band, participating in choral groups, collecting records, attending concerts, singing in the church choir, or joining a dancing group. If handicapped students are so inclined, teachers should encourage the development of such hobbies and provide an opportunity for the hobby to be shared with the class. Sharing hobbies within class can help build the bridge to sharing outside the school.

Some musically talented handicapped students may achieve more in this curriculum area than in any other. Being at a significant disadvantage in some subjects makes it particularly important for them to shine in others. If music is the student's strength, teachers should capitalize on this successful experience to help the handicapped student receive the respect of peers. The student might be asked to conduct the class's singing, write a class song, demonstrate how to play an instrument, play the lead in a musical performed by the class, participate in school-sponsored and community-based special events in music, or act as a peer tutor on music activities. This should not be viewed as favoritism to the handicapped student, and certainly similar opportunities should be extended to non-handicapped students talented in music.

Whether it is experienced through radio, television, stereo, or lessons, music is a part of the everyday lives of all students. Students who are academically gifted may be less gifted musically than many of their peers. This is an area in which they can relate to and learn from other students. If they are musically talented, their talent can be a means to entertain, teach, and share with all students.

ART

In responding to the back-to-basics controversy, Goodlad (1987) states:

> The response to individual differences among students must not be a narrowing of the curriculum, with accompanying lowered perceptions of human potential. What is good, beautiful, and just for the economically advantaged is also good, beautiful, and just for the impoverished. To neglect the arts in childhood is to impoverish not only the child, but the child become adult. (p. 53)

Exceptional students can be successfully mainstreamed in art programs. Blandy (1989) claims that a special, segregating art curriculum is no longer warranted or defensible, and that no physically or mentally disabling condition prevents any person from reaping the specific cognitive and affective benefits from study in art.

Concept Development

Lowenfeld and Brittain (1987) believe strongly that cognitive development relates to creative and artistic expression. They state that "children use art as a means of learning, through the development of concepts which take visible form, through the making of symbols which capture and are an abstraction of the environment, and through the organization and positioning of these symbols together in one configuration" (p. 2).

Art activities allow students to develop and participate at individual rates and ability levels and to study and adapt to their environments. Because basic skills and subjects can be taught through art, it has proven to be valuable in remedial instruction (List, 1982).

Art enables handicapped students to initiate their own ideas and materials, rather than to assume passive roles. As with music, the full benefits of art for handicapped students can be derived through clarifying goals and modifying curriculum and teaching strategies.

Clarifying Goals

Art instruction, like music and other creative art forms, has many purposes. As part of the general curriculum, art should promote social, personal, and perceptual/conceptual development. As a discipline, art should help students understand and appreciate the feelings, ideas, and values that major traditions of art communicate (Clark & Zimmerman, 1981).

The following are general outcomes for art programs:

- The arts develop creativity in children.
- Art experiences assist in the development of intelligent consumers and producers.
- Cooperative endeavors and social adjustments result from participation in group art activities.
- The visual experience promotes the growth and development of the child.
- Art activities and experiences provide for the release of emotion and feelings. (List, 1982, p. 5)

For handicapped students, art has many benefits. It provides a medium of communication for students with limited speech and writing abilities; it helps expand the student's frame of reference by providing new experiences; it is useful in developing manual dexterity; it provides opportunities to work cooperatively with others; it can be coordinated with other classroom learning experiences to help develop various concepts; and it can help in preparing for work situations (Krone, 1978).

Modifying Curriculum and Strategies

As in other disciplines, the content of art instruction must be ordered in developmental sequences that meet the individual needs of learners (Clark & Zimmerman, 1981). Lowenfeld and Brittain (1964) suggested that a knowledge of the developmental stages of art can be useful in assessing a student's developmental level and in planning appropriate art activities. The stages in their hierarchy are the preschematic stage (4 to 7 years), the schematic stage (7 to 9 years), and the stage of dawning realism (9 to 11 years). A new instrument, Clark's Drawing Abilities Test, is used as a screening and identification instrument. This test has been shown to be effective for screening or identifying candidates for a gifted/talented program in the visual arts (Clark, 1989).

After initial assessment has been accomplished and teachers have an idea of a particular student's strengths and weaknesses, adaptations in the art curriculum may be needed to accommodate the student's unique needs. Adaptations may have to be made in what is to be taught (content), how the content is to be taught (methods/materials), and when the content is to be taught (timing/sequence).

Many characteristics associated with handicapping conditions necessitate content modifications of the art curriculum. Students who are learning disabled or mentally retarded may have short attention spans or difficulty in remembering directions. These characteristics often require curriculum adaptation in timing and sequence. Additionally, lowered functioning in some academic subjects may create problems in art. For example, if the students are expected to read a poem and illustrate it with a painting, students with learning problems may be unable to read the poem. The use of a peer tutor or a tape presentation can eliminate this particular problem. Some students with learning problems have difficulty with spatial orientation, which is an important prerequisite to higher level artistic functioning. These students may be unable to draw a human figure without gross body distortions. The spatial problems of some students can be remediated through sound instruction and practice; other students will always have significant spatial problems.

Teachers should help students compensate for their deficiencies by developing interests and talents in other artistic endeavors that they can perform successfully. Many students with learning problems have strong talents in art. In these cases, teachers should use the artistic channel to teach other academic skills and to improve self-concepts.

Students who are blind and partially sighted, as well as those who are orthopedically handicapped with hand and arm involvement, often require adaptations in all areas of the art curriculum—content, methods/materials, and timing/sequence. Because of limitations imposed by the handicap, students may be below the developmental level in art that is predicted on the basis of chronological age. Teachers have to determine student performance levels and provide instruction at those levels in order to establish a strong foundation of artistic skills and concepts. The teaching/learning style options described in the earlier section on physical education also apply to art education. These options include visual guidance, verbal guidance, multisensory instruction, and the movement exploration approach.

As for multisensory instruction, students who are blind typically learn best through a combination of auditory, tactile, and kinesthetic experiences. When teaching macramé to students who are blind, the teacher might provide verbal instruction in how to make a particular knot, have the student feel the texture of the knot (loose, tight, smooth, pointed), and guide the student's hands and fingers through the sequence of steps involved in making the knot. Other art activities that have been mastered and enjoyed by students who are blind include experiences with clay, sculpture, printmaking, collages, finger painting, papier mâché, and ceramics. A variety of textures should be used and explored to familiarize students who are blind with their environment and to refine the tactile skills necessary for learning braille. Art media are plentiful, including paper (regular, sandpaper, tracing paper, wax paper), wood, textiles, wet sand, string, yarn, pipe cleaners, wires, rubber, plastic, and glass.

The adaptation that is usually necessary for concept development to proceed is in the sequencing of art activities.

The sixth-grade class was making crayon collages by coloring a sheet of paper with different colors. After the coloring was completed, they outlined each different color section by gluing string around its border. David, a student who is blind, participated in the activity by reversing the procedure: first, he glued string in various patterns on the sheet and then he colored the inside of each section. His collage, depicted in Figure 11.4, was one of the best in the class.

The range of individual differences in approach and ability is tremendous in art productions. Examples of the range are shown in Figure 11.5, drawn by a 7-year-old nonhandicapped student, and Figure 11.6, drawn by an 11-year-old student with mental retardation.

Even when drawings are not used to make judgments about students, they can be used to plan activities appropriate for them. Using Lowenfeld and Brittain's developmental stages (1964), students can be grouped into levels of instruction based on their art samples. Art lessons can be developed that meet individual student needs within a class and still provide common experiences. Examples of individualization are cited in Table 11.3.

Mobility

Art experiences and activities frequently require movement. Some are gross movements, such as finger painting; others require very fine control, such as sketching or carving very small figures. Students who are orthopedically handicapped, particularly those who have limited mobility in their arms, hands, and fingers, may require adaptations in the art curriculum. For some students who cannot hold a pencil, crayon, or paint brush in the typical fashion, a ball of clay or foam rubber sponge attached to the tool provides a better grip. Students who have jerky or uncoordinated

FIGURE 11.4 Collage by a Student with Visual Impairment

FIGURE 11.5   Drawing by a 7-Year-Old Student

movements frequently have papers slip off their desks, spill paint, or knock crayons to the floor. Teachers can use masking tape to position the paper on the student's desk or table. Students who have uncontrolled movements or who are particularly clumsy can work at a special table away from the major material storage areas in the classroom. Limits can be placed on how many materials they may have on their table at one time, and a special area of the table can be set aside for materials and supplies. Reserving one area of the table for materials encourages students to be particularly careful with haphazard movements in that direction. A sturdy rack with holes for paint jars also prevents spillage.

Some students with physical limitations may also have extreme difficulty manipulating small objects. Rather than making a collage or junk sculpture with small pieces of material, they may have to use larger materials that are easier to handle. Other students with more severe limitations will require more substantial adaptations.

Art activities involve a tremendous range of mobility requirements. Because of the variety of possible activities, teachers can be tremendously flexible when making needed adaptations for handicapped students.

FIGURE 11.6 Drawing by an 11-Year-
Old Student

Relevance to Academics

Art provides student-centered experiences that are adaptable to every
aspect of the school curriculum and to all skill areas. It is particularly
relevant to the language arts, mathematics, social studies, and science.

The Language Arts
Art is a method of expression. Through art, students can become more
sensitive to their own ideas and feelings and communicate these with
peers and adults. Art is an important form of communication for all
students, but it may have especially important implications for students
with language handicaps who are impaired in some channels of communication.

The language experience method of teaching reading (see chapter 8)
has traditionally been a vehicle for incorporating art. Students describe
their experiences; the teacher or peer writes down the words of the stu-

TABLE 11.3 Examples of Individualization

Level 1: Preschematic Stage
Level 2: Schematic Stage
Level 3: Stage of Dawning Realism

Level	Materials	Methods
1	Clay products from previous week Finger paints Large brushes Spray fixative	Use finger paints applied with brush. One color for entire product. Spray when dry.
2	Clay products Tempera paint Brushes	Children mix tempera; add liquid soap for smooth consistency. Several colors may be used.
3	Clay products Tempera paint Small brushes	Plan design on paper; transfer to clay product, using tempera. Spray when dry.

dent; and the student illustrates the words through art projects and learns to recognize and comprehend the words in written form. Art can be a very important component of the language experience approach to reading instruction.

Mathematics
Through art, concepts of form and shape can be developed. Art can also be used to teach counting, numbers, graphs, measurement, symbols, fractions, proportions, and time (List, 1982). The mathematically gifted student will enjoy making tesselations, geometric patterns that cover a surface with no gaps and no overlapping.

Social Studies
In the social studies curriculum, art can play a major role. For example, many students unable to read the textbook can learn concepts about foreign customs by analyzing pictures and other visual media; they can demonstrate their knowledge of these customs by constructing collages, shoebox stories, murals, and props for a play. This instructional strategy should not be used in a singular fashion, but rather combined with other strategies into a multisensory approach. Art also provides enrichment activities for gifted students who want to explore customs and cultures beyond the class assignment.

Science
Art can be used to teach science as it relates to concepts of texture, color, pattern, space, shape, and form. Specific topics can be interrelated through

science and art. As described in chapter 10, science and art activities have been particularly valuable in programs for students who are visually impaired.

Peer Relationships

Art education provides many opportunities for students to work together and to share their expertise. When handicapped students have special talents in art, they should have the opportunity to receive peer recognition and classroom status.

Art instruction can be planned to encourage small-group interaction. For example, group murals can be vehicles for learning artistic and academic skills and concepts and for increasing positive peer interaction. Teachers must try to insure that students with handicaps make positive contributions to the group and are regarded as assets rather than liabilities.

Art hobbies that stem from school experiences can carry over into neighborhood and community experiences. These hobbies can initiate lifelong leisure interests. As community experiences and leisure interests develop, handicapped persons increase their opportunities for interacting with peers. Art can serve as a bridge between people of similar interests.

The arts (music, art, dance, and drama) can enhance the cognitive, social, and emotional development of handicapped students and adults. The National Committee, Arts for the Handicapped, was created in 1975 for the purpose of coordinating the development of a nationwide program of all arts for all handicapped students. The organization is committed to the belief that "the arts can provide unique ways of acquiring skills and knowledge as well as bringing opportunities for beautiful experiences, and that handicapped people have a right to a full measure of both" (Apell, 1979, p. 74).

THE ARTS IN GIFTED EDUCATION

In 1972, when Commissioner of Education Sidney Marland reported to the Congress on the state of the gifted in schools in the United States, one major recommendation was to expand the definition of gifted from solely academic and cognitive areas to include high aptitude in the visual and performing arts (Gallagher, 1985). Some states use the term *academically gifted;* others use the label *gifted and talented* to identify students for special programming (see chapter 5). In general, talent refers to distinctly above average performance in fields of activities (e.g., math, music, astronomy, sculpture), as opposed to intellectual excellence (Davis & Rimm, 1989).

Characteristics of Talented Students

Research into talented students is much more limited than research that identifies intellectually and creatively gifted students (Parker, 1989). However, some traits have been identified and are classified into three categories: cognitive abilities, affective traits, and creative competencies. In the cognitive area, it has been noted that most talented individuals have a facility for learning rapidly, that they have keen senses of observation, the ability to recall visual detail, and skills of organization. Among the affective qualities appearing in persons talented in the arts are an intense interest in one or more art areas, self-confidence and a willingness to share ideas and products, a tendency to identify personally with subject matter and the medium used, high but realistic standards for self-evaluation, and sensitivity toward movement, content, and environment. Creative competencies include fluency, flexibility, originality, and elaboration. Other creative traits that characterize the talented individual are openness to new experiences and new ideas and a futuristic perspective, including plans for future artistic endeavors and future careers in the arts.

Curriculum Adaptations

Gallagher (1985) finds a greater tolerance by advocates of mainstreaming for the separation of talented students from the rest of the students in the visual and performing arts than in any other dimension of education. Special schools for dance, music, and drama are readily accepted as appropriate placements for students who have extraordinary talent.

Special programming in the arts should be based on several considerations:

1. Contrary to common practice, the arts program for gifted students should be individualized. This principle does not imply that there should never be whole-group or small-group instruction, but rather it demands that the teacher acknowledge, understand, and allow for the development of each gifted student's individual abilities, encouraging each potential artist to self-expression in accordance with his own styles and interests.

2. The classroom environment should be open, warm, and flexible, allowing students to feel free to use their imaginations in the application of the principles of art that are learned from the instructor.

3. Students should be offered a breadth and depth of experience in order that they may identify with the materials they use, understanding all of the nuances of color or tone, the possibilities for

coordinating and combining media, and the ways in which these learnings can be transferred to other contexts.

4. Regardless of the art form being studied, students should be encouraged—indeed, trained—to keep records of their work. To the visual artist, a record may be a sketchbook or a portfolio; to the music student, it may be a notebook of musical themes or original passages that spring from the subconscious during periods of rest or even other classes. These records, possibly accompanied by (or later added to) journals expressing their feelings about their work and the emotions that were present when it was being produced, can be of inestimable value in the artist's later years and should be a major part of the habits that are ingrained in all art students from the early days of the program.[2]

Most gifted students will not choose a career in the visual and performing arts. However, as with all students, experiences in the arts form an important part of their education. Boyer (1987) emphasizes the importance and necessity of arts in the curriculum:

> To be truly human, all of us must be able to respond to the subtle messages only the arts can convey. Children must learn from their earliest schooling that music and dance and the visual arts are basic. They enlarge the store of the images we use and make our understanding more discriminating and comprehensive. (p. 54)

REFERENCES

AMA. (1968). The epileptic child and competitive school athletics. *Pediatrics, 42,* 700.

American Association for Health, Physical Education, and Recreation. (1986). *Special fitness test manual for the mentally retarded.* Washington, DC: Author.

Apell, L. S. (1979). Enhancing learning and enriching lives: Arts in the education of handicapped children. *Teaching Exceptional Children, 11,* (2), 74–76.

Arbogast, G., & Lavay, B. (1986). Combining students with different ability levels in games and sports. *The Physical Educator,* (1), 255–260.

Aufsesser, P. M. (1981). Adapted physical education. *Journal of Physical Education, Recreation and Dance, 52,* (6), 28–31.

Beer, A. S., Bellows, N. L., & Frederick, A. M. D. (1982). Providing for different rates of music learning. *Music Educators Journal, 68,* (8), 40–43.

Blandy, D. (1989). Ecological and normalizing approaches to disabled students and art education. *Art Education, 42,* (3), 7–11.

Boyer, E. L. (1987). Keep arts in the schools. *Music Educators Journal, 74,* (4), 52–55.

[2]From *Instruction Strategies for Teaching the Gifted* (p. 267) by J. P. Parker, 1989. Boston: Allyn and Bacon. Copyright 1989 by Allyn and Bacon. Reprinted by permission.

Buell, C. E. (1982). *Physical education and recreation for the visually handicapped* (rev. ed.). Washington, DC: American Alliance for Health, Physical Education, Recreation, and Dance.

Chambless, J. R., Anderson, E., & Poole, J. H. (1981). IEP's and mastery learning applied to psychomotor activities. In G. R. Roice (Ed.), *Teaching handicapped students physical education* (pp. 20–22). Washington, DC: National Education Association.

Clark, G. (1989). Screening and identifying students talented in the visual arts: Clark's drawing abilities test. *Gifted Child Quarterly, 33*, (3), 98–105.

Clark, G., & Zimmerman, E. (1981). Toward a discipline of art education. *Phi Delta Kappan, 63*, (1), 53–56.

Coates, P. (1985). Make mainstreaming work. *Music Educators Journal, 72*, (3), 31–32.

Cratty, B. J. (1980). *Adapting physical education for handicapped children and youth.* Denver: Love.

Davis, G. A., & Rimm, S. B. (1989). *Education of the gifted and talented* (2nd ed.). Englewood Cliffs, NJ: Prentice-Hall.

Davis, R., Woolley, Y., & French, R. (1986). Reverse mainstreaming. *The Physical Educator, 44*, (1), 247–249.

Epley, C. (1972). In a soundless world of musical enjoyment. In M. E. Bessom (Ed.), *Music in special education* (pp. 142–154). Washington, DC: Music Educators National Conference.

Fait, H. F. (1978). *Special physical education.* Philadelphia: Saunders.

Flowers, A. M. (1980). *The big book of sounds.* Austin, TX: Pro Ed.

Folio, M. R., & Norman, A. (1981). Toward more success in mainstreaming: A peer teacher approach to physical education. *Teaching Exceptional Children, 13*, (3), 110–113.

Futrell, M. H. (1987). Keep arts in the schools. *Music Educators Journal, 74*, (4), 52–55.

Gallagher, J. J. (1985). *Teaching the gifted child* (3rd ed.). Boston: Allyn and Bacon.

Gfeller, K., & Darrow, A. (1987). Ten years of mainstreaming: Where are we now? *Music Educators Journal, 74*, (2), 27–30.

Goodlad, J. I. (1987). Keep arts in the schools. *Music Educators Journal, 74*, (4), 52–55.

Graham, R. M. (1988). Barrier-free music education: Methods to make mainstreaming work. *Music Educators Journal, 74*, (5), 29–33.

Haubenstricker, J. L. (1982). Motor development in children with learning disabilities. *Journal of Physical Education, Recreation and Dance, 53*, (5), 41–43.

Hope, S. (1987). Keep arts in the schools. *Music Educators Journal, 74*, (4), 52–55.

Johnson, L., & Londeree, B. (1976). *Motor fitness testing manual for the moderately mentally retarded.* Washington, DC: American Alliance for Health, Physical Education, and Recreation.

Karper, W. B. (1986). Childhood asthma and physical education. *The Physical Educator, 44*, (1), 250–254.

Kenny, A. (1987). Counseling the gifted, creative, and talented. *Gifted Child Today, 10*, (5), 45–51.

Krone, A. (1978). *Art instruction for handicapped children.* Denver: Love.

Lam, R. C., & Wang, C. (1982). Integrating blind and sighted through music. *Music Educators Journal, 68*, (8), 44–45.

List, L. K. (1982). *Music, art and drama experiences for the elementary curriculum.* New York: Teachers College Press.

Lowenfeld, V., & Brittain, W. L. (1964). *Creative and mental growth* (4th ed.). New York: Macmillan.

Lowenfeld, V., & Brittain, W. L. (1987). *Creative and mental growth* (8th ed.). New York: Macmillan.

Marlowe, M. (1979). The games analysis intervention: A procedure to increase the peer acceptance and social adjustment of a retarded child. *Education and Training of the Mentally Retarded, 14,* (4), 262–268.

McCoy, M. (1982). In the mainstream. *Music Educators Journal, 68,* (8), 51.

Miller, S. E., & Schaumberg, K. (1988). Physical education activities for children with severe cerebral palsy. *Teaching Exceptional Children, 20,* (2), 9–10.

Mooney, M. K. (1972). Blind children need training, not sympathy. In M. E. Bessom (Ed.), *Music in special education* (pp. 24–38). Washington, DC: Music Educators National Conference.

Parker, J. P. (1989). *Instructional strategies for teaching the gifted.* Boston: Allyn and Bacon.

Perkins, C. E. (1979). Music to their ears. *Instructor, 89,* (4), 134–136.

Reichard, C. L., & Blackburn, D. B. (1973). *Music based instruction for the exceptional child.* Denver: Love.

Santomier, J., & Kopczuk, W. (1981). Facilitation of interactions between retarded and nonretarded students in a physical education setting. *Education and Training of the Mentally Retarded, 16,* (1), 20–23.

Sava, S. G. (1987). Keep arts in the schools. *Music Educators Journal, 74,* (4), 52–55.

Schmidt, S., & Dunn, J. M. (1980). Physical education for the hearing impaired. *Educating Exceptional Children, 12,* (3), 99–102.

Seaman, J. A. (1988). The challenge. *Journal of Physical Education, Recreation, & Dance, 59,* (1), 32–33.

Sherrill, C. (1986). *Adapted physical education and recreation* (3rd ed.). Dubuque, IA: William C. Brown.

Stein, J. U. (1979). The mission and the mandate: Special education, the not so sleeping giant. *Education Unlimited, 1,* (2), 6–11.

The school music program: Description and standards (2nd ed.). (1986). Washington, DC: Music Educators National Conference, 19–26.

Thompson, K. (1982). Education of handicapped learners. *Music Educators Journal, 68,* (8), 25–29.

Vodola, T. M. (1978). Developmental and adapted physical education. A.C.T.I.V.E. Motor ability and physical fitness norms: For normal, mentally retarded, learning disabled, and emotionally disturbed individuals. Oakhurst, NJ: Township of Ocean School District.

Welsbacher, B. T. (1972). More than a package of bizarre behavior. In M. E. Bessom (Ed.), *Music in special education* (pp. 86–95). Washington, DC: Music Educators National Conference.

White, L. D. (1982). How to adapt for special students. *Music Educators Journal, 68,* (8), 49–50, 63–67.

Winnick, J. P. (1988). Classifying individuals with handicapping conditions for testing. *Journal of Physical Education, Recreation & Dance, 59,* (1), 34–37.

Winnick, J. P., & Short, F. X. (1985). *Physical fitness testing of the disabled.* Champaign, IL: Human Kinetics.

Zakrajsek, D., & Carnes, L. A. (1986). *Individualizing physical education.* Champaign, IL: Human Kinetics.

—12—

Managing Classroom Behavior

Managing the behavior of exceptional students is one of the primary factors in determining successful mainstreamed placements. Two facets of behavior have to be considered. First is the curtailment of inappropriate behavior:

> *David never enters a room; he falls into it. He stalks about the room, breaking things, creating confusion, and being the class clown. The other children laugh at him, and he destroys all my well-laid plans.*

Second is the increase of appropriate behavior:

> *I have 25 fourth graders and Tony. Tony rarely completes his assignments. How can I help him complete his work and still meet the needs of the other students?*

Handicapped children and youth can acquire immature or antisocial behavior for many reasons. They may be overprotected at home, where temper tantrums, interruptions, or overbearing attitudes are permitted. They may have been enrolled in special schools or special classes, where behavior standards were not as high as in other situations. They may function at a level at which most persons do not expect normal behavior from them. They may have experienced chronic failure in school that has resulted in rebellious behavior. They may have special problems, such as hyperactivity or serious emotional disturbances, that contribute to their behavior problems. Children and youth who are gifted may also exhibit inappropriate behavior for many of the same reasons that other children do. Regardless of the reason, inappropriate behavior can be replaced by acceptable behavior. This change alone can make a tremendous difference in the degree to which students are accepted by teachers and peers.

> *After talking with David about his behavior, we listed things that needed to be changed. We made a chart, with space for check marks each time he entered the room quietly, put his books away promptly, etc. With each five checks, David can spend 30 minutes working on his string art, which he loves to do. We also set up a check system for the other students, giving them checks for not laughing at David, and removing checks when they do laugh. I feel that David is gradually assuming responsibility for his own behavior.*

DEFINING TEACHER EXPECTATIONS

Behavior problems occur when there is a discrepancy between what the teacher expects and what students do. Teachers might expect attention in class—but some students want to sleep; teachers might expect class members to get along with each other—but some students fight; teachers might expect work to be handed in on time—but some students are chronically late. Thus, the two important dimensions that need to be examined are teacher expectations and student behavior. This section focuses on teacher expectations; it is followed by strategies for recognizing and defining student behavior.

A necessary first step to increasing the appropriate behavior of all students is for the teacher to define behavioral expectations. Such expectations evolve from the teacher's values and beliefs about how students should behave in the classroom. Remember that the same behavior is seen *differently* in *different* situations and by *different* people (Barnes, Eyman, & Engolz, 1974). One teacher stated her values and beliefs as follows:

> I believe that teachers should operate in a highly authoritarian manner. Students should be told what is expected of them, and any infraction of the rules should bring an automatic detention period. Without exception, rules and sanctions should be consistently applied.

Another teacher stated an alternative philosophy:

> *Classroom discipline is an area where I usually don't have too many problems. Part of the reason for that is that I am a very relaxed teacher and many things don't bother me. I am not a reactor. At the beginning of each year, we jointly discuss what is acceptable behavior and what is not. They help set the rules and if I can't live with something, I tell them so and we compromise, and vice-versa.*

Obviously, the basic beliefs of these teachers will influence the actual rules they devise and their methods for applying contingencies to both appropriate and inappropriate behavior. There is no set of correct beliefs and values; rather, teachers need to delineate a philosophy that is consistent with their personality and instructional style.

The clarification of beliefs and values is a foundation for specifying actual classroom rules. Clear rule setting is helpful for all students with a history of behavior problems. Such students benefit from expectations that are explicit, fair, and within their range of achievement. An elementary teacher reported rules that he and his students developed:

1. Stay on task and follow directions
2. Have school supplies ready and assignments completed
3. Raise your hand to receive permission to talk
4. Walk to and from classes in line with no talking.

Once rules are developed, they should be put in writing and posted in class. Particularly at the beginning of the year, students may need reminders and clarifications of the rules. A secondary social studies teacher described the procedures she uses.

I believe the first week of class is very important and can set the tone for the year. During that week I spend 90 percent of my time deciding with the students what the ground rules will be, how routines will be handled, and what the operational mechanics of the classroom will be. Future problems can be avoided by putting the rules down in writing. By taking care of these things during the first week, we can spend the rest of the year more beneficially learning about government.

Once rules have been established, it can be helpful to review those rules with the class on a periodic basis to discuss any needed changes. Students can also be encouraged to identify areas in which they have made progress and areas that need more improvement.

DEFINING STUDENT BEHAVIOR

In recalling our definition of behavior problems—a discrepancy between what teachers expect and what students do—it is necessary for teachers to recognize and define student behavior that deviates from their expectations. Educators frequently use ambiguous terms in describing student behavior. For example, the phrase "short attention span" could refer to an inability to sit still for five minutes, inability to listen for half an hour, inclination to roam about the room, or any number of behaviors. Behavior should be defined in observable, countable, and repeatable terms.

Once the behavior is defined, it is helpful for teachers to explore factors that are contributing to the problem. Questions that teachers should consider in identifying factors include (Regan, 1979):

1. Does the student have the prerequisite skills to complete the expected tasks? Assessment of the student's current level of performance may reveal skill deficiencies requiring instructional changes. When instruction is delivered at the appropriate level, behavior problems may disappear.
2. Are there personal, family, classroom, or environmental factors contributing to the student's behavior problems? Such factors include the student's health, whether the student is hungry, the existence of competing responsibilities limiting sleep and attention to school work (e.g., outside employment) and whether the classroom arrangement is conducive to the student's learning style.
3. Does the student have motivational problems? In such cases, the student may not have the initiative or desire to conform to teacher expectations as set forth in classroom rules.

Analyzing student problems according to these three questions can assist teachers in planning intervention strategies. In the first case, the problem is primarily an instructional one that will likely require instructional strategies tailored to individual needs. In the second case, the problem is created by barriers, and the most effective intervention is the removal of those barriers.

> *Sandra, a sixth-grade student from a low income background, kept her head on her desk for most of the school day. She did not pay attention to class discussions and would not complete assignments. Her withdrawn and passive behavior greatly interfered with her performance. Her teacher was quite concerned, even irritated with her. One afternoon when she was reprimanding Sandra, the teacher noticed that Sandra's gums were bleeding. Upon inspection, she realized that Sandra had permanent teeth growing under permanent teeth. The teeth were cutting through the tops of her gums. Sandra then told the teacher, "All I think about is how much I hurt." The school nurse worked with Sandra, her family, and a local dentist in arranging for the dental surgery needed to correct this problem. Once Sandra returned to school, her attention increased dramatically.*

In the third case, the problem is primarily a motivational one requiring intervention strategies to increase the student's interest and initiative. It is important to recognize that student problems rarely fall neatly into one of these categories. Students frequently have combinations of problems; thus, a comprehensive approach to ameliorating problems is often needed.

GENERAL MANAGEMENT STRATEGIES

A teacher's selection of management strategies is influenced by many considerations. As previously discussed, the teacher's behavioral expectations—including both values and classroom rules—are critical determinants of how problem behaviors are actually managed. Other important considerations are the definition of the student's problematic behavior and the factors contributing to that behavior. This section focuses on general management strategies that are effective in preventing behavioral concerns from becoming major problems. These general management strategies include teacher preparation, individualized instruction, communication, room arrangement, assigned responsibility, signals to students, and parental involvement. The next section focuses on strategies based on behavioral principles.

Sufficient Teacher Preparation

Sufficient preparation is a key to successful classroom management (Sabatino, 1987). If a teacher has prepared only 20 minutes of work for a 55 minute class period, behavioral problems are likely to occur. Students should be busy and interested. They should be engaged in activities that are appropriate to the needs of the students. Typically, the busier the students, the fewer the behavior problems. That is not to imply that students should be busy only for the sake of doing something whether it is appropriate or not. However, there is therapeutic value to being engaged rather than having nothing to do. Although thorough preparation is a time-consuming task for teachers, it can save time in the long run by preventing teachers from spending inordinate amounts of time dealing with problems. The decision is really to spend time preventing problems rather than with problems after they occur. A teacher described her support of this strategy as follows:

> *My best defense has always been an aggressive offense. I try to keep the students so busy that they do not have time to make trouble. There are many activities available to suit each child's learning level and interests. This takes much advance preparation to be sure, but I am convinced that it is worth it. I rarely have behavior problems and that makes classroom time much more productive.*

As with all strategies discussed in this chapter, no approach is successful with all students. In some cases, thorough teacher preparation still does not curtail behavioral problems, as in the case of a student who is highly aggressive.

Individualized Instruction

Closely related to the issue of teacher preparation is the need to individualize instruction as a strategy for improving behavior. It is impossible to separate totally instructional and management interventions. As discussed earlier, a major factor contributing to some students' behavior problems or lack of learning is that instruction is not tailored to their performance level and to the input/output modes most effective for their learning (see chapter 7). Students engaged in productive, challenging, and interesting tasks that have successful outcomes are much more likely to behave appropriately. Frequently, task requirements need to be adapted for students with behavioral problems. One strategy for individualization follows:

> *Teaching in a middle school learning center was a new experience for me. The middle school student has that "constant bouncing energy"—particularly one of the students in my English class. Joe is short on attention span, giving 10 minutes at most to his work and then wandering about the room. I tried to channel his interests to other activities and then have him return to the initial task until it was completed. If Joe began to "wander," I would have him take his turn on the computer if it was not in use. He loved to work with it. He was also a good speller. After perhaps 15 to 20*

minutes of the period had elapsed, he could be steered back to the original English assignment for another 10 minutes. For the remainder of the time, I would let him choose a book from the reading area, if his tasks had been completed. Reading was his second love, after the computer. Joe was able to do special assignments if his attention could be focused long enough. He also enjoyed teaching other students how to use the computer.

Such task variation can be done for one student or for the entire class. Not every student can or needs to read *Canterbury Tales.* Some behavior problems are the result of frustration with material that is too difficult or too easy for the particular student. Activities can be varied to include class discussions, completing short written assignments, locating reference materials in the library, writing review questions, engaging in small-group work, taking a short quiz, and grading papers. Such variation helps students keep active and directed. A substitute teacher made the following observation:

The biggest behavioral problem I have encountered is students talking while I was lecturing. I noticed that they paid attention when I started writing notes using the overhead projector.

It is helpful for teachers to ask when behavior problems arise: Can I change the way I teach or approach this subject to meet the individual needs of the students?

Communication

The nature of communication between the teacher and students can substantially influence whether behavior problems increase or decrease. When frustration arises because of the discrepancy between teacher expectations and student behavior, communication can become difficult. Teachers should consider these four guidelines when communicating with students in conflict situations:

1. Focus communication on the student's behavior without judging or attacking. A helpful strategy is to use "I" rather than "you" messages (e.g., "I'm concerned about the number of times you interrupt the conversations of others," rather than "You are rude and annoying").
2. Be firm and consistent in applying rules and assigning consequences. It can be helpful to remind students that they have the choice to abide by the rules or accept the consequences of breaking them (e.g., "Connie, I know you don't want to be on Bill's team because you feel most of your friends are on another team. Per-

haps next time you can get on the team you want, but for now you have the choice to play on Bill's team or sit out this game"). Once the choice is stated, the teacher should not respond to the student's protests or complaints.

3. Angry feelings are natural, particularly when the student has engaged in behavior that is dangerous to others. Strive to express angry feelings in a rational and clear fashion without escalating the intensity of your feelings or those of the student. The old adage "to proceed like the ticking of a clock in a thunderstorm" is a good strategy for handling situations charged with emotion. A teacher who is able to exercise self-control and moderate reaction is much better equipped to deal with students who have emotional problems and still need to learn these skills.

4. Teacher confrontations should never occur in front of an entire class. When that happens, the student can gain sympathy and support from other class members. Also, the teacher is placed in the position of proving to be in control. Often, the amount of time it takes to walk out of the classroom can diffuse anger enough so that the teacher can calmly explain how the behavior was inappropriate and what consequences will be necessary. Without an audience, the student may no longer feel it necessary to demonstrate a lack of fear. The student should not be given the opportunity to swagger back into the classroom.

Conflict situations rarely call for just one of these guidelines. Frequently, they must be used concurrently.

Ongoing communication can also be used to prevent conflict. As is discussed in the next section on behavioral techniques, praise is a powerful contributor to promoting positive behavior. Frequently, communication with students focuses on correction or criticism. Communication should also hinge on catching students being good. A physical education teacher reported that positive communication is an effective strategy in her class:

> I usually walk up and down my squads when I take attendance and make comments to my students. I often comment on general rules that had been neglected in the past but are now being followed. "Thanks for taking off your jewelry." "Gee, you remembered your gym clothes on a Monday." "You got an A on the test for the first time—I'm proud of you!" It is amazing how often the students remind me that they remembered. They like the positive attention.

Another strategy for maintaining ongoing communication with students is to have classroom meetings. As described by Glasser (1969), this approach involves providing specific opportunities for students to discuss relevant issues, build trusting relationships with peers, and increase their sense of cohesiveness in the classroom. Zeeman and Martucci (1976) reported the successful use of classroom meetings in a special education class with students who are learning disabled. The classroom meeting strategy is discussed further in the next chapter regarding its use in enhancing the social integration of handicapped and nonhandicapped students.

Room Arrangement

The arrangement of the room can influence the degree to which students meet the behavioral expectations of the teacher. For students with short attention spans, it is particularly helpful to have a portion of the room set up for change-of-pace activities. Children who are gifted also benefit from such arrangements. One possible arrangement is illustrated in Figure 12.1.

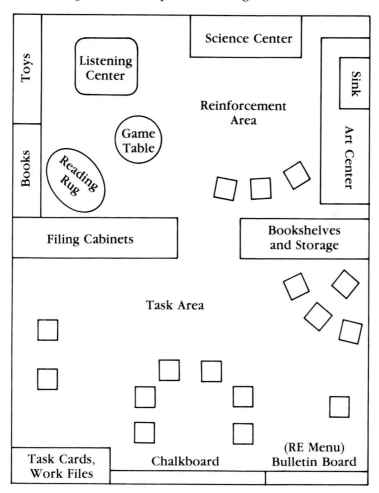

FIGURE 12.1   Classroom Arrangement

Such an arrangement enables students to work on center and reinforcement activities without disrupting the concentration of their peers. Another alternative is to arrange separate areas for students who are distracted by the movement and noise of peers. These areas should be used as aids to concentration rather than as punishment for disruptions.

Another environmental feature that can minimize behavioral disruptions is adequate storage for personal belongings. When students have a specified and private place to keep their belongings, conflicts over lost materials or disputes over ownership can be minimized.

Assigned Responsibility

Some students engage in inappropriate behavior as a way of seeking attention. An effective strategy for dealing with such students is to provide extra attention by assigning them classroom responsibilities. A secondary history teacher used this approach with success:

> I had been warned to "watch out for Robert" long before he entered my class. He had created chaos in one class after another, year after year. I decided to give him extra attention and responsibility starting on the first day he walked into my class.
>
> The duties delegated to Robert were running audiovisual equipment and collecting and filing student papers. He liked to work with audiovisual equipment and also seemed to like the leadership role of collecting papers given to him by other students. I found that he was eager to please and to have someone place trust in him. I never had any real problems with him but did remind him on a couple of occasions, when I sensed he was slipping a little, that he had certain responsibilities and would need to show that he deserved to keep them.

Other special duties that can be assigned to students needing extra attention include taking attendance, being on the school safety patrol, caring for plants, fixing bulletin boards, writing the daily schedule on the chalkboard, keeping a class calendar, running errands, and straightening the room. Handicapped students often get overlooked in the assignment of special responsibilities, yet these duties can have many positive benefits. In addition to providing extra attention, other outcomes can include heightened status among peers (discussed in the next chapter) and a recognition that the teacher trusts them and values their contribution to the class.

Signals to Students

Some students can be reminded to redirect their attention to the task at hand by verbal and nonverbal signals from teachers (Evertson, Emmer, Clements, Sanford, & Worsham, 1989). Direct verbal signals are requests to students to behave appropriately. Indirect verbal signals also are effective.

> *Eileen is an excessive talker. She not only fails to get her work done on time, but she also disrupts her classmates. Her teacher sometimes uses Eileen's name in a sentence that has to do with what he is presenting. Consistently, Eileen stops talking when she hears her name.*

Other nonverbal signals include gestures, facial expressions, and turning lights on and off.

Often the teacher's immediate presence is a signal to students to behave appropriately. An effective technique is for the teacher to move about the classroom while students are working on assignments. Physical proximity allows for individual assistance and also enables teachers to deal with problem behavior in a discreet manner.

Parental Involvement

The involvement of parents in decision making about intervention strategies and in actually delivering consequences for school behavior can be very effective for some students. The IEP conference provides an opportunity to discuss intervention strategies and to determine parental willingness to work cooperatively with the teacher. At this time, the teacher can explain classroom rules for appropriate behavior and the consequences for misbehavior.

When behavior problems arise, parent conferences can be held to discuss the problem and obtain suggestions from parents on management strategies that have been effective. After such a conference, continued communication with the parents regarding the student's progress can help the student realize that both teachers and parents are serious about the need for behavior change. Such communication can include notes, phone calls, or additional periodic conferences (Schulz, 1987). An important point to remember is that parents need to be told about good behavior as well as about problems. Also, many parents of handicapped students have repeatedly witnessed instances in which their child was rejected or isolated. Thus, it is particularly important for teachers to convey to these parents that their handicapped child is accepted and respected (Hallenbeck & Beernink, 1989).

BEHAVIOR MANAGEMENT PRINCIPLES AND STRATEGIES

The techniques for changing specific student behaviors discussed in this section are based on the work of B. F. Skinner and his associates (Skinner,

1953). They involve the systematic application of behavioral principles and procedures.

The effectiveness of behavior management with handicapped students has been documented (Alberto & Troutman, 1986; Gresham, 1981; MacMillan & Forness, 1970) with reference to all categories of handicapping conditions. Behavior management strategies have been used with the full range of classroom problems, including reducing disruptive behavior, increasing peer interactions, and improving performance in academic subjects. There has been some criticism that behavior management is a tool for manipulating people (Alberto & Troutman, 1986). With the understanding that this technique is primarily a positive approach, embodying strategies long used by parents and teachers, such criticism may dissolve.

When presented with the principles of behavior, many teachers exclaim, "Why, I've been doing that for years!" They have been rewarding good behavior and ignoring or punishing bad behavior. Certainly, behavior management is not new. The new aspect is the *systematic* approach to using the principles of behavior. In other words, the techniques formerly used at random are now being used in an organized, scientific way. Because behavior is predictable, the systematic use of behavior management is effective.

Once understood, the principles of behavior can be explained to peers, paraprofessionals, and volunteer helpers in the classroom. Because the objectives are specific, communication between the teacher and other assistants is increased. Teachers can give procedural directions for behavioral programs that others can implement.

Principles of Behavior

> *A young mother took her 3-year-old daughter to an egg hunt. Because there were older children participating and the competition was keen, Mary found no eggs. Her mother was surprised, therefore, to see that she had one of the prizes. Asked how she got the prize, Mary replied, "I cried for it."*

Children learn at a very early age that their behavior produces consequences. In contemplating behavior change, therefore, the teacher seeks to arrange the consequences to promote the desired behavior.

Two kinds of behavior are delineated: respondent and operant. Respondent (reflex) behavior refers to responses that are elicited by special stimulus changes in the environment (Alberto & Troutman, 1986). It is usually associated with involuntary muscular movements, such as the contraction or dilation of the pupils of the eyes, response to touching a hot stove, and watering of the mouth at the sight or smell of some appetizing food.

Operant (voluntary) behavior, on the other hand, is the conscious response to one's environment, maintained through reinforcement. Thus, operant behaviors are of major concern to teachers who wish to change a student's behaviors. Whether operant behaviors are changed depends on what happens following each operant behavior (Alberto & Troutman, 1986). The general rules in behavior management are that desirable behavior should be rewarded (reinforced) and that undesirable behavior should not be rewarded. Behavior that is reinforced tends to be repeated: behavior that is not reinforced tends not to be repeated (Kerr & Nelson, 1983).

Increasing Behavior

One way to increase the likelihood of a behavior recurring is to follow that behavior with a positive or favorable event. This is called positive reinforcement.

> *In the school cafeteria, Henry picked up Miss Lassiter's lunch tray and carried it to the table for her. Miss Lassiter smiled and said, "Thank you, Henry. That was very thoughtful."*

It must be remembered that one can increase the likelihood of undesirable behavior as well as desirable behavior by positive reinforcement.

> *Jamie pulled at Mr. Owen's jacket, "Mr. Owen, let me have the ball." Mr. Owen ignored Jamie; Jamie continued to pull at his jacket. Mr. Owen said, "Oh all right, Jamie, you can have the ball, but stop pulling my jacket!"*

It also must be noted that sometimes teachers inadvertently *punish* desirable behavior rather than reward it.

> *"Teacher, I've finished all my math problems." "Fine. Here are ten more for you to do."*

Two conditions are required to make positive reinforcement work:

1. Make the positive event come *after* the desired behavior.
2. Be sure the consequence is favorable (Mager, 1972).

Another way to increase the likelihood of a behavior recurring is to follow the behavior by taking away an unpleasant event. This is called *negative reinforcement*.

> *Tom was very annoyed by Cindy, who chattered constantly. When he did not do his work, Cindy was instructed to sit next to Tom. When Tom was working well, Cindy was moved to the other side of the room.*

In many cases, a desired behavior must be broken into small steps. This is done for two reasons: first, the student may not be able to perform the entire behavior and therefore cannot be reinforced for it; second, teaching a task through a series of small steps minimizes the number of errors made by the student. In behavior management there are several techniques for breaking tasks into small steps.

Shaping

Shaping is the process of reinforcing a student for closer approximations to the desired response. The first step is to state the desired (or target) response. The first response (approximation) that occurs which roughly resembles the target behavior should be reinforced. When the student has been reinforced for this response repeatedly, a closer approximation is required before reinforcement occurs again.

> *"Susan, sit on the chair." The first approximation is for Susan to look in the direction of the chair. She is reinforced. When Susan has been reinforced for this response several times and is looking at the chair often, more is required. The next approximation is for her to take a step toward the chair in order to be reinforced. The sequencing of events continues until sitting in the chair is all that is reinforced.*

It is important to raise the standards for reinforcement so the student will go on to the next step. However, standards should not be raised so rapidly that the student cannot receive reinforcement.

Chaining

For most learning tasks, one response does not complete the criteria for learning the entire behavior. Chaining techniques are used to teach behaviors that occur in a sequence. The complex behavior is broken into simple components to be learned one at a time and chained together to obtain the complete behavior. The distinguishing characteristic of chaining is that reinforcement is delivered after the last step. Frequently referred to as *backward chaining*, this technique requires completion of the task before reinforcement; it is a powerful teaching device.

> *A picture puzzle is assembled except for the last piece, which is placed adjacent to its proper place. Only a small effort is required for the student to complete the task and see the final product. Reinforcement is delivered for finishing the task. Later, two pieces are omitted from the puzzle and reinforcement is delivered for completion. Finally, the child completes the entire task and is reinforced.*

There are several conditions to chaining. First, the student must know how to perform each unit; second, the student must perform each unit in the proper sequence; third, the units must be performed in rapid succession to be sure they are linked together; fourth, the chain must be repeated until the learning has taken place; fifth, reinforcement must be present in the learning of chains and the reinforcement must be immediate.

To set up a chain of events, the teacher must acquire the skills of task analysis, pertinent to any target behavior. Task analysis is defined and described in chapter 7.

Fading

In using fading, the stimuli are varied or reduced until a response made in one situation is made in another. Changes are made in the condition under which the behavior occurs rather than in the nature of the task itself. An example cited by Thompson and Grabowski (1972) is teaching children to color inside a heavy raised outline (cardboard template or yarn); later the height of the outline is reduced and still later replaced by a heavy drawn outline. Ultimately, the outline is the usual printed one. A similar technique is illustrated in Figure 12.2 in teaching a student to print his name. Fading can be effectively used to teach skills and improve performance in several academic areas, such as arithmetic and reading (Sulzer-Azaroff & Mayer, 1986).

Decreasing Behavior

Behavior is weakened or suppressed by punishment or extinction. When a behavior is followed by punishment, the likelihood of the behavior's recurring decreases. The use of an aversive event (such as a verbal reprimand or detention) is the form generally used. A second type of punishment (response cost) is used when positive reinforcement is withdrawn. A third type of punishment (time out) involves isolating the student from reinforcement for a stated time.

To be effective, punishment must be intense and must last long enough to be viewed as aversive, and it must be administered every time

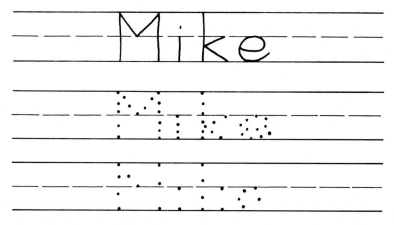

FIGURE 12.2 Example of Fading

and immediately following the undesirable behavior (Blackham & Silberman, 1975).

The effects of punishment are less predictable than those of reinforcement. Some undesirable side effects can include avoidance of the punisher; modeling aggression; and increase of fear, withdrawal, and tenseness.

Blackham and Silberman (1975) present guidelines to avoid such side effects from punishment:

> Use punishment infrequently and never as the only method for controlling or eliminating undesirable behavior.
>
> Specify clearly the acceptable and unacceptable behavior and the consequences for each. When a child is punished, he or she should know the reasons for the punishment.
>
> Punish the undesirable behavior as soon as it appears; do not wait until the behavior has run its course.
>
> Provide desirable behavioral alternatives for the child.
>
> While punishing the undesirable behavior, reinforce the behavior you wish to promote.
>
> Be consistent in punishing behavior you wish to eliminate. Inconsistent punishment may make the undesirable behavior more durable (p. 71).

A second way to reduce the likelihood of a behavior's occurring is *extinction*. Because behavior is maintained by positive or negative reinforcements, withdrawal of the reinforcement weakens the behavior.

> *Jamie pulled on Mr. Owen's jacket, "Mr. Owen, let me have the ball." Mr. Owen ignored the pulling. Jamie continued to pull his jacket, but when she didn't get the ball, she stopped.*

Ignored behavior usually increases at first; this is part of the extinction process. Many teachers do not allow the behavior to continue long enough; it is difficult to do. However, it does help eliminate nonproductive and disruptive responses because these behaviors are often attention-getters.

Certain potentially dangerous behaviors cannot be ignored. Physical attacks, horseplay with scissors, and self-injurious behavior cannot always be handled by removal of reinforcement. In such cases, various forms of punishment should be considered. The choice of aversives may progress from those for students functioning at very low levels to those that apply to mature persons: spanking in some districts; withdrawal of love, affection, or approval; denial of privileges or removal from a rewarding setting; scolding or social disapproval; and self-disappointment. The punishment should be selected in terms of the functional maturity of students and should be perceived by them as aversive. When punishment is used, it is important to use it consciously and systematically.

BASIC PROCEDURES

Observing and Recording

Once the principles of behavior are understood, there are basic procedures to follow to insure maximum success from the method. The first procedure is to *define and describe operationally the behavior to be changed.* As discussed earlier in the chapter, behavior should be defined in observable terms. The test for observable behavior is: Can other persons (who agree on the definition of the behavior) see the same behavior at the same time? Do they all agree as to when the behavior did or did not occur? Do they agree on how many times it occurred and the force or intensity with which it occurred? If such agreement can be reached, the behavior is observable.

When the behavior has been pinpointed, a target must be set in observable terms. Thus, the goal "to decrease John's aggressiveness" would be inappropriate. The target "to decrease John's kicking" would be observable, countable, and therefore subject to change. In addition to the previous questions, a very simple test of observable behavior is: Can you count it?

When the target behavior has been identified and stated in operational terms, the teacher should *observe and record* that behavior. Sometimes viewed as a chore and a time-consuming effort, this process is a timesaver and an essential element in successful behavior management strategies. Many trial-and-error methods that have been used traditionally in the classroom are not discarded because there is no proof that they do or do not work. If good records are maintained, the teacher can easily keep or reject a particular intervention, depending on the recorded results. Another important advantage is that such records are reinforcing to the teacher, to the parent, and to the student.

In observing and charting behavior, the teacher often realizes that the behavior does not occur at the originally perceived frequency. On consideration, the behavior may be seen as annoying to the teacher only and not of sufficient frequency or duration to need altering.

There are two types of observation of concern in the classroom. The *frequency count* is a measurement of the number of times a behavior occurs. A frequency count could be taken of the number of times Ann cries during a stated observation period. The *time interval* observation is a measurement of the length of time a behavior is exhibited. The length of time Ann cries may be more pertinent than the number of times she cries.

An accurate measurement of behavior before intervention is referred to as the *baseline*. Because the purpose is to record an average of the behavior, the recording can be done for a short length of time each day over a 5-day period. It is desirable that the behavior be recorded in the setting in which change is desired. Data obtained during the baseline period are usually plotted on a graph (see Figure 12.3). The line and bar graphs are most frequently used. The horizontal axis in both graphs usually identifies the time period, and the vertical axis denotes the criteria used to evaluate intervention effects.

Frequency can be counted by recording a mark on a sheet of paper each time the behavior occurs (see Figure 12.4) or by using a mechanical counter or stopwatch. One effective method called *time sampling* involves setting a timer to correspond with target intervals indicated on the chart. When the timer bell rings, the teacher glances at the student and identifies what he or she is doing at that instant. After recording the behavior, the teacher immediately resets the timer and proceeds with instruction.

Teachers who feel they cannot manage recording while teaching can use other methods. If paraprofessionals, volunteer aides, or parents are available, they can be classroom recorders. Students themselves can record certain behaviors. Moving the recording task from the teacher to the students in sequenced steps increases the students' potential for self-direction. For example, if the teacher is recording class behaviors, such as

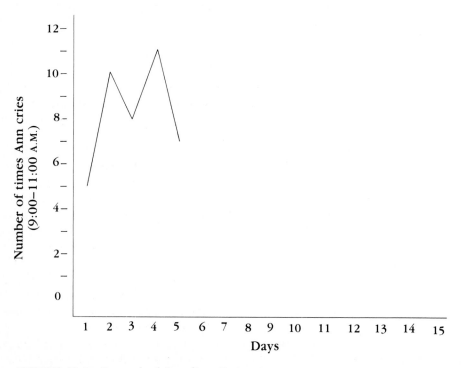

FIGURE 12.3 Record of Baseline Data

Number of times Ann cries
(9:00–11:00 A.M.)

Day	1	2	3	4	5	Weekly Total	Average
	‖‖‖ ‖‖‖	‖‖‖ ‖‖‖	‖‖‖ ‖‖‖	‖‖‖ ‖‖‖ ‖	‖‖‖ ‖‖	41	8.2
	6	7	8	9	10		
	‖‖‖ ‖‖‖	‖‖‖ ‖‖‖ ‖‖	‖‖‖ ‖‖‖	‖‖‖ ‖‖‖	‖‖‖‖	46	9.2
	11	12	13	14	15		
	‖‖‖‖	‖‖		‖		7	1.4

FIGURE 12.4 Form of Recording Frequency

in seat on time, on a daily chart, students can assume this responsibility. Individual behaviors can be recorded on a piece of masking tape on each child's desk. After observing the teacher's method, students can record their own behavior (Sarason, Glaser, & Fargo, 1972). Heady and Niewoehner (1979) describe a system of self-charting in which a student recorded on a piece of paper taped to her desk the number of times she interrupted during a target period. One positive outcome of self-recording is that it frequently decreases the student's disruptive behavior (Heward, 1979; Kerr, Nelson, & Lambert, 1987). This decrease is probably attributable to the fact that the student becomes more aware of the problem behavior.

Recording is continued after the intervention is introduced (see Figure 12.5) to determine the effectiveness of the plan. Although day-to-day fluctuations will occur, a well-planned program usually produces the desired effects. If the teacher is uncertain about what produced the desired effect, or suspects that other variables have contributed, the intervention can be stopped and the recording continued. The results will indicate whether or not the intervention is effective. However, most teachers are reluctant to withdraw a plan that is working!

Recording behavior change is useful even if the particular intervention does not appear to be effective. For example, Bill is sent from the room every time he kicks a classmate. The kicking behavior is recorded and does not decrease with the intervention. Rather than being discouraged, the teacher may discard this intervention and seek another one. At the least, one technique has been tried and proved ineffective. This is certainly more productive than continuing a poor strategy.

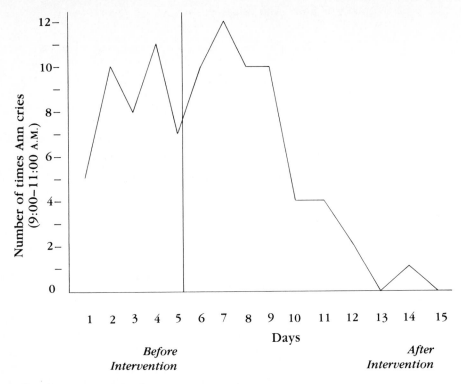

FIGURE 12.5 Record of Intervention Effect

Once the baseline data have been charted, the teacher can decide whether or not to proceed with an intervention. The successful arrangement of consequences requires specific attention to behaviors and how they are affected by reinforcement. Arranging consequences requires the teacher to decide which reinforcers to use, how much reinforcement is necessary, and the schedule of reinforcement to employ.

Reinforcers

Because reinforcement is contingent on the student's response, it can be used to increase appropriate behavior or to decrease inappropriate behavior. The *selection of the reinforcer* demands sensitivity from the teacher. Care must be exercised that the chosen event is rewarding to the student.

Tommy made an outstanding score on his achievement tests. As a reward, the teacher suggested that he go home an hour early. Tommy walked home, miserable and lonely, and waited for his friends to join him.

Because a reinforcer is defined by its effect on behavior, it is a highly individual event; it is the teacher's task to find reinforcing events for specific students. This can be done by observing what the student does with free time, asking what the student would work for, or systematically arranging a consequence and observing its effect on the student's behavior (Wallace & Kauffman, 1973).

Neisworth and Smith (1973) present a hierarchy of reinforcer categories:

1. Self-generated reinforcers (satisfaction with a job well done, etc.)
2. Self-management of tangible reinforcers (allowing yourself to watch television only after you've completed an unpleasant chore)
3. Social approval, attention
4. Management of tangible reinforcers (tokens, trinkets, food, water) by others (p. 87).

It is suggested that one should use reinforcers as high in the hierarchy as possible and revert to basic reinforcers only if the higher ones are unsuccessful.

Interventions

The final step in the behavior management process is *to choose and implement a particular strategy*. The choice will depend on the behavioral level of the students, the resources available, and the preference of the teachers. There are advantages and disadvantages to each system presented. The teacher is encouraged to experiment with each and to discover techniques appropriate for particular situations and students. Reinforcement systems used in schools can be classified as primary, social, modeling, token, and contingency management.

Primary Reinforcement

Primary (tangible) reinforcers are particularly effective with students who exhibit immature or bizarre behavior. When paired with praise and approval, they can be starting points toward nontangible reinforcers. Most students respond to edibles, such as cookies, popcorn, or nutritional snacks.

Although the use of primary reinforcement is usually considered most appropriate for younger children, older students sometimes need to begin a reinforcement program at this level. Additionally, primary reinforcement can be used as an occasional treat for students at middle and secondary levels. An eleventh-grade teacher described how she used food as a reinforcer.

The students in my study hall were always quiet and well behaved. The rules I set for them were always followed. I routinely used praise as a reinforcement technique. One day I brought them each a cupcake and told them how much I appreciated their cooperation. They appreciated the special reward of cupcakes.

There are several precautions to take when using primary reinforcers. The reinforcers need to be changed frequently so the student does not become satiated and therefore not reinforced. The strength of edible reinforcers may be increased if used prior to meal time. Special consideration must be given to the choice of edibles. Diet colas, crackers, raisins, or cereal can be used instead of the usual cookies and candy.

The cost of primary reinforcers must be taken into consideration. Some schools allow instructional material funds to be used for purchasing reinforcers; some reinforcers can be obtained from the school cafeteria. A team of fourth-grade teachers devised an ingenious method. Rather than asking several parents to furnish refreshments for a school party, they asked every student to bring something. The leftover cookies, potato chips, and candy were put into canisters to be used for primary reinforcers. Again, health concerns should be considered when using food. Many teachers purchase reinforcers out of personal funds. Because this can be expensive, teachers are advised to use the resources available to them.

Because reinforcement systems are chosen to suit the students, there may be just a few children who receive edible reinforcers. It is important for the class members to understand that rewards may differ. This difference will not present a problem if each student knows that appropriate behavior will be rewarded in some way.

Social Reinforcement
Social interaction or attention is another powerful reinforcer. The strength of social reinforcement is demonstrated in a study reported by Dmitriev and Hawkins (1974). A child had refused to speak for 2 years and had been placed in a remedial class. After many trial-and-error patterns of treatment, a behavior management specialist suggested that teacher attention be withdrawn. The child was prompted to speak selected words and when she did not speak, all teacher attention was withdrawn. Within 22 days of this treatment, the child was speaking more than 400 words a day and was reinstated in a regular classroom. She had been receiving teacher attention (social reinforcement) for *not* speaking.

Approval from the teacher and from peers promotes desirable behavior in most students. Smiles, pats, and verbal approval have worked well for teachers for many years. Easy to administer, inexpensive, and adaptable to any age group, social reinforcers are ideal. However, depending on the teacher's interaction with the student, the student's previous experience with teachers, and the severity of the student's behavior problem, social reinforcement may not be totally effective. In this event, it can be paired with a primary or token reinforcer. As appropriate behavior increases, the tangible reinforcer can be faded out. One teacher, who wished to establish good behavior in his classroom, gave a Cheerio (cereal) for attention, academic performance, and so on. Inappropriate behavior was ignored. With the cereal, he always said something like "I like a good worker." He later discontinued the cereal, relying on the praise as a social reinforcement.

A classic study of the effects of teachers' behavior on students' behavior (Thomas, Becker, & Armstrong, 1968) indicates that teachers who use approval for good behavior will find that frequency and duration of appropriate behavior will increase. It further suggests that teachers who try pleasantly to get students to stop inappropriate behavior and who talk to them in an attempt to get them to understand what they're doing wrong will find an increase in inappropriate behavior. The authors conclude that "unless an effort is made to support desirable classroom behaviors with appropriate consequences, the children's behavior will be controlled by others in ways likely to interfere with the teacher's objectives" (p. 45).

The rule that seems to work is to give praise and attention to behaviors that facilitate learning. Tell the students what they did to deserve the praise. Try to reinforce behaviors incompatible with those you wish to decrease. Inappropriate behavior may be strengthened by paying attention to it even though you think you are punishing (Madsen, Becker, & Thomas, 1968).

Modeling
Modeling refers to implementing systematic strategies to teach students to imitate appropriate peer behaviors. Many proponents of mainstreaming suggest that a major benefit of such placements is that handicapped students will emulate the behavior of their nonhandicapped classmates. Such emulation does not automatically occur (Gresham, 1981); however, teachers can structure opportunities for students having problems to recognize precisely the more appropriate behavior of their classmates.

A veteran teacher, convinced of the power of modeling, described techniques she uses:

> *When I see William not holding his pencil correctly, I praise Virginia for what a good job she is doing and ask her to show us how she is doing it. William is not feeling bad because he was not correct; he has learned what is correct and will try hard to do what Virginia is doing. When I want the group's attention, I announce that table three really wants to learn about (anything) and is ready to listen. Other students then have an example of the behavior I expect from them.*

For modeling to be effective, students must attend to the appropriate behavior of peers, retain the information they learned, practice the behavior on their own, and receive some incentive for their efforts (Bandura,

1977). In providing incentives to students, teachers can use social reinforcement or tokens (discussed in the next section).

Peer tutoring and cooperative learning activities described in chapter 7 are excellent formats for using modeling as an intervention strategy. An important consideration for teachers is to choose carefully the tutors and group members who will provide positive examples of behavior based on the particular needs of a handicapped student.

Token Economy

The token system of reinforcement is usually implemented in classrooms when social reinforcers such as praise have been ineffective in controlling a student's behavior. Skinner (1953) defines the *token* as a generalized reinforcer distinguished by its physical specifications. He cites money as the most common example, because it can be exchanged for primary reinforcers of great variety. This system involves the presentation of a token (checkmark, poker chip, star, school money, points) following specified behaviors. When students have accumulated a sufficient number of tokens, they can exchange them for back-up reinforcers, such as nutritional snack food, toys, school supplies, or desirable activities.

The tokens initially function as neutral stimuli, acquiring reinforcing properties by being exchangeable for back-up reinforcers. Teacher praise and approval will increase in effectiveness as reinforcers when paired with the tokens. A general goal of token systems is to transfer control of responding from the token systems to other conditioned reinforcers, such as teacher praise and grades (Kuypers, Becker, & O'Leary, 1968).

Token systems have been used effectively with handicapped students in many situations. Their success has been demonstrated with students who are retarded (Birnbrauer, Wolf, Kidder, & Tague, 1965), with students who are emotionally disturbed (Hewett, 1967), with students who have cerebral palsy (Stone, 1970), with students who are learning disabled (McKenzie, Clark, Wolf, Kothera, & Benson, 1968), and with nonhandicapped students (O'Leary & Drabman, 1971). Token economies have been used in a variety of settings, including special education classrooms (Broden, Hall, Dunlap, & Clark, 1970), regular classrooms (McLaughlin & Malaby, 1972), and the school cafeteria (Muller, Hasazi, Pierce, & Hasazi, 1975).

The system is highly individualized. It also overcomes many of the objections to a primary reinforcement system, such as one student's asking, "How come Johnny gets a treat for sitting still and I don't?" Tokens can be made available to all class members and can be earned by achieving individual goals.

Several organizational patterns to token economies have been suggested. Hewett (1967) refers to his highly structured situation as an engineered classroom, in which the emphasis is on alerting students to the work efficiency orientation of the classroom. As students enter the class in the morning, they pick up a work record card ruled into squares. As they move through the day, the teacher and aide recognize their accomplishments by checking off squares on each student's card. The students save their completed work cards and exchange them weekly for snacks, small toys, or trinkets. An exchange board in the room displays tangible rewards available for one, two, or three cards filled with checkmarks. The philosophy of the program says to students, "We want you to succeed at all costs. If you will meet us half way and function reasonably well as a student, we will give you tasks you can do, need to do, and will enjoy doing, and we will reward you generously for your efforts" (p. 466).

Another token system uses a point system (O'Leary & Becker, 1967). On the first day of the token period, instructions are written on the chalkboard: In Seat, Face Front, Raise Hand, Working, Pay Attention, Desk Clear. The procedure is explained to the students; the tokens are ratings placed in booklets on each desk. Ratings from 1 to 10 are given, reflecting the extent to which the students follow instructions. The points can be exchanged for back-up reinforcers. The frequency with which ratings are given is gradually decreased, and the number of points required to obtain a prize is gradually increased. Group points are also given for total class behavior, to be exchanged for popsicles at the end of the week. Because teacher time may be a factor, it is interesting to note that in this particular program the ratings took only 3 minutes.

In a program for students who were orthopedically handicapped and who exhibited deviant behavior, the class day was divided into five learning periods. A behavior chart was supplied for each period. At the end of each period, the students were given 1 penny if they had carried out all the behaviors and lessons on the chart. At the end of class, the students who had earned 5 pennies could buy a toy from the teacher (Stone, 1970).

One of the greatest advantages of the token system is that tokens can be dispensed immediately following the desired behavior, providing an ideal situation for building new behaviors. They can be dispensed by the teacher or the aide, and should be accompanied by a comment such as "Good work, Sue!"

To help the student learn to delay reinforcement and thus deal with society's reward systems, the time for exchange of tokens is gradually extended. In the beginning, tokens can be exchanged at the end of each day; later, at the end of each week. The exchange period is reinforcing in itself and may follow a less desired activity. Tokens should be easy to dispense, easy to carry to the area of exchange, and their value should be understood by all the students. They can be given for approximations of the desired behavior and for progress in any specified activity.

An efficient token system should gradually withdraw material reinforcers (e.g., snacks, toys) and rely on reinforcing activities. If this is the goal, the teacher should consider advancing to a contingency management program.

Contingency Management

The term *contingent* implies a relationship between what one does and what happens afterward. Salaries are contingent on job performance; teaching positions are contingent on certification. The contingencies of our environment control our behavior. Therefore, a teacher can control (change) a student's behavior by arranging contingencies (Haring & Phillips, 1972). A contractual agreement between the teacher and the student, contingency management helps the student assume responsibility for motivating personal behavior and facilitates the shift from external control to self-management (Homme, Csanyi, Gonzales, & Rechs, 1970).

> *In a preschool class for youngsters with mental retardation, a little girl was observed to go to her teacher for a task (a lacing board), go to her desk and complete the task, return the board to her teacher, and go to the sand table to play.*

Contingency management is based on the Premack Principle (Premack, 1959), which states that a low-probability behavior (such as working math problems) can be increased in frequency when its performance is followed by the opportunity to engage in a high-probability behavior (such as listening to a favorite record). This system, like the token system, is particularly suitable for use with handicapped students in a regular classroom, since it can be individualized. It has been used successfully with handicapped as well as with nonhandicapped students.

Langstaff and Volkmor (1975) outline the procedures in planning a contingency management program:

Setting up a reinforcement (RE) menu. A list of reward activities (high-probability behaviors) from which students may choose. RE activities are available to the student only upon completion of a specified task (low-probability behavior) [see Figure 12.6].

Arranging the classroom. In the beginning, it is helpful to divide the room into two areas—a task area where students can work quietly and an RE area where they may spend their free time [see Figure 12.1]. Arrangements may be flexible to accommodate a self-contained classroom, a resource room, or an open situation.

Scheduling task and RE time. At first, the schedule should be designed so that all students start tasks at the same time, finishing within 2 to 3 minutes of each other. When the child finishes, he signals for the teacher to come and check his work and he is immediately excused to the RE area. The RE time should be kept to 5- to 8-minute periods.

A desk signal [such as raising a hand] is used by the student to indicate task completion. A teacher signal [such as ringing a hand-held bell or rapping a small wooden gavel] is used to call the students back to the task area from the RE area.

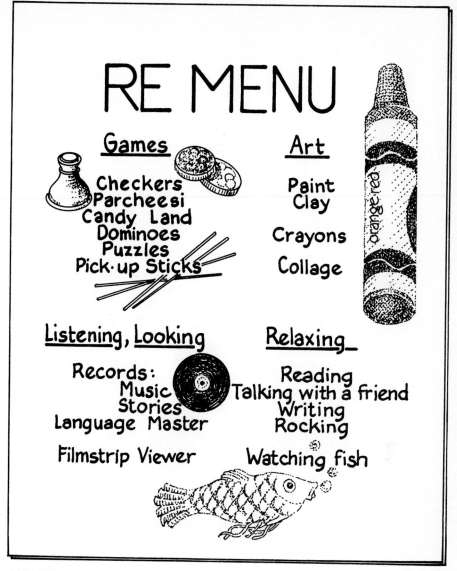

FIGURE 12.6 RE Menu

Preparing tasks for students. Initial tasks should be slightly below competency level to insure success when the program begins. Directions should be clear; task cards or individual folders should be presented. Students should be observed as they work and helped if they are confused. Group work may be conducted while individual students are working on assignments.

Explaining the system to the students. A chart may be posted explaining the system:

Do some work . . .
Have some free time . . .
Do some more work . . .
Have some more free time . . .
Work is whatever is assigned,
Free time is whatever you want to do

IF

1. Your work is finished correctly.
2. You respect the right of others.
3. You remember safety rules.
4. You remember school rules. (Langstaff & Volkmor, 1975, p. 63)

One teacher evaluated her program in a resource room for students with learning disabilities:

My recent experience with contingency management had produced a much more effective and successful learning atmosphere. The implementation of the program involved a great deal of organization and preparation. I explained the program to the children and made it possible for them to offer suggestions in regard to their potential reinforcers.

The reward area consisted of an art center, listening center, game area, and relaxation area. It is crucial to remove activities which have little or no reinforcement value from the reward area.

The task area was structured to provide easy access for teacher-student interaction and emphasized individualized instruction. A horseshoe-type seating arrangement permitted me to sit in the center, easily accessible for each child.

The students became involved by having the opportunity to make a nonverbal sign that was used for signifying they were working, needed help, or had finished their assignment. A timer was used to indicate a return to the task area from the reward area, or to return to their regular classes.

An individual folder was prepared for each student to contain the work for that day. Folders were given to the students each day and assignments explained.

I was pleased with the results I saw; the children enjoyed the program and expressed a desire to continue with it.

Besides promoting desirable behavior, contingency management has other advantages. Because the RE items are not consumable, there is little expense involved. There is little opposition from parents or school critics because the reward is an activity. Most important, this system involves the student in the decision-making process and leads toward self-direction.

Teachers may suspect that behavior management techniques will not be effective with students who are gifted or perhaps that such students will not require decreasing or eliminating inappropriate behaviors and increasing appropriate behaviors. The fact is that all students will exhibit behaviors that teachers want to discourage and behaviors that teachers want to increase. The techniques discussed here are built on behavior principles and are effective with all individuals, including children and adults, handicapped and gifted, and those not labeled as handicapped or gifted.

Some changes in the use of behavior management techniques and the menu of reinforcers and the schedules of reinforcement may be required. For example, playing games is a powerful reinforcer for many children. The kind of games preferred by children varies. Children with mental handicaps will probably prefer games that are much more simple than those enjoyed by children who are the same chronological age but intellectually gifted. Children who are gifted may need external reinforcement such as praise less often than some children who are behaviorally disordered.

Many students are aware of being obviously manipulated and they dislike it. Students who are gifted may be more sensitive to perceived manipulation and thus may be more likely to object or rebel. Motivational techniques such as challenging activities and providing choices are likely to be more effective with students who are intellectually and academically gifted than are apparent attempts to force conformity to rules instituted for the sake of control. A teacher of gifted students explains:

> *My students constantly want to know why they can not do things in different ways. Students in the school were asked to participate in an essay contest on the value of a free enterprise system. Two of my students wanted to submit a video essay. I told them that it was a writing contest. They countered that they were doing more. They would write an essay within the number of words allowed and accompany with video. That isn't unusual. They don't like going places in single-file lines, which is a practice in our school. They say that if they don't disturb others that a line serves no purpose. In many cases, I agree with them.*

Toward Self-Management

It is hoped that the value of tokens, tangible items, and reinforcing events will give way to the satisfactions of succeeding in school and receiving recognition as a student from one's peers, teachers, and parents. Teachers are interested, therefore, in building study behavior. In order to do so, teachers must first teach students how to learn and how to behave appropriately in the classroom.

If students are to learn to manage their own behavior, they should be involved in changing it.

> *Tommy, who was considered incorrigible, was asked by his teacher to list things about himself that he would like to change. Without hesitation, he stated that he would like to "quit talking so much and learn to ignore troublemakers."*

Teachers can help students achieve this self-management goal by encouraging them to make behavioral choices systematically by:

1. considering all their alternatives for a given decision,
2. identifying consequences for each alternative,
3. considering how each alternative would make them feel,
4. choosing the most appropriate alternative, and
5. evaluating their choice after they have acted on their decision (Silverman, 1980).

Many students who respond to reinforcement systems with enthusiasm decide at a later time that they do not need them. This is the ultimate goal of behavior management: to help students realize that their actions produce consequences and that they, themselves, can change their actions and thus achieve goals that they set.

REFERENCES

Alberto, P. A., & Troutman, A. C. (1986). *Applied behavior analysis for teachers* (2nd ed.). Columbus, OH: Merrill.

Bandura, A. (1977). *Social learning theory.* Englewood Cliffs, NJ: Prentice-Hall.

Barnes, E., Eyman, P. D., & Engolz, M. D. (1974). *Teach and reach: An alternative guide to resources for the classroom.* Syracuse, NY: Human Policy Press.

Birnbrauer, J. S., Wolf, M. M., Kidder, J. D., & Tague, C. (1965). Classroom behavior of retarded pupils with token reinforcement. *Journal of Experimental Child Psychology, 2,* 219–235.

Blackham, G. J., & Silberman, A. (1975). *Modification of child and adolescent behavior.* Belmont, CA: Wadsworth.

Broden, M., Hall, R. B., Dunlap, A., & Clark, R. (1970). Effects of teacher attention and a token reinforcement system in a junior high special education class. *Exceptional Children, 36,* 341–349.

Dmitriev, V., & Hawkins, J. (1974). Susie never used to say a word. *Teaching Exceptional Children, 6,* 68–76.

Evertson, C. M., Emmer, E. T., Clements, B. S., Sanford, J. P., & Worsham, M. E. (1989). *Classroom management for elementary teachers* (2nd ed.). Englewood Cliffs, NJ: Prentice-Hall.

Glasser, W. (1969). *Schools without failure.* New York: Harper and Row.

Gresham, F. M. (1981). Social skills training with handicapped children: A review. *Review of Educational Research, 51,* (1), 139–176.

Hallenbeck, M., & Beernink, M. (1989). A support program for parents of students with mild handicaps. *Teaching Exceptional Children, 21,* (3), 44–47.

Haring, N. G., & Phillips, E. L. (1972). *Analysis and modification of classroom behavior.* Englewood Cliffs, NJ: Prentice-Hall.

Heady, J., & Niewoehner, M. (1979). Academic and behavior management techniques that work. *Teaching Exceptional Children, 12,* (1), 37–39.

Heward, W. L. (1979). Teaching students to control their own behavior: A critical skill. *Exceptional Teacher, 1,* (4), 3–5, 11.

Hewett, F. M. (1967). Educational engineering with emotionally disturbed children. *Exceptional Children, 33,* 459–467.

Homme, L., Csanyi, A. P., Gonzales, M. A., & Rechs, J. R. (1970). *How to use contingency contracting in the classroom.* Champaign, IL: Research Press.

Kerr, M. M., & Nelson, C. M. (1983). *Strategies for managing behavior problems in the classroom.* New York: Random House.

Kerr, M. M., Nelson, C. M., & Lambert, D. L. (1987). *Helping adolescents with learning and behavior problems.* Columbus, OH: Merrill.

Kuypers, D. S., Becker, W. C., & O'Leary, D. K. (1968). How to make a token system fail. *Exceptional Children, 35,* 101–109.

Langstaff, A. L., & Volkmor, C. B. (1975). *Contingency management.* Columbus, OH: Merrill.

MacMillan, D. L., & Forness, S. R. (1970). Behavior modification: Limitations and liabilities. *Exceptional Children, 37,* 291–297.

Madsen, C. H., Jr., Becker, W. C., & Thomas, D. R. (1968). Rules, praise, and ignoring: Elements of elementary classroom control. *Journal of Applied Behavior Analysis, 1,* 139–150.

Mager, R. F. (1972). *Who did what to whom?* Champaign, IL: Research Press.

McKenzie, H.S., Clark, M., Wolf, M. M., Kothera, R., & Benson, C. (1968). Behavior modification of children with learning disabilities using grades as tokens and allowances as back-up reinforcers. *Exceptional Children, 34,* 745–752.

McLaughlin, T. F., & Malaby, J. E. (1972). Intrinsic reinforcers in a classroom token economy. *Journal of Applied Behavior Analysis, 5,* 263–270.

Muller, A. J., Hasazi, S. E., Pierce, M. M., & Hasazi, J. E. (1975). Modification of disruptive behavior in a large group of elementary school students. In E. Ramp & G. Semb (Eds.), *Behavior analysis: Areas of research and application* (pp. 269–276). Englewood Cliffs, NJ: Prentice-Hall.

Neisworth, J. T., & Smith, R. M. (1973). *Modifying retarded behavior.* Boston: Houghton Mifflin.

O'Leary, D. K., & Becker, W. C. (1967). Behavior modification of an adjustment class: A token reinforcement program. *Exceptional Children, 33,* 637–642.

O'Leary, D. K., & Drabman, R. (1971). Token reinforcements programs in the classroom: A review. *Psychological Bulletin, 75,* (6), 379–398.

Premack, D. (1959). Toward empirical behavior laws: I. Positive reinforcement. *Psychological Review, 66,* 219–233.

Sabatino, D. A. (1987). Preventive discipline as a practice in special education. *Teaching Exceptional Children, 19,* (4), 8–11.

Sarason, I. G., Glaser, E. M., & Fargo, G. A. (1972). *Reinforcing productive classroom behavior.* New York: Behavioral Publications.

Schulz, J. B. (1987). *Parents and professionals in special education.* Boston: Allyn and Bacon.

Silverman, M. (1980). *How to handle problem behavior in school.* Lawrence, KS: H & H Enterprises.

Skinner, B. F. (1953). *Science and human behavior.* New York: Macmillan.

Stone, M. C. (1970). Behavior shaping in a classroom for children with cerebral palsy. *Exceptional Children, 36,* 674–677.

Sulzer-Azaroff, B., & Mayer, G. R. (1986). *Achieving educational excellence: Using behavioral strategies.* New York: Holt, Rinehart and Winston.

Thomas, D. R., Becker, W. C., & Armstrong, M. (1968). Production and elimination of disruptive classroom behavior by systematically varying teacher's behavior. *Journal of Applied Behavior Analysis, 1,* 35–15.

Thompson, T., & Grabowski, J. (Eds.). (1972). *Behavior modification of the mentally retarded.* New York: Oxford University Press.

Wallace, G., & Kauffman, J. M. (1973). *Teaching children with learning problems.* Columbus, OH: Merrill.

Zeeman, R., & Martucci, I. (1976). The application of classroom meetings to special education. *Exceptional Children, 42,* (8), 161–162.

13

Enhancing Social Integration

As defined in chapter 1, mainstreaming is the instruction *and* social integration of exceptional students in a regular education class. The primary emphasis in preceding chapters has been on instructional integration; this last chapter focuses on the equally important component of social integration.

Social integration refers to the teacher and peer interaction in the classroom. Such interaction has at least three components: affective, cognitive, and behavioral. The affective component of social integration focuses on feelings toward or perceptions of exceptional students. A perception that is essential for successful mainstreaming is the acceptance of and respect for human differences. The second component, characterized as cognitive, includes the knowledge and understanding that students have of individual differences, in general, and of handicapping conditions, in particular. Finally, the behavioral component focuses on students' actions—verbal, nonverbal, and physical—toward classroom peers. The affective, cognitive, and behavioral components interact to determine the degree to which social integration of handicapped and nonhandicapped students is actually achieved in mainstreamed classrooms and schools.

The Regular Education Initiative (REI) proposed by Will (1986), who was then assistant secretary for the Office of Special Education and Rehabilitative Services, U.S. Department of Education, may have led educators to think that social integration would naturally follow. The Regular Education Initiative is a proposal for classroom teachers and special educators to form a new partnership to share in the education of all children, including those with exceptionalities in an integrated environment. Instructional integration does not guarantee social integration, but it would certainly help foster it. The fact is, however, that there is no guarantee that REI will result in instructional integration because of the resistance encountered (Kauffman, Gerber, & Semmel, 1988). Social integration as defined here will require effort by educators and will result in a variety of benefits for both students and educators. If the REI helps achieve social integration, it will realize one of its major purposes.

There are many benefits to the achievement of social integration for handicapped and nonhandicapped students, as well as for teachers. All persons involved in mainstreaming have the opportunity to recognize and value the uniqueness of all people, to increase their knowledge about the body and its functioning, to expand their friendships, and to enhance their own self-confidence and self-esteem in learning to handle new situations with success. It is very important to be aware of the reciprocity of the beneficial outcomes of social integration. Nonhandicapped people have a great deal to gain from handicapped friends, just as handicapped individuals can learn from their nonhandicapped peers.

Just as the integration of handicapped students into the mainstream is essential, the social integration of students who are gifted is important and not to be taken for granted. There is little agreement about optimal educational managements for students who are gifted, and many educators and parents believe that such students need the company of gifted peers as much as possible. Surely, there is merit in interaction among students who are gifted. Likewise, the benefits of social integration of students who are gifted with other students in heterogeneous settings are the same in many ways as the benefits of socially integrating handicapped students. The strategies for integrating gifted students are also similar.

This chapter addresses the issue of social integration according to the following four dimensions:

1. need for social integration intervention,
2. teacher variables associated with social integration,
3. student variables associated with social integration, and
4. resource materials.

NEED FOR SOCIAL INTEGRATION INTERVENTION

A consistent theme in the literature is that handicapped students are frequently rejected and alienated in regular class settings. Most research on the degree of social integration has been conducted with mentally retarded and learning-disabled populations. The rejection of mentally retarded students by nonhandicapped classmates has been documented in a sizable number of studies (Bruininks, Rynders, & Gross, 1974; Goodman, Gottlieb, & Harrison, 1972; Gottlieb & Budoff, 1973; Gottlieb & Switzky, 1982; Iano, Ayers, Heller, McGettigan, & Walker, 1974; Reese-Dukes & Stokes, 1978; Sandberg, 1982). In synthesizing the findings from a number of these studies, Gottlieb (1975) and Gresham (1984) concluded that mildly retarded students are accepted less frequently and reacted to more negatively than are their nonhandicapped peers.

Similar trends of rejection have also been documented with the learning-disabled population. From a series of studies on sociometric status and social behavior, Bryan (1978) reported that a substantial number of learning-disabled students have a difficult time establishing friendships with peers. Specific findings indicated that as compared to nonhandicapped peers, learning-disabled children received significantly fewer votes on social attraction, were less accurate in comprehending nonverbal communication, and made significantly more competitive statements. A related finding was that teachers, as well as peers, make negative evaluations of these children. These findings have been corroborated in other studies (Bruininks, 1978; Chapman, 1988; Gresham, 1984; Pearl, Bryan, & Donahue, 1983; Pearl & Cosden, 1982).

Social integration problems have also been identified in children with other types of handicaps. Force (1956) reported that elementary students preferred nonhandicapped class members over physically handicapped ones for friends, playmates, and workmates. Similar findings regarding physically handicapped students have been reported (Farina, Sherman, & Allen, 1968; Kleck, 1968; Thompson, 1982). Emotionally handicapped students have also been reported to be more socially isolated and to have lower self-concepts than nonhandicapped classmates (Gaylord-Ross & Haring, 1987; Nelson, 1988; Vacc, 1972), as have deaf and hearing-impaired students (Antia, 1985; Craig, 1965; Wilson, 1971).

The age at which nonhandicapped students are aware of differences associated with handicaps is an important consideration in documenting the need for intervention. Research has shown that young children, including preschoolers, are aware of handicapping conditions and favor nonhandicapped peers (Brown, Ragland, & Bishop, 1989; Jenkins, Speltz, & Odom, 1985; Levy & Gottlieb, 1984; Peterson & Haralick, 1977; Richardson, 1970). Thus, it appears that rejecting attitudes on the part of nonhandicapped children develop early, and that these attitudes tend to be consistently predisposed across handicapping conditions.

A major void of information exists on the social acceptance of handicapped students by similarly handicapped students and by those with different types of handicaps. It can be speculated, however, that handicapped children and youth are likely to have stronger preferences for interacting with some individuals and not others. To the extent that they might reject peers with some types of handicaps, the need for social integration is just as important for them as it is for nonhandicapped classmates.

Another reason for such intervention with handicapped children and youth is that frequently they need assistance in understanding the nature of their own handicap and in developing an acceptance and respect for their individuality, including the strengths and weaknesses associated with their handicap. This need is poignantly expressed by Bill Hartford, who has a stuttering handicap:

> *There is a certain self we present to people, and we use the words beautiful and ugly to describe the self. Stuttering is an aberration of the self, an aberration of vocal expression. Stuttering is ugly and I have always thought myself ugly. One of the things that was ugly about me was stuttering. I was ugly, period.*
>
> *Because this most expressive part of me—the vocal musculature—is not reliable, I can't depend on it. It is likely to fail me. My whole body image goes to hell with that. It's affected the way I look at myself. From body image to whole self-concept, and it starts with the fact that this most important and expressive part of my body, my speech, is unreliable.*
>
> *I was the only one in my grammar school who stuttered, until the eighth grade, when another person came in who stuttered. She was a beautiful girl. It sounds juvenile, but I learned that I really couldn't blame stuttering for my ugliness any more. I knew that this girl stuttered, and that she was a beautiful girl.*
>
> *I was kind of a shy kid and I didn't talk to girls often. I certainly would never talk to*

this girl about her speech. That is common among us stutterers; we never talk about our stuttering even to another stutterer. I've changed a lot since then—I now talk about my stuttering with anyone.[1]

This statement reflects a major need to assist handicapped students in developing an understanding of their handicap and a positive self-image.

In summary, it is obvious that positive social integration of non-handicapped and handicapped children and youth is unlikely to occur spontaneously in mainstreamed classrooms. Social integration, similar to academic areas of the curriculum, warrants a systematic approach to inter-vention. The encouraging aspect of such intervention is that it has been quite successful in ameliorating patterns of rejection and alienation.

It is difficult to isolate and identify the precise reasons for the occur-rence of social integration problems. A complex set of variables interact leading to negative attitudes. These variables can be classified into two major groups: teacher and student variables. A description of variables and intervention strategies for each of these groups follows.

TEACHER VARIABLES

Teacher variables that can influence the degree of social integration include teachers' attitudes toward handicapped students and their level of compe-tency in teaching handicapped students.

Teacher Attitude

It has been documented repeatedly that teachers' views of students are a strong force in determining the nature of the interaction between teachers and students and, in turn, the students' achievement (Brophy & Good, 1974; Good, 1970; Purkey, 1970; Rosenthal & Jacobson, 1968). Teachers constantly communicate important attitudinal messages to students about individual differences. It becomes obvious to all students whether teachers favor high-achieving students; feel respect, pity, or disgust for students who have special problems; believe that every person has inherent value; or are prejudiced against those who are different. Teachers generally are much more transparent than they care to believe.

Based on a comprehensive literature review of teacher attitudes to-ward handicapped students, Clark (1980) concluded that teachers typically

[1]From *Voices: Interviews with Handicapped People* (p. 27) by M. D. Orlansky and W. L. Heward, 1981. Columbus, OH: Charles E. Merrill Publishing Co. Copyright 1980 by Charles E. Merrill Publishing Co. Used by permission.

are uncomfortable with handicapped students and have negative attitudes about their placement in regular classes. This attitude is still evident despite the emphasis on mainstreaming since the mid-1970s and the Regular Education Initiative (REI) supported by the Office of Special Educational and Rehabilitative Services (Will, 1986; Idol-Maestas & Ritter, 1985; Margolis & McGettigan, 1988; Munson, 1987).

Furthermore, teacher attitudes have been identified as being crucial to the success of any mainstreaming program (Alexander & Strain, 1978; MacMillan, Jones, & Meyers, 1976; Madden & Slavin, 1983). Teacher attitudes not only set the tone for the relationship between teachers and handicapped students, but they also substantially influence the attitudes of nonhandicapped classmates.

> *Kate, a third grader, has been classified as educable mentally retarded on the basis of formal diagnostic tests. Kate goes to the resource room for 1½ hours every day. Her classroom teacher tends to exclude her from almost all activities on the basis that "no child with her limited development can effectively participate in the regular classroom." When other students in the class fail to achieve according to the teacher's expectations, the threat voiced by the teacher is, "If you cannot do your assignments, you will have to go with Kate to work with the other EMR's in the resource room." Both Kate and her peers get the message.*

Although this is an extreme example, it is a true story. A teacher's views and behavior can be extremely influential in defining respect for differences within the classroom.

When considering attitudes toward handicapped students, the most basic question teachers should ask themselves is: Does less able mean less worthy? Teachers might analyze their response to this question by documenting whether they genuinely believe that handicapped students should be entitled to consideration for placement in a regular class and whether they deserve the same rights, privileges, and responsibilities as their nonhandicapped peers. If teachers can honestly affirm that less able does not mean less worthy, they must make a commitment to implement the intervention strategies that will be subsequently discussed. Additionally, teachers should check themselves constantly, because people sometimes tend to avoid handicapped persons without realizing it. If students who stutter take longer to say something, teachers may avoid the fact that they want to communicate rather than allow them to stammer throughout their response. Similar situations occur with students representing the range of handicapping conditions. It often requires more time and effort for the teacher to make curriculum adaptations and to arrange situations that promote social integration for handicapped students who need this help than for students who are automatically accepted by their peers. If teachers believe that handicapped students are just as worthy as other students, the extra investment of time and effort does not create negative barriers between teachers and handicapped students.

Furthermore, the attitudes of other school personnel are critical. Many students look to other people in the school for cues about how to act. If these people demonstrate negative or even neutral attitudes by their lack of positive, natural interactions with handicapped persons, they influence teachers and nonhandicapped students. Although the focus here is on teacher attitudes and in the next section on student attitudes, one must be cognizant of the influence of other people. In a study of superintendents' attitudes toward integration of handicapped students in one state, researchers discovered an overall positive disposition toward integration. However, approximately 15 percent of the principals held negative attitudes and 34 percent were uncertain (Stainback, Stainback, & Stainback, 1988). These results underscore the need to consider attitudes toward the integration of handicapped students in a broad context.

Many teachers and other adults may believe that less able does mean less worthy. This does not mean that these people are cold and insensitive and have no place in the education profession. It may mean that they have had extremely limited contact with handicapped persons, probably because separate classes, schools, and residential centers for handicapped students were favored in the past over educational settings that bring together handicapped and nonhandicapped persons. Given this lack of exposure, many people tend to imagine more differences than really exist. Sometimes, negative stereotypes based on imaginations or myths can cloud a person's perception of other human beings. This is an understandable phenomenon, but it does not have to become a lifelong attitude. People's attitudes toward handicapped individuals can be changed through accurate information and positive encounters (Johnson & Johnson, 1984; Stainback & Stainback, 1982; Stainback, Stainback, Courtnage, & Jaben, 1985).

Theresa had just graduated from college and was considering the possibility of entering graduate school in the field of education. Her roommate, who was a member of the local Association for Retarded Citizens (ARC), convinced Theresa to come along on an ARC recreational function that involved taking approximately 45 handicapped children (mentally retarded, severely emotionally disturbed, and multiply handicapped) on a hayride and picnic. Theresa was hesitant about going along for several reasons. Although she had never been around handicapped persons to any significant degree, she had the idea that it might be dangerous to be with them. She wondered if they would bite her, make inappropriate sexual advances, or start a fire in the hay. On the one hand, Theresa told herself that she was being ridiculous, but on the other hand, she had strong reservations. Theresa's roommate insisted that she come along, and Theresa hesitantly decided to go. As the trucks were loaded with children, Theresa began to relax a little as she began to join in with the children's singing. She looked closely at the children. Some were attractive, and some were unattractive. Some were talkative, and some were shy. There seemed to be a great variety of shapes, colors, sizes, and personalities. When they arrived in the country at the setting for the picnic, the children started running through the meadows, playing games, eating hotdogs, laughing, fighting, joking, and generally doing the things that children do. Toward the end of the picnic, Theresa wandered over to her roommate and whispered, "Where are the handicapped children?" Not understanding Theresa's question, the roommate gave her a puzzled look. Theresa repeated, "Where are the handicapped children? These are just children."

The fact that teachers have had limited opportunities to develop positive attitudes toward handicapped persons does not mean that they cannot begin to develop them.

An important strategy for teachers is to get to know handicapped people as *people*. The fear of the unknown can be overcome by finding out handicapped persons' likes and dislikes, strengths and weaknesses, hobbies, interests, and future plans. Sometimes teachers only get to know handicapped children and youth as students. They know a student's level of performance, particular disability, curriculum needs, and learning styles; but that is not enough. It is also important to know the student as an individual and, furthermore, to find joy and naturalness in the relationship.

When teachers and nonhandicapped students encounter handicapped children and youth for the first time, perhaps before they are entirely comfortable with their new relationships, they might follow some helpful guidelines. People should behave naturally in the presence of handicapped persons. Being tense, oversolicitous, or sympathetic toward handicapped persons can be offensive. Carry on a normal conversation; attitudes of pity or charity are unproductive. Ideally, attitudes of equality and respect should form the foundation of associations with handicapped individuals.

The disadvantages associated with people's handicaps may be inconvenient for them, but these handicaps may not prevent them from full participation in regular class activities. Debora Ann Butler, a teacher of visually impaired children, expressed this point of view:

I've been blind since birth, so I don't feel I'm really missing anything by not seeing. I don't feel handicapped; to me it is more an inconvenience than a handicap. The only things I can't do are drive a car and just pick up a printed book and read it. It bothers me when people say, "Oh, you're handicapped." I feel I can do the same things a sighted person does, even though I might do some things differently.[2]

Handicaps are often in the eye of the beholder. Teachers and peers need to guard against negative attitudes and perceptions that might impose a greater handicap on the person than really exists.

[2]From *Voices: Interviews with Handicapped People* (p. 77) by M. D. Orlansky and W. L. Heward, 1981. Columbus, OH: Charles E. Merrill Publishing Co. Copyright 1980 by Charles E. Merrill Publishing Co. Used by permission.

Overprotectiveness represents an unfavorable attitude toward handicapped persons. Encouraging independent behavior in handicapped students is often more difficult than with their nonhandicapped peers. Sometimes, there is a natural tendency to want to protect or to prevent failure; however, it is important for teachers to strike the proper balance between needed support and encouragement of independence. This balance may have a slightly different definition in each individual situation.

Teacher Competency

A second teacher variable influencing the degree of social integration is competency, which refers to the teacher's knowledge and skill in teaching handicapped students. Unfortunately, this variable is not easy to understand. For example, some evidence suggests that classroom teachers who are most competent may also be most resistant to accepting handicapped pupils in their classes (Gersten, Walker, & Darch, 1988; Walker & Rankin, 1983). What is needed for effective integration are effective teachers with positive attitudes toward integrating handicapped students with nonhandicapped peers. Therefore, teacher competency influences social integration in a variety of ways.

First, a relationship has been documented between a teacher's knowledge about handicapping conditions and the existence of positive attitudes (Shaw & Gillung, 1975; Yates, 1973). It is obvious that people are more enthusiastic about engaging in experiences in which they feel confident and competent rather than in experiences in which they feel threatened and apt to fail. Second, the competence of the teacher can determine whether handicapped students achieve academic success in the classroom and thus receive the status and respect that are outcomes of such success. A third important factor in teacher competency is the teacher's skill in systematically implementing the student-oriented social interventions discussed later in this chapter.

The effects of increasing teacher competency regarding social integration interventions were documented by Leyser and Gottlieb (1980). They provided a 2-hour workshop to teachers, a training manual, and periodic consultation on implementing strategies, such as classroom discussions, peer tutoring, and simulations to improve the social status of handicapped students. An analysis of pre- and posttest sociometric data, focusing on the four most socially rejected students in the classroom of each teacher receiving training, revealed a significant improvement in social acceptance at the end of a 10-week period. Thus, a short-term training program aimed at increasing teacher's skills resulted in substantial gains for the students. Helping to achieve social integration by increasing teacher competency regarding social integration interventions has been supported by other researchers (Brown, Ragland, & Fox, 1988; Madden & Slavin, 1983; Putnam, Rynders, Johnson, & Johnson, 1989; Twardosz, Nordquist, Simon, & Botkin, 1983).

STUDENT VARIABLES

Most of the research, general literature, and training guides developed on the subject of social integration among handicapped and nonhandicapped students is aimed strictly at improving the attitudes of nonhandicapped children and youth toward handicapped peers. As indicated previously in this chapter, handicapped students may have negative perceptions of handicapped and nonhandicapped classmates. Also, students in both groups may have negative perceptions of themselves that interfere with their ability to interact with peers. Thus, a broad intervention program is required that focuses on improving the interaction skills and self-esteem of *all* students.

Student variables that can influence the degree of social integration in mainstreamed classrooms include knowledge about handicapping conditions, structure of peer interactions, and degree of classroom status achieved by the students.

Knowledge

All students need information about the nature of handicapping conditions, in general, and the specific effects that these conditions have on their classmates or on themselves. It is natural for children and youth to be curious about differences.

> *Joe is hearing impaired. His second-grade classmates wonder why he wears "the funny wires that go in his ears." At the beginning of the year, they frequently asked Joe and Mr. Parks, their teacher. Mr. Parks quickly told them to "mind their own business" and "not be so cruel." They finally stopped asking, but they still wondered. The main thing they figured out from Mr. Parks's response was that it must be something shameful. Joe was also confused by Mr. Parks's reaction. He decided that Mr. Parks must not like hearing aids. That meant, in his way of thinking, that Mr. Parks must not like him either.*

Such curiosity should not be interpreted as cruel, but rather as genuine interest in learning about differences.

Students frequently have misconceptions about handicapped people. In a survey of 400 high school students (*IRUC Briefings*, 1977), many misconceptions were documented, such as:

- people with muscular dystrophy are also retarded (47%),
- epilepsy is related to emotional illness (47%),
- blind people are unable to attend college or work (59%), and
- speech deficits are usually related to mental retardation (55%) and/or emotional problems (53%).

More than half of the respondents indicated a desire to broaden their knowledge about handicaps by hearing speakers who are handicapped, seeing films, and visiting facilities.

In planning instructional activities to increase student knowledge, consideration should be given to the similarity-attraction model as discussed by Asher (1973). This model postulates that attraction to an individual increases as the perceived similarity of that individual to one's self increases. As applied to classroom interventions, the similarity-attraction model suggests that as knowledge about handicapping conditions is presented and discussed, the emphasis should be on similarities between handicapped and nonhandicapped persons. This model, however, should not be interpreted to mean that differences should be masked or denied.

Several different strategies can be used to increase student knowledge. Three such strategies include instructional programs, classroom discussions, and simulations of handicaps.

Instructional Programs
Units of instruction can be taught on many different topics. Social studies is an obvious curriculum area in which such topics as handicapping conditions, architectural accessibility, the handicapped activist movement, and media stereotypes of handicapped persons can be developed into meaningful and comprehensive instructional units.

Instructional units can also be developed in other curriculum areas, including:

1. civics—federal and state legislation pertaining to rights for handicapped people,
2. health—individual differences, etiology, prevention,
3. science—the mechanics of hearing aids and auditory trainers,
4. music—contributions of blind composers and musicians,
5. biology—genetic screening and amniocentesis, and
6. home economics—adapting the home environment for physically handicapped persons.

An increasing amount of literature on the topic of handicaps is available for children and adolescents. It can be excellent resource material for instructional units, learning centers, or independent reading. A comprehensive annotated bibliography that is continually updated is *Special Needs Bibliography*, with information about current books for exceptional children, their parents, and educators. It also covers other topics, such as illness/disease, social/emotional concerns, and death and dying.

When choosing books for classroom use, teachers should be aware that media portrayals of handicapped persons through books (Biklen & Bogdan, 1977; Mullins, 1979; Schwartz, 1977) and television (Donaldson, 1981) have frequently presented a negative stereotypic image. Persons evaluating resource material should avoid the following stereotypic views:

- presenting disabled persons in a sensational manner;
- one-dimensional characterizations of disabled persons;
- having disabled persons as targets of ridicule;
- reference to superhuman attributes; and
- reference as objects of pity (Biklen & Bogdan, 1977).

If the goal of intervention is to enhance the student's knowledge, then the teacher should judiciously choose materials to avoid these stereotypic perspectives.

An excellent instructional activity for a secondary English composition class would be to evaluate critically a range of literature with handicapped characters. Examples of books to include are *Treasure Island, Of Human Bondage, Moby Dick,* and *Of Mice and Men.*

Classroom Discussions
It is likely that the use of instructional units, learning centers, books, and media will result in the need for classroom discussions on particular areas of student interest. Caution should be taken to insure that the discussions are based on accurate information, avoiding the possibility that uninformed biases would form the core of the exchanges (Siperstein, Bak, & Gottlieb, 1977). An excellent strategy for classroom discussions is to invite handicapped adults to meet with the class and discuss the nature of their disabilities and the feelings associated with them. This strategy has several major advantages including the opportunity for students to get first-hand information about the day-to-day reality of handicaps, the placement of a handicapped person in the status position of teacher, and the identification of a role model for handicapped students.

> *Ron, a handsome and muscular adult, talked with a kindergarten class about his physical disability. He explained how he plays basketball in his wheelchair and even demonstrated some expert shooting. He got a big laugh from the students when he described his softball technique of sliding into first base on his back wheels and handlebars. Many questions were asked during the discussion, such as: "Can you drive a car?" "Will you ever be able to walk?" "Do you wish you could walk?" As the open and lively discussion drew to a close, one of the children commented to Ron, "I have been looking at your wheelchair the whole time. But next time I see you, Ron, I will be able to look you in the eyes."*

When handicapped adults were used as speakers to college classes, Donaldson and Martinson (1977) reported a significant increase in positive student attitudes. Their research also indicated that videotaped discussions of handicapped adults resulted in similar positive attitudinal changes. In implementing such a strategy, they pointed out the importance of selecting handicapped individuals who present nonstereotypic images and who are not overly sensitive or self-pitying about their handicaps.

In addition to having handicapped adults discuss the nature of their handicaps, meaningful learning experiences can be provided by having these adults share their interests, talents, and career responsibilities. These topics help students identify common characteristics and interests; this identification is consistent with the previously discussed similarity-attraction model. A blind poet might read his poems; an adult paralyzed from the waist down might demonstrate methods of increasing upper body strength; and a deaf person might give a pottery lesson. Such situations provide opportunities to accentuate similarities rather than differences.

Discussions can provide opportunities for handicapped students in the classroom to share information about their own disabilities or to answer questions about them. The teacher might talk with the handicapped students, parents, and the school counselor when planning a method of providing information to nonhandicapped classmates at the beginning of the school year. Many handicapped children and youth can explain the nature of their handicaps succinctly to their peers. This ability to provide a self-explanation is very important, because handicapped students are frequently quizzed about "what's wrong" when the teacher is not around.

Sherry has a physical disability referred to as cerebral palsy. She uses a walker to get around her third-grade class. When her peers ask her about why she uses the walker, she immediately tells them that the walker's name is Hi-O Silver and that Hi-O can help her get anywhere she wants to go. She goes on to tell them that she has cerebral palsy, which means that her muscles have not developed in the same way as most other people's. Sherry's parents helped her learn to respond to questions in this fashion. Her teacher established the type of classroom atmosphere in which questions and responses could be discussed in an honest and open fashion.

Some students may prefer to have the teacher provide classmates with information about their individual handicaps. Such information can be provided before a student enters the class or during a classroom discussion. When the student is present, it is preferable for the student to participate in some way in the discussion—demonstrating special equipment, such as a wheelchair, large-print books, or a hearing aid; sharing a description of physical therapy sessions; or describing what it is like to be in a hospital and to have surgery. Such communications should be characterized by openness, respect for differences, and identification of similarities among all students.

Parents can be excellent resources for classroom discussion. A third-grade teacher described a way she capitalized on the expertise and willingness of a parent to expand the knowledge of her students:

> *Janie had a severe hearing impairment. She attended a special class next door to ours. The biggest problem was communication with Janie during recess and at school functions. How could my third graders feel comfortable communicating with her? They were afraid to talk to her.*
>
> *Janie's mother came to my class and taught the children sign language. The whole class loved it! They learned very fast. They started going to Janie every day and asking for her help in learning more signs. This gave them a common ground. The children were no longer hesitant in approaching her.*
>
> *Like all children, they always think of more than one way to skin a cat. How could they talk to their friends in the lunchroom when they were supposed to be silent? Sign language—it was great for everyone!!*

Although many parents are interested in such participation, other parents are uncomfortable explaining their child's handicap to others. One parent stated such a perspective.

> *I get so tired of always being asked to explain Larry's handicap. It seems like every time Larry enters a new situation—school, church, scouts, community recreation—I am always asked to come in and explain mental retardation. I often want to say, "Can't someone else do it?" I almost feel like it puts me in the position of asking or begging other people to be nice to him. As a parent, that feeling makes me sad.*

Several cautions apply to classroom discussions. First, insure that handicapped students and their parents are comfortable being the focus of classroom discussions. Teachers should adhere to their preferences and recognize that some people prefer to maintain a lower profile. Second, respect for the student should be maintained at all times. The mother of a student who was orthopedically handicapped provided an illustration of an unintended insult:

> *In high school, a teacher didn't mean harm but upset Sara's friends, who later came to her very indignant. Sara came to us in tears. This was the first time my husband and I went to see the principal; and once again the teacher had done what she thought was a kind thing. But neither the children, nor Sara, nor we saw it as that: After Sara's first day in class, she told subsequent classes about Sara, and said they should all be thankful they were not like Sara. Sara's friends did not see her as such a deformed person, and they resented the implication.*
>
> *We thought it very bad taste to single out a person—handicapped—to make others feel fortunate. The teacher apologized but not to Sara, nor did she mention it to the children.*[3]

[3]Excerpt from *Understanding and Working with Parents of Children with Special Needs* by James L. Paul, copyright © 1981 by Holt, Rinehart and Winston, Inc., reprinted by permission of the publisher.

Thus, such discussions should in no way portray the handicapped person as pitiful or pathetic. Rather, the discussion should focus on ability as well as on disability, on feelings, and on coping.

Teachers are encouraged to deal with issues and concerns directly related to the handicap, rather than to avoid them. When classroom peers ask specific questions about the handicap, these questions should be viewed as natural and worthy of honest answers. When peers are provided with adequate understanding, they in turn can provide explanations to other students when questions arise. Thus, the handicapped individual does not always have to provide the explanations. Once classmates clearly understand handicaps and develop a sensitivity to differences, questions of "what's wrong" with a particular student become practically nonexistent.

Simulation

A third strategy that can be used to increase student knowledge is the actual simulation of handicaps. Simulation requires nonhandicapped students to act as if they have a handicap through the use of special equipment and according to specified instructions.

Resource materials listed at the end of the chapter include a variety of simulation activities for use with students. With younger age groups, puppets can also be used as a mode for simulation. Puppets with handicaps can be made by the students or community volunteers. Puppets can

also be purchased commercially (see *The Kids on the Block* in the resource list at the end of this chapter).

The effects of simulation on the modification of attitudes was studied by Clore and Jeffrey (1972). They had one group of students use a wheelchair to travel a specified route; another group followed along at a distance of 20 feet and observed the person simulating the orthopedic handicap. Using several attitudinal assessments, they found a significant increase in positive attitudes for the students who participated. This difference was evident immediately and was maintained over a 4-month period. The authors attributed this positive change to the development of empathy.

Several guidelines should be considered when using simulation. Wright (1979) cautions that simulations can result in negative emotions, such as fear, loneliness, and helplessness, as students experience difficulty with coping. Such negative emotions could be projected on the handicapped population as a whole. The immediate simulation of a handicap without the prior development of coping skills is not at all the same situation as that of a classmate who has had a particular handicap for a period of time and has learned to compensate for it. Thus, when simulation is used as a teaching strategy, nonhandicapped students need to experience successful coping responses rather than just frustration and awkwardness. Successful coping responses can be accomplished by such activities as requesting the installation of a paper cup dispenser when the student cannot reach the water fountain (Wright, 1979) or learning to ask for assistance in a nondefensive manner when maneuvering a wheelchair onto an elevator. The important point is that students conclude simulation experiences with a greater insight about the nature of handicaps and about possibilities for adaptation. An excellent concluding activity, after students have participated in simulations, is to have a handicapped speaker discuss the types of adaptations he or she has learned to make. Students are likely to have a much greater appreciation of such adaptations after they have participated in simulations.

Combination Approach

One project initiated by a high school English teacher and her husband, a university educator, involved an instructional program, classroom discussion, and simulation by studying a unit titled "Handicaps in Literature and Life" (Grantham & Grantham, 1987). They described the purpose of the unit for ninth-grade students:

> Development of the unit offered an opportunity to teach the students several important concepts. First, many fine works exist in the world of literature which either were produced by persons with handicaps, or are good descriptions of persons who experience life with a handicap. A second concept of the special study was to offer the students the opportunity to interact with persons who might have handicaps and to ask the questions. Finally, the

simulation activities of the study provided some of the other students a special time to experience, to some degree, the physical limitations, as well as the emotional strains, of living with a handicap. (p. 11)

Students in the class were able to have experiences that allowed them to gain understanding of handicapped persons. Whether this understanding generalizes to social integration is not guaranteed; however, without it, social integration of handicapped pupils is an uphill battle.

Structured Peer Interactions

Interaction among handicapped and nonhandicapped students usually does not occur spontaneously in mainstreamed classrooms (Gresham, 1984; Johnson & Johnson, 1986). Furthermore, unstructured contact does not lead directly to more positive attitudes on the part of nonhandicapped persons (Donaldson, 1980). An effective type of intervention, however, is to structure experiences systematically to provide opportunities for students to work or enjoy leisure activities together. Structured interactions can be planned using a variety of strategies, including planned activities to increase communication, peer tutoring, cooperative instruction, and teaching friendship skills.

Planned Activities to Increase Communication

Teachers can plan a variety of activities to increase communication among students. A frequently used technique is to have regularly scheduled sharing times throughout the school year to enable students to share their experiences, special activities, feelings, and ideas. Sharing time can be structured to accomplish various purposes. A teacher described a strategy for structuring as follows:

> Sometimes we get a ball of yarn and throw it from one person to another. The person who catches the yarn has to say something good about the person who threw it. Another time we used the yarn, the persons catching it had to say something nice about themselves. I have seem some really good results in class morale and closeness.

Another strategy for structuring communication through planned activities is to use a communication wheel (see Figure 13.1). This wheel can be used at the beginning of school to increase peer interaction. All students should be provided with a copy of the wheel and should be encouraged to seek help from each other.

Peer Tutoring

Peer tutoring, discussed in chapter 7, is a familiar concept. As related to social integration, it represents an effective strategy for bringing hand-

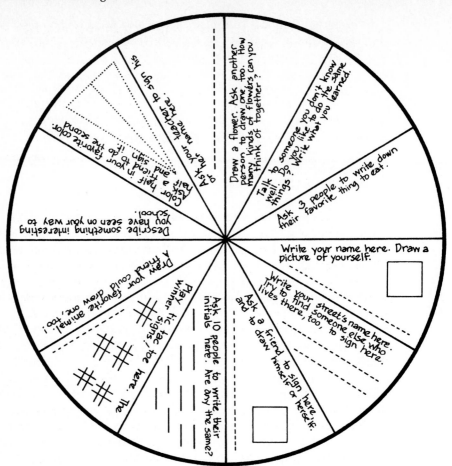

FIGURE 13.1 Communication Wheel

icapped and nonhandicapped students together to accomplish a defined
goal. It is very important that handicapped students have the opportunity
to provide tutoring as well as to receive it.

> *Jazmina is an active, energetic second grader. She has boundless energy for everything
> except reading. She stumbles over words and is still reading at a primer level at the
> end of second grade. Her peers tease her sometimes and it makes her afraid she will be
> laughed at in her reading group. She gets very tense during reading period. Jazmina
> excels in gymnastics. Her teacher planned a unit on tumbling in the physical
> education class and asked Jazmina to help some of her classmates learn to do head-
> stands, handstands, and cartwheels. Jazmina was delighted to serve as a peer tutor,
> and the students who had been teasing her quickly learned a side of Jazmina they had
> never known.*

Helping relationships often turn into friendships. The nonhandicapped students may be amazed at the adaptations and compensations that a handicapped peer is able to make. As students become aware of each other's strengths and weaknesses, respect for individual differences and spontaneous interactions can be natural by-products.

Opportunities for both nonhandicapped and handicapped students in regular classes to provide peer tutoring to moderately and severely handicapped students in special classes can also be arranged. Poorman (1980) has outlined a detailed program to prepare regular class students for these tutoring experiences.

Cooperative Instruction

Cooperative instruction refers to the structuring of learning situations so that students work together to achieve common goals. In contrast, individualistic instruction results in independent student achievement, for example, a goal accomplished by one student is not tied to that of other students. Cooperative instruction is discussed in chapter 7. Documentation exists on the value of cooperative instruction in enhancing peer interactions of handicapped and nonhandicapped students. Johnson and Johnson (1981) compared the outcomes of cooperative and individualistic learning experiences for handicapped and nonhandicapped third graders. The instruction consisted of a daily 25-minute math lesson for 16 days. In the cooperative condition, students were divided into five small groups; four of the groups included one handicapped student. The students were instructed to work together to complete assignment sheets. All students were expected to contribute ideas, and the teacher rewarded the group as a whole. The individualistic condition had students working alone and the teacher rewarding students on an individual basis. The results for each variable investigated in the study are summarized here:

Variables	*Results*
1. Interaction between handicapped and nonhandicapped students during instruction	1. In cooperative condition, nonhandicapped students asked handicapped peers more questions, offered more suggestions, and provided more help
2. Amount of off-task behavior	2. No significant differences between the two conditions
3. Interaction between handicapped and nonhandicapped students during free time after instructional sessions	3. More cross-handicap interactions occurred in the cooperative condition
4. Nomination of friends	4. Trend for more nominations of friends among handicapped and nonhandicapped students in the cooperative group

A major finding of this study is that the interaction occurring during the structured activities generalized to unstructured situations in which students could choose classmates with whom to interact.

These finds have been replicated (Johnson, Johnson, Warring, & Maruyama, 1986) and have shown that nonhandicapped students also benefit (Putnam, Rynders, Johnson, & Johnson, 1989). The findings suggest that group activities, such as sociodrama, art projects, science projects, and games, can be used to structure successful interaction among handicapped and nonhandicapped students. Rather than providing singular or isolated instruction to handicapped students, teachers should try to meet their individual needs within small working groups.

Teaching Friendship Skills

Friendship skills involve a range of behaviors including sharing, cooperation, communication, verbal complimenting, nonaggressiveness, and participation. Because of previous rejection and alienation, handicapped students may have had limited opportunities to develop these skills. There is a paucity of research on the level of friendship skills of handicapped students; however, one study at the junior high level indicated that mentally retarded students were more limited in interpersonal skills than were their nonhandicapped classmates (Kingsley, Viggiano, & Tout, 1981).

Behavior management techniques discussed in chapter 12 apply to teaching friendship skills. Gresham (1981) provides a comprehensive review of research on the application of these techniques to social skills training.

Setting clear behavioral standards has particular relevance for students with learning and behavior problems. Often, these students are not attuned to some of the subtle nonverbal cues that reflect peer approval or disapproval of their behavior. Thus, they may behave inappropriately because the rules and standards of behavior are not clear to them.

> *When Cindy started her menstrual period, she did not understand what was happening or why she had physical cramps. It was a source of great anxiety to her. Anytime a teacher or classmate asked her how she was, she always responded in terms of whether it was just before, during, or after her menstrual period. Her reactions became a class joke, and classmates increased the frequency of asking only to laugh when she responded in her stereotypic manner. Her teachers felt sorry for her, because she did not have any friends and lived at an institution for mentally retarded persons in the community. They did not want to embarrass her by telling her that her frequent comments about menstruation were socially inappropriate. When the school counselor heard some of Cindy's classmates laughing about her conversation, she set up an appointment with Cindy and explained the bodily changes associated with menstruation and guidelines for appropriate conversation. They brainstormed about other responses Cindy could make when she was asked how she was feeling. The counselor also talked with Cindy's teachers and peers and encouraged them to praise Cindy for appropriate conversation. Cindy kept a diary of her conversations and reviewed it with*

the counselor on a weekly basis. After her initial meeting with the counselor, Cindy never made any more inappropriate comments about menstruation.

Nonhandicapped students also frequently need assistance with friendship skills as they relate to handicapped peers. One problem that can arise in mainstreamed classrooms is name calling, such as "retardo," "crip," and "four-eyes." Such negative interactions can be handled in a variety of ways in teaching more appropriate social behavior. Salend and Schobel (1981) described an instructional unit they taught to a fourth-grade class on the function of names. The major topics within the unit were acquisition and meaning of names, how names are different, and positive or negative effects of nicknames. On the last topic, one activity was a discussion of the negative effects of nicknames and of the importance of considering another person's reaction to the nickname.

Just as it is important for all students to develop sensitivity to the feelings of their classmates, it is also important for handicapped people to develop strategies for dealing with name calling. Mothers of young hand-icapped children identified the greatest benefit of mainstreaming for their children to be preparation for the real world. One mother stated this perspective as follows:

Some of the other kids would pick on him or beat him up or something, and he'd just let them pick on him. They'd call him some real names . . . really surprised me . . . 'retarded,' 'cripple,' or stuff like that . . . really bad names. . . . But as far as I know, they've quit doing that. He's finally learned to stand up for himself.

Schulz (1979) discussed the importance of facing the label in prepar-ing her mentally retarded son for successful employment as an adult.

The strongest example I can present is the experience of my son, who is mentally retarded. Although aware of his retardation, he was raised and educated in protective environments; he was never called "stupid," "fat," "dumb." When he went to work he failed, not because he lacked the necessary skills, but because he had not learned to deal with the threats and jeers of his co-workers. (p. 51)

Teachers need to be comfortable in helping handicapped students deal with name calling as they simultaneously work with them in develop-ing friendships.

Nellie, a student in Ms. Wilson's third-grade class, goes to the resource room for instruction 30 minutes each day. The resource room is referred to as the EMR class around the school. Some of Nellie's peers teased her about going to the resource program and started calling her "EMR" and "retardo." Nellie came to Ms. Wilson and asked "What does it mean to be an EMR?" Ms. Wilson's heart dropped. How should she respond? She did not want to hurt Nellie's feelings; yet she valued honest communication with her students. She responded to Nellie by indicating that EMR stands for educable mentally retarded. She went on to explain that the term educable mentally retarded is sometimes used to refer to students who have more difficulty learning school subjects than some of their classmates.

She asked Nellie if sometimes her reading and arithmetic lessons were hard for her to understand. Nellie affirmed that they were. Ms. Wilson reassured Nellie that educable mentally retarded does not mean that Nellie cannot learn at all nor that she has difficulty learning everything. Nellie's performance in art projects was pointed out as an area where she had less difficulty than many of her classmates. Ms. Wilson reminded Nellie that all people have difficulty learning some things. The point that individual people have different strengths, weaknesses, interests, and learning rates was strongly stressed. Ms. Wilson told Nellie that she could understand how she did not like being called EMR. Ms. Wilson encouraged Nellie to remember the progress she was making from going to the resource program and to ignore students who have not yet learned that name calling is unkind.

After this initial conference, Ms. Wilson and Nellie jointly chose some representative work assignments that Nellie had done in the resource room. These were shared with the class during "show and tell" period, along with a description of the types of work done in the resource room. Ms. Wilson also worked with the class during language arts in writing scripts and producing puppet shows on sensitivity to feelings. Some of the students who had been doing the name calling had puppets cast in roles of needing special help in order to understand their school work. Through the simulated experience with the puppets, these students began to get the message of what it is like when the shoe is on the other foot. Ms. Wilson realized that name calling would not be eliminated immediately, but that systematic steps could be taken to teach respect for differences. She knew that merely punishing the students who were teasing Nellie might only teach them to call others names when they knew the teacher would not find out. Replacing the negative attitudes and behavior with positive attitudes and behavior was Ms. Wilson's goal.

Degree of Classroom Status

Classroom status refers to the prestige or recognition that students have among their peers. Students who have status in the classroom are likely to have fewer problems with social integration. In a sociometric study of students who were learning disabled (Siperstein, Bopp, & Bak, 1978), it was found that this group was less popular than their nonhandicapped classmates. An interesting trend detected, however, was that of the six best-liked children with learning disabilities in the study, five received nominations for best athlete in the class. Thus, it was speculated that the status gained through athletics helped compensate for some of the students' other areas of deficit.

To help develop status, teachers first need to insure that students have an opportunity to achieve success. Success is important for all students, but it can be of special significance to handicapped students. Some handicapped students, unfortunately, experience overwhelming amounts of failure in their school careers. Sometimes the failure is more teacher-

based than student-based, as when teachers routinely set expectations for handicapped students on a much higher academic level than their achievement level warrants. Inaccurate or insufficient assessment can lead directly to failure. Teachers can eliminate a large number of failure experiences by planning appropriate instruction. The IEP can be the focal point of successful instruction.

Purkey (1970) suggests questions that teachers might consider in developing a classroom atmosphere characterized by success. These questions include:

- Do I permit my students some opportunity to make mistakes without penalty?
- Do I make generally positive comments on written work?
- Do I give extra support and encouragement to slower students?
- Do I recognize the success of students in terms of what they did earlier?
- Do I take special opportunities to praise students for their successes?
- Do I manufacture honest experiences of success for my students?
- Do I set tasks which are, and which appear to the student to be, within his abilities? (p. 56)

As handicapped students experience success, they can become more confident about their strengths and more positive in their self-concept. Likewise, their nonhandicapped peers have the opportunity to recognize their strengths. All of these factors can contribute to the enhanced, social integration of handicapped and nonhandicapped students.

The status of handicapped students can be increased by insuring their successful inclusion in extracurricular activities and prestige positions in the school. In many situations, handicapped students are not chosen to be captains of the ball teams, stars in the class play, or editors of the school newspaper. These positions, however, typically have status in most elementary and secondary schools. Teachers cannot always arrange peer relationships or determine which students are chosen by their classmates for special honors, but the teacher's influence and guidance can serve as a strong model. It is important for teachers to be sensitive to classroom and school opportunities that might capitalize on the strengths and interests of handicapped students. These opportunities should also be generally associated with status and prestige.

> *Charles is in his last year of elementary school. He is mentally retarded and has low academic achievement in all areas. He also has some emotional problems. At the beginning of the year, his teacher was acutely aware of his inferior class position. When basketball season started, Charles was very disappointed because he knew he was not skilled enough to go out for the team. He loved basketball and spent every afternoon practicing. His teacher had a great idea. Would the coach allow Charles to be the basketball manager? The teacher carefully described the situation to the coach and stated reasons he thought Charles would do a very good job as team manager. The coach agreed to give Charles a chance to prove himself. When the teacher told Charles of this opportunity, he was overwhelmed with excitement. He could hardly wait until the first day of practice. Faithfully and diligently, Charles worked at his job and performed in an outstanding manner. The coach and team grew to respect him as their manager and friend. Charles had the opportunity to travel with the team to all out-of-town games and was awarded a plaque at the sports banquet. The opportunity to be basketball manager was the beginning of new peer perceptions toward Charles. No longer was he the "kid with problems" or the "EMR student." Charles was the basketball manager. This position carried status.*

In addition to being managers, some handicapped students successfully participate in interscholastic athletics.

> *Kathy and Frances were upper elementary students with significant learning problems. They were first-string players on the school's volleyball team. Their classmates came to games to cheer them on. The school letter each received is their most prized possession.*

Handicapped students can be members of the school chorus, members of an honor club, active in drama productions, members of the safety patrol, members of the school newspaper staff, or peer tutors of other students.

> *James Oates is not your typical sixth grader. He serves on the Safety Patrol in the cafeteria before school starts each day. He relies on his ears to help him maintain order, since he is totally blind. James has a full day splitting time among his sixth-grade class, his vision resource teacher, and the gifted and talented program. In addition to his studies, James is serving his second term as the student council president.* (Lauber, 1980, p. 38)

Whatever the nature of involvement, the important point is that handicapped students have opportunities to excel in areas valued by other students. The end result is usually increased peer and self-respect.

Achieving Social Integration

Social integration can be enhanced when careful attention is given to developing positive attitudes toward handicapped students and to establishing a classroom environment characterized by open and honest communication, success, and respect.

> *Mark has a long history of school failure. He has been ostracized frequently by his peers. When Mark reached the fourth grade, his teacher made a commitment to try to create for him an environment more conducive to learning. She first referred him for special education services. Mark was tested, and it was found that he qualified for services from the learning disabilities resource program. A committee comprised of Mark's classroom teacher, resource teacher, coordinator of special education services, and parents was established to develop an IEP for him. The committee worked very hard to pinpoint Mark's level of achievement and to plan the next steps.*
> *When the IEP was completed, Mark's teacher, Ms. Turner, felt that she had a good idea of where to start. With the help of the resource teacher, she gathered some instructional materials on Mark's level. As the year progressed, Mark systematically moved toward higher levels of mastery. He was proud of what he learned and appeared to be a happier and more outgoing child overall.*
> *Ms. Turner arranged for Mark to lead storytime in a first-grade class one day a week. Because of the work he had done and knowledge he had obtained at home in his parents' garden, he became "Chief Advisor" for the classroom window garden. He took excellent care of the plants and always seemed to know what to do when one began to droop. Mark's peers admired him for his gardening skills.*
> *Ms. Turner observed that classroom peers gradually began to include Mark in more and more activities as one of the guys. This pleased her very much, and one day she expressed her pleasure to a nonhandicapped peer who invariably included Mark in informal classroom groups. The peer was puzzled that Ms. Turner would make such a statement. The peer's reply was, "What's the big deal about including Mark? He's neat."*

Perhaps the ultimate goal is for social integration for handicapped and nonhandicapped students to be so natural that it is not a "big deal."

RESOURCE MATERIALS

Only in recent years have commercial materials been developed on the topic of enhancing social integration. Representative samples of these resources are included in this section (to order, see Appendix A). Readers are also urged to contact the professional and volunteer organizations listed in Appendix A. Many of these organizations have resource lists of materials aimed at the special needs of the handicapped people whom they represent. These organizations also offer pamphlets that can be extremely useful in planning social integration activities. One strategy for collecting this information would be to have students write these organizations for information as an activity in a language arts lesson.

MAINSTREAMING: WHAT EVERY CHILD NEEDS TO KNOW ABOUT DISABILITIES   Units of instruction designed for grades 1 through 4 are provided in the areas of blindness, deafness, physical disabilities, and mental retardation. Instructional activities include using classroom discussions; simulations; exposure to aids and appliances; guest speakers; and books, movies, slides, and videotapes. Excellent resource lists are also included. The Exceptional Parent Press.

KIDS COME IN SPECIAL FLAVORS: CLASSROOM EXPERIENCE COLLECTION   This collection of social integration materials includes a teacher's guide book of detailed activities and resource lists, storybooks, cassette tapes for acquainting students with hearing impairments, paper and pencil tasks for simulating problems of the students who are mentally retarded and learning disabled, and equipment related to the special needs of students who are visually impaired and orthopedically handicapped. It is aimed at the elementary level. Kids Come in Special Flavors.

EVERYBODY COUNTS! A WORKSHOP MANUAL TO INCREASE AWARENESS OF HANDICAPPED PEOPLE   A collection of simulation activities covering the full range of handicapping conditions is included in this guidebook. Detailed instructions and graphic illustrations enable the reader to implement the activities with success. The activities are geared to the secondary level. Council for Exceptional Children.

PUT ON A HANDICAP   A teacher's manual and a record provide a range of instructional activities including simulations, discussions, and examining prosthetic aids and appliances. The record contains songs that are educational and fun. Kimbo Educational Materials.

I AM, I CAN, I WILL   This series featuring Mr. Rogers includes 15 titles aimed at helping handicapped children understand their feelings. The titles are available in several media formats including films, videotapes, audio cassettes, and books. Teacher guides are also available with suggestions for follow-up activities to encourage the expression of feelings. Hubbard Scientific.

THE KIDS ON THE BLOCK   Engaging handcrafted puppets representing a range of handicaps are available in this program. A teacher's guide is also available that includes scripts, numerous ideas for follow-up activities, and an extensive bibliography of children's literature related to handicaps. The Kids on the Block.

SPECIAL PEOPLE BEHIND THE EIGHT-BALL   This book is a compilation of an extensive annotated bibliography of literature categorized according to handicapping conditions. Books appropriate for both elementary and secondary levels are included. The Exceptional Parent Bookstore.

PEOPLE YOU'D LIKE TO KNOW   Ten films focusing on handicapped youth, ages 11 to 14, are included in this series. The films focus on the similarities of these young people to the nonhandicapped population. Encyclopedia Britannica Education Corporation.

DIFFERENT FROM YOU AND LIKE YOU TOO   This filmstrip explores the concept of individual differences and encourages children to ask questions of their handicapped peers. It is suitable for an elementary audience. Lawren Productions, Inc.

GIFTED CHILDREN SPEAK OUT   Cited in Griffin (1986). Divided into two parts, the first part is a compilation of lively and thoughtful responses to a questionnaire given to gifted children across the country. It asked for their perceptions on the high points and hurdles of growing up gifted. Part Two presents a series of activities and discussion problems to correspond with the contents of Part One. These activities are appropriate for groups of children and are designed for use with those identified as gifted.

REFERENCES

Alexander, C., & Strain, P. (1978). A review of educators' attitudes toward handicapped children and the concept of mainstreaming. *Psychology in the Schools, 15,* 390–396.

Antia, S. (1985). Social integration of hearing impaired children: Fact or fiction? *The Volta Review, 87,* 279–289.

Asher, N. W. (1973). Manipulating attraction toward the disabled: An application of the similarity-attraction model. *Rehabilitation Psychology, 20,* 156–164.

Biklen, D., & Bogdan, R. (1977). Media portrayals of disabled people: A study in stereotypes. *Bulletin, 8,* (6–7), 4–9.

Brophy, J., & Good, T. (1974). *Teacher-student relationships—causes and consequences.* New York: Holt, Rinehart and Winston.

Brown, W. H., Ragland, E., & Bishop, N. (1989). A naturalistic teaching strategy to promote young children's peer interactions. *Teaching Exceptional Children, 21,* (4), 8–10.

Brown, W. H., Ragland, E. U., & Fox, J. J. (1988). Effects of group socialization procedures on the social behavior of preschool children. *Research in Developmental Disabilities, 9,* 359–376.

Bruininks, R. H., Rynders, J. E., & Gross, T. C. (1974). Social acceptance of mildly retarded pupils in resource rooms and regular classes. *American Journal of Mental Deficiency, 78,* 377–383.

Bruininks, V. L. (1978). Peer status and personality characteristics of learning disabled and nondisabled students. *Journal of Learning Disabilities, 11,* (8), 29–34.

Bryan, T. H. (1978). Social relationships and verbal interactions of learning disabled children. *Journal of Learning Disabilities, 11,* (2), 58–66.

Chapman, J. W. (1988). Learning disabled children's self-concepts. *Review of Educational Research, 58,* 347–371.

Clark, F. I. (1980). The development of instrumentation to measure regular classroom teachers' attitudes toward mildly handicapped students. Doctoral dissertation, University of Kansas.

Clore, G. L., & Jeffrey, K. M. (1972). Emotional role playing, attitude change and attraction toward a disabled person. *Journal of Personality and Social Psychology, 23,* 105–111.

Craig, H. B. (1965). A sociometric investigation of the self-concept of the deaf child. *American Annals of the Deaf, 110,* 456–478.

Donaldson, J. (1980). Changing attitudes toward handicapped persons: A review and analysis of research. *Exceptional Children, 46,* (7), 504–513.

Donaldson, J. (1981). The visibility and image of handicapped people on television. *Exceptional Children, 47,* (6), 413–416.

Donaldson, J., & Martinson, M. C. (1977). Modifying attitudes toward physically disabled persons. *Exceptional Children, 43,* (6), 337–341.

Farina, A., Sherman, M., & Allen, J. G. (1968). Role of physical abnormalities in interpersonal perception and behavior. *Journal of Abnormal Psychology, 73,* 590–593.

Force, D. G. (1956). Social status of physically handicapped children. *Exceptional Children, 23,* 104–107.

Gaylord-Ross, R., & Haring, T. (1987). Social interaction research for adolescents with severe handicaps. *Behavioral Disorders, 12,* 264–275.

Gersten, R., Walker, H., & Darch, C. (1988). Relationship between teachers' effectiveness and their tolerance for handicapped students. *Exceptional Children, 54,* 433–438.

Good, T. (1970). Which pupils do teachers call on? *Elementary School Journal, 70,* 190–198.

Goodman, H., Gottlieb, J., & Harrison, R. H. (1972). Social acceptance of EMR's integrated into a nongraded elementary school. *American Journal of Mental Deficiency, 26,* 412–417.

Gottlieb, J. (1975). Public, peer, and professional attitudes toward mentally retarded persons. In M. J. Begab & S. A. Richardson (Eds.), *The mentally retarded and society: A social science perspective* (pp. 99–125). Baltimore: University Park Press.

Gottlieb, J., & Budoff, M. (1973). Social acceptability of retarded children in non-graded schools differing in architecture. *American Journal of Mental Deficiency, 78,* 15–19.

Gottlieb, J., & Switzky, H. N. (1982). Development of school-age children's stereotypic attitudes toward mentally retarded children. *American Journal of Mental Deficiency, 86,* 596–600.

Grantham, L., & Grantham, D. C. (1987). A high school literature course with emphasis on the study of handicaps. *Counterpoints* (Nov.–Dec.), 11.

Gresham, F. M. (1981). Social skills training with handicapped children: A review. *Review of Educational Research, 51,* (1), 139–176.

Gresham, F. M. (1984). Social skills and self-efficacy for exceptional children. *Exceptional Children, 51,* 253–261.

Griffin, B. K. (1986). *Special needs bibliography: Current books for/about children and young adults regarding social concerns emotional concerns the exceptional child.* DeWitt, NY: The Griffin.

Hollinger, J. D. (1987). Social skills for behaviorally disordered children as preparation for mainstreaming: Theory, practice, and new directions. *Remedial and Special Education, 8,* (4), 17–27.

Iano, R. P., Ayers, D., Heller, H. B., McGettigan, J. F., & Walker, V. S. (1974). Sociometric status of retarded children in an integrative program. *Exceptional Children, 40,* 267–271.

Idol-Maestas, L., & Ritter, S. (1985). A follow-up study of resource/consulting teachers: Factors that facilitate and inhibit teacher consultation. *Teacher Education and Special Education, 8,* (3), 121–131.

IRUC Briefings. (1977). Washington, DC: Information and Research Utilization Center, Physical Education and Recreation for the Handicapped, American Alliance for Health. Physical Education and Recreation.

Jenkins, J. R., Speltz, M. L., & Odom, S. L. (1985). Integrating normal and handicapped preschoolers: Effects on child development and social interaction. *Exceptional Children, 52,* 7–17.

Johnson, D., & Johnson, R. (1984). Classroom learning structure and attitudes toward handicapped students in mainstream settings: A theoretical model and research evidence. In R. Jones (Ed.), *Attitudes and attitude change in special education* (pp. 118–142). Reston, VA: Council for Exceptional Children.

Johnson, D. W., & Johnson, R. T. (1986). Mainstreaming and cooperative learning strategies. *Exceptional Children, 52,* 553–561.

Johnson, D. W., Johnson, R. T., Warring, D., & Maruyama, G. (1986). Different cooperative learning procedures and cross-handicap relationships. *Exceptional Children, 53,* 247–252.

Johnson, R. T., & Johnson, D. W. (1981). Building friendships between handicapped and nonhandicapped students: Effects of cooperative and individualistic instruction. *American Education Research Journal, 18,* (4), 415–423.

Jones, R. L., & Sisk, D. (1967). Early perceptions of orthopedic disability. *Exceptional Children, 9,* 42–43.

Kauffman, J. M., Gerber, M. M., & Semmell, M. I. (1988). Arguable assumptions underlying the Regular Education Initiative. *Journal of Learning Disabilities, 21,* 6–11.

Kingsley, R. F., Viggiano, R. A., & Tout, I. (1981). Social perception of friendship, leadership and game playing among EMR special and regular class boys. *Education and Training of the Mentally Retarded, 16,* (3), 201–206.

Kleck, R. (1968). Physical stigma and nonverbal cues emitted in face-to-face interaction. *Human Relations, 21,* 19–28.

Lauber, A. (1980). James Oates. *Education Unlimited, 2,* (4), 38–39.

Levy, L., & Gottlieb, J. (1984). Learning disabled and non-LD children at play. *Remedial and Special Education, 5,* (6), 43–50.

Leyser, Y., & Gottlieb, J. (1980). Improving the social status of rejected pupils. *Exceptional Children, 46,* (6), 459–461.

MacMillan, D. K., Jones, R. L., & Meyers, C. E. (1976). Mainstreaming the mildly retarded: Some questions, cautions and guidelines. *Mental Retardation, 14,* 3–10.

Madden, N. A., & Slavin, R. E. (1983). Mainstreaming students with mild handicaps: Academic and social outcomes. *Review of Educational Research, 53,* 519–569.

Margolis, H., & McGettigan, J. (1988). Managing resistance to instructional modifications to mainstreamed environments. *Remedial and Special Education, 9,* (4), 15–21.

Mullins, J. B. (1979). Making language work to eliminate handicapism. *Education Unlimited, 2,* 20–24.

Munson, S. M. (1987). Regular education teacher modifications for mainstreamed mildly handicapped students. *Journal of Special Education, 20,* 489–502.

Nelson, C. M. (1988). Social skills training for handicapped students. *Teaching Exceptional Children, 20,* (4), 19–23.

Orlansky, M. D., & Heward, W. (1981). *Voices: Interviews with handicapped people.* Columbus, OH: Merrill.

Paul, J. L. (Ed.). (1981). *Understanding and working with parents of children with special needs.* New York: Holt, Rinehart and Winston.

Paul, J. L., & Beckman-Bell, P. (1981). Parent perspectives. In J. L. Paul (Ed.). *Understanding and working with parents of children with special needs* (pp. 119–155). New York: Holt, Rinehart and Winston.

Pearl, R., Bryan, T., & Donahue, M. (1983). Social behaviors of learning-disabled children: A review. *Topics in Learning and Learning Disabilities, 3,* 1–13.

Pearl, R., & Cosden, M. (1982). Sizing up a situation: LD children's understanding of social interactions. *Learning Disabilities Quarterly, 5,* 344–352.

Peterson, N., & Haralick, J. (1977). Integration of handicapped and nonhandicapped preschoolers: An analysis of play behavior and social interaction. *Education and Training of the Mentally Retarded, 12,* 235–245.

Poorman, C. (1980). Mainstreaming in reverse with a special friend. *Teaching Exceptional Children, 12,* (4), 136–142.

Purkey, W. W. (1970). *Self concept and school achievement.* Englewood Cliffs, NJ: Prentice-Hall.

Putnam, J. W., Rynders, J. E., Johnson, R T., & Johnson, D. W. (1989). Collaborative skill instruction for promoting positive interactions between mentally handicapped and nonhandicapped children. *Exceptional Children, 55,* 550–557.

Ray, B. M. (1985). Measuring the social position of the mainstreamed handicapped child. *Exceptional Children, 52,* 57–62.

Reese-Dukes, J. L., & Stokes, E. H. (1978). Social acceptance of elementary educable mentally retarded pupils in the regular classroom. *Education and Training of the Mentally Retarded, 13,* (4), 356–361.

Richardson, S. A. (1970). Age and sex differences in values toward physical handicaps. *Journal of Health and Social Behavior, 11,* 207–214.

Robinson, M. G. (1979). Awareness program helps children understand needs. *Education Unlimited, 1,* (2), 25–27.

Rosenthal, R., & Jacobson, L. (1968). *Pygmalion in the classroom: Teacher expectation and pupils intellectual development.* New York: Holt, Rinehart and Winston.

Salend, S. J., & Schobel, J. (1981). Coping with name calling in the mainstreamed setting. *Education Unlimited, 3,* (2), 36–38.

Sandberg, L. D. (1982). Attitudes of nonhandicapped elementary school students toward school-aged trainable mentally retarded students. *Education and Training of the Mentally Retarded, 17,* 30–34.

Schulz, J. B. (1979). Facing the label. *Education Unlimited, 1,* (4), 50–53.

Schwartz, A. V. (1977). Disability in children's books: Is visibility enough? *Bulletin, 8,* (6–7), 10–15.

Shaw, S. F., & Gillung, T. B. (1975). Efficacy of a college course for regular class teachers of the mildly handicapped. *Mental Retardation, 13,* (4), 3–6.

Siperstein, G. N., Bak, J. J., & Gottlieb, J. (1977). Effects of group discussion on children's attitudes toward handicapped peers. *Journal of Educational Research, 7,* 131–134.

Siperstein, G. N., Bopp, J. M., & Bak, J. J. (1978). Social status of learning disabled children. *Journal of Learning Disabilities, 11,* (2), 49–53.

Stainback, G., Stainback, W., & Stainback, S. (1988). Superintendents' attitudes toward integration. *Education and Training in Mental Retardation, 23,* 92–96.

Stainback, S., & Stainback, W. (1982). Influencing the attitudes of regular class teachers about the education of severely retarded students. *Education and Training of the Mentally Retarded, 17,* 88–92.

Stainback, W., Stainback, S., Courtnage, L., & Jaben, T. (1985). Facilitating mainstreaming by modifying the mainstream. *Exceptional Children, 52,* 144–152.

Thompson, T. L. (1982). "You can't play marbles—You have a wooden hand": Communication with the handicapped. *Communication Quarterly, 30,* 108–115.

Twardosz, S., Nordquist, V. M., Simon, R., & Botkin, D. (1983). The effects of group affection activities on the interaction of socially isolated children. *Analysis and Intervention in Developmental Disabilities, 3,* 311–338.

Vacc, N. A. (1972). Long-term effects of special class intervention for emotionally disturbed children. *Exceptional Children, 39,* 15–22.

Walker, H. M., & Rankin, R. (1983). Assessing the behavior expectations and demands of less restrictive settings. *School Psychology Review, 12,* 274–284.

Will, M. C. (1986). Educating children with learning problems: A shared responsibility. *Exceptional Children, 52,* 411–415.

Wilson, E. D. (1971). The influence of deafness simulation on attitudes toward the deaf. *Journal of Special Education, 5,* 343–349.

Wright, B. A. (1979). The coping framework and attitude change: A guide to constructive role playing. Paper presented at the American Psychological Association Conference, New York.

Yates, J. R. (1973). Model for preparing regular classroom teachers for "mainstreaming." *Exceptional Children, 39,* 471–472.

APPENDIX A

Addresses of Publishers

Allyn and Bacon
160 Gould Street
Needham Heights, MA 02194–2310

American Association on Mental
   Deficiency
5210 Connecticut Avenue, N.W.
Washington, DC 20015

American College Testing Program
P.O. Box 168
Iowa City, IA 52240

American Guidance Service, Inc.
Publishers' Building
Circle Pines, MN 55014

American Newspaper Publishers
   Association Foundation
The Newspaper Center
Box 17407
Dulles International Airport
Washington, DC 20041

American Printing House for the Blind
1839 Frankfort Avenue
P.O. Box 6085
Louisville, KY 40206

Bell Telephone System
American Telephone and Telegraph
   Co.
195 Broadway
New York, NY 10007

Benefic Press
10300 West Roosevelt Road
Westchester, IL 60153

Bennett Publishing Co.
866 Third Ave.
New York, NY 10022

Butterick Publishing
Division of American Can Co.
708 Third Avenue
New York, NY 10017

John D. Caddy
Box 251
Canoga Park, CA 91305

Children's Book Centre
140 Kensington Church St.
London W8, England

Council for Exceptional Children
1920 Association Drive
Reston, VA 22091

Creative Publications
P.O. Box 10328
Palo Alto, CA 94303

Creative Teaching Press
10701 Holden St.
Cypress, CA 90630

Cuisenaire Company of America, Inc.
12 Church Street
New Rochelle, NY 10805

Developmental Learning Materials
7440 Natchez Avenue
Niles, IL 60648

The Dushkin Publishing Group, Inc.
Guilford, CT 06437

Edmark Associates
655 South Orcas Street
Seattle, WA 98108

Educational Design Associates
P.O. Box 915
East Lansing, MI 48823

Educational Insights
19560 S. Rancho Way
Dominquez Hills, CA 90220

Educational Service, Inc.
P.O. Box 219
Stevensville, MI 49127

Educational Teaching
159 West Kinzie
Chicago, IL
(calculator)

Educational Teaching Aids
657 Oak Grove Plaza
Menlo Park, CA 94025
(Veri Tech Math Lab)

Encyclopedia Britannica Education
  Corporation
310 S. Michigan Avenue
Chicago, IL 60604

Exceptional Child Center
UMC–68
Utah State University
Logan, UT 84322

The Exceptional Parent Bookstore
296 Boylston Street
Boston, MA 02116

The Exceptional Parent Press
Room 700, Statler Office Building
Boston, MA 02116

Fearon Publishers
6 Davis Drive
Belmont, CA 94002

Field Education Publications
609 Mission Street
San Francisco, CA 94105

Follett Publishing Company
Customer Service Center
Box 5705
Chicago, IL 60680

Garrard Publishing Co.
1607 N. Market Street
Champaign, IL 61820

Globe Book Co., Inc.
175 Fifth Avenue
New York, NY 10010

The Goodheart-Wilcox Co., Inc.
123 West Taft Drive
South Holland, IL 60473

Goodyear Publishing Co.
Santa Monica, CA 90401

Harcourt Brace Jovanovich, Inc.
1250 Sixth Ave.
San Diego, CA 92101

Harper and Row Publishers, Inc.
10 East 53rd Street
New York, NY 10022

The Haworth Publishers, Inc.
10 Alice St.
Binghamton, NY 13904–1580

Houghton Mifflin Company
1 Beacon St.
Boston, MA 02108

Hubbard Scientific
P.O. Box 104
Northbrook, IL 60062

Incentive Publications, Inc.
Box 12522
Nashville, TN 37212

Janus Book Publishers
3541 Investment Blvd.
Suite 5
Hayward, CA 94545

Jastak Associates, Inc.
1526 Gilpin Avenue
Wilmington, DE 19806

Junior League of Spartanburg, Inc.
Spartanburg, SC 29301

Kendall/Hunt Publishing Company
2460 Kerper Blvd.
Dubuque, IA 52001

Kids Come in Special Flavors
Box 562
Forest Station
Dayton, OH 45405

Kids on the Block
c/o Barbara Aiello
Suite 1040
Washington Building
Washington, DC 20005

Kimbo Educational Materials
Box 477
Long Branch, NJ 07740

Lawren Productions, Inc.
P.O. Box 666
Mendocino, CA 95460

Learning Concepts, Inc.
7622 Palmerston Dr.
Mentor, OH 44060

Lectro-Stik Corporation
3721 North Broadway
Chicago, IL 60613

Lexington Educational Aids Workshop
3413 Montavesta Road
Lexington, KY 40502

Library of Congress
Washington, DC 20540

Little, Brown & Company
34 Beacon Street
Boston, MA 02106

Little Brown Bear Learning Associates,
Inc.
P.O. Box 561167
Miami, FL 33156

Longman, Inc.
95 Church Street
White Plains, NY 10601

Love Publishing
1777 S. Bellaire St.
Denver, CO 80222

McGraw-Hill Book Co. and McGraw-
Hill Films
330 West 42nd Street
New York, NY 10036

Charles E. Merrill Publishing Co.
1300 Alum Creek Drive
Columbus, OH 43216

Midwest Publications Co., Inc.
P.O. Box 448
Pacific Grove, CA 93950

ModuLearn, Inc.
San Juan Capistrano, CA 92675

National Braille Association
Reader-Transcriber Registry
5300 Hamilton Ave., Apt. 1404
Cincinnati, OH 45224

The National Committee
Arts for the Handicapped
1701 K Street, N.W.
Washington, DC 20006

New Readers Press
Division of Laubauch Literacy, Inc.
Box 131
Syracuse, NY 13210

Northwestern University Press
P.O. Box 1093
Evanston, IL 60201

Olympus Publishing Co.
1670 East 13th Street
Salt Lake City, UT 84105

Perry-Neal Publishers, Inc.
P.O. Box 2721
Western Durham Station
Durham, NC 27705

Prentice-Hall, Inc.
Route 9W
Englewood Cliffs, NJ 07632

Pruett Publishing Co.
2928 Pearl Street
Boulder, CO 80301

Psychological Corporation
304 East 45th Street
New York, NY 10017

Random House, Inc.
Microcomputer Software
201 East 50th Street
New York, NY 10022

Reading Joy
Naperville, IL 60540

Frank E. Richards Publishing Co., Inc.
324 First Street
Liverpool, NY 13088

William H. Sadlier, Inc.
11 Park Place
New York, NY 10007

Scholastic Book Services
906 Sylvan Avenue
Englewood Cliffs, NJ 07532

Science Research Associates, Inc.
259 East Erie Street
Chicago, IL 60611

Scott, Foresman and Company
Brown College
1900 E. Lake Avenue
Glenview, IL 60025

Southwest Educational and
  Psychological Service
P.O. Box 1870
Phoenix, AZ 85001

Teaching Resources Corp.
100 Boylston Street
Boston, MA 02116

Texas Instruments Inc.
P.O. Box 655303–8338
Dallas, TX 75265

United Graphics, Inc.
1401 Broadway
Seattle, WA 98100

Wadsworth Publishing Company
10 Davis Dr.
Belmont, CA 94002

J. Weston Walch, Publisher
Box 658
Portland, ME 04104

Webster Division
McGraw-Hill Book Co.
30th Floor
1221 Avenue of the Americas
New York, NY 10020

Western Psychological Services
12031 Wilshire Blvd.
Los Angeles, CA 90025

Word Making Productions, Inc.
60 West 400 South
Salt Lake City, UT 84101

Professional and Consumer Organizations

For more information on exceptional students, contact the following organizations:

Alexander Graham Bell Association
  for the Deaf, Inc.
3417 Volta Place, N.W.
Washington, DC 20007

American Association for Gifted
  Children
15 Gramercy Park
New York, NY 10003

American Association on Mental
  Retardation
1719 Kalorama Road, N.W.
Washington, DC 20009

American Foundation for the Blind,
  Inc.
15 West Sixteenth Street
New York, NY 10011

American Printing House for the Blind
1839 Frankfort Avenue
P.O. Box 6085
Louisville, KY 40206

American Psychological Association
1200 Seventeenth Street, N.W.
Washington, DC 20036

American Speech and Hearing
  Association
10801 Rockville Pike
Rockville, MD 20852

Association for Children and Adults
  with Learning Disabilities
4156 Library Road
Pittsburgh, PA 15236

Captioned Films for the Deaf
Special Office for Materials
  Distribution
Indiana University
Audio-Visual Center
Bloomington, IN 47401

Closer Look
Box 1492
Washington, DC 20013

Council for Exceptional Children
1920 Association Drive
Reston, VA 22091

Council for Learning Disabilities
P.O. Box 40303
Overland Park, KS 66204

Cystic Fibrosis Foundation
3379 Peachtree Road, N.E.
Atlanta, GA 30326

Epilepsy Foundation of America
1828 L Street, N.W.
Washington, DC 20036

Gifted Child Society
P.O. Box 120
Oakland, NJ 07436

The Library of Congress
Division for the Blind and Physically
    Handicapped
Washington, DC 20542

National Association for Gifted
    Children
4175 Lovell Road, Suite 140
Circle Pines, MN 55014

National Association for Retarded
    Citizens
2501 Avenue J
Arlington, TX 76011

National Association of State Directors
    of Special Education, Inc.
1201 Sixteenth Street, N.W.
Washington, DC 20036

National Association for the Visually
    Handicapped
305 East 24th Street
New York, NY 10010

National Association of the Deaf
814 Thayer Avenue
Silver Spring, MD 20910

National Easter Seal Society for
    Crippled Children and Adults
2023 West Ogden Avenue
Chicago, IL 60612

National Epilepsy League
6 North Michigan Avenue
Chicago, IL 60602

National Federation of the Blind
1629 K Street, N.W.
Washington, DC 20006

National Foundation
March of Dimes
1275 Mamaroneck Avenue
White Plains, NY 10605

National Society for the Prevention of
    Blindness, Inc.
79 Madison Avenue
New York, NY 10016

TASH: The Association for Persons
    with Severe Handicaps
7010 Roosevelt Way, N.E.
Seattle, WA 98115

Name Index

446

Shaw, S. F., 417
Shea, T. M., 65
Sheldon-Wildgen, J., 115, 206
Sherman, J. A., 115, 206
Sherman, M., 412
Sherman, P., 255
Sherrill, C., 344, 346, 350, 352
Shoemaker, D. J., 82
Short, F. X., 347
Silberman, A., 392
Silberman, R., 66
Silverman, L. K., 19
Silverman, M., 406
Simon, R., 418
Simpson, R. D., 322–323
Singer, J. D., 6, 49–50
Siperstein, G. N., 420, 430
Sirvis, B., 41, 47, 52
Skinner, B. F., 387–388,
    400–401
Slavin, R. E., 414, 417
Smith, M. D., 206–208, 212,
    216–217
Smith, P. B., 173
Smith, R. J., 209, 224,
    234–235, 243, 250
Smith, R. M., 397
Smitherman, D. W., 243
Sowell, V., 290
Speckels, J., 231
Speltz, M. L., 412
Spungin, S. J., 62
Stafford, D. G., 324
Stainback, G., 415
Stainback, S., 415
Stainback, W., 415
Stanley, J., 133
Stannard, R., 8
Stefanich, G. P., 320
Stein, R., 158
Stephens, I. M., 20
Stephens, T. M., 306, 308
Stewart, J., 329
Stokes, E. H., 411
Stokes, S., 146
Stott, D. H., 245
Stowitschek, E. E., 252
Stone, M. C., 400
Strickland, B., 156, 158–159,
    197
Strickland, D. B., 17, 19, 147,
    150, 152, 158–159
Streibel, M., 329
Sugai, G., 146
Sulzer-Azaroff, B., 391
Sund, R. B., 329, 335
Suterko, S., 60
Swartzbaugh, T., 255
Switzky, H. N., 9, 411

Tague, C., 400
Taylor, G., 137, 333
Taylor, L., 143

Taylor, M. K., 30
Taylor, S. E., 206
Taymans, J., 188
Tecca, J. E., 72
Temple, C., 210
Tessier-Switlick, D., 164
Thier, H. D., 325, 326
Thomas, D. R., 399
Thompson, B. J., 244
Thompson, G. B., 136
Thompson, K., 355, 357
Thompson, T., 391, 412
Thornton, C. A., 293–294,
    299–300
Thorpe, L. P., 307
Tiedt, I. M., 209, 251
Tiedt, S. W., 209, 251
Tiegs, E. W., 307
Tobin, D., 130
Tomlin, J. G., 206
Torgeson, J. K., 186, 187–188
Torgeson, J. L., 187–188
Torrance, E. P., 129
Trief, E., 66
Trout, I., 428
Troutman, A. C., 388–389
Truan, M. B., 60
Turnbull, A. P., 9, 16, 17, 19,
    147, 150, 152, 156,
    158–159, 197
Turnbull, H. R., 19, 159
Turner, T. N., 307, 335–336
Twardosz, S., 418

Utley, C. A., 104

Vacc, N. A., 246, 412
Vacc, N. N., 187, 246, 249,
    260
Van Houten, R., 172
Van Nagel, C. B., 111
Van Reusen, A. K., 158
Van Riper, C., 80, 81
Vardian, E. R., 307
Victor, E., 323
Viggiano, R. A., 428
Vockell, E. L., 273
Vodola, T. M., 347
Volkmor, C. B., 404

Walberg, H. J., 25
Walker, D. K., 6, 44, 49–51
Walker, H. M., 417
Walker, V. S., 7, 411
Wallace, G., 98, 204, 213, 220,
    229, 233–234, 242, 397
Wang, C., 359
Wang, M. C., 4, 25
Ward, M. E., 22, 59
Warner, M. M., 99
Warren, S. F., 85
Warring, D., 415, 428
Wasylyk, T. M., 249

Watt, D., 186
Weber, M. C., 324
Wechsler, D., 230
Weill, M. P., 131
Weiner, B. B., 159
Weintraub, F. J., 10
Weir, S., 186
Welsbacher, B. T., 357
White, L. D., 358
Whitmore, J., 131
Whorton, D., 183
Wieck, C., 186
Wilen, W. W., 316
Wilhide, J. A., 249
Will, M., 4, 25, 257, 410, 414
Willeford, J. A., 70
Williams, F. E., 136
Williams, J. M., 65
Wilson, E. D., 412
Wilson, M. A., 187
Wilson, R. M., 225, 230, 235
Winkeljohann, R., 221
Winnick, J. P., 345, 347
Wiseman, D. E., 238
Witt, B. T., 218
Wolf, J. S., 20
Wolf, M. M., 400
Wolfinger, D. M., 321, 323,
    337
Wolfthal, M., 223
Wood, J. W., 276
Wood, S. P., 49
Wood, T. A., 206
Woodcock, R., 209
Woodford, C. M., 72
Woodward, J., 187
Woolley, Y., 355
Worsham, M. E., 386
Wray, D., 74
Wright, B. A., 424

Yager, R. E., 323
Yard, G. J., 111
Yates, J. R., 417
Yeager, R. F., 186
Yin, R. K., 189–190
Yoder, D. E., 219
Yoshida, R. K., 7
Ysseldyke, J. E., 20, 99–100,
    225

Zakrajsek, D., 347
Zeeman, R., 384
Zettel, J. J., 19
Zigler, E., 102
Zimmerman, E., 136, 365–366

Subject Index